Chicago, in1982, at the request of th
pertaining to Hinduism, including ab
Maharaj. Revered Maharaj conveys h
inmates of Kauai's Hindu Monastery.

Swami Asimatmananda, for Srimat Swami Ranganathanandaji, President, Belur Ramakrishna Math and Mission, West Bengal, India

True conversion is not a mere change of label but an inner transformation of mind and heart. The great task that lies ahead of us is that of converting Hindus—in India and abroad—into true Hindus, acutely aware of the rich heritage that belongs to them as children of the ancient rishis of Bharatvarsha. The emphasis of the rishis was not on words but on life. When the Hindus bear witness in deeds of daily living to the great ideals of Sanatana Dharma, then indeed will India shine once again in the splendor of the new morning sun. Hence the value of How to Become a Hindu. It has been written with clarity of thought, perceptivity of mind, a depth of feeling and a great sense of commitment. It answers many questions that perplex the youth of today. ¶India is passing through a dark period of her destiny, because Hindus have forgotten how to live as Hindus. They need to be taught the truths proclaimed by their prophets and avataras and by Him who said, "Renouncing all rites and writ duties, come unto Me for single refuge. I shall liberate thee from all bondage to sin and suffering. Of this have no doubt!" Millions of Hindus are waiting to be converted into true Hindus. I am one of them. I welcome this publication and breathe out an aspiration that it may find a place in every Hindu home—and heart.

H.H. Dada J.P. Vaswani, head of the worldwide Sadhu Vaswani Mission, renowned Sindhi religious leader and eloquent lecturer, Pune, India

Since ancient times Hinduism has been known as Sanatana Dharma, which means the Eternal Truth. As such, the Hindu religion has a long history of accepting anyone and everyone who is on the path toward eternal truth. Hinduism does not discriminate against any sincere seeker. Whosoever is devoted to the search for that Eternal Truth is embraced by the religion of Hinduism. Therefore, Hinduism is perhaps the most universal and welcoming faith of all time. ¶How to Become a Hindu, by revered Satguru Sivaya Subramuniyaswami, is the first authoritative book to give those who wish to embrace Hinduism more formally and more fully all the inspiration and guidance to enable them to do so. This book is encyclopedic in its breadth and depth, answering any and every question regarding Hindu faith, its beliefs and rituals. Finally, there is a book that teaches aspirants how to embrace the faith that is always ready to embrace the true seeker.

H.H. Sri Swami Satchidananda, Founder/Spiritual Head of Satchidananda Ashram; Founder, Light of Truth Universal Shrine (LOTUS); renowned yoga master and visionary; Yogaville, Virginia

How to Become A Hindu

हिन्दु कथं भवितुं

Second Edition, First Printing, 3,000 copies

How to Become a Hindu, A Guide for Seekers and Born Hindus is published by Himālayan Academy. First published as *Śaivite Names* in 1989. Designed, typeset and edited by the sannyāsin swāmīs of the Śaiva Siddhānta Yoga Order, 107 Kaholalele Road, Kapaa, Hawaii, 96746-9304, USA.

Published by
Himālayan Academy
USA • India

PRINTED IN USA

Library of Congress Control Number: 00-132420
ISBN 0-945497-82-2

Cover art: *Chennai artist S. Rajam depicts some of the typical steps a soul takes in adopting Hinduism (clockwise from upper left): confronting previous religious leaders to inform them of this change; Lord Śiva looks on; young aspirant studies the scriptures and philosophy of Sanātana Dharma; Western convert learns to wrap a sari as part of her cultural immersion; Chinese seeker worships Lord Gaṇeśa; priests conduct the traditional homa rites for the final ceremony, the name-giving sacrament, nāmakaraṇa saṁskāra.*

How to Become A Hindu

A Guide for Seekers And Born Hindus

हिन्दु कथं भवितुं

विद्यार्थीच जाति हिन्दु पथदर्शनमं

Satguru Sivaya
Subramuniyaswami

உ

Dedication

Samarpaṇam

समर्पणम्

H*OW TO BECOME A HINDU* IS DEDICATED TO MY SATGURU AND ALL THOSE BEFORE HIM IN OUR LINEAGE, DATING BACK 2,200 YEARS. Satguru Śiva Yogaswāmī (1872–1964), *paramaguru* of over two million Sri Lankan Hindus, had the vision, the foresight, to fulfill my request to enter the Śaivite religion in 1949 and receive my *nāmakaraṇa saṁskāra* and the love and support to this day of the Tamil religious community for over fifty years. Today he and I work together, he in his world and I in mine, to stabilize, encourage and enlighten the Sri Lankan Hindus, who for a decade and a half have experienced an unexpected diaspora into all major and minor countries. We have established temples and dedicated shrines, published books in their language, and given solace to those suffering in leaving their homeland, so fraught with war. We have worked to keep them reminded of their ancient and historic culture of music, art drama and the dance, literature and so much more, to keep it all as it once was, without a break in continuity. This book is also dedicated to all swāmīs who for decades have taught the ancient Sanātana Dharma in the West and thus effectively brought tens of thousands of devout souls half way into the Hindu religion, and now, through a more carefully defined ethical conversion, will complete the process. Swāmī Vivekānanda (1863–1902), one of the foremost progenitors of Hinduism in the Western world, noted: "Why, born aliens have been converted in the past by the thousands, and the process is still going on."

Contents

Vishayasūchī

विषयसूची

Dedication—*Samarpanam* v
Introduction—*Bhūmika* ix

CHAPTER . . . . PAGE
1 Personal Encounters with Hinduism 1
2 Religious Loyalty and Commitment 103
3 Gurudeva Speaks on Entering Hinduism 113
4 Gurudeva Speaks on Ethical Conversion 131
5 Does Hinduism Accept Newcomers? 149
6 Beliefs of All the World's Religions 169
7 Six Steps of Conversion 257
Real-Life Severance Letters and
Other Personal Documents 267
8 Choosing a Hindu Name 281
Sanskrit Birthstar Syllables 291
A Collection of Hindu Names 297
9 Embracing Hindu Culture 337
10 Nine Questions About Hinduism 351

Conclusion—*Nirvāhaṇam* 369
Sanskrit Pronunciation—*Ucchāraṇa Vyākhyā* 372
Glossary—*Śabda Kośa* 373
Index—*Anukramaṇika* 413
Colophon—*Antyavachanam* 435

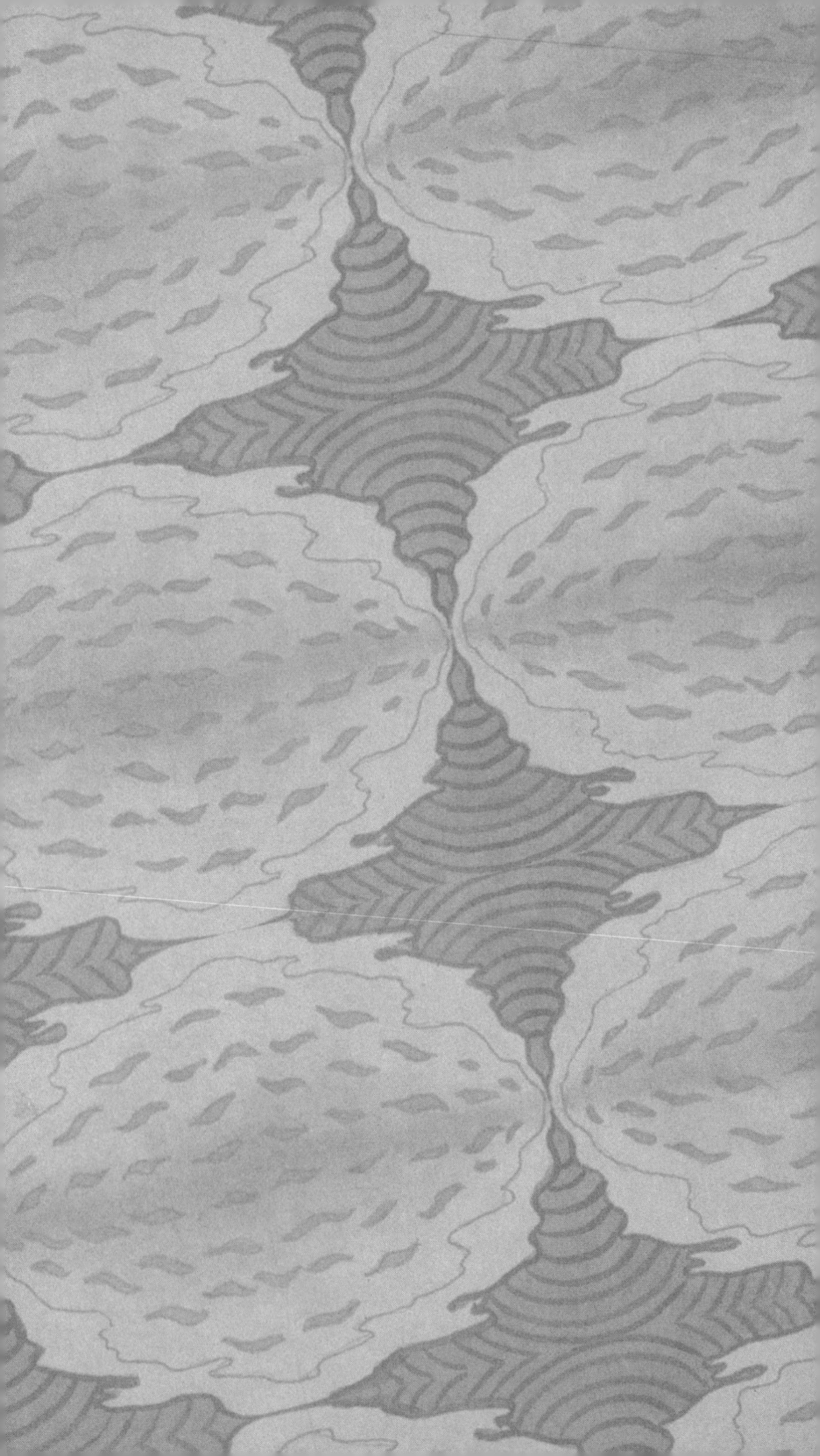

Author's Introduction

Granthakāra Bhūmikā

ग्रन्थकारभूमिका

THOSE WHO KNOW HISTORY KNOW THAT THE concept of changing one's faith is nothing new to Hinduism. Long before Islam or Christianity had even begun, Jainism and Buddhism contended with the Sanātana Dharma for the allegiance of India's masses. Great Hindu saints, such as Ādi Śaṅkara (788-820), Appar (ca 700) and Sundarar (ca 800), gained fame in large part through their opposition to these nascent religions—an opposition so aggressive and so successful as to practically abolish both in the land of their birth. The other edge of conversion's sword figured when South Indian kings colonized Cambodia, Bali and other parts of Southeast Asia, for in those days the way of things was the way of kings: the religion of the ruler was the religion of his subjects. The Indian kings who dominated regions like Indonesia brought their new subjects into Śaivite Hinduism.

While Hindus today are worried about Christian efforts to "save the Pagans," millions in the West are quietly adopting Hinduism in a remarkable and little-discussed silent conversion, a conversion no less powerful and far more extensive than in the past. Sincere seekers in Europe, Africa and the Americas are starting to call themselves Hindu and seek formal entrance into the faith. They are the result of 150 years of Hindu philosophy surging out from India in several waves: first as scriptural translations, then itinerant holy men such as Swāmī Vivekānanda, and most recently as part of the diaspora of Hindus out of India, Sri Lanka and Nepal, and the resulting establishment of temples and *āśramas* in nearly every country of the world. The central Hindu concepts of karma, dharma, reincarnation and the presence of the Divine in all things are now understood by tens of millions not born in the faith but exposed to it through music, film and television, and even commercial advertising.

To the born-Hindu of today, the question of entering Hinduism may seem unnecessary, for by one common definition Hinduism is a way of life, a culture, both religious and secular. The Hindu is not accustomed to thinking of his religion as a clearly defined system, distinct and different from other systems, for it fills his every experience. It encompasses all of life. This pure, simple view has to do, in part, with Hinduism's all-embracing quality, to accept so many variations of belief and practice into itself. But this view ignores the true distinctions between this way of life and the ways of the world's other great religions. There is no denying that Hinduism is also a distinct world religion, and to hold otherwise in today's world is fraught with risk.

If Hinduism is not a religion, as many Western academics and nonreligious Indians still assert, then it is not entitled to the same rights and protections given to religion by the nations of the world. As just one example, in colonial Trinidad, Hinduism was not recognized as a religion, Hindu marriages were therefore considered illegal, Hindu children illegitimate and unqualified to inherit property. A great deal of Hindu ancestral property was forfeited to the colonial Christian government. The claim that Hinduism is "not a religion" weakens its position socially and legally with respect to other religions in the world community.

Among Hinduism's four major denominations—Vaishnavism, Śaivism, Śāktism and Smārtism—only certain Smārta lineages, those represented by the Śaṅkarāchāryas of Sringeri and Puri, do not accept converts. Smārta priests serving in American temples have consistently refused to perform the *nāmakaraṇa saṁskāra*, the name-giving ceremony for non-

Hindus by which they could enter the religion. But the spiritual leaders and priests of the remaining sects—representing perhaps 85 percent of Hindus—actively engage today in conversion rites.

The hundreds of Hindu swāmīs, pandits and lay persons who regularly travel outside India are a relatively passive band, offering a reasoned presentation of beliefs that listeners are only expected to consider and accept or reject. There is no proselytizing, no tearing down of other faiths and no active attempt to gain new followers. Hindu philosophy is free from the missionary compulsion to bring the whole world into its fold in a kind of spiritual colonialism and cultural invasion. This latter form of conversion, which has gone on in India for centuries, ever since Muslims and Christians discovered the subcontinent, has seriously disrupted communities, turned son against father, wife against husband, friend against friend. Coupled with the enticement of material gain and destruction of ancient traditions, it has destroyed lives. The Hindu form of preaching does none of this, and ironically this nonintrusive attitude itself is bringing many toward Hinduism.

How One Enters Hinduism

A direct result of hundreds of swāmīs and yogīs coming to the West, and of tens of thousands of Westerners journeying to India, is the desire by some non-Hindus to enter Hinduism. This is an issue I began facing five decades ago.

In answer to the question, "Gurudeva, how did you become a Hindu?" I would answer that it wasn't a dramatically awesome, big experience for me to enter the oldest religion in the world. I grew up in Hinduism. As with many Americans, I had no prior religion, though I was raised by those who had lived long in India and were enamored of its culture and worldview. Hinduism was, therefore, my first faith. A very dear friend of our family, a graduate of Stanford University in California, had the opportunity to be the guest of the Mahārāja of Mysore for five years. There she learned Indian art, dance, culture and the Śaiva religion. When my mother passed on, when I was nine years of age, she assisted my father in raising me, and from that moment on India was a vital part of my life.

I knew at ten years of age how to wear a dhotī, how a turban should be wrapped, how women drape a sārī, how the dance of Śiva Naṭarāja should be danced, how incense should used to purify the atmosphere of the home and how Indian food should be eaten. My father passed on when I was eleven, and the drama continued.

Thus, I was brought up in Hinduism first through culture, music, art, drama, dance and all the protocols of Indian life. This remarkable person lectured and gave presentations to the public on the beauty and glory of Indian culture. At that time there were only five or six Hindu families living in the Northern California area. So what she had to offer was very welcome to the western people. At youth summer camps held at her beautiful chalet on Fallen Leaf Lake, near Lake Tahoe, I learned the worship of Lord Śiva Naṭarāja. At the beginning of my teens, this was very important to me, and it led me into the Vedānta philosophy, which I pursued through listening to lectures of Indian swāmīs at the Vedānta Society in San Francisco and in reading books. I was most inspired by the life of Swāmī Vivekānanda and his four small volumes: *Rāja Yoga, Bhakti Yoga, Karma Yoga* and *Inspired Talks.* I was especially impressed by his masterful poem, "The Song of the Sannyāsin." Only years later would I discover that my *satguru,* Yogaswāmī, as a young man about my same age, had been inspired by a personal encounter with Swāmī Vivekānanda when the Indian monk visited Colombo on his way back from America to India.

So, following the path of *charyā,* which leads into kriyā which leads into yoga—the culture, the protocols and philosophy, which lead into practice—I started learning yoga: diaphragmatic breathing, concentration, meditation. Then I was told,"Now you need to find your guru. This is the next step. You need to find your guru, and your guru is in Sri Lanka." At twenty years of age, I took the first ship to leave for India after the Second World War and celebrated my twenty-first birthday days before going ashore and walking through the grand Gateway to India in Mumbai. Traveling by train to Chennai and then to Sri Lanka was a remarkable and remarkably hot experience.

During my first year in Sri Lanka, everyone wanted me: the Muslims, the Buddhists and the Christians. I felt very, very special, being appreciated by so many people. Being an orphan, you are not often wanted. But I found that their way of thinking, their protocols and their philosophy didn't compare with what I had learned of Indian culture, art and the philosophy of Vedānta.

After I was in Sri Lanka for about a year, Satguru Śiva Yogaswāmī sent one of his closest disciples to Colombo from Jaffna, in the northern part of the island, to fetch me, an elegant gentleman from the vaiśya caste, the Chettiar community. Kandiah Chettiar began taking me to the Hindu temples. For the first time, I experienced how Śaivites worship the Gods, about pūjā and the priests, about the mysteries of the temples and their connection to the inner worlds. Now the pattern was complete. I had been taken into the Tamil Hindu community and was preparing myself to formally enter Hinduism when the timing was auspicious.

Kandiah Chettiar finally took me to Jaffna to prepare me to meet my *satguru*, whom Chettiar called "a living God." This was the very last increment to this adventure. When we finally met in 1949, I asked Satguru Śiva Yogaswāmī, "Please bring me into the Hindu religion, fully and formally." And he did just that, giving me the name *Subramuniya* through the *nāmakaraṇa saṁskāra,* name-giving sacrament. That's how I became a Hindu. I also later received my *dīkshā* as a sannyāsin from the great saint of Sri Lanka, who instructed me to "build a bridge between East and West" for all his devotees to the lands beyond Sri Lankan shores—Malaysia, Singapore, Mauritius, Europe, Canada, the United States, Australia, New Zealand and many other countries—preparing the way for the *visarjana*, the diaspora, of the Sri Lankan Tamil people forced by the great civil war that started in 1983. Until his departure he communicated with me, year after year, through Kandiah Chettiar. Upon returning to the US, the first thing I did was to change my name legally to my new Śaivite Hindu Name. The judge took it in stride and quickly granted the request. In 1957, at age thirty, I began my public teaching mission in San Francisco.

It later became clear to me that I was a Hindu in my last life and that I was born in the West to perform the mission that I am performing now. I learned about the mission that I am doing now from psychics when I was 17 or 18 years of age. I am performing it now. I have a Western body, an American passport and free transportation from India to the US, with the natural sequence of events.

In my life, I went from charyā, to kriyā, to yoga, to jñāna, following dharma's progressive path, which we must remember is a progressive path. It begins with finding out what the path is in the charya stage, then living the path through *sādhana* in the kriyā stage, then going in and realizing the Self in the yoga stage, which culminates in the jñāna stage of bringing out what you have realized. Some people think, "When you get to the yoga stage, you don't have to do the worship, you don't have to do the service. You just do the yoga." In our Śaiva Siddhānta philosophy, when you get to the yoga stage and the jñāna stage, you still enjoy the worship, you still enjoy the service. These are dear and intricate parts of your life.

While in Sri Lanka, I was taken to Christian gatherings,

to Catholic gatherings, to Islamic gatherings, to Parsi gatherings, and I found them all very nice people. But at that time I was on the yoga path, and those religions did not include the yoga *mārga.* They did not encourage meditation and Self Realization, which was my particular path that I got started on very early in life—seeking full identity of my own inner Self. Having been orphaned at a young age, I was independent and free. I didn't have to answer to anyone, except myself. So, I was on the path to find the Self to answer to. Finding the Self within, which is solid, immovable, which is the same year after year as the mind fluctuates and goes around it, was a great realization, a great stability.

Also, these other religions didn't have the understanding of reincarnation and karma, which provided me a logical explanation of so many things that happen in life. I did meet wonderful people, though, from the Islamic, the Christian, the Protestant, the Catholic and the Buddhist communities. I would say Buddhism influenced me most in the monastic path, because I visited and lived in many Buddhist temples in Sri Lanka. I was received by the monks there. I saw how they lived, saw how they dressed, and that influenced in a very strict way the monastic protocols that we later put into action in our own monastic order. I was being prepared to go to the northern part of the country, the Tamil Hindu area which was quite strict at that particular time, very orthodox.

Formalizing the Process

The experience of my own entrance into Hinduism in my twenties set the pattern for my ministry in the years to come, when I worked to apply the same pattern for others who wished to fully enter Hinduism through self-conversion. I ultimately developed a six-step pattern of ethical conversion that results in a sincere and lasting commitment to the Hindu faith, or any faith for that matter. I found it useful to distinguish between the *convert,* a person with clearly defined prior commitments to another faith, and the *adoptive*, a person with no prior religious affiliations, who is free, without severance formalities, to embrace and enter the faith of his or her choice.

The most innovative step in this form of ethical conversion—and what truly makes it ethical—is the mandatory severance from any former faiths. The devotee is asked to go back to his prior religious leader, priest, rabbi, minister, imam, etc., and explain his change of belief, culture, etc., in a face-to-face meeting. Typically, the leader may attempt to talk the devotee out of his intention, though some will immediately honor the depth of his new commitment and understanding.

It was in 1977 that I imposed the strict conversion/adoption edict that stands in place to this day among my congregation. Only as full-fledged Hindus, committed 100 percent to the Hindu religion, with no other religious obligations inhibiting their participation in the culture, philosophy and lifestyle, could they settle at last into the religion of their soul. Anything less, and they would remain half-Hindus. Only in completely entering the Hindu fold, I perceived, would followers be able to pass the fullness of our teachings on to their children. Many, I realized, had lived as Hindus in past lives, and now, born in the West, were merely rediscovering the religion of their soul. Having found it, they would be content with no other religion. To not provide a way for formal entrance to Hinduism would be to leave them between religions, stranded, in a sense, with no religion at all.

Research began, and it was soon discovered that, indeed, Hinduism does and always has accepted newcomers, though the issue is generally handled discreetly. Formal entry is accomplished through a simple ceremony, no different that the naming of a young Hindu child. The procedure was formalized and performed in our Kadavul Hindu Temple on the Garden Island of Kauai. Each devotee repeated a verbal oath before God, Gods and guru and gathered devotees, promising to be eternally faithful to the principles of the Sanātana Dharma as he entered the Śaivite Hindu religion through this "sacramental name-giving." I asked that a certificate be issued which devotees could use later for the legal name-change, and which also proved useful for entering strict temples in India when on pilgrimage.

The pattern was set, and hundreds entered Śaivite Hinduism in this way, joyously bringing their children into Hinduism in the same manner thereafter and raising them as orthodox Hindus. The process continues to this day. Soon a new generation of born Hindu children emerged from these converted and adoptive Hindu parents. A new *gotra,* or spiritual clan, was quick to form in the West, called the Subramuniya Gotra.

Entrance into Hinduism was simpler for those who had little early training in the religion of their parents. This group made up the majority of the clan, which continues to be the case. For those confirmed or baptized or deeply indoctrinated in a non-Hindu religion or philosophical system, the transition was more involved. I established a counseling office at our Himālayan Academy in San Francisco to assist aspirants in identifying their religious loyalties and convictions. Many students chose not to take this serious step and drifted away. Thus, the Śaivite souls, as I call those who are inwardly destined to follow Śiva, were distinguished from those who had yet another path to follow.

After 1977, only those who formally entered the religion were accepted as my *śishyas,* though non-Hindus were and are availed an introductory study of Śaivism through the Academy's *Master Course* study programs. Students with predominant non-Hindu backgrounds who wished to enter Hinduism, having completed Book One of *The Master Course,* were advised of the requirement to first sever their prior religious commitments. This generally meant returning to the religious institution of their childhood, there to obtain a severance through convincing their former religious leader that they had embraced the Śaivite Hindu religion and intended to enter it formally. This severance was also documented in writing, in most cases through a letter from that institution. It soon became clear that this honest approach, with the burden of severance falling entirely on the devotee, was a vital step in the personal spiritual unfoldment of these individuals, resolving long-standing subconscious conflicts between the old faith and the new.

In cases of deep former commitment devotees were asked to study their former faith so as to prepare a point-counterpoint of its beliefs and those of Śaivite Hinduism. They were also asked participate in the activities of their former faith, attend services and share in social events with the congregation. In several instances, devotees became reinspired with their original religion and changed their minds about converting to Śaivism. We were happy for all who rediscovered their path in life in this way, having reawakened their spiritual/religious nature through their participation in the vibrant and compellingly uplifting ceremonies of Hinduism. It was not a surprise to us, for Hinduism has such a power, such a magic, being the oldest living tradition, being so full of the divine, having never put their Gods into exile, as did most other ancient faiths when they encountered the newer religions. Hinduism kept the original path intact, pure and unashamed, rich and bold in its ways, colorful and so profound. No wonder some souls upon seeing and experiencing this were reinspired inwardly and returned to their born religion with a new hope and vision.

Among those who have entered Hinduism in recent years in the West are former Jews, Taoists, Buddhists, Christians of all denominations, Muslims, atheists, existentialists, agnostics, materialists, new age seekers and others. *Nāmakaraṇa saṁskāras* are now performed in the West by many qualified

Indian priests—Śaivites, Śāktas, Vaishṇavites and Smārtas—each performing the name-giving for adults and their children as is traditionally done for each Hindu child.

In the early eighties, when Hindu devotees of other lineages, such as Smārtaism, Vaishṇavism and Śāktism, began seeking admittance to Śaiva Siddhānta Church, I established similar procedures to help them make the transition to Śaivite Hinduism. This was found necessary, for while the great Hindu lineages share many common beliefs, each is also different and distinct enough to be considered a separate religion in its own right. Devotees who had been initiated by other gurus were not allowed initiation from me unless they obtained a formal release from their former initiator. Those with strong non-Śaivite backgrounds were required to study the differences in belief between those school and the Advaita Śaiva Siddhānta of my Church so that they could make the necessary inner adjustments to becoming a good Śaivite, all based on the principle that former commitments must be dissolved before new ones can be made.

Why Is a Formal Process Needed?

In 1966, the Vishva Hindu Parishad (VHP), a prestigious, multi-million member Hindu organization, issued this definition: "*Hindu* means a person believing in, following or respecting the eternal values of life, ethical and spiritual, which have sprung up in Bharatkhand [India] and includes any person calling himself a Hindu." While self-declaration remains the basic way to enter the faith, the VHP's 1998 Dharma Samsad, an annual meeting of Hindu spiritual leaders held that year in America, called for the development of "a process for accepting willing non-Hindus into the Hindu fold, which is an important concern among Hindus living in America." Those concerns include intermarriage, including the need for a non-Hindu spouse to adopt the religion of his or her mate and for the couple to raise their children in a purely Hindu home. These are some of the reasons a formal process is needed.

Another reason is the standing policy of most Indian swāmīs in the West to not formally convert their devotees to Hinduism. They generally give an informal Hindu first name only, and thereby create what may be called an *ardha*-Hindu—"half-Hindu"—who finds himself separated from his old faith by newfound beliefs and practice, but not fully embraced by his new one. The situation gets especially precarious when it comes to raising children. Are they Hindus, Christians, Jews? The practical outcome I have observed in the last twenty years is that such offspring are raised with no formal religion at all and are left adrift to fend for themselves in an unforgiving world.

Also, by setting a standard of ethical conversion, Hindus can help alter the oftentimes predatory nature of religious conversion. Applying this idea to another faith, if every Hindu who wanted to become a Christian went successfully through an ethical conversion, there would be no claims by Hindus that he had been bribed, coerced, enticed or otherwise forced into the change. Of course, there would also be fewer conversions! Finally, at this time in history religions are looking for ways to get along better and work for humanity's common spiritual good rather that fight over followers. Unfortunately, the continuing disruptive conversion tactics of the aggressive Abrahamic missionary religions are rarely on the agenda at global conferences. By advocating ethical conversion, Hindus can help the world overcome the single greatest obstacle to interfaith harmony.

Entering Hinduism has traditionally required little more than accepting and living the beliefs and codes of Hindus. This remains the basic factor of conversion or adoption, although there are, and always have been, formal ceremonies recognizing an individual's entrance into the religion. The most obvious sign of the adoptive is the Hindu name. People can feel uneasy about changing their name, but a look into Western names reveals them to be remarkably fluid, frequently changed as the result of minor circumstances. Those names which are not descriptive of one's occupation or family are most frequently derived from the Christian Bible and signify a follower of Christianity. An individual who rejects belief in the doctrines of Christianity must also reject the name given him under that religion, for reasons that we will explain later.

The Audience of This Book

If you are a student of comparative religions, a truth-seeker, an onlooker or a devout Hindu, you will enjoy this book. Perhaps you have studied Hinduism and now feel it is your religion. If this is the case, as it has been for so many who have been exposed to Eastern thought and beliefs, and if you are of another religion and sincerely wish to become a Hindu formally, you will be happy to know that it is possible to do so. The process is not at all difficult, and though each situation is unique, it generally follows the pattern outlined herein. Should you be a born Hindu, especially if you were educated in a Catholic or Protestant Christian school or studied existentialism or secular humanism in a university, this book will certainly broaden and enhance your understanding of religious loyalty and belief and inspire you to rededicate yourself consciously and subconsciously to the Hindu dharma. This book is designed to serve three audiences: first, non-Hindus interested in entering the Hindu religion; second, Hindus changing from one Hindu sect or denomination to another; and third, mature Hindu elders who can help converts and adoptives make the necessary adjustments for full entrance into the community; as well as derive inspiration about their own faith and deepen their own spiritual life. To some, the mention of the last purpose may seem out of place, but let it be known that everyone's faith can be strengthened and self-conversion even applies to those born to the religion, spiritually speaking.

Yes, I am referring to "bringing Hindus into Hinduism." It is another well kept secret that I have been bringing Hindus into Hinduism most of my life. Hindus by and large don't understand the basics, let alone the depths, of their religion. For those seeking deeper waters, soul-searching, education and steps toward severance may be required to pave the way for a clear understanding of their born faith, leading to a happier future. Many Hindus, though born into the religion, have grown up attending Catholic schools. But if you ask them about the effects, they generally say, "I really didn't pay much attention to what the nuns and fathers were saying." We know from experience that this is impossible. Because of such influence and other programming, many Hindus are Hindus in name only.

When serious Hindu seekers discover the path, and the more esoteric, metaphysical aspects of their born religion, they must face and deal with the dragons that may lurk in their subconscious. You will discover a wonderful example of this in the Chapter One story of our friend Sri Sita Ram Goel, one of India's greatest living thinkers. Though born in a Hindu family, He became an atheist and a communist in his youth, a disbeliever and a heretic to his father's faith. Yet, due to his sincerity and intelligence, one experience led to another and he, too, became a Hindu, after fully reconciling with his former mentors.

Again, a few may inquire whether such emphasis is necessary, whether it may be more efficient to focus solely on matters of spiritual discipline, *sādhana* and philosophy and avoid these technical tangents. Our answer is that these matters are really not so tangential as they might seem. For those once involved in another religion, the subject of this book is a most crucial one. What is being discussed is commitment, and commitment precedes the practice of deeper spiritual disciplines and meditations. By commitment I mean fully embracing one's religion, fully practicing one's religion, fully serving one's religion. Only in this way will the spiritual disciplines, *sādhana* and philosophy take hold and produce lasting results. Only in this way, no longer as an onlooker, will the convert or adoptive become an intrinsic part of an ever-growing international community constituting one sixth of the human race.

Are You a Hindu?

Belief is the keynote of religious conviction, and beliefs vary greatly among the different religions of the world. Psychologically speaking, what we believe forms our attitudes, shapes our lives, defines our culture and molds our destiny. To choose our beliefs is to choose our religion. Compare your beliefs to the beliefs of Sanātana Dharma. If you find yourself at home with Hindu beliefs, the attitudes they produce and the culture that is lived by a billion-plus souls, then obviously you are a Hindu. It is that easy.

But formally entering any new religion is a serious commitment, one which must certainly be considered deeply. This book outlines the purpose and the requirements of that auspicious and important step. It is a most individual experience, often joyful, sometimes painful and always challenging, especially for those severing from other loyalties. That is as it should be. Severance from a former religion or philosophy should be a memorable experience, sharp, clean-cut, with no ragged edges left. Then entrance into Hinduism is clear and completely positive.

Entrance to Hinduism should not be sought because friends are doing it or because this is the next step in a course of study. It must come from the heart, from a deep, inner sense, an inner knowing that this is the natural dharma of your soul. This book records the conclusions of over fifty years of work and research in the field of personal belief and religious conviction which occasionally culminates in the need to transcend the boundaries of one's born faith and seek solace in another. *How to Become a Hindu* is thus a practical manual to help guide those seeking to ratify their self-declared commitment to the Sanātana Dharma in all its dimensions: spiritual, social, cultural, economic and educational. It's a package deal.

How do you know if you are a Hindu deep inside? If an elder, your guru or a friend has given you a Hindu name? If you have met a swāmī or yogī, pandit or *satguru* who speaks out the truths you always knew to be the way of the universe? If you feel in your heart of hearts that no other religion suits you better, expresses your native spirituality more profoundly, offers you a way to personally know the Divine within you?

Let's analyze and through the process of elimination find out. If you believe, as your guru does, in the existence of God everywhere and in all things, you are certainly not a Christian, Muslim or Jew. If you believe in one Supreme God and many Gods, you are certainly not a Christian, Muslim, Jew or Buddhist. The Buddhists, like the Jains, don't believe in a personal God. They don't like to use the word *God.* They don't feel the concept of God is part of their deepest understanding. They do not accept a creator, or a knowing God who guides His creation. I was deeply impressed at hearing the Dalai Lama and the head of a Japanese Buddhist tradition make a strong and articulate point of this to several hundred spiritual leaders at the Presidents' Assembly at the Parliament of the World's Religions' 1993 centennial in Chicago, where they appealed to the other religions to please not include the use of the word *God* in a key declaration, called "Toward a Global Ethic," that all faith leaders were asked to affirm and to sign. Significantly, the word *God* was left in that document.

If you believe in the law of karma, action receiving its

comparable just due, you might be a Buddhist, but then you have the personal God problem. But you are certainly not a Christian, Jew or Muslim, because their doctrines do not include karma. If you believe in reincarnation, *punarjanma*, "being born again and again," you might be a Buddhist or a Jain, but then there is the God problem again. But again, you are not a Christian, Jew or Muslim, because they adamantly reject these Vedic revelations, though Hasidic Jews do attest to reincarnation.

In summary, your religion is the group that you are the most comfortable with, those who think like you, share the same ideals, according to their similar philosophies. Another point: if you are attracted to Hindu temples, well then certainly you are not a Christian, Buddhist, Zoroastrian, Jew or Muslim. The 1993 Parliament of the World's Religions brought all these faiths together, and it became very clear to me that the religions of the world are happy to be different, unique, not the same. They celebrated these differences, while also affirming an inner oneness. As one of the three presidents of Hinduism at the Presidents' Assembly, along with Swāmī Chidānanda Sarasvatī and Māta Amṛitānandamāyī, I can say that each one of the leaders of the world's religions knows who the others are and is not about to change. The whole idea that all religions are one may be true in spirit, but in actuality, no. One path or another must be chosen and then lived fully. We don't hear born Hindus saying much anymore, "I'm a Christian; I'm a Muslim; I'm a Jew," as they used to proclaim in the '70s. Today they are proudly saying, "I am a Smārta, a Vaishṇavite, a Śākta or a Śaivite." Much of this change is due to the courageous stand that Hindu leaders of all denominations and traditions have taken.

If truly you find you are the Hindu an elder, friend or guru saw in you by giving you a Hindu name—they usually give Ananda, Shanti or Jyoti for starters—then take the next step and accept the culture, the conventions the fullness of the world's oldest spiritual tradition, with its yogas and its multitudinous wisdoms. Carefully choose the sect within the Sanātana Dharma, the old Sanskrit name for Hinduism, that you will devote your life to following.

Entrance Procedures

It is important to know that one cannot simply enter "the Hindu religion." That is not possible. It is necessary to enter one of Hinduism's specific sects or denominations. Even in these tempestuous times, the subtle differences of Hindu lineages are clearly and methodically demarcated by our priesthoods. After mind searching, soul searching and study, having assured yourself beyond question that yes, indeed, you are a devout follower of the Sanātana Dharma, go with your Hindu friends to a Hindu priest in a temple of your choice and arrange for the name-giving sacrament, *nāmakaraṇa saṁskāra.* Your beliefs and way of life have affirmed your inner decision to become a Hindu. This ceremony brings you formally into the Hindu community, recognizing and ratifying your proclamation of loyalty and wholehearted commitment to the Sanātana Dharma and validating, now and forever, your Hindu first and last name on all legal documents.

Chapter seven describes all the steps in detail. Included there is a model *nāmakaraṇa* certificate that you can photocopy or re-typeset to document the event, signed by the priest and several witnesses, especially members of the community you are entering, who will share your joy in becoming a full-fledged Hindu. Then have your new name made legal on your passport, social security or ID card, credit cards, insurance documents, driver's license, telephone listing and more. More information on arranging for the *nāmakaraṇa saṁskāra* and other matters can be found on our Website at www.himalayanacademy.com/basics/conversion/.

We call upon Hindu religious leaders to welcome and

embrace adoptive and converts and not say they disqualify for one reason or another. Leaders, priests, heads of *aadheenams, maṭhas* and *āśramas,* pandits, managers of temples and devotees, make it your duty to bring in those who were Hindus in their last life, those who are brand new to Hinduism but have a deep interest in it and those who were born into the religion but drifted away and now seek to return, who want to know in their aspiring hearts, "How can I enter Hinduism?"

Now we have the overview of what is to come. Travel with me through this documentary book about full and formal entrance into my beloved Hindu faith, the oldest spiritual tradition on Earth, the divine family that is over a billion strong and growing. You are interested, I know you are, as you have read this far. Read on, read on. You will never look back and regret that you did.

Love and blessings from this and inner worlds.

Satguru Sivaya Subramuniyaswami
162nd Jagadāchārya of the Nandinātha
Sampradāya's Kailāsa Paramparā
Guru Mahāsannidhānam
Kauai Aadheenam, Hawaii, USA
Satguru Pūrṇimā, July 15, 2000
Hindu year Vikrama, 5102

Hindudharmeṇasaha
Mama Saṅgamaḥ

हिन्दुधर्मेणसह मम सङ्गमः

Personal Encounters With Hinduism

Personal Encounters With Hinduism

HERE ARE TRUE HISTORIES OF INDIVIDUals and families who formally entered Śaivite Hinduism over the years. We begin with Hitesvara Saravan, a former Baptist who discovered Hinduism later in life and recently completed his conversion. Hitesvara and the others whose stories lie herein consented to share their firsthand experience in severing his former religious commitments and then entering the Hindu faith. These inspiring real-life stories illustrate the six steps of ethical conversion (see Chapter Seven) in captivating detail. Each story is written from a delightfully different angle. Enjoy.

My Conversion from the Baptist Church

How I Was Uplifted and Transformed by the Śaivite Hindu Teachings. By Hitesvara Saravan.

Gurudeva, Sivaya Subramuniyaswami, has blessed me with the name Hitesvara Saravan, which I interpret to mean One who cares for others born of the Lake of Divine Essence. My former name was Alton Barry Giles, a name from Scottish heritage.

It was not until I was in the *vānaprastha āśrama*, at 56 years old, that in July of 1997 I typed the word *Hindu* into a search engine on an archaic, text-only computer. This brought me into a new conscious realization as I came upon a text in Gurudeva's website about the five sacred vows of the sannyāsin, which I printed and studied. These words touched me at a soul level. Through exploration of the website over the next few days, I was brought into a small group of devotees in San Diego and then to the local *mandir.* My conscious journey into the beliefs of my soul intensified.

I had not met Gurudeva in person. I had not even seen a picture of him until my first *satsaṅga* in August. I had been aware, however, for many more than twenty years that I had an inner, spiritual guide—a gentle, kind man urging me onward. Now I know that Gurudeva has been with me all my life. I began the joy of being able to communicate with Gurudeva by e-mail and to be introduced to him by phone, but I was not to meet him in person until December of that year.

Why did I come in person to Gurudeva so late in life? I had many experiences from which to learn, many past life karmas to mitigate. I had many years of living below the *mūlādhāra.* I had the need to overcome fear of God from my fundamental Baptist upbringing in a very religious family. I had even been told by my mother that my lack of belief and lifestyle meant that I was going to go to hell. She cried. I had to overcome alcoholism and drug addiction and its effects, which I did in 1982, sexual promiscuity by becoming celibate in 1992, renouncing meat eating, also in 1992, and learning to rise above all of the lower emotions, such as fear, anger and resentment. I had to commence on the path toward purity to find and learn many lessons from experience before I would be ready to wholeheartedly and completely dedicate myself to the San Mārga, the straight path. I had previously rejected the idea of any one person being my teacher. Now I know this was just in preparation until I met my one teacher, the guru of my soul, Satguru Sivaya Subramuniyaswami.

I had been introduced to the Eastern religions in a fleeting way all throughout the 70s and 80s. I had heard Krishnamurti, had glimpses into Buddhism and Taoism, but it never fully formed in my mind that the beliefs of my soul were Hindu beliefs. I had only heard briefly about Hinduism and only from a Western perspective. In the 90s, after I renounced meat and sex, my spiritual path intensified. I read the Yogi Publication Society's books. I heard about Vivekananda and read his works, as well as *Autobiography of a Yogi*. I read some of the literature from the Theosophical Society; *Light on the Path* in particular struck home with me. From January, 1997, until I came into the Śaivite fold I attended SRF (Self Realization Fellowship) services in San Diego, but was put off by the fact that while I believed in the concept of "saints of all religions," the pictures of Jesus on the altar and the references to Jesus did not sit well with me.

Simultaneously with meeting Gurudeva's followers and having accessed the website, I began receiving the daily lessons from *Dancing with Śiva*. Every one of Gurudeva's beautiful words spoke to my soul. I realized that these were and had been always the beliefs of my soul. I had found my true path. From that day forward, and with greater intensity after my first beautiful experience of *darśana* and meeting Gurudeva in December of 1997, I have tried to undauntingly move forward as I have been guided and led.

I obtained and avidly read and reread *Dancing with Śiva* and *Loving Gaṇeśa*. I read "The Six Steps of Conversion." There has never been any doubt in my mind that this is what I wanted to do, not so much to convert to Śaiva Siddhānta but to return to it formally, albeit for the first time in this lifetime. I attended the local *mandir* for Śiva and Gaṇeśa pūjās starting the first month after accessing the website and mixed with Hindus during festivals. There was immediate welcoming and acceptance.

I wrote a point-counterpoint between Śaiva Siddhānta and Baptist belief. I realized that I had never been comfortable with my Baptist upbringing. I had, for example, never comprehended the concept that in the *Old Testament* God was vengeful, calling down plagues, killing first-born sons, but then it seemed that this God changed upon the birth of

Jesus and he was now kind and loving. It made no sense that God would change. I always believed in God, but the God of the Baptist religion did not equate with my inherent knowledge of God.

I commenced assigned *sādhanas,* books one and two of *The Master Course,* the teachers' guide, the *Loving Gaṇeśa sādhana* among them, and of course daily reading of *Dancing with Śiva.* I learned and began daily Gaṇeśa pūjā, rāja and haṭha yoga, and made efforts at meditation.

I let Gurudeva know that I wished to make a formal conversion. On March 9, 1998, I received the blessing of my Hindu first name based on my astrology and the syllable *hi.* My first name was *Hitesvara,* "God of Welfare," caring for others. I was now *ardha*-Hindu Hitesvara Giles. I was then permitted to pick three last names for Gurudeva to choose from. I chose *Kanda, Saravan* and *Velan.*

I attended several Baptist Church services locally, including Easter services. I made arrangements to travel to Boston on April 30 to meet with my father and brother and the minister of the church where I was brought up to fulfill the formal severance's third step of conversion and to inform my family of my decision. I had not been to the Baptist church for 38 years, except for my mother's funeral and one other occasion.

My father is a non-demonstrative person. He is very strict. He had never once said to me the words "I love you." The most physical contact we had since I was a small child was for him to shake hands with me. Mother and father had both lamented that I was going to go to hell because of my lifestyle. I had continued, however, a good though distant relationship with them in later years, but I was concerned that father would be upset by my decision, and there was a possibility that he could disown me. That was acceptable, but I wanted to try to honor and respect him for his ways and to not upset him, and it was important to me that I be clear and try to have him understand my decision and sincerity. I therefore wrote him some letters. I told him about my Hindu beliefs in God, and after meditation it came to me to write him a loving letter in which I reminisced about all of the good times that I could remember throughout my years of living at home.

I had received some advice and had listened to the testimony of several of Gurudeva's devotees on their experiences in conversion. There was no question that I did a great deal of introspective searching and meditation on the process and that it was fiery and humbling. However, I remained undaunted and firm, but I did need to expend great effort and newfound willpower.

I had some difficulty reaching and convincing long distance in advance the minister to meet with me, but before I left on my trip he agreed.

When I arrived at our family home after greeting my father and brother, I immediately set up a Gaṇeśa shrine and a picture of Gurudeva in my bedroom. The next day before dawn I performed Gaṇeśa pūjā and prayed for obstacles to be removed. I then spoke to my father, having prepared an outline in advance and explained to him the beliefs of my soul and also that I was in the process of receiving a Hindu name and that I would be giving up forever the family name.

My father's love remained outwardly hidden from me, however he listened and in his way showed his acceptance by remaining silent and not commenting on anything I had said. I invited him to join me in my meeting with his minister, Reverend Vars. My father declined, however my brother agreed to go with me. On Saturday I went to a brook where I had played as a child and performed Gaṅgā Sādhana, imparting to the leaves and flowing water all of my vestiges of Christianity and giving wildflowers I had picked to the water in thanks.

The meeting was set for the following Monday. I attended the Baptist church service on that Sunday with my brother and listened to Reverend Vars' sermon, which was on being joyful, gentle, having good, noble qualities. I introduced myself to him and also met briefly with many of my father's old friends. My father had stopped going to church at 86 due to fragility and weakness.

That Monday my brother and I arrived at the church at the appointed time. I believe that Lord Gaṇeśa and Gurudeva were there with me. Reverend Vars was very cordial. I spoke to him, explaining that I was grateful to have had a religious upbringing, talked about my years of spiritual questing, how his sermon had touched me, as it indeed was our belief as well to be gentle and to live a good life with good conduct. I had some trepidation that he might be spouting hellfire and damnation to me. However, I had prepared a great deal and sent prayers to the Kadavul Temple in Hawaii and had prayed to Gaṇeśa to remove obstacles and to smooth the way. I was so blessed.

I explained to the Reverend Vars my belief that I have, and always had, a Hindu soul, my belief in temple worship, divine beings, and in having a spiritual preceptor. I explained the Hindu beliefs of reincarnation and karma. Reverend Vars listened respectfully and told me that he had had chaplaincy training, where he had learned some about other religions, although he could not personally accept concepts like reincarnation. He turned to my brother and asked how he felt about what I was doing. My brother indicated that he would prefer it if I were to be a Christian but that he would support my choice.

I asked Reverend Vars if he would write me a letter of release. He stated that he would do so and mail it to me. I thanked him. I then offered him a copy of *Dancing with Śiva, Hinduism's Contemporary Catechism* to give him additional insight into the Hindu religion. He accepted and said, "I will read this."

FIRST BAPTIST CHURCH

330 EDGE HILL ROAD
P. O. BOX 327
MILTON, MASSACHUSETTS 02186
617-696-2119

May 3, 1998

To Whom it may concern:

I have today spoken with Barry Giles about his decision to convert to Hinduism. I found Barry sincere in his desire to follow his spiritual journey. I feel that he is honoring his past in the Baptist Church and showing concern for his family. My hope is that his subsequent journey is a satisfying one.

Rev. John R. Vars
Interim Minister

Baptist letter of severance received by Hitesvara Saravan.

Upon my return to San Diego I received the letter (p. 9) from the Baptist church. On May 28, 1998, I received word that Gurudeva had chosen *Saravan* for me as my Hindu last name. On May 31 I filed a petition in San Diego Superior Court to change my name. The court date was set for July 28. I also arranged that day for the name change to be published on four weekly dates prior to the court date.

It was as though my father had waited for me to tell him my news and that he had blessed me, for on July 16, 1998, my father made his transition quietly in his sleep. My mother had made her transition in 1992.

I appeared in court on July 28. The judge questioned the reason for my decision and promptly signed the decree. I immediately began the process of having legal papers changed, such as driver's license, social security and all of the many other places and documents that were necessary. I then informed all of my business associates and acquaintances of my decision.

After my thirty-one-day retreat subsequent to my father's death, I asked Gurudeva's blessing to have my *nāmakaraṇa saṁskāra.* Gurudeva sent a Church member, Sadhunathan Nadesan, and we met that day. I explained to him my Hindu beliefs, and he asked me some questions concerning these. I received Gurudeva's blessing, and subsequently Sadhu and I talked to the priest of our local *mandir.* The priest was somewhat surprised, as he had never performed a name-giving ceremony for an adult, but he consulted with his guru, who knew of our beloved Gurudeva, and we provided him with information concerning conversion, including a copy of the Six Steps to Conversion and a copy of a sample certificate. He agreed to perform the ceremony.

On the auspicious day of August 26, 1998, at a most beautiful ceremony performed by our local Hindu priest and looked over and blessed and attended by the Gods and devas and devotees of Gurudeva, I, Hitesvara Saravan, was "...thus bound eternally and immutably to the Hindu religion as a member of this most ancient faith," and guardian devas were invoked from the Antarloka to protect, guide and defend me. Jai Gaṇeśa.

I published in the newspaper a notice of my *nāmakaraṇa saṁskāra.* Our beloved Gurudeva was and is with me every step of the way. I received the following e-mail message from Gurudeva: "We are all very pleased that you have made this great step forward in your karmas of this life. Congratulations. Now the beginning begins. Don't proceed too fast. Don't proceed too slowly. Steady speed in the middle path."

My life changed forever. Continuous blessings have been flowing ever since from our beloved Satguru Sivaya Subramuniyaswami.

Hitesvara Saravan, 58, is the Administrator for the California Department of Health Services in San Diego and has oversight responsibilities for hospitals, nursing homes, home health agencies and hospices.

Our Release From the Jewish Faith

The Story of Facing Our Rabbi and Being Accepted by the Hindus of Denver. By Vel Alahan.

I was nervous as I sat with my former rabbi to discuss my change of religion. He turned out to be a fine, astute, intelligent man. We explained what we were doing, and he gave arguments in response. Basically he wanted us to give him a chance to start over with us. But we explained what we had been through and that we could not refute the inner knowing that had come from within ourselves about the truth of our Śaivism. We brought a witness with us, an old friend who lives in the neighborhood near the synagogue. We told him that based on our own inner experience we believed in Śaivite Hinduism and in Gurudeva as our guru. We explained how our worship is set up and the striving for eventual knowledge of Lord Śiva, merger in Lord Śiva. Based on the fact that I was a normal person, successful in the business world, with a family and children, he believed what I said and respected my convictions.

I explained to him why I had come: because I needed to A) test myself in the face of my former religious commitments and B) in the presence of my former rabbi and Jewish inner plane hierarchy, in the Jewish institution, state my inner commitment and my desire to leave Judaism. He had his arguments. We just had to stay strong. I held fast to my inner commitment. My outer mind was fluxing and swaying a bit, but I always had the inner part to hold onto.

He would not write a letter of severance. He felt that by writing such a letter he would be doing a wrong act himself. But he wished us well, gave his blessings and complimented us on our fine intellectual knowledge of our religion and of Judaism. We introduced the witness and explained why we had brought a witness, so that in the event that the rabbi would not write a letter, the witness could write a letter stating what had happened. We were well prepared, and that is a key point. If one were to go unkempt, unemployed, he would not get the respect. And if you are unprepared, you will fumble a bit.

Afterward the meeting was over I felt a sense of release. I felt wonderful. I couldn't believe I had actually done it. Of course, there were the details to be faced afterwards, the announcement and all. But it felt good. And we did not hurt the rabbi's feelings; though he did say he was sad to lose one of his fold and expressed his view that "Once a Jew, always a Jew." But he never had to face anything like this before and he said so, that it was something new to him and he would have to take it in on the inside and come to terms with it inside himself.

Actually, much of the experience of our severance took

place earlier, when we had been advised by the Academy to read some books on Judaism and then meet with the author and discuss Judaism with him. We also did extensive point-counterpoints comparing Judaism with Śaivism. At that time, that was a huge psychic battle, almost like a storm. And psychically it was not like fighting another person, but the other forces were defeated. It was a major inner struggle.

During the early years of our conversion process, we stayed away from the Denver Hindu community, though we visited the Indian food store regularly and paid our respects to the Gaṇeśa shrine there. We realize this would be the Deity of the future Hindu temple. At home, without fail, we did Gaṇeśa pūjā for a number of years with the whole family attending.

When we reached the stage to contact the Hindu community, and we made an appointment to meet with the Gangadharam family, Pattisapu and Sakunthala. We told them that we wanted to get to know the people and relate to them socially. They talked with us and took us into the community. They became our *appa* and *amma* and treated us very nicely. We explained that we intended to have a *nāmakaraṇa saṁskāra* later with our Gurudeva, and they immediately said, "We will do a *nāmakaraṇa*. We insist. It will be good for the community as a whole."

Interaction included playing tennis with some of the community, dinners, hiking, teas, Telegu new year, Tamil new year. Things progressed, and when the time was right and after we had seen the rabbi and chosen our names, the *nāmakaraṇa* was arranged. Mrs. Gangadharam planned the day according to Hindu astrology. And a priest was there from the Pittsburgh Temple, Panduranga Rao. Many people were there. A new sari was given to my wife to wear and a shirt and *veshṭi* was given to me. It was very nice the way they took care of us. During the ceremony, our "parents" signed our names in rice and repeated the required words

FILED IN THE COMBINED CLERKS OFFICE

JUN 16 1987

Eagle County, Colorado

By ________

DISTRICT COURT
COUNTY OF EAGLE
STATE OF COLORADO

CASE NUMPER 87CV2[illegible]

ORDER FOR CHANGE OF NAME

IN THE MATTER OF THE PETITION FOR THE CHANGE OF NAME OF:

LAWRENCE M. KANTROWITZ

The Court having read and considered the Petition for Change of Name and the Petitioner's Affidavit, and the Court being sufficiently advised:

FINDS: That the allegations made in said petition and affidavit satisfy all statutory requirements,

AND THE COURT FURTHER FINDS: That the desired change of name is proper and not detrimental to the interests of any other person.

IT IS THEREFORE ORDERED:

1. That the name of LAWRENCE M. KANTROWITZ is hereby changed to VEL ALAHAN

2. That pursuant to statute, petitioner shall give public notice of such change of name by publication of Public Notice, three times in VAIL TRAIL, a legal newspaper published in said county. This publication is to be made within twenty (20) days of date of this Order. Proper proof of publication shall be filed with the Clerk of the Court upon final publication.

BY THE COURT:

Jones

DISTRICT JUDGE

DATED: 6/16/87

COM[illegible]
Eagle County [illegible]
Certified to be full, [illegible] correct
copy of the original in my custody.
Date June 25, 1987
Clerk
By Deanna Rounsville Deputy Clerk

Vel Alahan's Colorado state name-change document.

before the community and Gods. Then we walked around and touched the feet of anyone who was an elder and gestured *namaskāra* to anyone younger. Food was served afterwards, *prasādam* from the pūjā.

Vel Alahan, 52, is a partner in a home building center in Vail, Colorado.

From Judaism to Hinduism

My Successful Struggle for Release From Judaism to Enter Hinduism. By Valli Alahan.

To convert from Judaism to Hinduism was a very big experience in this life. I didn't know that I would do it; it was nothing I ever planned on. But what happened in studying meditation and then later on, Hinduism, now seems inevitable and quite logical.

Our Gurudeva believes that it is best for a person to be fully of one religion, not half this and half that. When we began our inner study, I quite easily accepted Lord Gaṇeśa and what little I knew of Hinduism. I was ready to sign on right then. What I didn't know was that it is a very big process to consciously leave one's birth religion, especially Judaism at that time, with the confusion surrounding it as being a race-religion. So we were caught temporarily.

With the grace of Lord Gaṇeśa and Lord Murugan, our opportunity to convert moved along very slowly and with veiled sureness. I knew my true beliefs were in Hinduism and that I, the soul, had no binds. I felt that even if I could not convert in this life, I would hold my beliefs and it would work out later on. I also believed that Gurudeva would not have us go through this for nothing. Still it was discouraging to be halfway "there." I wanted to be the same religion as my Gurudeva. The longer it took, the more conviction and appreciation for Hinduism developed.

Minturn are hereby authorized to collect the emergency telephone charge imposed by this ordinance in accordance with Colorado Revised Statutes, 29-11-101 et. seq. 1973, as amended.

SECTION 4. This ordinance shall not be effective until the intergovernmental agreement creating the emergency telephone service authority and concerning the implementation of an emergency telephone service system is signed by representatives of all parties to the agreement.

INTRODUCED, READ AND ORDERED PUBLISHED ONCE IN FULL this 17th day of June, 1987.

TOWN OF MINTURN
Tito Peno
Mayor Pro-tem

ATTEST:
Darlene Lee Unger
Town Clerk

Published in The Vail Trail
on June 26, 1987

Public Notice

Letters of application to fill a vacancy on the Board of Councilmen for the Town of Minturn may be submitted to the office of the Town Clerk by July 1, 1987.

TOWN OF MINTURN
Darlene Lee Unger
Town Clerk

Published in The Vail Trail
on June 26, 1987

Public Notice

June 21, 1987

Vel and Valli Alahan, formerly Larry and Phyllis Kantrowitz and family, declared their apostacy to Judaism before Rabbi D. Goldberger, severing all ties to the Jewish religion in their conversion to Hinduism.

Explanations for their decision to convert were given in the meeting and were fully discussed.

As witnessed by me,
Robert L. Norman

Published in The Vail Trail
on June 26, July 3 and 10, 1987

Public Notice

ADVERTISEMENT FOR BIDS

PROJECT: Arrowhead at Vail — Water Tank Site Grading.

LOCATION: 1.5 miles west of Avon, Colorado along U.S. Highway 6

OWNER: Arrowhead Metropolitan District,

L. Kantrowitz was changed to John Alahan, the name of Ananda M. Kantrowitz was changed to Ananda Alahan; the name of Lese B. Kantrowitz was changed to Ambika Alahan.

CLERK OF THE DISTRICT COURT
Irene Carlow

Published in The Vail Trail
on June 19, 26 and July 3, 1987

Public Notice

NOTICE OF FINAL PAYMENT

NOTICE IS HEREBY GIVEN that the Town of Vail Recreation Department of Eagle County, Colorado, will make final payment at 292 West Meadow Drive, Vail, Colorado on July 9, 1987 at the hour of 11:00 a.m. to Richard T. Matthews of Matthews and Associates for all work done by said contractors in construction work performed within the Town of Vail.

Any person, copartnership, association of persons, company or corporation that has furnished labor, materials, provisions, or other supplies used or consumed by such contractors or their subcontractors, in or about the performance of the work contracted to be done, and whose claim therefor has not been paid by the contractors or their subcontractors, at any time up to and including the time of final settlement for the work contracted to be done, is required to file a verified statement of the amount due and unpaid, and an account of such claim to the Town of Vail Recreation Department, 292 West Meadow Drive, Vail, Colorado on or before the date and time hereinabove shown. Failure on the part of any claimant to file such verified statement of claim prior to such final settlement, will release the Town of Vail Recreation Department, its Board, officers, agents and employees of an from any and all liability for such claim.

BY ORDER OF THE
TOWN OF VAIL
By: Pamela A. Brandmeyer
Town Clerk

Published in The Vail Trail
on June 19 and 26, 1987

Public Notice

Per CRF 51.108(a)(b), regarding State of Colorado governmental audit compliance requirements, please be aware that copies of the 1986 Financial Report for the Town of Vail is available during regular office hours, Monday through Friday, 8:00 a.m. to 5:00 p.m. daily, for public inspection at the Office of the Town Clerk, Vail Municipal Building, 75 South Frontage Road West, Vail, Colorado 81657.

TOWN OF AIL
Pamela A. Brandmeyer
Town Clerk

Published in The Vail Trail
on June 19, 26 and July 3, 1987

P
A
PROJ
Transm
LOCA
along U
OWN
P.O. Bo
Wright,
ENGI
P.O. D
Arvada,
Pavelka
The
accepti
the Arr
Line a
Consol
Road, V
1987 at
and rea
not be
There
constru
Arrowh
Plans
the Eng
Copies
obtaine
upon p
each se
Each
accepta
least fi
payable
The
all bids
in any
The
approx
water l
indicate

Vel and Valli's notice announcing their conversion, authored by Robert L. Norman, the witness to their meeting with the rabbi.

We had to counterpoint our beliefs: Judaism and Hinduism. We (my husband and I) spoke to a rabbi in Israel over the telephone, after reading his book claiming Judaism predated and was the true source of Hinduism. And we wondered if we would ever resolve the conflicting karma of the birth religion and the religion of our soul. One morning I woke up from a dream where I was yelling at the Jewish angels in a fiery way, asserting that "I am not Jewish!" I read from the *Tirumantiram,* and it gave courage and security. This went on for seven or so years.

Then, with the grace of our Gurudeva, we were informed that we could amalgamate with the Denver Hindu community. It was a great joy to be around a generation of Indian Hindus that were very kind, open and understanding. Eventually they arranged for our *nāmakaraṇa.* The name-giving sacrament came after we formally declared apostasy to a rabbi in Denver. It was almost anti-climactic after the long wait, but still a little nerve-wracking because who could know what his reaction would be. We had a detached witness attend, and basically, without insult, the rabbi let us go. We published our change of religion in the local newspapers and with great joy began using our full Hindu names. This was a very meaningful experience that caused me to personally examine and pull up old roots and claim Hinduism as my true path.

Valli Alahan, 53, is a housewife, mother and grandmother in Vail, Colorado.

My Excommunication from Greek Orthodoxy

Sent Back To My Old Church, I Learned Hinduism Is The Only Religion for Me. By Diksha Kandar.

My present Śaivite Hindu name is Diksha Kandar; my former name was William Angelo Georgeson. I met Gurudeva in 1969, studied with him in California and India, and entered one of his monasteries in January of 1970. At that time a full conversion to Hinduism was not required, so I served in his monasteries until 1976, at which time he decided that a full conversion was necessary to thoroughly cleanse and clarify the minds of his devotees who had been involved in other religions prior to their exposure to Hinduism. I had been born and baptized in the Eastern Orthodox Christian religion, which is the original Christian religion that first emerged in Greece after the death of Christ. But beyond being baptized in it as a baby, I never participated in it and didn't know much about it. Yet as a monk, I had come to understand that this potent baptism had connected me up with inner world guardian angels who were obligated to guide me through life according to their Christian mindset, which I had previously adopted simply by being born into a Greek Orthodox family.

In 1976 Gurudeva informed me that because the Eastern Orthodox Faith is such an old and strong faith, it was considered a race-religion that I was bound to for life, and that I should return to that faith to participate in it fully and permanently. This was heartbreaking for me, and I remember openly crying about this unhappy situation of not being allowed into Hinduism.

I obeyed and returned to the city where I was baptized to practice Eastern Orthodox Christianity. I worked closely with the priest there and helped him with the church services. I very carefully studied this faith from its origins and learned its beliefs, which were very different than my Hindu beliefs, Orthodox Christian religion, which is the original Christian not only different, but very conflicting on many important points. Since I understood that Hinduism was not an option to me, I never discussed my Hindu beliefs with my Christian priest, because I could see that there was not a resolution in the discussion of them.

But in studying it out, I learned about a deep, mystical tradition that went back centuries in Greece. I felt if I could find a Christian monastery that lived the ancient spiritual tradition of the Church, then I would enter into that Christian monastery. I offered written prayers to Lord Gaṇeśa to help make this happen. Soon I was corresponding with an author in England who said he knew of such monasteries in Mount Athos, Greece. After six months of serving in the Greek Orthodox Church, I communicated all of this to Gurudeva. When he saw that I was clinging to my Hindu beliefs and did not share the beliefs of the Eastern Orthodox faith, he told me that now that I clearly understood the differences between the two faiths, if I wanted to, I could return to Hinduism after getting a letter of excommunication from the Christian Church, and after being refused the Christian sacraments offered by my priest and after getting my name legally changed to a Hindu name. What a happy day, and I did not hesitate to set all this into motion.

But the priest would not write such a letter, because to do so would be to consign me to everlasting hell, which he could not do in good conscience. The priest's wife came to me in tears, saying she was not crying because she was going to miss me but because of the condemnation of my soul to everlasting hell. I tried to console her, but it was no use. So then I went to the Church Bishop in San Francisco to see if he would write a letter of excommunication, but he would not discuss the issue with me. After another six months of effort, the Archbishop of North America in New York finally

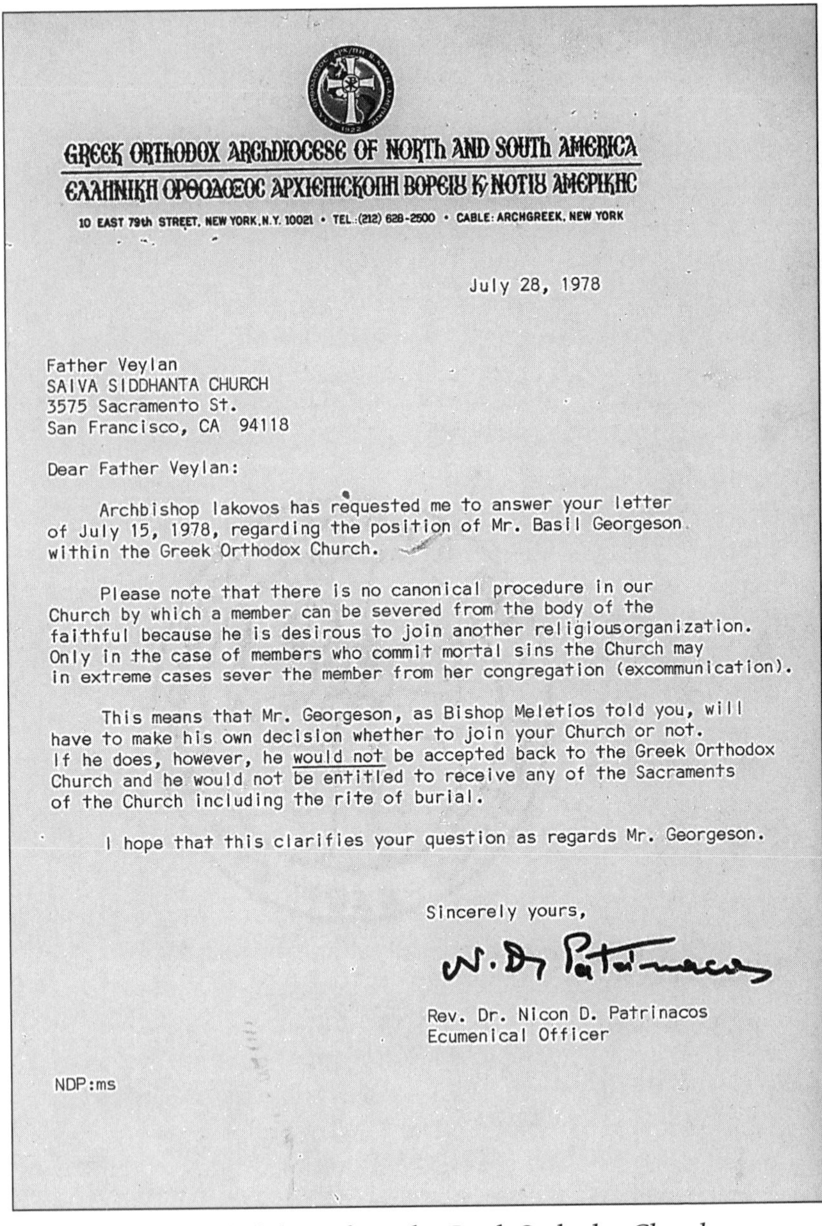

GREEK ORTHODOX ARCHDIOCESE OF NORTH AND SOUTH AMERICA

ΕΛΛΗΝΙΚΗ ΟΡΘΟΔΟΞΟΣ ΑΡΧΙΕΠΙΣΚΟΠΗ ΒΟΡΕΙΟΥ ΚΑΙ ΝΟΤΙΟΥ ΑΜΕΡΙΚΗΣ

10 EAST 79th STREET, NEW YORK, N.Y. 10021 • TEL.:(212) 628-2500 • CABLE: ARCHGREEK, NEW YORK

July 28, 1978

Father Veylan
SAIVA SIDDHANTA CHURCH
3575 Sacramento St.
San Francisco, CA 94118

Dear Father Veylan:

Archbishop Iakovos has requested me to answer your letter of July 15, 1978, regarding the position of Mr. Basil Georgeson within the Greek Orthodox Church.

Please note that there is no canonical procedure in our Church by which a member can be severed from the body of the faithful because he is desirous to join another religiousorganization. Only in the case of members who commit mortal sins the Church may in extreme cases sever the member from her congregation (excommunication).

This means that Mr. Georgeson, as Bishop Meletios told you, will have to make his own decision whether to join your Church or not. If he does, however, he would not be accepted back to the Greek Orthodox Church and he would not be entitled to receive any of the Sacraments of the Church including the rite of burial.

I hope that this clarifies your question as regards Mr. Georgeson.

Sincerely yours,

N. D. Patrinacos

Rev. Dr. Nicon D. Patrinacos
Ecumenical Officer

NDP:ms

Diksha Kandar's letter from the Greek Orthodox Church.

wrote a letter (see p. 20) that said I was no longer a member of the Eastern Orthodox Christian faith—another very happy day. It is this act by the Archbishop which severed my connection with the inner worlds and guardian angels of Christianity, and I felt a definite release.

My brother, an attorney, had my name legally changed for me. Finally, I had my *nāmakaraṇa saṁskāra* on January 5, 1979—Gurudeva's birthday—at Kadavul Hindu Temple in Kauai, which formally entered me into the inner and outer worlds of Hinduism and connected me up with Hindu guardian devas to guide me through life in accordance with my Hindu mindset, which to me accurately reflects the reality of all that is in all three worlds. I was given mantra *dīkshā*, initiation into the sacred Pañchākshara Mantra, by Gurudeva on September 9, 1982, at the famed Śiva Naṭarāja temple in Chidambaram, South India. These were two of the most important days of my life.

The whole excommunication process took exactly one year—to the day—to accomplish. There is no religion on Earth that comes close to comparing with the greatness of all that is Hinduism, most especially Śaivite Hinduism. In what sect of Hinduism would you find a woman weeping because someone's soul was eternally lost?

After returning to Gurudeva's monastery, I served for many years as a temple priest at the Palaniswami Sivan Temple in San Francisco and later in Concord, California. I was always treated with the utmost respect by the Indian community who came to the temple. They were always very impressed to hear my story of all the effort that I went through to become a Hindu, and I felt totally accepted by them as a Hindu and as a temple priest. Other Hindu priests also totally accepted me, and I am indebted to one very fine priest, Pandit Ravichandran, for his help in training me in priestly demeanor, protocol and the learning of the Sanskrit language for doing Hindu pūjās. Most importantly, I am indebted to my *satguru* for making it possible for me to be a Śaivite Hindu through and through, legally, physically, mentally, emotionally, socially, consciously, subconsciously and spiritually in this and inner worlds.

Diksha Kandar, age 58, lifetime brahmachārī for 31 years; served 23 years as a sādhaka in Gurudeva's monasteries, including serving as a priest in the temples in San Francisco, Concord and Virginia City. He presently works as a waiter in Seattle, while organizing outreach satsaṅgs.

Changing Over to a Śaivite Name

With My Family's Blessings, I completed the Legal Processes and Had a New Name-Giving Rite in Malaysia. By Sivaram Eswaran.

I was born into a Malaysian Hindu family and did not belong to any Hindu sect or religious group. Therefore, I didn't convert to become a Hindu and was free enough to chose to be a Śaivite Hindu. I am a student of Himālayan Academy preparing to become a member of Śaiva Siddhānta Church. One of the requirements was to bear and legally register a Śaivite Hindu name, first and last, and use it proudly each day in all circumstances, never concealing or altering it to adjust to non-Hindu cultures, as per *sūtra* 110 of *Living with Śiva.*

My original birth name was Raj Sivram Rajagopal. This name was incompatible with my Hindu astrology naming syllable, and the last name, *Rajagopal,* is a Vaishṇavite name. Therefore, I had to do a complete name change.

At this point my mother and relatives were unhappy about my proposed name change. Commonly in Eastern Hindu culture, especially in my family, a complete name change of an adult is discouraged. It's because they feel that this would indicate disrespect to parents and family elders,

BAHAGIAN KAD PENGENALAN,
IBU PEJABAT,
JABATAN PENDAFTARAN NEGARA, MALAYSIA,
WISMA PENDAFTARAN,
PERSIARAN BARAT,
46551 PETALING JAYA,
SELANGOR DARUL EHSAN

Telefon: 7560044
Kawat: COMNATREG, K.L.
Fax: 7575818

Ruj. Tuan:

Ruj. Kami: Bil.(12)dlm.JPN.KP: 163/683/PD /APN/0631(4) 98

Tarikh: - 6 AUG 1998

RAJ SIVRAM A/L RAJAGOPAL,
144L Rifle Range Road,
11400 Ayer Itam,
Pulau Pinang.

Tuan/Puan,

Pembetulan Butiran Dalam Kad Pengenalan No: 761005-07-5025 /A3424994

Adalah saya dengan hormatnya memaklumkan bahawa permohonan tuan/puan mengenai perkara di atas telah diluluskan seperti berikut:-

BUTIRAN DI KAD PENGENALAN SEKARANG	PEMBETULAN/PINDAAN DILULUSKAN
1. Nama RAJ SIVRAM A/L RAJAGOPAL	SIVARAM ESWARAN @ RAJ SIVRAM A/L
2. Jantina: -	RAJAGOPAL .
3. Tempat Lahir: -	-
4. Tarikh Lahir: -	-
5. Lain-lain Hal: -	-

2. Oleh itu tuan/puan bolehlah memohon Kad Pengenalan gantian berdasarkan kelulusan pindaan tersebut di mana-mana Pejabat Pendaftaran Negara yang berhampiran.

Sekian dimaklumkan. Terima Kasih.

" BERKHIDMAT UNTUK NEGARA "

Saya yang menurut perintah,

(ZOREDA BINTI ABD HAMID)
b.p. Ketua Pengarah,
Jabatan Pendaftaran Negara
MALAYSIA

s.k.

Pengarah/Pegawai Pendaftaran/P.P.

....

....

Rujukan tuan Bil:
Bersama-sama ini dikembarkan dokumen-dokumen untuk disertakan.

Sivaram Eswaran's decree of name-change, Malaysia.

difficulties to legalize the new name, and it would be a hot topic among the surrounding society. However, I managed to convince them with my strong intentions of becoming a Śaivite Hindu, a member of Śaiva Siddhānta Church, to have a name compatible with my astrology chart and the numerological naming system. Understanding and respecting my decision, my mother and relatives gave their full blessings for the name change. With the blessings of my beloved Satguru Sivaya Subramuniyaswami and the guidance of Acharya Ceyonswami and Sannyasin Shanmuganathaswami, I accepted Sivaram Eswaran as the best and most suitable Śaivite name for myself.

According to Malaysian law, any addition, correction or complete name change in the birth certificate can only be done within the age of one year old. The birth name remains the same in the birth certificate and the new name is only considered an additional name to the original one, if a person intends to change his name after the age of one year old. However, this additional name would only be approved with valid reasons and supporting documents attached to the formal application

Knowing all this, I made a name change application to the Malaysian Registration Department. This application was attached with my valid reasons and supporting letters from Satguru Sivaya Subramuniyaswami, a relative and a close friend. About five months later, I received the approval letter from the department. At this point I was given a temporary identity certificate, and a year later I received my new identity card.

My name remained the same in the birth certificate but the addition was done in the identity card as Sivaram Eswaran @ Raj Sivram s/o (son of) Rajagopal. Once I received the new identity card, I went on to correct my name in all other departments, documents, certificates, passport, driving license and bank books. Everything went on well.

With the blessings of my beloved Gurudeva, on 26 May 1999 morning, my *nāmakaraṇa saṁskāra* was conducted by the priests at Waterfall Śrī Gaṇeśa Temple, Penang, Malaysia. The ceremony was done in a complete Śaivite tradition with a *homa* fire. The ceremony was witnessed by my mother, family members, close relatives and friends, and by the head of my Church extended family, Kulapati Thanabalan Ganesan and his wife.

After the name change, everyone started calling me Sivaram Eswaran, and my signature was also changed. I could also feel some physical changes in myself. The change didn't end here, but dragged on and started to uplift my life. After my *nāmakaraṇa saṁskāra*, I felt like a newborn baby at the age of 23 on the spiritual path. I could really feel the change and differences in my daily life when I compare this period to the time when I was known as Raj Sivram s/o Rajagopal. My life started improving well, plans started to manifest, needs were catered on time and life now seems to be more successful then ever. I really prefer and enjoy this new birth after the death of Raj Sivram s/o Rajagopal on 26 May 1999. Believe it or not, it's really a wonderful life after a name change!

Sivaram Eswaran, 24, lives in Penang, Malaysia. He is a final year undergraduate with University Utara of Malaysia pursuing a Bachelor's Degree in Public Management.

How I Found My Guru

Rejecting Christian Science Early in Life, I Discovered Hindu Yoga and a Śaivite Master. By Easan Katir.

When I was fourteen, an out-of-body experience revealed that there was more to life than this world, so I set out to find out all I could about inner things. I read lots of books, and the one book I used for spiritual practices said "this book is good, but it is much better if you have a spiritual teacher, a guru." I didn't have one.

I had taken Hindu yoga books to the Christian Science Sunday school my parents sent me to, and remarked to the teacher, "These books are saying the same thing as your books, aren't they?" He said, "No, they're not, and don't bring those books here again!" So I didn't, and I also never went back.

When I was nineteen I attended a haṭha yoga class at Fresno State University once a week. One week I showed up, and someone at the door said, "The class has been cancelled, but there is a speaker here instead, and you can stay if you want to." Not having anything else to do, I stayed. A few minutes later, in walked this tall being with white hair and huge eyes. He sat down in full lotus in the front of the room. He began speaking in a language I'd never heard before. A young monk sat next to him and translated into English. The language was Shūm, the language of meditation. I thought this was awesome, and knew that I had found my spiritual teacher.

I studied through correspondence, then went on Innersearch pilgrimages to India, Sri Lanka and Switzerland. I was a monk for four years at Gurudeva's monastery, Kauai Aadheenam in Hawaii, where I "grew up" and was educated. I vividly remember the day in 1975 when Gurudeva took a machete in hand, carved the San Mārga path through the Hawaiian jungle and discovered the *svayambhū* Śivaliṅga. My formal adoption of Hinduism took place at the Chidambaram Naṭarāja Temple in South India in an initiation ceremony conducted by the *dīkshitar* priests and Gurudeva.

For a few years, I didn't see Gurudeva or know of his whereabouts. I pilgrimaged to the Lord Gaṇeśa temple in Flushing, New York. Sitting in front of the Śivaliṅgam after the pūjā, I saw a vision of Gurudeva in orange robes with his hand on my head. About five minutes later, I felt something on my head. I opened my eyes, looked up, and there was Gurudeva in orange robes, with his hand on my head. He said, "Because you have come to this temple, your whole life will change."

Soon afterwards, a marriage was arranged in Sri Lanka to a Hindu girl. Now, twenty years later, we have two children who are carrying on the Hindu culture in the deep, mystical way Gurudeva has taught us. We've been blessed to help with parts of his grand mission as well. We toured China, Hong Kong and Malaysia to raise funds for Iraivan Temple, carried the *yantras* for Kadavul Hindu Temple from India, helped found the Concord Murugan Temple, resurrected the British subscription base of Gurudeva's international magazine, HINDUISM TODAY, helped Sri Lankan refugees and with Iniki hurricane relief in 1992 at Kauai Aadheenam, and helped the Mauritius devotees with the installation of the nine-foot-tall Dakshiṇāmūrti at Gurudeva's Spiritual Park on that beautiful island.

Truly, through Gurudeva's ever-flowing blessings, I've experienced much of the four noble goals of human life written of in the scriptures, with Śiva as the Life of my life on the path of Hindu Dharma, the broad four-lane expressway to Śiva's Holy Feet. Aum Namaḥ Śivāya.

Easan Katir, 48, lives in Sacramento, California, a Certified Financial Planner with American Express. He entered Hindu Dharma in 1972.

My Whole Family Became Hindus

Years of Study, Introspection and Praying, Brought Us Into The World's Greatest Religion. By Isani Alahan.

I was introduced to Gurudeva's teachings in 1970 through a local haṭha yoga class held at the Parks and Recreation Department in the town where I lived, Carson City,

Nevada. The woman teaching the class would lend the students weekly lessons written by Gurudeva, then known as Master Subramuniya, which we would return the following week in exchange for another.

As time went on I read more about yoga and the wonderful benefits for the body and mind, which I could feel after a few weeks. At this time I decided to become a vegetarian. I was sixteen years old. A few years passed in which I completed high school, experienced travel to Mexico and across the US and the worldly education of Śrī Śrī Śrī Vishvaguru Mahā-Mahārāja.

In 1972 my interest in studying Shūm, Gurudeva's language of meditation, manifested. After signing up to study *The Master Course* audio tape series, I attended the weekly *satsaṅga* in Virginia City, Nevada, where the vibration was very actinic. During the first *satsaṅga*, the monks chanted Shūm. I had a memorable vision of Lord Śiva Naṭarāja on the banks of the sacred Gaṅga. My life had changed.

I was, needless to say, impressionable, and Gurudeva, in his tape course, repeatedly said, "Travel through the mind as the traveler travels the globe." I went to Europe for four months, experiencing the great civilizations of Greece, Italy, Morocco and Turkey. I had my first encounter with people of the Muslim faith. I learned a lot and repeatedly read Gurudeva's books.

When I returned to the US, I moved to the Bay Area to be near Gurudeva's San Francisco center, as the monastery in Virginia City had been closed to women at the time. I met Gurudeva in the spring of 1973 at a festival at the San Francisco Temple. I went on Gurudeva's Himālayan Academy Innersearch Travel-Study Program to Hawaii that summer. Then, per Gurudeva's instructions, I moved back home with my parents.

In January, I attended another Innersearch to Hawaii. I really enjoyed what I was learning, and I took my *brah-*

macharya vrāta. I studied at home, but there wasn't a strong support group at the time, and I lacked the inner strength to really stay on track on my own to do the daily *sādhanas* well.

In 1975 I married my husband of 25 years. My husband was accepting of my beliefs, but wasn't interested in studying with Gurudeva at the time. I continued my studies, and in 1980 I legally changed my name to Isani Alahan from Ardith Jean Barton, but kept my husband's last name, Pontius.

In December of 1982 I completed my conversion to Śaivite Hinduism from Catholicism. I worked closely with the yogīs and swāmīs in Kauai as they guided me through the relatively easy process. I prepared a statement of apostasy and took it to the local priest. He looked at it and agreed to sign my formal release from the Catholic Church. As I took a deep sigh of relief and quietly said that I was grateful the process had been so easy, he hesitated and asked me to leave the room. When I returned, he had changed his mind. He told me he had called the Bishop in Reno and was told he could not sign the paper. Later I learned this was not true, and the Bishop had been out of town.

The swāmīs encouraged me to try another priest in the town where I was born. He was understanding, but also declined. During the next few weeks, all but one of my family members were very encouraging and understanding. Only my eldest sister, who was the last remaining practicing Catholic of my siblings, was emotional and angry. My parents even apologized for not being able to help me in some way.

Within a few weeks, I called the Bishop to make an appointment to meet with him. He told me to go back to the original priest, who would sign my declaration of apostasy. I returned to the local rectory and met a priest of Chinese descent. He was very warm and accommodating. He explained how he understood the Hindu concept of ethical conversion. He signed my declaration and wished me the best.

The next few weeks were extremely magical, as I had my *nāmakaraṇa saṁskāra* at Kauai Aadheenam on December 25, 1982, with my two-year-old daughter, Neesha, and an old family friend, Nilima Visakan, now Nilima Srikantha. Then we were off for six weeks of Innersearch with Gurudeva and forty pilgrims, visiting temples and ashrams throughout Malaysia, Sri Lanka (Yogaswami's shrine was a personal highlight) and Tamil Nadu, India. It was a fantastic spiritual experience that continues to reverberate in my mind today.

At the time, my husband was not a Hindu, but our three daughters were given Hindu first names at birth, while keeping his family name. We raised the children according to Hindu Dharma and Gurudeva's guidance. In 1984 we moved to the Seattle area. During the ten years we lived in Seattle, my children and I gathered with the other local Śaiva Siddhānta Church members for weekly *satsaṅga.* We also met with the local Hindu community for festivals. We studied Bhārata Nātyam and Carnatic vocal music. We had open house at our home for local Hindus to learn more about Gurudeva's teachings. My children attended the summer camps put on by Church members in Hawaii, and we stayed in the flow of Gurudeva's mind even though we lived far from the other communities of Church members.

All through these years, I prayed that my husband would become a Śaivite Hindu and accept Gurudeva as his *satguru.* With my husband's permission, I would write the same prayer weekly, and during our weekly *homa* I would burn the prayers, asking the devas to please help our family to worship together and to live in closer harmony with Gurudeva's teachings.

In 1993 my husband formally adopted Śaivism, legally changed his name from Victor Dean Pontius to Durvasa Alahan. He became a vegetarian, stopped smoking and gave up catch-and-release fishing, which was his favorite hobby. He had his *nāmakaraṇa saṁskāra* on Mahāśivarātri in Kauai in

1994 and became a member of Gurudeva's Śaiva Siddhānta Church. That fall we moved to the island of Kauai to live near the holy feet of our beloved Gurudeva.

In November, 1996, my husband and eldest daughter went on pilgrimage with Gurudeva to India for a month. My daughter was interested in studying Bhārata Nātyam, and my husband, under Gurudeva's guidance, left my daughter in India so that she could attend Kalakshetra College of Fine Arts and get a diploma in Bhārata Nātyam. She started college in June of 1997, and the rest of the family, my husband, myself and two younger daughters, moved to Chennai, Tamil Nadu, in November of 1997. The past three years have had their moments of difficulty, but overall they have been a peak experience of my life, a fulfillment of my heart's desires. I am now looking forward in the spring of 2000, following my daughter's graduation from Kalakshetra, to moving back to Kauai with my family and joining the other families there. Jai Gurudeva, Sivaya Subramuniyaswaminatha!

Isani Alahan, 46, has for the past three years lived in Chennai, India, where she works in the home, cooking South Indian āyurvedic meals for her family of five and does home-school with her youngest daughter. She is also studying Carnatic music, Sanskrit, haṭha yoga and the Kerala health system known as Kalaripayattu.

My Husband and I and Our Lifelong Quest

From Vietnam to Yoga; Austerity in British Columbia to a Fulfilling Life in Family Dharma. By Amala Seyon.

My first introduction to Hinduism was when I met my husband. He had been going through a very soul-searching time, asking God why the Vietnam war, why the rioting in the streets of America, and what does materialism have to offer the soul? While going through this trying time and praying, he took a world religion class at the university. One day a born Hindu man came to his class and talked about the Hindu religion. All the concepts of Hinduism were the truths my husband was looking for. This Hindu man had a meditation center and invited anyone in the class to come. My husband started going on a regular basis.

During this time my husband asked me to marry him. He explained to me about the Hindu religion and took me to the meditation center. I was so happy to hear some of the concepts, like God is within you, the law of karma, the evolution of the soul. I felt like I had been in a cage, like a bird, and someone opened the door, and I was able to fly into something much bigger and deeper.

My husband told me that if we got married this was the path he wanted us to take. I accepted that and supported it fully. This started the process, to our surprise, of a confrontation of Western and Eastern philosophies. Our first encounter was in finding someone to marry us. We wanted to have a religious blessing, and so my husband went to the Hindu meditation center and asked this saintly man if he could marry us. He explained that his visa did not allow him to perform the ceremony. So we went to my family's Christian minister and asked him to marry us. He asked us to meet with him as he did with all young couples wishing to marry.

During this meeting he asked my husband a series of questions. Do you believe Jesus Christ is the only Son of God? Do you believe that the *Holy Bible* is the only word of God? The questioning went on for some time, and at the end of the interview he told my husband that not only could he not marry us but he was going to call my parents and tell them that he was against having me marry someone who was not a Christian. My minister went on to say that he couldn't marry us because he didn't believe in marrying

JACQUELAINE ELAINE SCOTT
425 WALNUT STREET
SAN FRANCISCO, CALIFORNIA 94118
PH. 567-2269

IN PROPRIA PERSONA

THE ANNEXED INSTRUMENT IS A CORRECT COPY OF THE ORIGINAL ON FILE IN MY OFFICE. ATTEST, CERTIFIED

FEB 21 1979

CARL M. OLSEN, COUNTY CLERK OF SAN FRANCISCO, AND EX-OFFICIO CLERK OF THE SUPERIOR COURT OF THE STATE OF CALIFORNIA, IN AND FOR THE COUNTY OF SAN FRANCISCO

BY ______ DEPUTY

FILE

ENDORSED
FILED
San Francisco County Superior Court
FEB 21 1979
CARL M. OLSEN, Clerk
G. RASCH, DEPUTY

SUPERIOR COURT OF THE STATE OF CALIFORNIA

FOR THE COUNTY OF SAN FRANCISCO

In the matter of the application of:

JACQUELAINE ELAINE SCOTT

NO. 747959

DECREE CHANGING NAME

The petition of Jacquelaine Elaine Scott for an order changing Petitioner"s name from Jacquelaine Elaine Scott to Amala Seyon came on regularly for hearing before this court on Feb. 21, 1979.

Proof having been made to the satisfaction of the court, the court finds that the notice of the hearing was given in the manner required by law, that no objections were filed by any person, and that the allegations of the petition are sufficient and true.

IT IS THEREFORE ORDERED that said petition be granted and that the name of Jacquelaine Elaine Scott be and is hereby changed to Amala Seyon

DATED: FEB 21 1979

____
Judge of the Superior Court

Amala Seyon's decree of name-change, state of California.

couples from different religious beliefs.

We then had to confront my mother, who was very much a Christian. This was all emotionally hard for her because of the belief that you could only be saved through the belief in Jesus Christ. She was very disappointed, and the issue caused a major disruption in our family. Finally, they accepted our marriage, and my husband located his past minister, now a professor of world religions at the university close by, who agreed to marry us. This brought to the forefront our Hindu beliefs to our family and friends. It was puzzling at the time, because my husband's spiritual teacher had told us that all religions are one.

After our marriage, we started reading all we could on Hinduism. My husband mistakenly followed the statements in Hindu scripture that we now realize were intended for monks. We sold and gave away all our wedding gifts and went to live in very remote areas of British Columbia. He read from morning until night and sat by a river for hours on end, but we finally realized we were not making real spiritual progress, and I was lonely living in remote areas and even on a deserted island.

We started searching and praying, and one day someone invited us to meet our Gurudeva, Sivaya Subramuniyaswami. We recognized what a great soul he was immediately, and we started our studies with him. We had two daughters at the time, but had not had our name-giving sacrament into the religion as yet. So, when our children were five and three years old, we all had our name-giving together, formally entering the Śaivite Hindu religion.

Gurudeva was very patient with us and helped my husband and me understand the dharma of family people and the limitless depths of the Hindu faith. My children were raised in the Hindu religion, and we spent a lot of years living near a Hindu temple, learning the culture and mixing with born Hindus at the Flushing, New York, Gaṇeśa temple.

We learned so much and felt so naturally a part of the Hindu heritage. We followed a home school curriculum and taught our children in the home until they were twelve years old. We felt it important to get the Hindu convictions in strong, so they would know their religion. Our daughters are now both married and are wonderful mothers who stay home and care for their children. Our oldest daughter is married to a wonderful Hindu man from Mauritius in an extended family that showers her with love. We now live on the little island of Kauai and serve the community and the broader Hindu family through our many activities, all guided by Gurudeva himself. We are so very grateful to our guru. Aum Namaḥ Śivāya.

Amala Seyon, 51, entered Hinduism in May 1975. A homemaker on Kauai, she and her husband live within walking distance of the Kadavul Hindu Temple.

I'm So Proud to Be a Śaivite

Disillusioned with Catholicism, I Wound Up with No Faith at All, Then Discovered a Whole New Way of Perceiving Life and Beyond. By Asha Alahan.

It all seems like lifetimes ago. I had been raised in a Catholic family. My mother was a devout Catholic, my father had converted to Catholicism right before they were married. I was a happy child, believing in God, loving God and just doing as I was told. But when I reached my teens, I started to question many of the beliefs and became very disillusioned with the Catholic Church. So I left and became nothing!

At eighteen I moved away from my parents' home to live with my older sister in Santa Barbara, California. I loved God and knew that something was really missing, but did not quite know where to begin searching. My subconscious was so programmed that it was the Catholic Church or nothing. As children we were not even allowed to enter other places of worship; it was considered a sin. So I just did nothing! It wasn't until I was twenty-one that I knew my life was on a down-hill spiral and I had to do something. I returned to my parents' home and tried going to the local Catholic Church again. But I still felt that their religion did not hold the answers for me.

It was not long after that I was married to my wonderful husband, and he introduced me to Gurudeva's teachings. He showed me the "On the Path" book series and I listened to the original *Master Course* tapes that he had. It was all so new and exciting. The words were so true, and Gurudeva's voice was so penetrating. It was a whole new way of perceiving the world and beyond—almost a little scary, as my subconscious mind kept trying to remind me of all the previous programming from early childhood and the Catholic school I had attended.

Finally, we were able through an invitation from Gurudeva to come to Kauai for Satguru Pūrṇimā. I was about seven months' pregnant with our first child. When I saw Gurudeva I was so surprised at what a tall person he was, with his white, flowing hair. His *darśana* was so powerful, I was almost overwhelmed. I had never been in the presence of such a refined soul. This was all so new to me.

We continued our studies and finally came to a point where we were able to give Gurudeva three choices for our new Śaivite Hindu names. After receiving our new names, we went to tell our parents about this. Both sets of parents lived in the surrounding area, and we saw them often, so even though this was new (our name change), it wasn't a surprise. But they did take a while to adjust. It was interesting that it was my father who first started to call me by my new name, and it wasn't long after that my mother did also.

We continued our studies with Gurudeva and proceeded

Mission San Luis Rey Parish

October 25, 1982

TO WHOM IT MAY CONCERN:

RE: Asha Alahan

ASHA ALAHAN states to me she no longer wishes to practice her Catholic faith.

She states she is "giving up her Catholic Faith", to join your Saivite Hindu Religion, thus in the eyes of the Church she is apostosizing.

Sincerely,

Rev. Paul Feichter, O.F.M.
Associate Pastor

714/757-3250
4070 Mission Avenue
San Luis Rey, California 92068

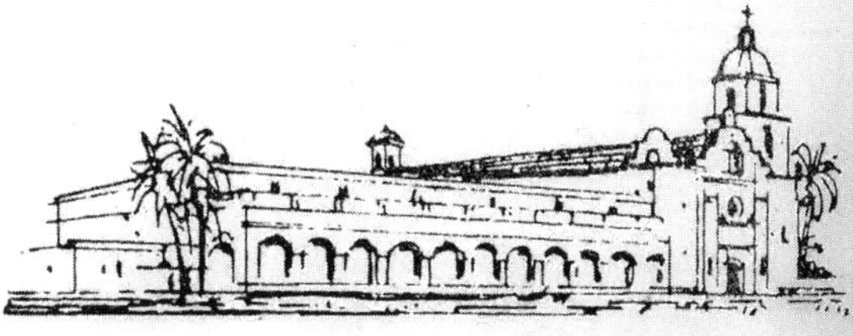

Asha Alahan's severance letter from her Catholic church.

to follow the steps towards severance. I had been confirmed in the Catholic Church so I needed to go back to the original parish where this had taken place and talk to the priest, have him understand my position and ask if he would please write a letter of severance for me. By the time I had finished speaking with him, he was unsure on what to say to me. He denied me the letter and suggested that I speak with the Archbishop of that diocese. I called and made an appointment with this person. I felt since I was going to a higher authority than the local priest that this should be easier. I was wrong. I thought he might understand my position and agree to write a letter for me. I was wrong. Well, he was not at all happy (even on the verge of anger) and totally refused to let me explain myself. So I left, wondering where I might go next.

In the area where we lived there were some old California missions that were still functional (as places of worship) so I decided to speak with a priest at the nearby mission. I knew the moment I walked into this priest's office that I had been guided by divine beings—he was the one to speak with. He had symbols of the major world religions hanging on his walls. We spoke for a while, and then he wrote me a letter (p. 37) stating that he understood that I wished to sever all previous ties with the Catholic Church and would soon be entering the Hindu religion and then wished me well.

Gurudeva suggested that I come to Kauai's Kadavul Hindu Temple to have my *nāmakaraṇa saṁskāra.* Which I did. It was a magical *saṁskāra.* At the time I don't think I realized the deep profoundness of that experience, finally finding the place where my soul knew it belonged.

I am so proud to be a Śaivite Hindu. I am proud of my Hindu name and often get compliments from people who hear it for the first time.

I am grateful and appreciate all that Gurudeva has done for me all these years, guiding me gently and offering me opportunities to make changes on the outside as well as on the inside. Jai Gurudeva. Jai!

Asha Alahan, 44, lives in the San Francisco East Bay, California. She formally entered Śaivism in 1985 at Kauai Hindu Temple. Asha, whose husband and children are also Hindus, is a wife, mother and housewife and a home-school teacher to all her children.

Excommunication and Facing the Family

The Priest Tested My Mettle, and My Parents Accepted My Decisions. By Kriya Haran.

I was born in New York City of a very strong Roman Catholic background. I went to church regularly. I was also an altar boy for a while. I made my communion and confirmation in the neighborhood church. I went to Catholic school for seventh and eighth grade, and my brother went into a monastery for a short time. I was formally excommunicated from the Catholic Church in 1978. I was lucky, as I was in New York City at the time, worshiping at the Gaṇeśa Temple in Queens.

I remember a few difficult parts of my excommunication. I think I was really coming to terms with my religious beliefs at that time. I was studying intensely with Gurudeva and one must have that total commitment and faith in your beliefs in Hinduism, because when you get excommunicated and are not of any religion it is a scary feeling. You realize how important religion is in one's life.

Facing my family was difficult and emotional. I didn't know how they would react to my decision. Also, I was worried about how they would react to my name change. Surprisingly, they accepted my decision with no arguments. They saw how much I had changed for the better since my association with Gurudeva, the swāmīs and other monks of Śaiva Siddhānta Church.

Chancery Office

Archdiocese of New York

1011 First Avenue • New York, N. Y. 10022
371-6100

December 29, 1978

This is to certify that, according to the Canon Law of the Catholic Church, Canon 2314, paragraph 1, as soon as the bearer, Leonard Santora, makes an act of public adherence to a religious faith other than Catholic, he is officially and automatically excommunicated from the Catholic Faith.

Edwin F. O'Brien

Reverend Edwin F. O'Brien
Vice Chancellor

Kriya Haran's letter of excommunication.

The other scary event I experienced was going to the archdiocese of New York City and facing the intimidating priests and nuns. I had to do this in order to get excommunicated. They simply do not want to let you go. They make excommunication an uncomfortable experience. I was (and still am) so sure of my Hindu beliefs that I would not take "no" for an answer, especially when the priest put his feet up on the desk and lit up a cigarette. The priest and I got into a heated discussion about Catholicism, Hinduism, heaven and hell, but my convictions and ties to Gurudeva were too strong for the priest. In the end, I succeeded in getting excommunicated (letter, p. 40).

Kriya Haran, 57, lives in Seattle, Washington, where he owns and operates his own taxi cab. He became a Hindu on January 4, 1979.

Reconciliation Was Arduous

I Had Been a Catholic, Mormon, Buddhist, New Age Person and More. By Damara Shanmugan.

In 1989 a friend and manager of a metaphysical bookstore gave me a little booklet as a thank you gift. She said, "It is by an American master known as Gurudeva." I read *I'm Alright, Right Now* every night for one month before going to sleep. Deep inside I knew that every word it contained was "the Truth," not just someone's interpretation of the Truth.

At the end of 1989 I sent away for *The Master Course* by mail and became a correspondence student of the Himālayan Academy. At this time in my life I was very active in the New Age movement. I worked full time and was also a massage therapist and rebirther. For years I had been going from teacher to teacher. All of them without exception taught, "Be your own guru, a real one is unnecessary," and "religion is

THE CHURCH OF
JESUS CHRIST
OF LATTER-DAY
SAINTS

MIRA MESA FIRST WARD
Penasquitos California Stake

June 16, 1992

Damara Shanmugan
10930 Summerdale Way #329
San Diego, CA 92126

Dear Sister Hunter:

I acknowledge your request to have your name removed from the records of The Church of Jesus Christ of Latter-day Saints.

Your request will be honored as you requested.

I am saddened by your decision but respect your free agency in this regard.

Sincerely,

Ross McCollum

Bishop Ross McCollum

Damara Shanmugan's letter from her Mormon church.

what is wrong with the world." For almost one year, I studied from afar, being careful not to get too close to this strangely familiar Hindu world.

I first met with Gurudeva in person on October 4, 1990. Any plans I had to only dangle my toes in the warm waters of Hinduism completely dissolved on that day. Just simply sitting in the presence of this wonderful enlightened being caused a shift within me that I could both feel and understand. I was forty-four years old at that time. I began to do pūjā every day as best I could and continued to study *The Master Course* teachings by mail and in seminars.

Unbelievably, I was moving toward membership in the only Hindu church on planet Earth. I probably hold the record for the most religions severed from! I had been born and raised a Catholic, attending ten years of Catholic school until 1960. In 1981 I became a Mormon and was very active as both a Ward and Stake Relief Society cooking teacher. By 1985 I found myself practicing Zen Buddhism and exploring the New Age movement. By nature, I do not have a very confronting personality, and over the years I had just drifted from one thing to another.

By December, 1991, I had completed all the necessary study to move toward becoming a Hindu. The next step was to reconcile what I now believed as a person aspiring to become a Hindu against all the beliefs I had held in the past. I took a whole month of vacation from work and spent that entire time searching my heart and soul, reconciling each belief as a Catholic, Mormon, Buddhist, New Age person and, yes, I even absorbed some beliefs from the drug culture and secular humanism.

I wrote over three-hundred pages of confessional prayers during that month. During this "gut-wrenching" time I had terrible pains in my stomach and more than a few times came very close to asking to be taken to the hospital. Why would I put myself through this? Was there some outside

A CENTER FOR SPIRITUAL AWAKENING
UNITY OF ESCONDIDO
Post Office Box 2396
Escondido, California 92033
(619) 745-2072

GREGORY E. PENN, D.D.
Minister

June 23, 1992

TO WHOM IT MAY CONCERN:

Please let it be known that Judy Hunter has completely severed ties with The Center For Spiritual Awakening, it's teacher, operations and her free-will funding of our Association. Judy has not been active in the Center's activities for more than a year, and without malice or prejudice, we freely let her go to continue her spiritual work wherever her heart so leads her. May she find happiness and well-being wherever her spirit takes her.

Respectfully and sincerely,

Gregory E. Penn, D.D.

LOCATION: 651 WEST SEVENTH AVENUE, ESCONDIDO, CALIFORNIA 92025

Damara Shanmugan's letter from her Buddhist teacher.

force making me do it? For the very first time in my life I knew from the inside out that I was finally on the right path for me.

My family did not take the change very well, and yet they all had to admit that I was happier and more content than they had ever seen me before. They decided to tolerate the changes. On January 1, 1992, I was given my new name, Damara Shanmugan. Such a beautiful and unique name. *Damara* means outstanding and surprising, an assistant of God Śiva. *Shanmugan* literally means, "six-faced," one of the many beautiful names of Lord Murugan, the God of Yoga.

Now began the formidable tasks of legally changing my name and obtaining a letter of severance from all former religious affiliations. But I was no longer just a drifter. A newfound courage was born of the knowing, without a shadow of a doubt, exactly what I believed from the inside out—not the outside in. I visited the Social Security Office, Department of Motor Vehicles, payroll department of my employer and filed a petition with the county of San Diego for a future court date in August of 1992. Every bill, card, account and license had to be corrected. Each phone call required an explanation, "Just as Cassius Clay became Muhammad Ali...."

I went back to the Catholic Church that I had attended until nineteen years old. As I attended mass each Sunday for a couple of months, I recognized the comfortable and soft feelings of this huge church. I realized that I had been guided and nurtured by kind, inner plane beings, angels, all through my childhood. I understood that there is no competition for souls in the inner worlds. And yet I also knew that what they were preaching I no longer believed.

I was bounced back and forth between the diocese and the parish when I called to get an appointment for excommunication. Finally one day when I was in the neighborhood, I just stopped by the rectory and asked to see the priest. They showed me in, and I told my story of wanting to be a Hindu and needing a letter of severance to move along my spiritual path. The forthcoming letter was beautiful, kind and loving beyond my wildest hopes and dreams. I understood the wisdom of closing this door with love and understanding.

When I went back to the Mormon ward I had attended for three years, I had a similar experience. The official letter of severance (p. 42) took months to arrive from Salt Lake City. And they sent many people to my home during that time to try to get me to change my mind. I discovered that I possessed an unwavering certainty within. This was a great surprise, for I had never been aware of this part of my character before.

Finally, I visited my New Age teacher, who loved and practiced Zen Buddhism. I could literally feel the deep karmic issues between us dissolving away. Another kind and loving letter was forthcoming (p. 44). My stomach was totally at peace now. Wow, I had done it! Not bad for a nonconfrontational person like myself.

I made plans to travel back to the Garden Isle of Kauai for my *nāmakaraṇa saṁskāra.* Just before leaving I had an incredible experience. One evening while sitting on the couch fully awake, I had a vision that is clearer today than it was on that night. I was surrounded by all the guardian angels who had helped me as a Christian. There were thirty or forty beautiful beings all around me. They were celebrating my becoming a Hindu! All around us was great celebration and joy. Then, off to the left, appeared another group of beautiful beings. I was lovingly escorted over to the new group, and I moved over to join them. I knew these to be my new guides, devas and Mahādevas of Hinduism. There was genuine celebration and pure joy among all these inner plane beings—no competition, no sorrow. I can still feel the love and well wishes of the former group.

The official ceremony took place in July of 1992, in the

small monastic Kadavul Temple on Gurudeva's paradise property in Kauai. There was a blazing fire in the *homa* pit and I was asked to stand between the Earthkeeper crystal and the six-foot-tall Śiva Naṭarāja during the last part of the ceremony. I don't remember my feet touching the ground. Gurudeva gave me a small *damaru*, Śiva's drum, symbolizing creation. I felt like a brand new person—new name, new religion, new culture, new way of dressing, new way of acting and a totally new way of seeing and relating to the world and people around me. It was an awesome day, and the feelings are stronger now than they were then.

Hinduism cannot be forced upon someone. Rather, Hinduism is found from the inside. Hinduism is a yearning vibration that can only be satisfied by finding and practicing Sanātana Dharma, the Eternal Truth. For me, Hinduism is none other than my own integrity, ever urging me on. On November 1, 1992, I became a member of Śaiva Siddhānta Church. I continue to make changes on the outside to match the unfolding truth and beauty from within.

Damara Shanmugan, 53, lives in La Mesa California with her 80-year-old mother. She became a Hindu on July 12, 1992. Damara is the Founder of The SHIVA (Saivite Hindu Information for the Visually Assisted) Braille Foundation. She has also been teaching haṭha yoga in the San Diego area since 1993.

From the Masonic Order and Roman Catholicism

How Our Quiet Life in Alaska Was Turned Inside Out When We Vacationed to Hawaii. By Shyamadeva and Peshanidevi Dandapani.

In February of 1994 we decided to take a relaxing vacation somewhere in the warm sunshine without a busy sightseeing schedule. Kauai presented itself in a roundabout way, and since we had visited Hawaii before (although not Kauai) it seemed to meet our needs. The roundabout got us to Kapaa, where we stayed at the Islander on the Beach.

Three days into our vacation we went into the Lazarus Used Bookstore, where Peshanidevi, my wife, began collecting books. She soon handed me a pile to purchase. On top was a copy of the second edition of *Dancing with Śiva.* I picked it up and looked at it, and on the back was a short biography and picture of the author, Satguru Sivaya Subramuniyaswami. Upon reading it, I said to my wife, "This author is right here on Kauai, and there is a temple here." We bought our books and went back to the hotel.

At this point we both seemed to be totally compelled, propelled and impelled to locate Gurudeva and the temple. We found a listing for Subramuniyaswami, Satguru Sivaya, in the local phone directory. There was also a phone listing for his Daily Sermonettes. We called, but there was no answer at the first number, so we called the Daily Sermonettes number and received *darśana* from Gurudeva for the very first time. After a few more attempts, Peshanidevi was able to talk with Yogi Rishinatha. She explained that we had found a copy of Gurudeva's book in the bookstore and would like to come to the temple and asked what the proper protocols were for visiting the temple. He gave instructions on what sections to read and directions for coming to the temple the next morning at 9:00 for pūjā.

We were both very excited the next morning as we drove up Kuamoo Road. With our Safeway flower bouquet in hand, we made our first walk up the path to the temple. Seeing the 16-ton black granite Nandi and the temple for the very first time was breathtaking. We washed our feet and entered the temple. It was beyond words. It was as if we had finally arrived back home after a long and arduous journey. Yogi very graciously welcomed us and guided us through the protocols, including prostrations to God and Gods. We sat down, the only two people in the temple that morning, as Ceyonswami began the pūjā. We did not know Sanskrit but somehow seemed to intuit the deeper beauty and meaning of the pūjā. Afterwards, we bought the newest edition of *Dancing with Śiva* and *Living with Śiva.* We purchased one of the tri-folds of Lord Gaṇeśa, Lord Murugan and Lord Śiva, plus postcards of the Deities, pamphlets and incense. We felt so alive that it was difficult to leave such an awesome experience and place.

Upon arriving back at the room, we made a small shrine with our pictures and flowers and began reading. The next day we returned to the temple. And this time, after the pūjā Ceyonswami came out to talk with us. It was so incredible to be in his presence. He was so loving, gentle and kind. We told him about finding Gurudeva's book and how we came to the temple. He explained some about Vedic astrology and asked if we would like to have our astrology done. We said, "Yes" and gave him our birth data. He said he would have it for us the next day. Again, we left dragging our feet, not wanting to leave the temple.

After the pūjā the next day, Swami asked us if we would like to meet Gurudeva. Yes, of course! When? Wait here. We can remember feeling His loving energy before he walked through the curtain. We could feel the love. And then we fully prostrated to our beloved Gurudeva for the very first time. It was as if we had done it many, many times before. As he sat down in his chair, he looked at us and said, "I see you are dancing with Śiva." At that moment we knew we had found our Guru, our Precious Preceptor, our Teacher. At that moment our lives were forever changed.

Later Ceyonswami gave us our astrology and explained some of it to us. He also talked about becoming vegetarian, which we were not. He gave us a wonderful little pamphlet entitled, "How to Win an Argument with a Meat-Eater." Unbeknownst to us, we had just become vegetarians. Our vacation had turned into a pilgrimage (in fact, it was the last vacation we have taken) and we had come back home to the Sanātana Dharma, the religion of our souls. During our two-week stay on Kauai, we received Gurudeva's *darśana* three times. Each time we were amazed at the power and how much we enjoyed it.

We left the island, full of both sadness and joy, and went home to Alaska. We set up a small shrine and every time we sat in the *darśana* of God, Gods and guru, we longed to return to Kauai and stay forever. We wanted to renounce the world to serve God and guru. That was not possible, but we did begin our first *sādhanas* in Himālayan Academy. In June we took our first three *vrātas*.

We pilgrimaged back to Kauai in November of 1994 for Kṛittika Dīpam. We stayed with the Katir family in their bed and breakfast, and we really increased our learning curve. We met and began merging with the island Church families. This was another special homecoming and a magical time with Gurudeva. During this pilgrimage, we truly began to embrace the Sanātana Dharma and returned home to Alaska with more *sādhanas*, to talk to our family and friends about becoming Hindus, and to begin merging with the Hindu community in Anchorage. For the most part everyone was tolerant of our enthusiasm about becoming Hindus, but no one wanted more information.

We had already leased out our house in preparation for moving to Kauai, so we rented an apartment and continued our studies and began the conversion and severance process with the most patient of *kulapatis!* Kulapati Deva Seyon gently nurtured us through this most intense time. It was our in-depth study to review our lives, to determine our true beliefs, where they came from and if they were still valid for us. There were many rewrites and surprises. We returned to our previous influences (myself to the Freemasons, and Peshanidevi to the Catholic Church), studying and participating with them again to be positive that we wanted to change our path. It was difficult to go back, because it did seem we were regressing. However, we knew that we were building a solid foundation on which to begin our new journey.

We returned to Kauai for the Pañcha Silanyāsa Stone Laying ceremony in April of 1995. It was an incredible pilgrimage. To be back on Kauai, at the holy feet of our beloved *satguru* and at this most auspicious time in the evolution and manifestation of Iraivan Temple, was such a remarkable and life-changing time. We met and merged with more of Gurudeva's global Church family, and we received our Hindu names, Shyamadeva Dandapani and Peshanidevi Dandapani. Such beautiful and long names! Gurudeva instructed us to legally change our names and to sever from our former religions by going back and fully embracing our former beliefs and writing a point-counterpoint for each one of them.

I returned to the Masonic Lodge and fully embraced Freemasonry for the next thirty days. I attended the lodge and participated fully in all its ceremonies and rituals. Everyone was glad to see me return, as it had been a few years since I had last attended lodge. At the end of the thirty days, I was completely convinced that I no longer held the inherent beliefs of the Masonic Order. Even with all the years of being a very active Mason—and my father also being a very well-known Mason—I knew it was neither my belief nor my path. The Masons say, "Once a Mason, always a Mason." The only way to sever the vows was to become a self-imposed apostate. I prepared a letter declaring that I was a self-imposed apostate to the Masonic vows and beliefs, and that I was converting fully to Śaivite Hinduism. I read the following letter in open lodge before all the members present and a copy was given to the secretary to be recorded into the minutes of the meeting on June 8, 1995, at Kenai Lodge No. 11.

To: *The Worshipful Master, Wardens,*
Officers and Members of Kenai Lodge No. 11
"I am here to terminate my Masonic membership as a self-imposed apostate. *Apostasy* means "an abandoning of what one has believed in, as a faith, cause, principles, etc." I am abandoning, and I have already abandoned, my former Masonic, Biblical and Christian beliefs. I do this of my own free will and accord and with a full understanding of the principles, landmarks, tenets and beliefs of Freemasonry. I also realize that taking this step will terminate my membership in all Masonic concordant bodies. My decision is made with the application of the strictest ethical principles of honesty and integrity. It is why I have chosen to do this in person at a stated communication of this Lodge. This is a personal decision. It is the spiritual path I have chosen to live. If I did not do this, I firmly believe it would affect my spiritual unfoldment as a Hindu. ¶I accept the finality of my decision. I would expect from this day forward to no longer have any privileges as a Mason. I have made my decision and will live by it. In fact, my decision to become a Śaivite Hindu includes adopting a Hindu name. Yesterday the Kenai Superior Court approved my legal name change to my new Hindu name, Shyamadeva Dandapani. It will be official in approximately thirty days. ¶In closing, I want each of you to know that this is my sole decision. It does not nor should it ever reflect on any member of my family or any member of this Lodge. I also want you to know that I acknowledge all the goodness that your friendship has brought into my life over the years. I am thankful to each and every one of you, for it has helped guide me on my path as a seeker of the Truth. I sincerely wish each and every one of you the very best that this life has to offer."

The only question came from the secretary, who asked, "Are you sure you do not want a demit?" to which I replied, "I am sure." I remained until the Lodge closed. Afterwards, a number of the members came up and wished me well on my path. I felt a great sense of relief and release.

Peshanidevi returned to the Midwest to attend mass and meet with the priest who had given her instructions for being baptized a Catholic. He had continued as a personal friend for some thirty years, even though she had not practiced that religion since her divorce in 1971. Two hours of discussion did not produce a letter of release, because he said, "Once a Catholic, always a Catholic." He took it very personally but promised a letter to follow. A month later it arrived (p. 54). The fire was strong but the bond was broken.

We applied for our legal name change and announced it in the newspapers. We made our court appearance, and the judge asked why we were doing it and if there was anyone in the court that objected. We told him for religious conversion to Hinduism, and no one objected. The whole process took less than five minutes and would become effective in thirty days. Gurudeva then blessed us with the news that we would have our *nāmakaraṇa saṁskāra* at Satguru Pūrṇimā. We were overwhelmed with his love and blessing.

On the auspicious day of July 9, 1995, in Kadavul Hindu Temple we made the irrevocable step of having our *nāmakaraṇa saṁskāra.* We felt the blessings of Lord Śiva and Gurudeva pour forth on us as we sat before God, Gods and Gurudeva and took this momentous, life-changing step onto the perfect path back to the lotus feet of our loving Lord Śiva. We "declared of our own volition acceptance of the principles of the Sanātana Dharma, and having severed all previous non-Hindu religious affiliations, attachments and commitments, hereby humbly petition entrance in the Śaivite Hindu religion through the traditional *nāmakaraṇa saṁskāra* and plead for recognition of this irrevocable conversion to Śaivite Hinduism." Thank you, Śiva! Thank you, Gurudeva! We had come home to the religion of our souls.

Our Lady of the Ozarks Catholic Church
P. O. Box 639
FORSYTH, MISSOURI 65653
Ph. 417/546-5208

January 17, 1995

Dear Francine,

It is with a heavy heart, and some reluctance, that I write this letter. I had hoped that you would be able to be an active and happy person as a Catholic. Even after your first marriage failed, I held out the hope that you could find a solution in your life to once more be active.

But this last move, it is so shocking that I could not react as I might have with more time. After your visit ended here, and you had gone, the impact of your decision became more scary. I can't imagine someone, who having been given the gift of Faith, could just set it aside. To make such a drastic change in your life makes one think that you have been brainwashed in some fashion. All that you guided your life by, is no longer revelant or has any meaning. I must confess to being amazed and not a little depressed. In a world that so desperately needs Our Savior, and needs to follow His teachings as a solution to the ills that we are enduring, to turn away from Him for a man-made philosophy is unbelievable. There has got to be another reason.

I can only hope that your desire to repair the errors of the past, has not led you to this decision. The past is past. It will never come again. The mistakes we made in the past can only be repented for, and the lessons we have learned by the wrong we have done, can and should guide our future decisions. But to so completely abandon the one saving supernatural mode of life for one that is based on natural knowledge, is to step backward into a realm of myth and conjecture.

I acknowledge that you are making this change in your life, and are embracing Saivite Hinduism. I do not approve. I do not give permission. I know this will not stop you in your determination to take this step. I also know that this step excommunicates you from the Catholic Church. I will pray every day that you come to your senses and return to the only true religion, The Catholic Faith.

I hope you will keep in touch as you promised to do. May the Blessing of Almighty God, Father, Son and Holy Spirit descent on you and remain forever.

Love and Prayers,

Father Mark Ernstmann

Father Mark Ernstmann

RECEIVED JAN 21 1995

Peshanidevi's heartfelt letter from her Catholic priest.

We experienced so much love, joy and emotion during the *nāmakaraṇa saṁskāra.* And it affirmed our beliefs that we are Śaivite souls and that we had been with Gurudeva in previous lives.

The fire of conversion was really roaring once we made our legal name change and *nāmakaraṇa saṁskāra* official in the newspapers and by mailing out a few hundred personal announcements to our parents, family, relatives, friends, clients and business associates. We mailed them the following announcement on a card with a beautiful Tamil Aum on the front: "To our dear family, friends, business associates, clients and customers: Eighteen months ago, Ron and Francine Moore went on a Hawaiian vacation to Kauai. While shopping in Kapaa at Lazarus Used Bookstore, we found the book, *Dancing with Śiva,* by Satguru Sivaya Subramuniyaswami. Since that moment our lives have forever changed. We discovered that Gurudeva, as he is affectionately known, was right there on Kauai. We located the Kadavul Hindu Temple. We attended the worship service. We had the privilege to meet Gurudeva. We knew we had found the religion of our souls and a preceptor to guide us on the path. ¶We have just completed our ethical conversion to Śaivite Hinduism and this is our announcement of that momentous event. We feel very grateful to live in a country that allows freedom of religion. We thank God and all of you for your love, understanding and support. We will be happy to assist anyone with pronunciations or to answer questions. Shyamadeva Dandapani (formerly known as Ronald Hance Moore) and Peshanidevi Dandapani (formerly known as Francine McPherson Moore) at a *nāmakaraṇa saṁskāra* (name-giving sacrament) held at their request on the auspicious day of July 9, 1995, at the Kadavul Hindu Temple on the Garden Island of Kauai, were duly given their Hindu names in accordance with the traditions of Śaivite Hinduism. They have made this irrevocable conversion to Śaivite

Hinduism, and they respectfully request everyone to use their new names in all instances from this day forward. Their new names have been legally changed by the courts and became effective July 7, 1995. The phonetic pronunciation is She-ah-ma-day-va Dawn-duh-pa-nee and Pay-shaw-nee-day-vee Dawn-duh-pa-nee."

The name change seemed to make our conversion very real to others, and many were quite alarmed. Our daughter was visibly frightened to enter our shrine room, and she forbid her young children to spend the night with us anymore. She was willing to use our new names and said that whatever we wanted to do was okay, but it was not for her. She would not accept any literature from us or talk about Hinduism. The two sons said about the same but were less rigid. My parents and siblings felt total rejection because of the family name, and they disowned us. They said that if their name was not good enough for us, then they had no son and daughter. Peshanidevi's parents are deceased, but she had been like an adopted daughter to my parents for years. My wife's grandmother and her brother were the only family members who were really happy for us. And they showed it by immediately beginning to learn how to pronounce and then use our new names. In my work, a few close friends fully accepted our new names and life without question. However, there was a period of about one year where I received a lot of fire and testing.

Many Śaiva Siddhānta Church members had shared their stories of conversion with us, so we were a little bit prepared. We felt so strongly in what we were doing, that we could continue on our path with love and joy. Life with Gurudeva just gets better and better, and there is so much more. Now we knew why we were here and where we were going. We thank you, Gurudeva, from the lotus of our hearts for all your gifts and blessings.

Shyamadeva and Peshanidevi Dandapani, both age 54,

live in Wailua, Hawaii on the island of Kauai. Shyamadeva is a commercial real estate broker specializing in site acquisitions and leasing for local, regional and national real estate clients. Peshanidevi is a domestic goddess and homemaker.

From the Sister Faith of Taoism

My New Hindu Name was Perhaps the Biggest Hurdle for My Chinese-American Family. By Indivar Sivanathan.

In retrospect, one can look at the journey of discovering why we are here, how we will get there, and appreciate the "chance" happenings, the signs, that have brought us to the present. For me the search really began in adolescence, and the awareness of being a religious seeker came in my early twenties. After meeting Gurudeva for the first time, and receiving my *nāmakaraṇa saṁskāra* several years later, I finally felt as if I had come home.

Early life was growing up in Hawaii in the 1950s and 60s. My parents are second-generation Chinese-American, and we were raised with a grandmother, uncles, aunts and lots of cousins. Father and Mother did not believe in imposing religious beliefs on their children; consequently no formal religion was taught at home. However there were small observances around births, deaths, auspicious and inauspicious times, and paying homage to our departed grandparents.

My mother would recount stories and beliefs held by her parents, about spirits, the nature of people by reading their faces, and myriad other observances about how to live life. We had one uncle who was a Southern Baptist! After his constant insistence we attend Sunday School, Mother finally assented. I remember sitting in the pulpit while the pastor was preaching at the top of his lungs that we were all "born in sin" and were "dirty" and "bad." Fortunately as a four-year old I thought, "I haven't done anything wrong" and dismissed the sermon. After sitting in the psalm singing group later, I definitely decided all this was not for me. Fortunately my parents did not force or encourage future visits to the church.

Then the university experience: humanism, existentialism, self-expression in the 1960s and getting as much experience as one can; then living in Europe and then becoming clear that this pursuit of experience for its own sake was a dead-end street. Perhaps the soul was starting to push itself forward, beginning thoughts of changing my life and direction entirely.

The first thing was to live a pure life, so I decided to become a vegetarian. The next was to start studying with a good teacher. But where to start? At this time came two inner-plane dreams, one taking place in Zürich, Switzerland. An elephant was running through town, its mahout unable to control him. Seeing him charge toward me, I projected a thought to him, and he answered rather humorously. He then hoisted me up on his back with his trunk and carried me around the lake which surrounds the town.

In December of the same year the Śaiva Siddhānta Church conducted an Innersearch Study Program on the Big Island of Hawaii. One very chilly morning we gathered in a room where a picture of a being with an elephant's head and a human body was displayed. I thought, "My God, what have I gotten myself into!" and in a split second remembered the dream in Zürich. It was then I realized our Great Lord Gaṇeśa had brought me to this point, and would always be there for me.

After the dreams in Switzerland, a major chapter of my life was coming to an end. Many of the aspirations and self-propelled ambitions had come to naught. At my lowest point, I was fortunate to have a session with a psychic healer (Betty Bethards) who had just returned from Hawaii where she had visited a mystical bookstore. She read material written by a "white-haired man" who had an *āśrama* on Kauai. She said the books were "right on" and suggested I start studying there, as "he wasn't very high" (chuckle).

After reading *The Clear White Light* and other "On the Path" books by Gurudeva, wonderful inner things began to happen. On January 5, 1974, I met him for the first time, and the connection was cemented.

When students were informed that in order to continue studying with Gurudeva and the reasons for doing so, like many others who were born and raised in a non-Hindu culture, all the anxieties and fears of disassociation came up to the forefront: loss of friends, strained work relations because of being thought different, not to mention the same happening in one's family.

Interestingly, Gurudeva had to tell me what religion I had to sever from: Taoism. Fortunately a Ta Chiao Festival of Renewal was being conducted in Honolulu at that time, so there was an opportunity to experience religious practices directly. My "advisor" was a Catholic Sicilian-born professor of Chinese Religion at the University of Hawaii. What was discovered were the similarities between Taoism and Hinduism, in ritual as well as in approach and attitude. The Taoist scripture being followed by the priest was in Sanskrit. *Mudrās* were used to communicate with the Gods. The Hawaiian Deities were propitiated to accept the Taoist Gods. There were guardians of the eight directions. There was no sermonizing in the temples, and the resident priests facilitated interaction between the Gods and people by performing rituals, burning prayers and translating the responses through their psychic vision and hearing.

The process of comparing the two religions done, it was necessary to speak to my parents and convince my mother that changing my name was not a repudiation of the family, but accepting an identity which felt closer to me than my given name. While on a walk with Mother I tried to explain that I never felt comfortable with my own name, and she became even more hurt. Finally I reminded her she had changed her own Chinese name to a Western one. When she replied, "That was different," I blurted out, "If I had your name, I would have changed it, too!" She laughed, as her Cantonese name was less than melodic.

After that, everything went smoothly. Back in 1980 we chose names from a very long list. I picked three first names and some last names and asked friends to call me by them. The combination which felt right and flowed together nicely was the one chosen. All was approved for the ceremony on Mahāśivarātri night in February of 1980 at Kadavul Temple on Kauai. All in all, the process of entering the Hindu religion for me was more one of acceptance rather than the "burning by fire" that comes from a difficult severance. This was probably because of Taoism being so similar to Hinduism, my being raised in an Oriental family, and in the more tolerant environment of Hawaii, where so many beliefs and cultures blend together.

Indivar Sivanathan, 52, lives in Bend, Oregon, where she is a photographer, primarily of architecture and interiors. She entered Hinduism formally on February 14, 1980.

Being Refused Communion Was the Test

I Felt the Catholic Angels Withdraw When I Said "I No Longer Believed In Jesus as the Son of God." By Aran Sendan.

I was in the process of formally converting from Roman Catholicism to Hinduism, having done my point-counterpoint belief comparisons between the two religions and having gone back to the Catholic Church to try practicing that faith again.

I had resolved that, yes, indeed I felt more comfortable with Hindu beliefs than those of Catholicism or Christianity.

I needed a clean break with Catholicism, so went back to Sacred Heart Church, the parish in which I was baptized, confirmed and received my first holy communion. I had an appointment with the monsignor and met with him in the rectory office. It was a old room, filled with glass-doored bookcases piled up with books and papers. The desk was a jumble of more books and papers as well.

I would have preferred a frank and rational discussion along the lines of the point-counterpoint; I was ready for that, but we were not going there. He was a little non-plussed by my statements, like it really wasn't happening, and said that, well, Buddhists or whatever were good people, too, and if I wanted to study, that it was alright with him. I insisted that he write "declared apostate" next to my name in the Parish record book where my baptism, confirmation and first holy communion dates were recorded. He wouldn't do it, but allowed me to. I wrote "declared apostate" and dated it. I left the meeting a little unsatisfied by the interaction and felt that I needed to do something else.

I decided to attend mass the next morning and went up to the communion rail where the same priest was giving out holy communion to the faithful. It seemed to me that his faith would prevent him from giving me holy communion and thus my point would be made. At the rail he asked if I "believed in Jesus Christ as the son of God and the savior of mankind." I said that I didn't and that he couldn't give me holy communion. At that moment it became real. I could feel the Catholic angels withdrawing from me, as clearly as I could feel the wind. I now understood Catholicism better than I had ever understood it before. It isn't a religion of belief. It's a religion of faith, and clearly not my faith. I was no longer a Catholic.

Aran Sendan, 50, is a builder and general contractor in El Sobrante, California. He and his wife Valli entered Hinduism formally on February 14, 1980.

At Home in Hinduism

Attending a Guru Pūjā, I Knew Without Doubt That I Was a Hindu. By Chamundi Sabanathan.

I first met Gurudeva just over 32 years ago, in 1967, at the age of 19, having married one of his devotees and begun my study and practice of *The Master Course.* My background to that point had been nonreligious. My father was an unconfirmed Presbyterian, my mother an unconfirmed Episcopalian, and neither a church-goer. In my teen years, out of curiosity, I had accompanied several of my friends to their respective churches—Catholic, Baptist, Presbyterian, and a Jewish synagogue—but had felt no sense of recognition in any of them. It was like staring blankly at a piece of modern art and wondering, "Why?"

During those years, though, I was also avidly reading whatever books I could find that dealt with the Eastern religions. These—especially the *Upanishads* and the *Dhammapada*—awakened in me a strong sense of recognition, a feeling of rightness.

Oddly enough, although I had expected to feel Gurudeva's presence very powerfully on meeting him, this did not happen at first, which disturbed me deeply. It wasn't until that first wonderful *pādapūjā* (ceremonial worship of his holy feet) in San Francisco that I knew beyond doubt that I was a Hindu. I had read about *pādapūjā* before. I had known that after the guru's feet are ceremonially bathed, the devotees are offered the water to drink—and I had worried that when that time came I might react in a Western way. Indeed, doubtless to make things easier for any who did feel reluctant, Gurudeva sort of chuckled and told us, "You don't have to drink it; I didn't wash them."

But far from feeling any reluctance, I was completely overcome with the feeling one might have upon reaching an oasis after wandering for days—a lifetime, in this case—without water in the desert. At that point I knew I was a Hindu and that Gurudeva was my *satguru*, although it was not until years later that my husband and I were actually able to take our family to Kadavul Hindu Temple in Hawaii and have our *nāmakaraṇa saṁskāras.*

Chamundi Sabanathan, 52, lives with her daughter and son-in-law and their three home-schooled children in Santa Rosa, California. She was accepted into Hinduism through the nāmakaraṇa saṁskāra on Mahāśivaratri, March 4, 1981 at Kadavul Hindu Temple.

Constant Nourishment and Solace

I Took up Gurudeva's Hindu Teachings as a Teen and Entered the Faith at Age 25. By Shama Vinayaga.

I first learned about Gurudeva when I was about sixteen years old. A group of my girl friends ordered *The Master Course* and started listening to it every Friday, at which time we also started doing haṭha yoga. We had no religious foundation at this time and were blundering along.

However, it was not until I was almost twenty that I decided to go to Hawaii and meet Gurudeva. A friend came with me. We stayed in the outdoor cabins on the Mauna Kea hillside on the Big Island, attended daily pūjās and started studying Shūm, the language of meditation. You can imagine my shock and surprise when the winter air descended on the Mauna Kea slopes. I thought that I was coming to Hawaii. I was warmer back home in the Canadian North. After two weeks of a very arduous schedule, we flew to Kauai to meet Gurudeva. The daily pūjās had reached deep into my soul, and I felt that I was starting to climb out of an abyss. Upon arrival on Kauai, we attended a pūjā at the Kadavul Hindu Temple. The Śiva Naṭarāja Deity was the only icon there at that time, and it was housed in a small shelter with a thick white sand floor. The pūjās were extremely powerful and drew me inward.

However, nothing compared to my meeting with dear, sweet Gurudeva. I was sitting with a group of ladies on the grass outside the temple when Gurudeva came along. He commented on the group of flowers ornating the lawn. It was at this time that I was blessed with Gurudeva's presence, the *śaktipāta* from a realized soul and *satguru.* It was a gift that I will always cherish.

The years ahead proved to be very arduous, as I was forced to face myself again and again. My belief structure had to be reformatted. I became a vegetarian, and I had to learn to combat instinctive desires.

After many years of doing regular pūjā and *sādhana,* I was able to have my *nāmakaraṇa saṁskāra* at the Kadavul Hindu Temple. I was almost twenty-five years old. The after effects of the ceremony permeated the depths of my being. The congregation sang "Śaṅkara Śiva." To this day, when I sing this song I feel as if I have come home.

The Hindu religion has given me constant nourishment and solace. It has given me the strength to face seed karmas. It has magically lifted me up again and again. There are no words to express the gratitude that I feel to Gurudeva, the philosophy and the Gods. There is no doubt in my mind that Hinduism is the root religion. It feels so ancient and yet so close.

I pray that I will always have the humility to move forward in the San Mārga path, that I will have the courage to face myself at all times and that I will be able to slowly build my inner temple while maintaining a spirit of upliftment toward each human being that I may encounter—none of which I could begin to do without the guidance of Gurudeva Sivaya Subramuniyaswami.

Shama Vinayaga, 46, is a Compliance Officer at Wain-

wright Credit Union Ltd. in Wainwright, Alberta, Canada. She became a Hindu on January 5, 1979.

Breaking the Idol Barrier

How the Hindu Way of Worship Changed My Life. By Rudite J. Emir.

I grew up in a Christian family. Not only was it Christian, it was Protestant. Protestants tend to be austere in their ritualism and in their portrayal of holy images. The typical church holds a cross, perhaps a statue or painting of Christ. Stained glass windows may depict the life of Christ or of his apostles—that is all. The Catholic propensity for richer symbolism was viewed through my Protestant family's eyes as a strange kind of extravagance, colored by a touch of something almost pagan. I remember looking skeptically at Catholics kneeling in front of statues of saints and burning candles by their images to invoke their blessings.

That's the kind of mind that came in contact with the religious thought and culture of the Hindus. Around the age of sixteen the impact of spiritual India began to enter my life. The influence came first through contemplative literature—the poetry of Rabindranāth Tagore, the *Bhagavad Gītā,* and the *Upanishads.* Though they touched my heart and initiated new stirrings deep within, still, the heart was not blasted wide open. I had not yet met my guru.

Then I met Gurudev, Swami Chinmayananda. I was twenty-six, with an unappeased hunger that had begun ten years earlier and had still not been satisfied. Swāmījī blasted my heart wide open as his love-drenched intellect pierced through my rational mind to reach the sanctuary within.

Around that time the symbolic and ritual aspect of Hindu worship also became known to me through *bhajanas* and *kīrtana,* prostrations to the teacher, receiving of *prasāda* from the hands of the guru, and the first tentative, uncertain, yet strangely overpowering experiences with a *pādapūjā*, worship of the guru's sandals. Still, the Protestant in me affirmed, "I am a Vedāntin, not a Hindu. The ritualistic aspect of the spiritual search is for the Hindu, not for me, a Westerner. I am striving for the essence behind the symbol; the symbol itself I can forego."

My first trip to India, about ten years after I had met Swāmījī, included a few unforgettable visits to temples and some dutiful prostrations in front of idols. I did it out of respect for the spiritual traditions of a country I had grown to revere and out of my intellectual appreciation that each symbol stood for a deeper meaning behind it. But the Protestant in me still persisted in her protest against worship of inanimate stone and wood.

In the fall of 1987 I had the good fortune to participate in a Chinmāyā Spiritual Camp at Sidhabari, Himachal Pradesh, at the foothills of the Himālayas. The spiritually charged setting, the meditative stillness of the Himālayas, left my mind in awe. One morning after meditation I found myself walking toward the temple. After doing my *pranāms* in front of the idols in the sanctuary, I followed the other worshipers to the rear of the temple. I must confess I had no idea what I might find there. As I turned the corner, my eyes fell upon a wooden image of Gaṇeśa. A blast of overpowering emotion almost pushed me to the ground. I was reeling inside. Lord Gaṇeśa, through the idol, had just come alive for me. In fact, He had caught me totally unawares, had taken me by surprise by this unexpectedly powerful announcement of His undeniable presence. "Lord Gaṇeśa, what have You done? Of all the idols that I had contemplated upon in my intellectual studies of Hindu symbolism, You of all the many Deities left me quizzical and wondering—You with the strange animal head, the bloated belly, the broken tusk. I could never take You seriously. I wondered how so many Hindus could. And now, what have You done? Among the bevy of beautiful, statuesque, inspiring images of Hindu Gods, dear Lord, You chose to speak to me through the strange, even comical, form of Gaṇeśa!"

I left the temple as though struck by a bolt of lightning. My mind later pondered over what had transpired. Perhaps my encounter with Gaṇeśa was simply the extension of a fulfilling hour of contemplation that had ended just moments before my visit to the temple. The experience would most likely not be repeated. The next day I decided to test the previous day's newfound reality. As I rounded the corner toward the back of the temple, I found myself talking to Gaṇeśa, half-reverently, half-jokingly (as He had left me with a very intimate, slightly jovial feeling of His presence the day before): "Gaṇeśa, will You really be there for me again? Will you assert Your reality through the dead image of carved wood? Go ahead, prove it to me!" He did it again. And again and again, for many days afterward.

The Protestant in me no longer protests. How can she? Not only does Gaṇeśa speak to me through the idol now, He has also proven His presence as the Remover of Obstacles for me. On my return trip from Sidhabari, I had no train reservations. Gathered in a huddle on the station platform, my friends were valiantly trying to persuade the railway personnel to allow me to use a ticket unused by another passenger. In vain. The conductor's face remained stern; his head continued to shake in an adamant "No!" Departure time was approaching fast. By the minute, it looked less and less likely that I would reach New Delhi in time to meet Swāmījī when he arrived there. Only one thing to do. "Gaṇeśa!" I cried in my mind, "You must come to help me now! Remove this obstacle!" The very instant I shouted those words in my mind, a smile broke across the conductor's face. "OK," he said, "we'll arrange for a seat."

The Protestant protests no more.

The idol barrier has been broken.

You may wonder if I took the step of converting to Hinduism. The answer is that I did not. I feel more of a universalist than a Hindu, although, through Vedānta, Hinduism became very close to my heart. I don't feel that I have fully severed my ties with my Christian roots, nor have I through my study of Vedānta disallowed loving, for instance, Rumi's intense love for God and worshiping Him through Rumi's poems. I see myself as someone who has a universal outlook on spirituality, with openness to many of the great religions of the world (which I have learned to understand from a deeper perspective through Vedānta), but with a particular love for Hinduism because of my many years of study with my guru from India.

Rudite Emir lives in Los Altos, California. She conducts business workshops incorporating the principles of Vedānta into business management.

An Unexpected Life-Changing Pūjā

How the Goddess Captured Me Forever.
By Stephen P. Huyler.

I had been to Padmapoda, a village in eastern India, a number of times previously to visit the family of a close friend. Each time, I was taken to see the sacred tree that embodies the local Goddess, Gelubai, the Deity of the community. But this visit brought an unprecedented honor: being allowed to witness the ceremony of invocation in which the dynamic power of the supreme Goddess Chandi was requested. It was a very special ritual, enacted on rare occasions to implore the aid of the Goddess in overcoming a difficult domestic problem. The entire ritual had already taken two priests two hours: preparing and dressing the image of the Goddess, drawing a sacred diagram upon the ground, building a fire on it, and feeding that fire with clarified butter (ghee), all the while singing Her names and praises. As a middle-aged cultural anthropologist and art historian who had already spent more than half my life studying India, I prided myself with my objectivity. I might feel empathy toward a particular subject or situation, but as a scholar I tried to distance myself, to observe and take notes.

Despite my resistance at that moment, as the fire flared brightly and the spirit of the Goddess was invoked to enter the tree and be available to the village, I actually felt Her presence. I felt a change in the atmosphere: a palpable sense of power, pulsating, vibrating energy, the strength of which I had never before sensed. I was completely surprised, overwhelmed beyond any expectation. In that one moment I, who had come as an observer, had become a participant.

That insight altered and enriched my perception, allowing me to release decades of self-identity as an objective outsider. My personal and professional life was changed. I was transformed.

I have always found the Indian people to be remarkably hospitable, opening their hearts and their lives to me with generous candor. People have always invited me into their homes, to witness and share in their private lives and feelings. I have been fascinated by Hindu spirituality, by the ways in which conscious awareness of the Divine permeates every aspect of daily and seasonal life. But for a young American raised in a strong Christian family, much of it seemed obtuse and confusing.

Now when I am invited to attend a sacred ceremony, I no longer withhold myself in critical appraisal. I am fully present. I realize my earlier distance was merely the consequence of my own limitations. The many Indians I have interacted with always invited my full participation. For years it was I who held myself apart. My Western heritage and my unconscious miscomprehension of image worship blinded me from deeper understanding. Now I can admire and even be in awe of the ways in which the sacred permeates the lives of the Hindu people, while still maintaining strong attachments to my own home, family, friends, culture and ideals. Awareness of one only enriches awareness of the other.

Long before I knew what was happening, I was being offered a deep trust. By opening their homes and their hearts to me, in sharing their private, personal and sacred thoughts with me, countless individuals in India have consciously and unconsciously made me an emissary. I understand now that I can serve as a bridge between two cultures. I have long felt the deep need to set aright the extraordinary imbalance of Western opinions of India. Projections assert that India will be a leading world power within the next few decades. It is remarkable that as India modernizes, as her people grow into leading proponents of an innovative and contemporary world, their sense of religion and spirituality is not diminished. Hinduism is still as vital to the lives of the Indian people as it has ever been. It is a belief system in complete harmony with change, adaptation, modernization and growth.

Stephen P. Huyler is an art historian, cultural anthropologist and photographer, living in Camden, Maine.

How I Became a Hindu

The Story of My Rejection of Communism, Existentialism, Catholicism and Materialism. By Sita Ram Goel—Excerpts From His Book, "How I Became a Hindu."

I was born a Hindu. But I had ceased to be one by the time I came out of college at the age of twenty-two. I had become a Marxist and a militant atheist. I had come to believe that Hindu scriptures should be burnt in a bonfire if India was to be saved. It was fifteen years later that I could see this culmination as the explosion of an inflated ego. During those years of self-poisoning, I was sincerely convinced that I was engaged in a philosophical exploration of cosmic proportions.

How my ego got inflated to a point where I could see nothing beyond my own morbid mental constructions is no exceptional story. It happens to many of us mortals. What is relevant in my story is the seeking and the suffering and the struggle to break out of that spider's web of my own weaving. I will fit in the filaments as I proceed.

My earliest memory of an awakening to interests other than those with which a young boy is normally occupied goes back to when I was eight years old. My family was living in Calcutta. My father was a total failure as a broker in the jute goods market. But he was a great storyteller. He could hardly be called an educated person, having spent only two or three years in a village school. But he had imbibed a lot of the traditional lore by attending *kathās* and *kīrtanas* in his younger days. His knowledge of Hindu mythology, legendary heroes and the lives of saints was prolific.

One fine evening he started telling me the lengthy and complex story of the *Mahābhārata*. The narrative lasted for more than a month, each installment lasting over an hour or so. I absorbed every event and episode with rapt attention and bated breath. The sheer strength of some of the characters as they strode across the story lifted me up and above the humdrum of everyday life and made me dwell in the company of immortals.

The Arya Samaj of my young days in the village had three main themes to which they devoted the largest part of their programs—the Muslims, the Sanātanis, the *Purāṇas*. The Muslims were portrayed as people who could not help doing everything that was unwholesome. The Sanātani brāhmins, with their priestcraft, were the great misleaders of mankind. And the *Purāṇas*, concocted by the Sanātanis, were the source of every superstition and puerile tradition prevalent in Hindu society.

There was not much of traditional Sanātanism in my family, due to the influence of Sri Garibdas, a saint in the *nirguṇa* tradition of Kabir and Nanak. Our women did keep some fasts, performed some rituals and visited the temple and the Śivaliṅga. But the menfolk were mostly convinced about the futility of image worship and did not normally participate in any rituals. The brāhmin priest was not seen in our homes, except on occasions like marriage and death. The great religious event in our family was the *patha* of the Granth Saheb performed by Garibdasi *sādhus* who stayed with us for weeks at a time. I remember very vividly how lofty a view I took of my own *nirguṇa* doctrines and how I looked down upon my classmates from Sanātanist families whose ways I thought effeminate. I particularly disliked their going to the annual *mela* (festival) of a Devī in a neighboring town. God for me was a male person. Devī worship was a defilement of the true faith.

But as my moral and intellectual life was preparing to settle down in a universe of firm faith provided by Mahātma Gandhi, my emotional life was heading towards an upheaval which I had not anticipated. Let me hasten to clarify that this upheaval had nothing to do with love or romance. The dimensions of this disturbance were quite different. I started doubting, first of all slowly and then rather strongly, if there was a moral order in the universe at large and in the human society in which I lived. The sages, saints and thinkers whom I had honored so far were sure that the world was made and governed by a God who was Satyam (Truth), Śivam (Good), Sundaram (Beauty). But all around me I saw much that was untrue, unwholesome and ugly. God and His creation could not be reconciled.

This problem of evil arose and gripped my mind, partly because of my personal situation in life. In spite of my pose of humility, learned from Mahatma Gandhi, I was harboring a sense of great self-esteem. I was a good student who had won distinctions and scholarships at every stage. I had read a lot of books, which made me feel learned and wise. I was trying to lead a life of moral endeavor, which I thought made me better than most of my fellow men. Standing at the confluence of these several streams of self-esteem, I came to believe that I was somebody in particular and that the society in which I lived owed me some special and privileged treatment. All this may sound ridiculous. But people who take themselves too seriously are seldom known for a sense of humor.

My objective situation, however, presented a stark contrast to the subjective world in which I loved to live. I was very poor and had to lead a hard life. My learning, whatever it was worth, did not seem to impress anyone except my teachers and a few classmates. Most people around me thought that I was a bookworm and a crank. My interest in Arya Samaj, the freedom movement and Harijan uplift had alienated the family elders in the village. I had even suffered physical assault from one of them. But the unkindest cut of all was that whenever I visited the home of some city classmate who liked me, his family people made it a point to ignore me as a village bumpkin outside the ken of their class. I was always so poorly dressed as to be mistaken for one of their servants. It took me a long time to forget and forgive the father of a close friend who chided his son in my presence for having fallen into bad company; I did not know at that time that our upper classes are normally very uppish and that their culture and good manners are generally reserved for their social superiors.

Over a period of time, I found that I was getting overwhelmed by a great sense of loneliness and self-pity. This black mood got intensified by my voluminous readings of the great tragedies from Western literature. Thomas Hardy was one of my most favorite novelists. I read almost all his works. The comedies of Shakespeare I always gave up midway. But I lapped up his tragedies. I knew by heart all the soliloquies of *Hamlet.* And I thought that my situation was summed up by the following stanza in Grey's *Elegy:* "Full many a gem of purest ray serene, the dark unfathomed caves of ocean bear; full many a flower is born to blush unseen, and waste its sweetness on the desert air." I was sure that I was one of those gems and flowers which would never get the appreciation they deserved by virtue of their brilliance and fragrance. I translated the whole poem into Hindi verse.

My mental defenses in support of Gandhism were giving way one by one under assault after assault mounted by a philosopher friend whom I loved as a remarkable human being and to whom I conceded a superiority of intellect and knowledge. But I refused to share his conviction that this world was created and controlled by the Devil, who off and on spread some grains of happiness over his net in order better to trap the helpless human beings. I was not prepared to give up all hope so fully and finally. But the evolutionistic explanation of the world, inanimate and animate, which I had read in H. G. Wells' *Outline of History* a year or two before, now suddenly started coming alive in my consciousness. So far I had remembered only some unconventional observations made in this big book, namely, that Ashoka was the greatest king in the annals of human history, and that Alexander and Napoleon were criminals. Now I started wondering whether this world was really a chance concourse of atoms with no purposive consciousness leading it towards a godly goal and no moral order governing at the heart of its matrix.

Now I was in a desperate hurry to get a good knowledge of the doctrine of socialism. It was prescribed reading also for my next year's course in the history of Western political thought. But I did not want to wait till the next year.

A desire to read Karl Marx now became irresistible.

First, I read the *Communist Manifesto*. It was simply breathtaking in the breadth and depth of its sweep over vast vistas of human history. It was also a great call to action, to change the world and end exploitation and social injustice for all time to come.

At the same time I concluded that God as a creator of this world could be conceived only in three ways—either as a rogue who sanctioned and shared in the roguery prevalent in his world, or as an imbecile who could no more control what he had created, or as a sannyāsin, who no more cared for what was happening to his creatures. If God was a rogue, we had to rise in revolt against his rule. If he was an imbecile, we could forget him and take charge of the world ourselves. And if he was a sannyāsin, he could mind his business while we minded our own. The scriptures, however, held out a different version of God and his role. That version was supported neither by experience nor by logic. The scriptures should, therefore, be burned in a bonfire, preferably during winter when they could provide some warmth.

Four years after leaving college, I was ready to join the Communist Party of India when it declared war on the newly born Republic of India in February, 1948. I conveyed my decision to my friend Ram Swarup, whom I had met after leaving college and who was to exercise a decisive influence on my intellectual evolution. He wrote back immediately: "You are too intelligent not to become a communist. But you are also too intelligent to remain one for long."

This was a prophecy which came true. It was only a year and a few months later that I renounced Marxism as an inadequate philosophy, realized that the Communist Party of India was a fifth column for the advancement of Russian Imperialism in India, and denounced the Soviet Union under Stalin as a vast slave empire.

My encounter with Sri Aurobindo, on the other hand, came about almost inadvertently. I had heard his name from my father who extolled him as a great yogī. My father literally believed that Sri Aurobindo could levitate as much as five feet above ground. But I had never read anything written by Sri Aurobindo, nor was he on my list of masters whom I aspired to read some day. The intellectual elite in the college talked a lot about Spengler, Bergson, Marcel Proust, Bernard Shaw and Aldous Huxley. But I had never heard the name of Sri Aurobindo in this exclusive club.

As I look back, I can see that the greater part of Sri Aurobindo's vast vision as expounded in *The Life Divine* was beyond my grasp at that time. The heights to which he rose as a witness of the world process and the drama of human destiny left me literally gasping for breath. But this much was clear at the very start: that his concept of man had dimensions which were radically different from those I had come across in any other system of thought. He was not dealing with man as a producer and consumer of material goods. He was not dealing with man as a member of a social, political and economic organization. He was not dealing with man as a rational animal or a moral aspirant or an aesthete. Man was all these, according to him, but man was also much more at the same time. He was a soul, effulgent with an inherent divinity which alone could sustain and give meaning to the outer manifestations of the human personality.

And the promise made by Sri Aurobindo regarding the ultimate destiny of the human race was far more stupendous than that held out by Marx. The international proletarian revolution anticipated and advocated by Marx was to lead to a stage at which mankind could engage itself in rational, moral and aesthetic endeavors, free from the distortions brought about by class interests. But the supramentalization of the mental, vital and physical nature of man envisaged and recommended by Sri Aurobindo would enable mankind to bridge the gulf between human life as a terrestrial turmoil and human life as a spiritual self-existence.

The conceptual language I am using now to draw the distinction between Marx and Sri Aurobindo was not accessible to me in those days. Most of this clarity is wisdom by hindsight. But howsoever vague and inchoate my vision might have been at that time, I did feel that Sri Aurobindo was talking about fundamentally different dimensions of the universe and human life. The gulf between my mundane interests and the grand aspirations dictated by Sri Aurobindo's vision was very wide, and I could hardly muster the care or the courage to cross over. But in the inner recesses of my mind, I did become curious about the nature of the universe, about man's place in it and about a meaningful goal of human life.

My problem now was to reconcile Sri Aurobindo with Marx, in that order. Marx, of course, came first. He was the exponent par excellence of the social scene with which I was primarily preoccupied as well as extremely dissatisfied. Sri Aurobindo had to be accommodated somewhere, somehow, in the system of Marx. The reconciliation was achieved by me several years later to my own great satisfaction. I came to the conclusion that while Marx stood for a harmonized social system, Sri Aurobindo held the key to a harmonized individual. The ridiculousness of this reconciliation did not dawn on me, even when a well known exponent of Sri Aurobindo, to whom I presented it as a triumphant intellectual feat, dismissed it with a benevolent smile. I dismissed the exponent as wise by half because while he had studied Sri Aurobindo, he had most probably not studied Marx, at least not so well as I had done.

My plight was pretty serious after I left college. I was now a married man and the father of a son. There was a family to support, which included my parents in the village. But I had not a penny in my pocket. I gave up the only job I could get, as a clerk in the Central Secretariat, after exactly sixty-five days, because I was ashamed to be a cog in the British imperialist machine. My supreme aspiration was to be a lecturer in some college. But every interview to which I was called ended with the employers' pointing out that I had no previous experience of teaching!

I was present in the Second Party Conference of the Communist Party of India which was held in the Maidan at Calcutta in February, 1948. I was really thrilled and made up my mind to join the Party immediately. But Destiny was determined, as it were, to deny me that "honor" also. My friend Ram Swarup suddenly appeared on the scene and expressed his intention to stay with me for quite some time. It was his first visit to Calcutta. I was very happy because he was my nearest and dearest in the whole world. I did not know that Ram Swarup had by now come to regard communism as a very great evil threatening to engulf the future of mankind. There had been nothing in his letters to indicate this decisive turn. After I failed to put my three best communist friends against Ram Swarup, I had to face him myself and all alone. The discussions spread over several months. Most of the time I repeated party slogans, sometimes very vehemently. Ram Swarup dismissed them with a smile.

One day in my exasperation I struck a superior attitude and said, "We find it difficult to come to any conclusion because I have a philosophical background while you proceed merely from economic, social and political premises." Ram Swarup enquired what I meant by philosophy, and I rattled out the list which I had ready in my mind—Locke, Berkeley, Hume, Descartes, Spinoza, Leibnitz, Kant, Hegel, Schopenhauer and so on. Ram Swarup told me that at one time or the other he had studied all of them but had found them irrelevant and useless. I was surprised as well as pained. Ram Swarup explained: "Suppose one knows this philosophical system or that. Does it make a better man out of him in any way? These systems are mere cerebrations and have little to offer towards practical purposes of life." The word *cerebra-*

tion got stuck in my mind and made it impossible for me to read any abstract philosophy anymore. I had been very fond of Western metaphysics and epistemology till then.

Finally, I was back to square one. My faith in Gandhism had lost the battle to Marxism. Now I was no longer a Marxist. I asked myself again and again: Where do I go from here?

The business of life can go on very well without an ideological frame of reference. One reads books and papers and gossips and goes about passing conventional judgments on current events. One has a family, a vocation, a circle of friends and some hobbies to keep one occupied in leisure time. One grows old, collects his own share of diseases and looks back with anguish towards earlier times when one was young and active. For most of us ordinary mortals, this is the whole of human life. We take very seriously our successes and failures and our loves and hates, without spending a thought on what it is all about.

Ram Swarup had tried his best to rescue me from the twin morass of a false self-esteem and a degrading self-pity. He had encouraged and assisted me with timely advice to take an impersonal interest in higher ideas and larger causes. As I shared his ideas and concern for social causes, I could not question his command for action. Now I was invited by him to join a group to serve the new values we shared with him. The cultural and political atmosphere in India had become over the years chock full with communist categories of thought. The main task we took upon ourselves was to expose communist categories of thought as inimical to human freedom, national cohesion, social health, economic development and political and cultural pluralism, to which we were wedded as a people. Simultaneously we went out to explode the myths about communist countries so that our people, particularly our national and democratic political parties, could see them as they were—totalitarian tyrannies with low standards of living and regimented culture.

In due course, we became acutely aware of the progressive degeneration of politics in India. A similar degeneration was taking place on the international plane as well. In this atmosphere of declining political standards, we decided to withdraw our anti-communist campaign as we had conceived it to start with. We were convinced that a larger battle, couched along deeper cultural contours, was needed if the nation was to be saved from the corrosion of its soul.

Ram Swarup was now becoming more and more meditative and reflective in his comments on the current political scene. He often talked of a cultural vacuum which communism was using to its own great advantage. Communism, he said, was deriving support from a deeper source, a new self-alienation amongst our political and cultural elite and advancing with the help of forces which on the surface seemed to be allied against communism. It was not our democratic polity alone which was under attack from communism. There were several other forces which had come together to suffocate and render sterile the deeper sources of India's inherent strength.

It was at this time that I fell seriously ill and lost a lot of weight, which I had never had in plenty. A Catholic missionary whom I had known earlier in connection with our anti-communist work, came to visit me. He was a good and kindly man and had a strong character. He had insisted upon his religious right to sell our anti-communist literature in melas and exhibitions in spite of his mission's advice that this was no part of his ordained work and that, in any case, the government of India frowned upon it.

The Father, as I called him, found me in a difficult condition, physically as well as financially. He felt sure that it was in such times that Jesus Christ came to people. He asked me if I was prepared to receive Jesus. I did not understand immediately that he was inviting me to get converted to Catholicism. My impression was that he wanted to help me with some spiritual exercises prescribed by Christianity. Moreover, I had always admired Jesus. I had, therefore, no objection to receiving him. Only I was doubtful if someone was really in a position to arrange my meeting with Jesus. But I became aware of the Father's true intentions as I travelled with him to a distant monastery. He asked every other missionary he met on the way to pray for his success.

At this monastery, which was a vast place with very picturesque surroundings, I was advised by the Father to go into a retreat. It meant my solitary confinement to a room. I was not supposed to look at or talk to anyone on my way to the bathrooms or while taking my morning and evening strolls on the extensive lawns outside. And I was to meditate on themes which the Father prescribed for me in the course of four or five lectures he delivered to me during the course of the day, starting at about 6:30 in those winter mornings. I was not used to this way of life. I had never lived in such solitude by my own choice. My only solace was that I was allowed to smoke and provided with plenty of books on the Christian creed and theology.

I tried to read some of the books. But I failed to finish any one of them. They were full of Biblical themes and theological terminology with which I was not familiar. Most of the time they made me recall Ram Swarup's observation about mere cerebration.

Or they were simplistic harangues to love Christ and join the Catholic Church. They had a close similarity to communist pamphlets which I had read in plenty. The Father had asked me again and again to invoke Christ and meditate upon him. But he had not told me how to do it. I had no previous practice in meditation. I did not know how to invoke Christ, or any other godhead for that matter. All I could do was to think again and again of Christ preaching the "Sermon on the Mount" or saving an adulteress from being stoned to death.

While delivering a lecture about creation, the Father said that God in his wisdom and kindness had made all these fishes and animals and birds for man's consumption. I immediately rose in revolt. I told him very emphatically that I was a Vaishṇava and a vegetarian and that I had absolutely no use for a God that bestowed upon man the right to kill and eat His other creatures simply because man happened to be stronger and more skilled. I added that in my opinion it was the duty of the strong and the more skilled to protect the weak and the less wily.

The Father also suddenly lost his self-possession. He almost shouted: "I can never understand you Hindus who go about seeking a soul in every lice and bug and cockroach that crawls around you. The *Bible* says in so many words that man is God's highest creation. What is wrong with the higher ruling over the lower?"

I kept quiet. I could see the pain in his eyes. I did not want to add to his anguish. He recovered his self possession very soon and smiled. Now I went down on my knees before him and asked his forgiveness for my lack of strength to go on with the retreat. He agreed, although rather reluctantly. His sense of failure was writ large on his face. I was very sorry indeed. I now wished that it would have been better for both of us if Christ had come to me.

On our way back to the big city where his mission was housed, he became his old normal self again. There was not, a trace of bitterness on his face or in his voice as we talked and joked and discussed several serious and not so serious matters. Now I took my courage in both my hands and asked him my final question: "Father, am I not already a Christian? I do not normally tell a lie. I do not steal. I do not bear false witness. I do not covet my neighbor's wife or property. What more can a man do to demand God's grace and kinship with Christ? Why should you insist on a formal conversion which in no way helps me to become better than

It was at this time that Sri K. R. Malkani, the soft-spoken and ever-smiling editor of the *Organiser*, extended the hospitality of his weekly to me. I wrote more or less regularly in the *Organiser* for several years. One of my long series was devoted to a political biography of Pandit Nehru which ultimately cost me my job. Some friends frowned upon my writing for the *Organiser*. My invariable reply was that one paid court at the portals of the so-called prestigious papers only if one had nothing to say and if one's only aspiration was a fat check. I found Sri Malkani to be a very conscientious editor. He never crossed a "t" or dotted an "i" of whatever I wrote, without prior consultation with me.

I was using my spare time during these three or four years to brush tip my Sanskrit. I made quite a headway because I relinquished the help of Hindi or English translations and broke through some very tough texts with the help of Sanskrit commentaries alone. At last I was able to read the *Mahābhārata* in its original language.

In the long evenings I spent with Ram Swarup I compared with him my notes on the *Mahābhārata*. But Ram Swarup's way of looking at the *Mahābhārata*, was quite different. He related it directly to the *Vedas*. He expounded how the mighty characters of this great epic embodied and made living the spiritual vision of the Vedic seers. What fascinated me still more was Ram Swarup's exposition of dharma as enunciated in the *Mahābhārata*. To me, dharma had always been a matter of normative morals, external rules and regulations, do's and dont's, enforced on life by an act of will. Now I was made to see dharma as a multidimensional movement of man's inner law of being, his psychic evolution, his spiritual growth and his spontaneous building of an outer life for himself and the community in which he lived.

The next thing I did was to read and reread the major works of Sri Aurobindo and discuss his message with Ram Swarup day after day. Sri Aurobindo would have remained an abstract philosopher for me, in spite of all his writings on yoga, had not Ram Swarup explained to me how this seer was the greatest exponent of the Vedic vision in our times. Sri Aurobindo's message, he told me, was in essence the same old Vedic message, namely, that we are gods in our innermost being and should live the life of gods on this Earth. He made me see what Sri Aurobindo meant by the physical, the vital, the mental and the psychic. He related these terms to the theory of the five *kośas* in the *Upanishads.*

But Sri Aurobindo was not an exponent of Vedic spirituality alone. He was also a poet, a connoisseur, a statesman and a superb sociologist. His *Human Cycle* was an interpretation of history which placed man's striving for spiritual perfection in his inner as well as outer life as the prime mover of the world matrix. His *Foundations of Indian Culture* made me see for the first time that our multifaceted heritage of great spirituality, art, architecture, literature, social principles and political forms sprang from and revolved round a single center. That center was Sanātana Dharma, which was the very soul of India. Sri Aurobindo had made it very clear in his Uttarpara Speech that India rose with the rise of Sanātana Dharma and would die if Sanātana Dharma was allowed to die.

In my earlier days I had read the biography of Sri Ramakrishna written by Romain Rolland. I had read the talk which Vivekānanda had delivered long ago about "My Master." I had visited Sri Ramakrishna's room at Dakshineshwar. I had also seen a Bengali film on his life. But what brought me into an intimate and living contact with this great mystic and *bhakta* and Śākta and *advaitin* was his *Kathamṛita.* He had not used a single abstraction, nor discussed any of the problems which pass as philosophy. His talks embodied expressions of a concrete consciousness which had dropped every trace of the dirt-land dross and inertia which characterize what is known as normal human consciousness. The metaphors which sprang spontaneously from this purified consciousness were matchless in their aptness and illumined in a few words the knotted problems which many voluminous works had failed to solve. I was now having my first intimations of immortality towards which Kabir and Nanak and Sri Garibdas had inclined me earlier.

The final breakthrough came with the publication of Ram Swarup's long article, "Buddhism vis-à-vis Hinduism," in the *Organiser* sometime in 1959. The Buddha's parable of the man struck by an arrow and refusing medical aid until a number of his intellectual questions and curiosities were satisfied struck me in my solar plexus, as it were. I had spent a lifetime reveling in intellectual exercises. What was the nature of the universe? What was man's place in it? Was there a God? Had he created this cosmos? Why had he made such a mess of it? What was the goal of human life? Was man free to pursue that goal? Or was he predetermined and destined and fated for a particular path and towards a particular goal by forces beyond his control? And so on and so forth. It was an endless cerebration. The Buddha had described it as Dṛishṭi-Kantar, the desert of seeking. Ramakrishna had also ridiculed the salt doll of an intellect which had gone out to fathom the great ocean but got dissolved at the very first dip.

I was now sure that the quality of questions I raised was controlled by the quality of my consciousness. Ram Swarup told me that what we called the normal human consciousness had to be made passive before one could establish contact with another consciousness which held the key to the proper questions and the proper answers. Wrestling with and stirring up the normal consciousness with all sorts of questions and curiosities was the surest way to block the way of a purer and higher consciousness which was always waiting on the threshold.

I now requested Ram Swarup to initiate me into the art of meditation. He told me that no very elaborate art was involved. I could sit and meditate with him whenever I liked, wait and watch, go within myself as far as I could manage, at any time, dwell on whatever good thoughts got revealed in the process, and the rest would follow. I acted upon his simple instructions with some measure of skepticism in my mind. But in the next few days I could see some results, which encouraged me for a further endeavor.

One day I meditated on ahiṁsā, which had remained an abstract concept for me so far. After a while I found myself begging forgiveness from all those whom I had hurt by word or deed, or towards whom I had harbored any ill will. It was not an exercise in generalities. Person after person rose into my memory, going back into the distant past and I bowed in repentance before each one of them. Finally I begged forgiveness from Stalin, against whom I had written so much and upon whom I had hurled so many brickbats. The bitterness which had poisoned my life over the long years was swept off my mind in a sudden relaxation of nerves. I felt as if a thousand thorns which had tormented my flesh had been taken out by a master physician without causing the slightest pain. I was in need of no greater assurance that this was the way on which I should walk.

One day I told Ram Swarup how I had never been able to accept the Devī, either as Sarasvatī or as Lakshmī or as Durgā or as Kālī. He smiled and asked me to meditate on the Devī that day. I tried my best in my own way. Nothing happened for some time. Nothing came my way. My mind was a big blank. But in the next moment the void was filled with a sense of some great presence. I did not see any concrete image. No words were whispered in my ears. Yet the rigidity of a lifetime broke down and disappeared. The Great Mother was beckoning her lost child to go and sit in her lap and feel safe from all fears. We had a gramophone record of Dr. Govind Gopal Mukhopadhyaya's sonorous *stuti* to the Devī. As I played it, I prayed to Her.

There were many more meditations. My progress was not fast; nor did I go far. But I now felt sure that this was the method by which I could rediscover for myself the great truths of which the ancients had spoken in Hindu scriptures. It was not the end of my seeking, which had only started in right earnest. But it was surely the end of my wandering in search of a shore where I could safely anchor my soul and take stock of my situation.

Ram Swarup warned me very strongly against letting my reflective reason go to sleep under the soporific of inner experience, however deep or steep. This was the trap, he said, into which many a practitioner had fallen and felt sure that they had found the final truth, even when they were far away from the goal.

The soul's hunger for absolute Truth, absolute Good, absolute Beauty and absolute Power, I was told, was like the body's hunger for wholesome food and drink. And that which satisfied this hunger of the human soul, fully and finally, was Sanātana Dharma, true for all times and climes. A votary of Sanātana Dharma did not need an arbitrary exercise of will to put blind faith in a supernatural revelation laid down in a single scripture. He did not need the intermediacy of an historical prophet nor the help of an organized church to attain salvation. Sanātana Dharma called upon its votary to explore his own self in the first instance and see for himself the truths expounded in sacred scriptures. Prophets and churches and scriptures could be aids, but never the substitutes for self-exploration, self-purification and self-transcendence.

I had come back at last, come back to my spiritual home from which I had wandered away in self-forgetfulness. But this coming back was no atavistic act. On the contrary, it was a reawakening to my ancestral heritage, which was waiting for me all along to lay my claim on its largesses. It was also the heritage of all mankind, as proved by the seers, sages and mystics of many a time and clime. It spoke in different languages to different people. To me it spoke in the language of Hindu spirituality and Hindu culture at their highest. I could not resist its call. I became a Hindu.

Sita Ram Goel, of Delhi, is a well-known renaissance writer on Hindu issues. He is associated with the Voice of India, a publishing house which guides understanding through enlightening tracts, books and articles. Ram Swarup (1920-1998) was a distinguished social observer, author and spokesman of renascent Hinduism which, he believed, can also help other nations in rediscovering their spiritual roots. His best-known book is The Word as Revelation, Names of God.

Author's note: It was with great pleasure that we received Sri Sita Ram Goel at our Hindu monastery on the Garden Island of Kauai in the mid '80s. His articulate message of strengthening the Hindu renaissance was profound, and his demeanor humble. To have among us a person held in such high esteem by the Indian intellectual community invigorated our many resident swāmīs, yogīs and *sādhakas.* Sita Ram's guru, Sri Ram Swarup, had for years been on our team of erudite, insightful writers for our public service, international magazine, HINDUISM TODAY, and his knowledge and insights into the needs of the times, based upon the failures of the past, sanctioned a mini-renaissance among our highly intellectual, Western-educated Indian readers living in America, Europe and Canada. Years later we enjoyed the long-awaited honor of a personal meeting with Ram Swarup when he came to visit me in our hotel in New Delhi in 1995 and spent valuable time with us, speaking on his views of the future of his beloved Sanātana Dharma, now called Hinduism, and the molding of the masses through systematic education meted out in little doses to an open and deserving few who would, in turn, belt it out with authority to those they influenced. He also commented that HINDUISM TODAY is the salvation, the blending together of worldwide seekers who have dedicated themselves to preserve the Sanātana Dharma within their communities.

Sri Ram Swarup elaborated in a later writing: "Hindu communities are now found in many countries, but with the exception of HINDUISM TODAY, there is no journal dealing with their problems and opportunities. In this respect, this journal is unique. It reveals to us an important face of Hinduism, its international face. Every time one picks up its copy, one becomes aware of Hindus not only in India but also in Fiji, Mauritius, Trinidad, South Africa, Southeast Asia and now also increasingly in Europe and North America. Its pages bring them together so often under the same roof that they begin to feel and live together."

Vedic Mysticism Brought Me Into Hinduism

My Soul's Search Found in Hinduism What it Couldn't Find in Catholicism, Existentialism and Buddhism. By David Frawley (Pandit Vamadeva Shastri), Excerpts from His Book, "How I Became a Hindu."

In my case it was not a question of a quick conversion like accepting Jesus as one's personal savior or surrendering to Allah. Nor was it the result of a concerted effort to convert me by religious preachers speaking of sin or redemption, or of religious intellectuals trying to convince me of the ultimacy of their particular philosophy or theology. It was a personal decision that occurred as the result of a long quest, a finishing touch of an extensive inner search of many years.

For most people in the West becoming a Hindu resembles joining a tribal religion, a Native American or Native African belief with many gods and strange rituals, rather than converting to a creed or belief of an organized world religion. Discovering Hinduism is something primeval, a contacting of the deeper roots of nature, in which the spirit lies hidden not as an historical creed but as a mysterious and unnameable power. It is not about taking on another monotheistic belief but an entirely different connection with life and consciousness than our Western religions provide us.

I came to Hindu Dharma after an earlier exploration of Western intellectual thought and world mystical traditions, a long practice of yoga and Vedānta and a deep examination of the *Vedas.* In the process I came into contact with diverse aspects of Hindu society and with Hindu teachers that few Westerners have access to, taking me far beyond the range of the usual perceptions and misconceptions about the subject. Such direct experience, which was often quite different than what I had expected or was told would be the case, changed my views and brought me to my current position. Hopefully my story can help others change from taking Hinduism as something primitive to understanding the beauty of this great spiritual tradition that may best represent our spiritual heritage as a species.

I always had a certain mystical sense, going back to early childhood. Whether it was looking at the sky and gazing at the clouds or seeing distant snow covered mountains, I knew in my heart that there was a higher consciousness behind the world. I felt a sacred and wonderful mystery from which we had come and to which we would return after our short sojourn on this strange planet.

I had trouble reconciling this mystical sense with the idea of religion that I contacted through my Catholic background. Both my parents grew up on dairy farms in the Midwest of the United States (Wisconsin) and came from strong Catholic backgrounds. My mother's family in particular was quite pious and a pillar of the Church where they lived, following all the Church observances and donating liberally to its causes. One of her brothers was a priest, a missionary in South America, and he was regarded very highly, pursuing a very noble and holy occupation.

The figure of Jesus on the cross that we saw during mass was rather gruesome and unpleasant. One didn't want to look at it. We were told that we had all killed Jesus. We were responsible for his death by our sins, which were terrible in the eyes of God. But then I never knew Jesus and since he lived two thousand years ago, how could my actions have affected him? I could never really relate to the image of the sacrificed savior who saves us, we who cannot save ourselves. I also began to notice that we all have our personal failings, including the nuns that taught us who had evident tempers and not much patience. The whole thing didn't seem to be as God given as we were told it was.

At the age of fifteen I had a remarkable school teacher

who taught a class on ancient history that opened my eyes about the ancient world. This began my fascination with ancient cultures that eventually led me to the *Vedas.* I sensed that the ancients had a better connection to the universe than we moderns and that their lives had a higher meaning.

About the age of sixteen I underwent a major intellectual awakening. It came as a powerful experience that radically changed my thoughts and perception. Initially it was quite disturbing and disorienting. While some sort of intellectual ferment had been developing in me for several years, this one resulted in a profound break from the authorities and ideas of my childhood and the vestiges of my American education. It initiated a series of studies that encompassed Western intellectual thought and first brought me in contact with Eastern spirituality. It marked an important transition in my life. Throughout this intellectual revolt I never lost sight of a higher reality. I fancied myself to be a "mystical atheist" because though I rejected the Biblical idea of a personal God, I did recognize an impersonal consciousness or pure being behind the universe.

The law of karma and the process of rebirth that I had learned about through Eastern philosophy made more sense to me than such Christian teachings. After reading a number of different scriptures and spiritual texts from all over the world, the Christian fixation on Jesus seemed almost neurotic. It was clear to me that there have been many great sages throughout history and Jesus, however great, was only one of many and that his teachings were not the best preserved either. I failed to see what was so unique about him or what his teachings had that could not be found with more clarity elsewhere. The mystic feeling I once had in Christianity was now entirely transferred to the East.

At the beginning of 1970 in Denver I found a local guru who introduced me to many spiritual teachings. While in retrospect he was limited in his insights, he did serve as a catalyst to connect me with the spiritual path. Through the encounter with various spiritual teachings that he initiated, I took to the yogic path as my main pursuit in life. He made me familiar with a broad array of mystical teachings: Hindu, Buddhist, Theosophist and Sufi. It included everything from occult teachings of Alice Bailey to Zen, and a prominent place for the teachings of Gurdjieff. I learned that a core of inner teachings existed behind the outer religious traditions of the world, an esoteric approach beyond their exoteric forms.

At this time I discovered the *Upanishads*, in which I found great inspiration, and it became my favorite book. It led me to various Vedāntic texts. I soon studied the works of Śaṅkarāchārya, which I avidly read in translation, particularly his shorter works, like *Viveka Chūḍāmaṇi*. Of the different teachings that I contacted Vedānta struck the deepest cord. I remember once climbing a hill by Denver with a friend. When we got to the top, I had the feeling that I was immortal, that the Self in me was not limited by birth and death and had lived many lives before. Such Vedāntic insights seemed natural, but the friend who was with me at the time didn't understand what I was talking about.

With my philosophical bent of mind I also studied several Buddhist *sūtras*, especially the *Laṅkāvatāra*, which I found to be intellectually profound. The Buddhist *sūtras* helped serve as a bridge between the Existentialism that I had studied earlier and Eastern meditation traditions. As I encountered these teachings at a young age before my mind had become fixed, I had the benefit of an almost Eastern education to complement my Western studies.

My study of Eastern traditions was not merely intellectual but involved experimenting with yogic and meditational practices. I began practicing intense *prāṇāyāma*, mantra and meditation teachings in the summer of 1970. These mainly came from the kriyā yoga tradition, which I contacted in several ways. I found that the techniques worked powerfully to create energy at a subtle level. I could feel the *prāṇa* moving through the *nāḍīs*, with some experiences of the chakras, and a general widening of consciousness beyond the ordinary sense of time and space. Mantra practices had a particularly powerful effect upon me. I felt that I had been some old Hindu yogī in a previous life, though in retrospect there was probably much fantasy in my approach. Another benefit from the *prāṇāyāma* was that it almost eliminated the allergies that I had suffered from for years. It cleared and cleaned my nervous system. I learned that yogic practices can heal both body and mind.

For a while I went back and forth between Buddhist and Vedāntic perspectives. The intellectuality of Buddhism appealed to me, while the idealism of Vedānta was equally impelling. Buddhist logic had a subtlety that went beyond words and the Buddhist understanding of the mind had a depth that was extraordinary, dwarfing that of Western Psychology. But Vedānta had a sense of Pure Being and Consciousness that was more in harmony with my deeper mystical urges. It reflected the soul and its perennial aspiration for the Divine that seemed obvious to me.

I felt the need of a cosmic creator such as Buddhism did not have. It was not the old monotheistic tyrant with his heaven and hell, but the wise and loving Divine Father and Mother, such as in the Hindu figures of Śiva and Pārvatī. I also found the existence of the ātman or higher Self to be self-evident. That all is the Self appeared to be the most self-evident truth of existence. The Buddhist non-ego approach made sense as a rejection of the lower or false Self but I saw no need to dismiss the Self altogether as many Buddhists do.

Among the spiritual teachers whose writings I studied, most notable in terms of my own thought and expression, was Sri Aurobindo. Aurobindo possessed an intellectual breadth that was unparalleled by any author I had ever read. One could swim in the field of his mind like a whale in the open sea and never encounter any limits. He dwarfed the Western intellectuals that I studied and even the Western mystics. Relative to Indian teachers, his teaching was clear, modern, liberal and poetic, not tainted by caste, authority or dogma. Aurobindo's vision encompassed the past, revealing the mysteries of the ancient world that I had long sought. But it showed the way to the future as well, with a balanced and universal vision of humanity for all time.

I studied a number of Aurobindo's works, notably the *Life Divine*, which unraveled all the secrets of the philosophies of India from Vedānta to Sāṁkhya, yoga and *tantra*. In it I noted the various verses from the *Ṛig Veda* that he used to open the chapters. I found these to be quite profound and mysterious and wanted to learn more of the *Vedas*. In looking through the titles of Sri Aurobindo, a book called *Hymns to the Mystic Fire*, which was hymns to Agni from the *Ṛig Veda*, struck a cord with my poetic vision. It led me to another book, *Secret of the Veda*, which more specifically explained the Vedic teaching and opened up the Vedic vision for me.

At that time I became a Vedic person, not simply a Vedāntin. While becoming a Vedāntin was the first level of my inner change, becoming Vedic was the second stage. These two transitions overlapped to a great degree. I followed the *Vedas* in the context of Vedānta. But later a more specific Vedic vision emerged and came to dominate over the Vedantic view. It brought a wider and more integral Vedānta and one that connected with poetry and mantra.

Then in summer of 1978 my Vedic work, which would dominate the rest of my life, first emerged. I was inspired by some inner energy to write a set of poems about the ancient dawns and the ancient suns that directed me back to the *Vedas*. I decided to study the *Vedas* in depth in the original Sanskrit. I wanted to directly confirm if Sri Aurobindo's view was correct that the *Vedas* did have a deeper spiritual and

Vedāntic meaning. I had studied a Sanskrit through the years and already had Sanskrit texts of the *Vedas* and *Upanishads* to start with.

Along a parallel line I had taken up the study of Vedic astrology. I first studied astrology in Ojai in the early seventies, which with a Theosophical center had good resources on the subject. I also discovered a few good books on Vedic astrology. I practiced Western astrology for several years, using Vedic astrology as a sidelight, but gradually shifted over to the Vedic system. Along with my āyurvedic work in the mid-eighties I focused on Vedic astrology, introducing classes and courses in it as well, starting with āyurveda students. With āyurveda and Vedic astrology I discovered a practical usage of Vedic knowledge that was relevant to everyone. The gap between my Vedic work and my actual career began to disappear. My Vedic work and my livelihood became interrelated. I focused on āyurveda and Vedic astrology for a few years and put my Vedic pursuits temporarily in the background.

My first trip to India occurred as part of my pursuit of āyurveda. It involved visiting āyurvedic schools and companies in Bombay and Nagpur, and sightseeing to other parts of the country. I also had two important visits of a spiritual nature, first to Pondicherry and the Sri Aurobindo Ashram, and second to the Ramanashram in nearby Tiruvannamalai, a pattern that was repeated in future visits to the country.

I came to the Ramanashram to contact Ramana and his path of Self-inquiry, which is a method to experience the non-dual state of pure awareness. What I actually discovered was the God Skanda, the child of fire, who demanded purification, death and spiritual rebirth. I encountered one of the Gods, not as a devotional or cultural image but as a primordial and awesome power. Ramana came to me through Lord Skanda, the son of Śiva, with whom Ganapati Muni identified him. I came to understand Ramana as Lord Skanda, the embodiment of the flame of knowledge.

Coming into Tiruvannamalai I felt the presence of a tremendous spiritual fire, which also had, in its more benefic moments, the face of a young boy. The image of a small boy carrying a spear, rising out of a fire, kept arising in my mind. This brought about an intense practice of Self-inquiry that was literally like death, though it was the ego's death, not that of the body. Going through that fire was perhaps the most intense spiritual experience of my life, to the point that I had at time to pray that it would not become too strong! Yet afterwards I felt refreshed and cleansed, with a purity of perception that was extraordinary.

Up to that point I had a limited understanding of the role of Deities in spiritual practice, I had almost no knowledge of Lord Skanda, though He is a popular Deity in South India and one sees His picture everywhere. I had not yet grasped the depth of His connection with Ramana. So I was shocked to come into a direct contact with such an entity, not as a mere fantasy but as a concrete and vivid inner experience penetrating to the core of my being. That the process of Self-inquiry, which starts out as a philosophical practice, could be aligned to a Deity in which my personality was swallowed up, was not something that I had noted in any teachings.

In time I learned much about both Skanda and Ramana. Skanda is the incarnation of the power of direct insight. He is the Self that is born of Self-inquiry, which is like a fire, the inner child born of the death of the ego on the cremation pyre of meditation. This child represents the innocent mind, free of ulterior motives, which alone can destroy all the demons, our negative conditionings, with His spear of discrimination beyond the fluctuations of the mind. Coming to Tiruvannamalai was an experience of that inner fire *(tejas)* which is Skanda and Ramana.

I felt Lord Skanda most keenly at the great temple of

Arunachaleśvara in the nearby town. Initially the experience of the temple was more important for me than the experience of the ashram. Arunachaleśvara temple still holds the vibration of Ramana, who was its child, where he stayed and practiced *tapas* when young and unknown. The temple has its own divine presence that has nourished many great sages and yogīs.

One day at the temple I decided to purchase a statue to take back home for my altar. I found a small statue of Lord Skanda, which I bought and put into my napsack. One of the brahmin priests in the temple noted my acquisition and asked for the statue, which I gave to him. He took my hand and led me through the temple, doing the pūjā to the main Deities. He started with the Devī temple and then to the Śivaliṅga and finally to the Skanda temple. My statue was placed on all these *mūrtis* and was consecrated as part of the pūjās. It was as if I myself was reborn as Skanda during these rites.

On my first trip to India I met an individual who would have a decisive influence on my life and thought. He would serve as my mentor for introducing me into Hindu thinking and to Hindu issues in India today. Dr. B.L. Vashta was an āyurvedic doctor working on product development for an āyurvedic company in Bombay. It was in that context in which I met him. He was then about seventy years of age, or about the age of my father.

In 1991 Dr. Vashta raised the idea that I formally become a Hindu. I thought, Why not? I have been following this tradition for twenty years and working with it had become my main spiritual path and career dedication. I thought about the many Hindus that have become Christians following the allure of the affluent West. The example of a Christian becoming a Hindu would be good for many Hindus and would encourage confidence in their own traditions.

Why shouldn't I express my appreciation and make a

more formal connection with Hindu Dharma? Personally, I am not much for formality and generally avoid ceremony or any kind of outer displays. But it didn't take much forethought to go ahead with this important project. It was also a way to create a new identity for myself that reflected the changes that I had gone through internally. Dr. Vashta told me that I was already a Hindu inwardly and so an outward ceremony wasn't necessary, but that the gesture would be appreciated by the community. I understood. The ceremony was called *śuddhi*, which means purification. It was short and simple, a ritual pūjā, a *kumbhābhishekam.* It was held at a local Mumbai ashram, Masurāshram that had once been connected to the Arya Samaj but in time became more traditionally Hindu. No preaching. No condemnation. No threats or promises. No swearing to go to a particular church or follow a prescribed path of action, just a promise to follow dharma.

While Vashta organized the event, Avadhuta Shastri, the head of Masurashram, performed the pūjā. His brother, Brahmachari Vishwanath, was one of the founders of the VHP. I took the name *Vamadeva* from the Vedic ṛishi Vamadeva Gautama. *Shastri* came from Avadhuta Shastri. *Vamadeva* was a name of Indra, the supreme Vedic God, particularly as a falcon *(śyena)*. It was also a name of Savitar, the Sun God, who dispensed his grace or beauty *(vāma)*. *Vamadeva* later became a name of Lord Śiva in His northern face. So it was an important and powerful name, and one that few people carried. By this ceremony I was accepted into Hindu society as a brahmin by my occupation. I realized that I was a kind of kshatriya as well, a warrior, at least on the intellectual plane, addressing not only religious but also social and political issues.

Pandit Vamadeva Shastri, a.k.a. David Frawley, is a Vedāchārya and Director of the American Insitute of Vedic Studies in Santa Fe, New Mexico. He is also a well-known author on āyurveda and Vedic astrology.

Dharmaśraddhā Tathā Dharmanishṭhā

धर्मश्रद्धा तथा धर्मनिष्ठा

Religious Loyalty And Commitment

Religious Loyalty And Commitment

THERE IS AN ENTIRE SCHOOL OF THOUGHT, supported by some Hindu swāmīs ministering in the West, which all but denies the differences between religions by claiming that "all religions are one." Because they are all one, the universalist reasoning goes, it is quite permissible for anyone to follow a Hindu religious life as much as he wants, with no need to formally accept Hinduism or sever loyalties to his previous religion. This school of thought states that it is also permissible for individuals to study and practice specific aspects of Hinduism, such as haṭha yoga or Vedānta philosophy, while remaining within another religion, on the theory that these practices and philosophies will make them better at their own religion—better Jews, better Christians, better Muslims.

My own personal observation is that without a complete and final severance from one's former religion or philosophy it is not possible to practice Hinduism fully and receive the full spiritual benefit, because of subconscious psychological confrontations that inevitably occur when the former belief and commitment make battle with the newly found ones. It is like trying to run a computer on two contradictory operating systems at the same time. Such inner conflict leads to confusion. In the spiritual aspirant it spells indecision and lack of commitment. For example, many problems may result if Hindu practices and beliefs are expressly forbidden by one's original religion. A Catholic accepting various principles of Vedānta is actually accepting beliefs contrary to the central dogmas of the Catholic Church, which he promised to believe, uphold and defend at his confirmation. A Jew who enters a Hindu temple and worships an idol is, according to Jewish law of the *Torah*, to be stoned to death by his own mother and father for worshiping a graven image.

To gain a clear subconscious for his future religious life, the individual must examine and reject those beliefs of his previous religion that differ from those of the Hindu religion he wishes to join. Then he must examine and accept the Hindu beliefs that are new to him. If he was confirmed or otherwise initiated in another religion or ideology, he must effect formal severance from his previous religion before formally entering the Hindu religion through the *nāmakaraṇa saṁskāra*, name-giving sacrament.

Belief is very important. Beliefs create attitudes. Each faith carries a number of community attitudes, or ways of thinking and responding, which have developed through time in the minds of its followers through the collective beliefs. *Attitude* originally meant "posture of the body" and has come to mean a person's state of mind as it can be deduced from the manner in which he holds himself. Therefore, a trained eye could, at a glance, distinguish in a crowd the Catholics, the Protestants, the Jews, the Hindus, etc., by the particular attitude and body language characteristic of their religion. The true sign of the change in beliefs is the change in attitudes that the inner transformation brings. Fully embracing a new religion brings a noticeable change in the posture of the physical and emotional body, and one starts to hear that he looks different and looks at things differently.

Each member of a certain religion has welcome access to all of its facilities, not only on the physical plane, but on the inner (astral) planes as well. As a Hindu, the great devonic realms of Hinduism, with its many great ṛishis, masters and devas, devotees and Mahādevas, welcome you each evening when you pass off to sleep, and when you finally drop your physical body at death. Likewise for the other religions.

These inner plane realms have been described as being like vast cities, and each embodied person is psychically and emotionally connected to one realm or more due to his karmic attachments, desires, aversions, promises and commitments. These inner bonds play a strong role throughout a person's life and are naturally felt during any consideration of new loyalties. Fully embracing Hinduism, for example, is a process of clearly defining one's attachments, positively attaching oneself to the Hindu realms while systematically detaching from other ties made in the past. The inner bonds are quite real, detailing responsibilities for the devotee to uphold, and various benefits, such as the protection of guardian devas, access to inner realms and special blessings in times of need. The final ceremony, the *nāmakaraṇa saṁskāra* (or in some cases the *vrātyastoma*), earned by fulfilling the stringent requirements that precede it, announces to one and all that the deed is done, a promise made, an inner contract made to live up to the lofty Sanātana Dharma to the best of one's ability.

Of course, although much karma may have had to be cleared to reach this point, this is only the beginning. Like a new student in a vast university, the supplicant begins a new life in the company of like-minded devotees, all worshiping God and the Gods in the same manner and approaching life through the same belief structure. This makes for a harmonious, happy, productive community, and for a rewarding spiritual life. The way for this clean start in a new religion is cleared by honestly looking at prior commitments and systematically resolving what needs to be resolved.

Entrance into Hinduism means becoming a member of a new community, a new tribe, a new group mind. What is a group mind? Every single human being on the planet is a member of a group mind—actually on several different levels. First, we are members of the group mind of our planet. Then, we are members of the human species. We are members of our race and ethnic group. And we are members of that group mind we call our nation.

While consciously or unconsciously sharing in group consciousness, mankind is also waking up to the tragedy of blind, separative consciousness, which breeds hatred, war, communal fighting, economic inequality and destruction of the planet itself. This awakening has led to a strong reaction. Thus, it is common to hear, "I am a universalist." "I am a citizen of all nations." "I consider myself a member of all religions." These New Age souls have become the expression of humanity's conscience, taking it upon themselves to assuage the guilt of eons of mankind's separative ignorance. But the fact of our membership in various groups remains. Even those who consider themselves independent of all groups are members of the group defined by the conviction to stand alone, or to stand with everyone.

Group consciousness, loyalty and commitment are not at fault. Ignorance of our oneness in God is the problem. The key, of course, is to transcend lower emotions and primitive group dynamics while sacrificing and committing oneself to working together with other people for higher ends. This is what should happen when one becomes a Hindu. The greatest spiritual work is done through religions. Temples and other facilities, printed scriptures, creeds of beliefs, codes of conduct, and the actual spiritual growth that religion seeks are all the combined results of groups of people. Religion exists and is sustained in the minds of groups of people.

We could say that the group mind of a religion is tribal. Tribe is the awareness that one has natural affinity and loyalties with certain people with whom one lives and associates on a daily basis. Hinduism is a tribal religion. You are either outside the tribe or within the tribe or disrespected by the tribe, but as long as you are remembered by the tribe and have at one time been accepted by the tribe, you belong to the tribe. That is the way we view our religion.

The tribes of old were territorial; centered in a certain geographical area, members cultivated the land, gathered food, hunted and lived, bound together by bloodlines and social need. A religion is a tribe of a different kind. Hinduism, for example, occupies a particular dimension of the inner plane. Its members cultivate spiritual seeds in the field of human consciousness. With faith they nurture, protect and preserve in themselves, in each other and their children, foundational beliefs for religious enterprise, spiritual unfoldment and mystical realization. Hinduism gathers together the power of particular forces from the inner worlds and brings those divine powers into manifestation on Earth as vehicles to carry members of its tribe forward into light and love. The tribe we call Hinduism is a great boat that carries souls across the turbulent and sometimes treacherous sea of life.

In many ways, religion also transcends the commonalities of lower orders of tribe and community—nationality, language and ethnic difference. Hindus have many different languages, are born in many different countries. The main common factor of this global tribe is religious belief. From the religious beliefs stem the traditions, culture and basic behavior patterns of the community. Members love and honor the tribe, its traditions, its culture. They mold their lives accordingly to great benefit for their own sake and for the sake of all other members of the tribe, for the sake of all Hindus. Entrance into Hinduism means becoming a part of all this. It may mean changing one's associations, commitments and community loyalties. Real entrance into Hinduism means spending one's time with Hindus, making friends with Indian, Sri Lankan, Nepalese, Balinese, African or Caribbean Hindus, enjoying an inspired Hindu culture.

Let's take the example of a young nurse who is a member of the Western, agnostic, materialist community. Suppose that her karma and the inner impetus of her soul are such that she learns and awakens to certain divine truths which she discovers are basic Hindu beliefs. After careful study, she comes to the conclusion that, at heart, she is a Hindu. She declares herself a Hindu. She begins to worship at a Hindu temple regularly. She may even change her name legally, on her passport and driver's license, and enter the religion formally through the *nāmakaraṇa saṁskāra* at the temple. In all aspects she has become a Hindu. But there is one further and most important step to be taken. She must enter the Hindu community.

Her other very sincere gestures will never have the full impact and depth if this merger does not take place. If she keeps associating only with non-Hindus, eating at McDonald's, spending her evenings at the disco, committing herself totally to the shallow social life of "fun," spending all her money on herself—we certainly could not call her a good Hindu. In fact, her entrance into Hinduism has meaning only insofar as she merges her lifestyle and her mind into the group mind, the tribal mind, the community mind, of other Hindus. She should begin making friends from within the Hindu community. If she were asked out on a date for hamburgers by a young atheist intern from the hospital, she might say, "No, I am a vegetarian and will be going to my Indian music class tonight." In other words, her commitments and loyalties should be to the traditions, the culture and the lifestyle of other members of her new tribe—which is now Hinduism.

Today, one who holds only a single Hindu name or who appreciates Hinduism's essence but has not accepted its totality is an *ardha*-Hindu, or "half-Hindu." *Ardha*-Hindus include not only Westerners who have taken a Hindu first name, but Easterners who have taken a Western name, first or last, to disguise their true Hindu name or to render it easier for Westerners to pronounce. Other religions abhor this.

For instance, in the Islamic community we would never meet Mohammed Ali Johnson or Joe Mohammed. They are proud to be who they are, abhorring all disguises. They set a good example for us.

Some Hindus, or *ardha*-Hindus, seeking to be ecumenical and all-embracing, observe Easter or celebrate Christmas, thinking themselves tolerant. But are they? In fact, they are not, for they do not equally celebrate the Prophet Mohammed's birthday; nor do they observe Jewish or Shinto or Buddhist holy days, or those of other faiths.

Hindudharmāṅgīkārasamaye
Gurudevasya Bhāshyam

हिन्दुधर्माङ्गीकारसमये गुरुदेवस्य भाष्यम्

Gurudeva Speaks on Entering Hinduism

Gurudeva Speaks on Entering Hinduism

IN THE LATE SEVENTIES, WHEN THE HImālayan Academy began its research into religious loyalties, many questions arose. Some came from family devotees and others from the Śaiva Swāmī Saṅgam of Śaiva Siddhānta Church. Their number and relevance grew, and I decided to dictate the answers myself. The monks recorded the following *upadeśa.* It covers an array of subjects, all relating to Hinduism in the modern world, focusing on the importance of religious roots and clear lines of loyalty for success on the eternal path.

Devotee: *How does one enter the Hindu religion?*
Gurudeva: There are two ways to enter a religion. The first is to be born into the religion. The second way is through adoption or conversion, and today this process is formalized and made complete through the name-giving sacrament. Among these individuals, some have had ties with prior religions, and these ties have had to be severed. This severance, though perfectly acceptable, especially if the wife wishes to be of the same religion as her husband, is an arduous, soul-searching task. History tells us that adoptives often become the strongest members of a religion due to their careful study prior to formal entrance and to their deep, soul-stirring convictions. The name-giving sacrament, also known as the *nāmakaraṇa saṁskāra,* is the sacred rite used in both forms of entry.

Devotee: *How is one born into Hinduism?*
Gurudeva: If both parents are Hindus, the child naturally is considered a Hindu and becomes a Hindu more fully by receiving a Hindu name and then other sacraments from time to time as he is growing up. The child is taught the tenets of the religion at home, in the temple and ideally in school as well.

Devotee: *How do born Hindus regard those who seek entrance into Hinduism?*
Gurudeva: Hindus are happy to include any sincere man or woman in their worship services. In fact, all temples in the West are open to people of all religions. Our religion is rich in symbolism, tradition and culture. Symbols are signposts, its unspoken language. Those seeking entrance who accept the symbols, traditions and culture are quickly accepted, loved and made to feel at home. Such devotees willingly wear the marks upon their forehead, decorate their home with the forms of our faith, go to our Gods for their needs, naturally hold their hands and their heads in a certain way when receiving the sacred sacraments, adore and prostrate before God, Gods and gurus, showing reverence and love. It's the look in the eye and the feel in the heart at seeing the images of the God and the Gods or a swāmī's feet that distinguish a Hindu as a Hindu. Yes, it is symbolism, it is tradition, it is the ancient Hindu culture and sincere worship that designate the Hindu home, the holy atmosphere that denotes the Hindu shrine. Yes, it is the crying need for yearly pilgrimage to a holy temple somewhere of the soul's choice, a *yātrā* that releases and removes the burdens accumulated throughout the year—it is all this which identifies the Hindu soul.

Devotee: *Can one simply declare himself a Hindu?*
Gurudeva: Yes, anyone can declare himself a member of the Hindu religion, but for one to be accepted into the commu-

nity, he must immerse himself in its traditions and lifestyle. This is the first step. Next he must practice Hinduism openly and thus prove his declaration in his own life and in the minds of others. A person seeking entrance to Hinduism must convince not only himself but his close friends and family that, in fact, he is a Hindu. Otherwise, it is just a secret "play pretend." Finally, he must change his name and use his Hindu name, first and last, in all circumstances and have it made legal so that it appears on his passport, driver's license and business letters. This is a clear sign to one and all that he has fully embraced the Hindu faith.

Devotee: *Why would someone not born into Hinduism wish to enter it later in life?*
Gurudeva: In the ancient days, people lived in small hamlets and reincarnated back into the same hamlet and even into the same family time and time again. The families, the hamlets and even the countries were, for the most part, all of the same religion. The evolving soul could experience different facets of his religion without a break in continuity, from layman to priest and so on. Now, with modern-day travel and worldwide communication, this tightly knit pattern of reincarnation is dispersed, and souls find new bodies in different countries, families and religions, which in some cases are foreign to them. A soul born to parents of a certain religion may not, therefore, be himself of the nature of that religion. There are different religions to accommodate different peoples at different places on the Eternal Path.
When a soul who has experienced the Hindu religion for many years in a small village in India or Sri Lanka suddenly finds himself incarnated, through desire, in the Western world in a family of no religion or in a Christian or a Jewish family that expects him to follow what is an alien faith to him, that soul intuitively seeks out and searches for the religion that is right for him. When he finds Hinduism, God

and the Gods become dear to him, Lord Gaṇeśa is a familiar friend. All layers of his mind are content, and wholeheartedly he declares himself a Hindu and later enters into the Hindu religion.

Conversion is a homecoming for the soul. Many people want to move from one religion to another because they have realized that they are not in the religion that is right for them. Their soul is not satisfied. Their beliefs have changed and they find themselves different from others within their birth religion. So, when the individual discusses his beliefs and his desire to enter Hinduism with his former religious leader, the priest, minister or rabbi intuitively realizes that truly this soul belongs to the religion of his belief. It is that easy. It is that final.

Devotee: *What are some of the other ways one might know if he is in fact a Hindu soul, having had deep impressions in that religion in past lives?*
Gurudeva: The Hindu soul is moved by the music, the pageantry and the rites of Hinduism. He intuitively understands the esoterics of temple worship and is content with the essence of the philosophy. When he finds the religion of his heart, he begins to lean on it, to use it. Our religion does not claim its path to be the only path. Thus, a soul drawn into Hinduism who was not born into a Hindu family is asked to become familiar with all religions before making a final choice. This is important, for entrance into the Hindu religion is irrevocable. There is no authority—no church, no aadheenam or other institution—empowered to sever a person from Hinduism, to disassociate him from this root religion.

Devotee: *Does this mean that someone born into the Hindu religion cannot leave it?*
Gurudeva: Yes, this means that should a member of the

Hindu religion embrace another faith, he nevertheless remains a Hindu for the rest of his life and only a follower of the second religion, for leaving Hinduism is impossible. He would still be a Hindu, but an apostate to one of the sects within Hinduism. The children born and raised in the parents' chosen religion, Christianity or Islam, for example, would be Christians or Muslims, provided they accepted the beliefs as they grew up. It is only their children, however, the third generation, that would be the true Christians or Muslims, not attached to or inclined to be pulled back to their Hindu roots. Therefore, Hindu religious leaders do proselytize among Hindus who have left the fold to follow another path in order to bring them back to the Hindu fold. These souls are considered to be Hindus who, for one reason or another, embraced another faith or abandoned all faiths for a time.

Devotee: *I have heard that it is not possible for one to leave the Jewish religion. Is this true?*
Gurudeva: Judaism does recognize apostasy, which is defined as the formal denial of the central tenets of Jewish faith—especially the "unity and uniqueness of God"—or as the formal conversion to a religion other than Judaism. Apostate Jews are denied certain privileges, but are taken back into Judaism if they repent. Many religions are like this, never denying former adherents the possibility of coming back and requiring some kind of purification ceremony if they do return.

Devotee: *If a Muslim wishes to embrace Hinduism, having found himself to truly be a Hindu soul, how can he do this?*
Gurudeva: The Vishva Hindu Parishad, the Madurai Aadheenam, the Masurāśrama and many other institutions are bringing Muslims into Hinduism through a simple ceremony. As in Christianity, one would become a *de facto*

apostate, for he no longer held the Muslim beliefs. He would be excommunicated, *ipso facto*. Like Christianity, Islam is based upon belief. One can enter Islam by simply declaring belief in Mohammed as Allah's true and final prophet, changing one's names and declaring a few other beliefs. Therefore, it is logical that when one no longer held this central belief, he would no longer be a Muslim.

Devotee: *Within Hinduism, can one change from one sect, or from one sampradāya within a sect, to another?*
Gurudeva: Yes, this happens quite often. It is part of the beauty of Hinduism that it allows for this kind of flexibility and change. After study of the new sect or *sampradāya* has been completed, the transfer is made through a special ceremony. Occasionally, Vaishṇavites adopt Śaivism through transfers of this kind. Certain Vaishṇavites place a small discus, sacred symbol of Vishṇu, on the shoulder of those who embrace their sect.

Devotee: *Can you explain more about apostasy? Is it the same as heresy or excommunication?*
Gurudeva: Usually excommunication is defined as a formal censure imposed by a bishop or other ecclesiastical authority by which an individual is excluded from the religious community, barred from the sacraments and denied a religious burial. The penalty of excommunication is generally imposed only on those who have committed a major offense against the religious body, such as heresy or schism. Schism is the offense of causing or trying to cause a split within the religious organization. Heresy is different. It is the rejection of one or more of the doctrines of a religion by one who still maintains an overall adherence to that religion, who has not abandoned it altogether. Some religions impose the penalty of excommunication on heretics, while others do not.

Apostasy is a voluntary act by which an individual formally denies the central tenets or beliefs of a religion, having completely rejected the religion itself. When the individual's rejection is formally recognized by the religious body, they consider him an apostate. As in the case of one who is excommunicated, an apostate is excluded from the religious community, barred from the sacraments and denied a religious burial. Some religious bodies only consider that an individual is an apostate after he has actually joined another religion. The rules vary. Some religions consider that an apostate incurs an *ipso facto* excommunication, meaning that by the very act of his apostasy he has automatically imposed on himself the penalty of excommunication. Generally, those who have been excommunicated or declared apostate can seek readmittance into the religion through repentance. However, some religious bodies never allow apostates to reenter.

Devotee: *Is it right to take a person away from his religion? Isn't there a negative karma involved?*
Gurudeva: Severance must be done by the person himself, not by the religionist or those seeking new members. It is a do-it-yourself path. All religious leaders should have a mutual respect for each other, a sense of professional ethics, an acknowledgement of the existence and the rights of every other religion in the world. None should seek to entice another into his religion, but rather encourage a deeper adherence to the beliefs and practices of each chosen faith. Hindus never set about to take a person away from another religion. We encourage Christians to return to their churches, Jews to their synagogues, Muslims to their mosques—there to become even more diligent and sincere followers. On rare occasions, severance is permissible, even preferable, but it should be totally on the part of the individual. We do not encourage such transfers, but if the individual devotee insists, if his sincerity is well tested, his reasons well founded, if

his persistence and purity prove him to be a Hindu soul beyond a doubt, and if he would suffer through life in an alien religious tradition, then he is accepted into the Hindu fold through the *nāmakaraṇa saṁskāra* in the traditional way.

Devotee: *How important is religious education?*
Gurudeva: All the eleven great religions of the world and each of the various faiths have some definite form of education for young and old alike. Religious education trains an individual how to use his religion to better his life by coming closer to God. It teaches him what to believe and what to reject. That individual, well trained, eventually becomes a defender of his faith, and the religion is preserved, protected and defended, and sometimes it is expanded by him. Man does not have horns or claws to protect himself. He is neither swift nor strong compared to the animal kingdom. His intelligence and knowledge are his weapons, his strength.

Each religion educates its young in a sectarian way, for religionists believe that to learn one specific path is sufficient and necessary. Therefore, education should not be diluted by taking in all religions under one banner for the sake of something called "universality." Rather, religious education should be faithful to tradition. Religious schools are essential, Śaivite schools for the Śaivites, Vaishṇavite schools for the Vaishṇavites and Śākta schools for the Śāktas, Christian schools for the Christians and Muslim schools for the members of Islam. In the spirit of honesty and good faith in fulfillment of the duty to educate the young of our religion, this should be observed. The Christians do not send their children to Hindu schools, nor do the Muslims send their children to Christian or Jewish schools. The truly devout discriminate in this way for the sake of their children, whom they dearly love. Thus, they dispatch their sacred duty by passing their religion, their faith, on to the next generation.

Devotee: *If a Hindu swāmī talks of reincarnation and karma and convinces Christians, Jews or Muslims of the validity of these concepts, since these are not official beliefs of these religions, has he not made them apostate to their religion?*
Gurudeva: Yes, indeed. Hinduism is so insidiously profound that it is capable of turning many people away from their born religion, none of which can match its depth. Through the Hindu swāmīs, thousands, millions, have been brought to the doorstep of Hinduism. How can these basic beliefs, inherent in all mankind, be erased once learned? Truly, the Jew and the Christian and the Muslim who learn that God is everywhere and within all things, that the soul returns from birth to birth and is responsible to its own actions through the principle of karma, that all souls are destined to full merger into God—can they forget these things? Can we forget the law of gravity? Can we change the nature of electricity if, once comprehended, we deny all knowledge of it? The swāmīs, however, have gone as far as they feel ethically permitted to go, since many of their devotees were born into Christian or Jewish families.

It is really up to the devotees to take further steps toward embracing Hinduism. The swāmīs, respecting their acceptance of the basic Hindu beliefs of karma, reincarnation, dharma and all-pervasive Divinity, have given them each a Hindu "ashram" name. They have done their part. Next the devotees must, if they are really sincere in embracing the path which the swāmī privately practices, complete their severance, have their name made legal and enter the Hindu religion formally through the traditional *nāmakaraṇa saṁskāra.* Then they will have the fullness of our religion in all its increments and will raise their children in the beliefs and with the sacraments of their chosen sect within the multifaceted religion called Hinduism.

Devotee: *Does all the responsibility fall on the devotees?*
Gurudeva: The situation in the West has been building since the 1920s, when Hindu monks began attracting congregations in America and other Western countries. As we have said in the past, they as a rule have disguised their Hinduness. We might say this was done to avoid overstepping the ethical bounds of religious propriety. Sincerely they sought to spread the universal message of Hinduism without drawing anyone away from their root religion. But they, too, have learned, especially as Hinduism has grown up in the West with the coming of thousands of Hindu immigrants, that their teachings have had a powerful impact. Many hundreds of devotees are betwixt and between—no longer good Christians and not yet fully Hindus. The most potent catalysts of all are the children of these devotees, who for all intents and purposes are born Hindus, raised in the Hindu culture, beliefs and attitudes, which permeates the yoga, universalist presentation of so many swāmīs and gurus. It is up to the devotees to declare their religious loyalties—if not for themselves, then for the sake of their children. They know this, and the swāmīs know this, too. For some, this is a difficult step, for there is subconscious conflict between the old impressions and beliefs and the new. The *sādhana* then, if they are to enter Hinduism fully, is to make the inner adjustments, to resolve the conflict. The swāmīs are there on the inside, ready to assist.

We feel most of the swāmīs are simply waiting for their devotees to take the next step, as they have given as much as they can without overstepping their protocol. One of the purposes of this book is to show devotees how this is possible. The priests, whose duty it is to perform this important rite of passage, are the final link to orthodoxy for these hundreds of sincere souls.

Devotee: *Is leaving one religion and entering another in any way objected to by government?*
Gurudeva: Not in the US, nor in most other countries which guarantee this right of personal religious choice, though some do restrict aggressive proselytization. This flow is well within the rights of citizens of the US. The founding fathers of this great country were anxious to not impose upon future generations the religious repressions they had suffered in Europe and, therefore, firmly established a personal freedom in religious matters that would allow members to come and go freely from one religion to another as they wished. Our nation explicitly provides for this freedom of religion in the Bill of Rights of the US Constitution.

Devotee: *Is severance a difficult process?*
Gurudeva: Withdrawing from one religion to enter another is not a difficult accomplishment. It is heart-breaking, of course, for a religious leader, a Catholic priest, Protestant minister, Jewish rabbi or Taoist master to realize his religion did not satisfy the needs of a member of the congregation while witnessing that member's severance and adoption of another religion such as the Hindu religion. Such dedicated religious leaders love their religion, as we do, and naturally feel personally hurt and perhaps helpless when one among their congregations seeks spiritual fulfillment elsewhere, especially if he holds to the belief that his is the only true religion. Outside of such personal matters, which are understandable, the laws of apostasy within all the religions of the world are clear and lenient. There may be challenges and difficulties involved in conversion, but these are generally due to the lack of understanding of the priest, minister, rabbi, family, friends or the individual himself.

Devotee: *What are the keys to successfully severing former ties before entering a one's chosen religion?*
Gurudeva: Severance is an individual affair, to be handled in a personal way between the individual and his religious leaders, family and closest friends. Once he has convinced those individuals that, indeed, he is a Hindu because of belief, practice and community, he will have fully convinced his own subconscious mind, the great impressionable computer within him, that this, in fact, is actually true. It is not at all necessary for family, friends and religious leaders to accept the principles and practices of Hinduism or even to understand them for this process to work. But it is necessary that the matter not be kept secret from them, especially before the full and formal conversion takes place.

For a full severance to happen, a certain emotional exchange has to occur among the people involved, and in some cases there may be quite a number of people involved. Therefore, a severance certainly cannot be accomplished by mail order or as a mere transfer of paperwork, where one is written off the register of one religion and added onto the membership rolls of another. It is not a procedure consummated by a clerk who adjusts the files and the mailing list simply because he has been asked to have a name removed. Such a severance cannot be taken seriously. The subconscious mind of the individual is convinced only through the experience of speaking with family, friends and former religious counsel. True severance is an inner matter; it is subconscious. It is not an organizational adjustment or mailing-list manipulation, which could then be readjusted in a year if the person changed his mind. For a severance to be true, strong and lasting, the process must make a strong, indelible impression within the subconscious mind of the religious leader—or his successor on the same physical premises where the devotee experienced the former religion and had its beliefs set into place in his mind.

Belief is another important aspect of severance. The individual must understand fully the beliefs that he was brought up with and compare them, one by one, to those of the new religion he wishes to join. Just prior to announcing to anyone his intent to enter Hinduism, the individual should participate for a short while, a day or two or more, in the religious services of his former religion. Then he should go to his minister or priest and explain that he now wishes to enter the Hindu religion. In this way he will update the subconscious mind and settle the minds of those who consider themselves his religious counselors, rather than just sneaking away, drifting away, from his former religion.

Devotee: *What can be the results if a full severance is not made and the person just drifts away?*
Gurudeva: If only a drifting away occurs, only half a severance is attained. The half-committed person may later drift on again into still another religion, or back into the one that he left, still dissatisfied. Drifting from one religious group to another, with no break in continuity for subconscious cleansing of the impressions which produced deep commitment, is much like the wandering nomad might who drifts from nation to nation, never becoming a citizen of any, never taking on the duties and responsibilities of any one community. Such indecisive devotees are like the perpetual tourist who, never satisfied, wanders from one place to the next.

This important protocol described above disallows the tendency of drifting away from one religion into another. Of course, many people do drift from one to another. We see this happening all of the time. It is easy to accept the new religion on blind faith, but without making a real commitment. This may be because, in some cases, it's too much of an effort or embarrassment to go back and face up to their former religious leaders, family and friends. It is, however, ethical and courteous to let them know that this very important, life-changing event is moving within them and about to occur. In the process of severance and adoption, there has to be a time when the devotee is in a limbo state, no longer holding the beliefs of the former religion and not yet fully accepted into Hinduism. This in-between state has to exist, if only briefly. Otherwise, nothing has happened subconsciously. An emptiness in the pit of the stomach should be felt for a time.

Devotee: *If someone had no previous religion, would there be no severance necessary before entering Hinduism?*
Gurudeva: Besides the great religions, there are other areas of belief to sever from as well, such as existentialism or the beliefs of the drug culture, communism, secular humanism. Severance from each one of these vast and powerful streams of thought should be taken as seriously as from a major religion. If the severance is not complete, right down to the most obscure belief, the individual may subconsciously try to adjust Hinduism to his own ideas, and this could be very frustrating to him. Each potential Hindu should study carefully all the beliefs within these other areas that have been impressed, knowingly or unknowingly, into his subconscious mind through the years. He must reject each one that does not concur with the beliefs of Hinduism. Only in this soul-searching will a true and successful preparation have occurred.

We want to stress once again that unless all alien beliefs are consciously rejected, unless former spiritual leaders, family and close friends are informed, and unless there is a definite break in continuity of leaving former religions or non-Hindu ways of thought before entering Hinduism, the purification and preparation process will not have been fully complete. Only by making this process as complete as possible can the new adoptive settle down as a full-fledged member of the Hindu community.

Devotee: *Do Hindus actively proselytize for converts?*
Gurudeva: No. Even though we are in the midst of strongly proselytizing faiths, Hindus do not actively proselytize among the members of other religions. We are over a billion strong and outnumber ourselves daily through the birth rate. However, we do welcome newcomers into the Hindu fold if they come knowingly and of their own volition. Hindu adoptives are expected to immerse themselves in philosophy, in temple worship, in protocol and earn their acceptance within the Hindu community.

We Hindus have always heartily recommended our philosophy to souls of other religions but have never overtly sought to dissuade them from their own religion. Yet, Hinduism has always proven itself to be the permanent home for the pilgrims who have knowledgeably sought it out, studied it and then lived its grand principles, performed the *sādhana* and entered the community. For the eternal truths of Hinduism are for the peoples of the world. They are the heritage of all humanity.

Dharmantarasya Neetiśāstravishaye
Gurudevasya Bhāshyam

धर्मान्तरस्य नीतिशास्त्रविषये गुरुदेवस्य भाष्यम्

Gurudeva Speaks on Ethical Conversion

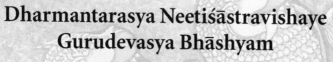

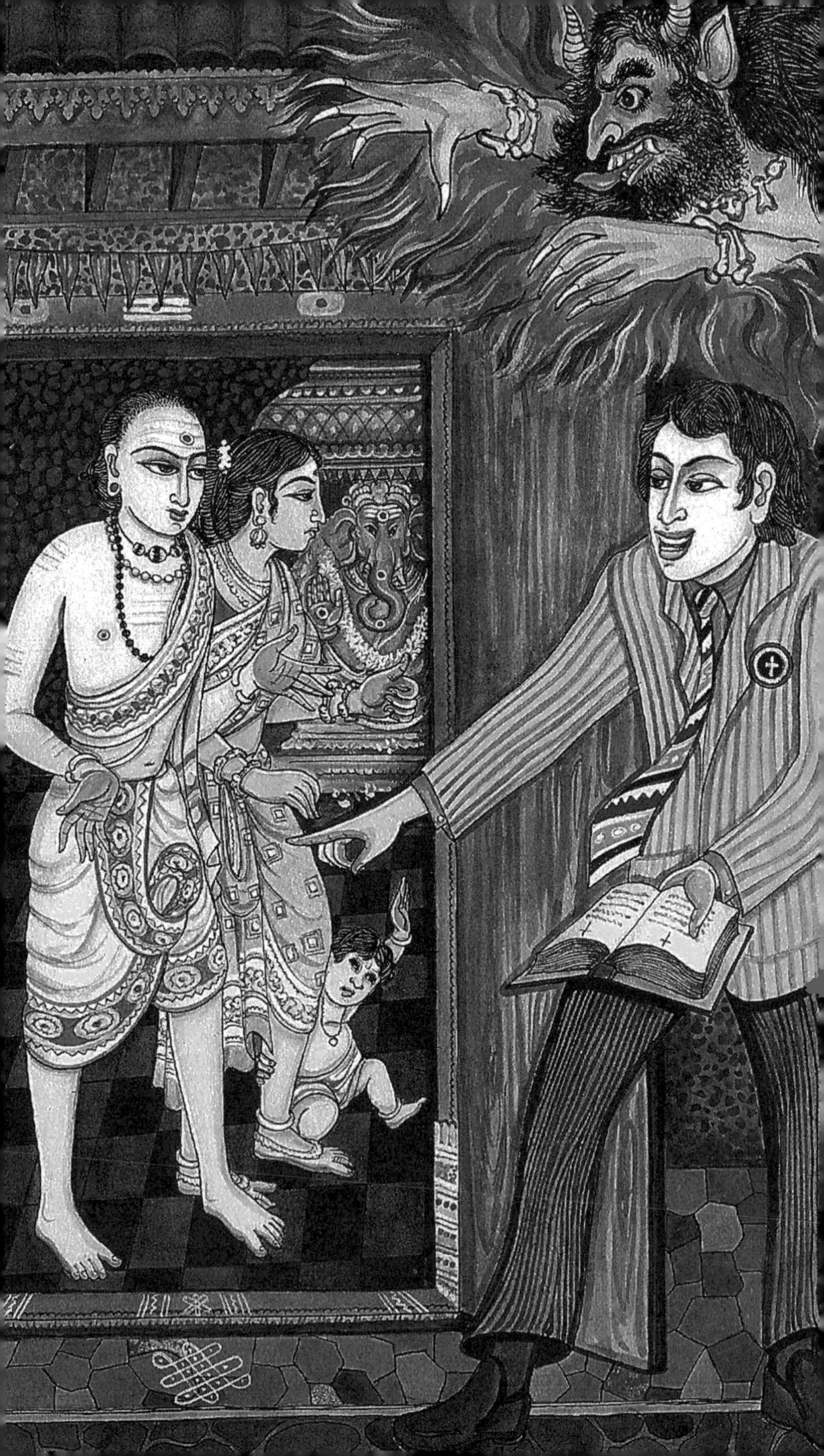

Gurudeva Speaks on Ethical Conversion

THE FOLLOWING IS A QUESTION-AND-ANSWER session, known in Sanskrit as an *upadeśa*, in which we respond to devotees' queries on ethical conversion, sectarianism, paths of attainment, spiritual unfoldment and more.

Devotee: *How do you view the practices of religious persons who embrace all at once Christianity, Buddhism, Hinduism and all the religions in a kind of universal ecumenism?*
Gurudeva: This is a perfectly understandable phase of spiritual evolution, but it is not the true or final path for sincere seekers. It is certainly not what Śrī Rāmakṛishṇa was trying to tell people, nor was it what our own beloved *satguru,* Śiva Yogaswāmī, stood for. They were both staunch Hindus, one a Śākta and the other a Śaivite, who understood their religion deeply. Śrī Rāmakṛishṇa did not cease being a Śakti devotee, but so fully embraced Her worship that he came to know Her vastness in embracing everything. Nor did Śiva Yogaswāmī abandon God Śiva to become everything to everyone, but was everything in being the perfectly devout Śaivite.

They were simply indicating, as I do, that religions are one in their movement toward God, some offering knowledge, others service, others love, attainment and direct experience. At the same time, they are different in their practices and attainments, and most assuredly distinct in their beliefs, the foundation of the attitudes of their members. It is good to love and respect all religions; it is a necessary condition of spiritual unfoldment. But it is necessary to keep firmly to a single path toward God. Our Śiva Yogaswāmī taught that a train can only run on the tracks. Following the path given by our religion leads one onward through religious practices and *sādhana* into divine realization. Otherwise, there is no longer a path, but a trackless plane where each wanders totally on his own, as his own guide, often without experience, in a desert of ignorance seeking solace in a mirage, an imaginary enlightenment he can see just on the horizon but which, in reality, does not exist.

Devotee: *Some Hindus, particularly in the West, embrace all religions as if they were one, feeling that sectarianism is too narrow, too prone to conflicts. Why do you disagree with that view and prefer instead to promote sectarianism?*
Gurudeva: Religious people do not cause conflicts. They resolve them and bring peace into the world. The Anglican British in India played upon sectarianism to create strife among the members of the sects toward one another to fulfill their own divide-and-rule policy, hoping the sects would destroy each other. They did the same with the caste and sub-caste positions, as well as with money exchange between the provinces. Much strife was created through communalism, stirring dissension between Hindus and Muslims, which was exactly what the British were attempting to do.

I argue against nonsectarianism because it doesn't work. It may have been good for a time, but proved to be a dead-end street, leading well-intentioned followers into an abyss of mental confusion, divorce, abortion and suicide, leading its followers to the question, "Where is the true path of Hinduism?" Our final answer to that question is the path of Hinduism is Śaivism; it is Vaishṇavism; it is Śāktism; it is Smārtism. It is not in a Hinduism that is divorced from sectarianism, because Hinduism does not exist without its four major sects or denominations. It is a four-fold religion, the sum of its four sects. If you destroy the parts, you destroy the whole. If you eliminate the four denominations, you also eliminate Hinduism.

In theory, the idea that all religions are one, or that all religions are the same, is a convincing notion. But the great experiment to abandon one's religion to embrace all others or to relinquish one's sect to become nonsectarian has not worked. Nor was this the first effort to create an eclectic, man-made religion, one that took a little of this and a little of that and a few ideas from its founder and a few improvements by its successors, and so on into an idealistic emptiness. This is always true of religious efforts which do not uphold dharma. Throughout history utopian movements have risen and fallen, bright and promising in their birth, neglected and forgotten in their demise.

Devotee: *What about the principle of Ishṭa Devatā? Isn't every Hindu free to choose the form of the Deity he or she wants to worship?*

Gurudeva: Of course, within each denomination the idea of Ishṭa Devatā—that one may choose the form of the Deity he is naturally drawn to worship—is most proper and traditional. A Śaivite, for example, is free to choose Gaṇeśa as his Deity, or to become a devotee of Lord Murugan or Śiva. But the modern Smārta trend of accepting a Devatā outside of one's sect is not good. I believe that this was begun in an effort to break down sectarianism. We are proud to be Śaivites, and Vaishṇavites are proud of their religion, too. But there are those who sought to be free from their father's religion, even to embrace Christianity or Buddhism. Even a statue of Jesus and Mother Mary are seen today as valid Ishṭa Devatās, and they stand next to a statue of Lord Gaṇeśa on a liberal, nonsectarian Hindu's home altar. On the positive side this is a sign of the broadness of our religion, which embraces all. But on the negative side it is a dilution of that same religion, which can lead to its destruction. Out of this comes a diluted religion, its strength sapped, its Gods exiled while foreign Gods hold sway. From my experience and inner findings, this idea of the Ishṭa Devatā chosen from any of the Gods or Goddesses, or none of them, should be closely looked at, as it can bring about a distortion of the traditional continuity of our religion.

Devotee: *There are those who teach a path to Truth through yoga and* sādhana *alone, without the temples, without the Gods. Would their followers succeed on such a spiritual path?*
Gurudeva: The first initiation that a traditional guru would give before *sādhana* is assigned and yoga is taught is to bring the truth-seeker fully into his religion. Then he would give his devotees *sādhana* to perform, basic religious practices to observe—such as japa and pilgrimage—and he would teach those devotees religious protocol and culture. Only after these matters were settled could experience of the deeper realizations be sought for. Of course, there could be peace of mind and a genuine devotion within those following yoga disciplines alone. But the deepest realizations of the yoga *mārga* and the *sādhana mārga* come when these are coupled with the rich traditions, with temple worship and so on. At this juncture, yoga can be taught and the disciple given permission to practice it. This is the magic. Then it will really work. Otherwise, it simply does not have the power that comes from the backing of the three worlds.

Therefore, those who seek Truth through yoga must enter the arena of *sādhana*—in our case, must fully embrace Śaivism in its entirety. Only then will *sādhana* bear the fruits of yogas well performed, as pūjā bears the fruits of *śakti* power, and *tapas* bears the fruits of *sānnidhya*. Only then will the fruit of *sādhana* ripen in the radiance of yoga, drawing its sustenance through the roots of the ṛishis' revelations in the Vedic-Āgamic way.

Devotee: *So often we have been told that Vedānta and yoga make a Christian a better Christian. How does that relate to your insights on sectarianism?*
Gurudeva: A strong religion births from within itself its own spiritual lights. You are correct. Christianity needs all the help that it can get, and yes, Vedānta and yoga have been a solace for millions of Christians. From personal experience in teaching Vedānta and yoga to Christians and Jews in the Western world, I assure you that it does not make them better Christians or Jews.

Those steeped in Christian/Judaic emotions and dogma in early years studied diligently with me later in life, striving for Self Realization. The more they strove in their yogic practices and philosophical understandings, the farther they moved from their goal. The Biblical theologies perpetuate a one-lifetime belief, inspiring a sense of hurried religious attainment. This very urgency of attaining a spiritual goal keeps the aspirant from the goal, keeps the mind agitated, the emotions frustrated, knowing that attainment has not yet been reached, knowing the time is shorter each day, and subconsciously believing that the soul has only one opportunity on this Earth to realize God.

Does the fruit upon the tree ripen because we wish it to? Is the energy in the sap, the kuṇḍalinī force, of the tree that ripens the fruit answerable to the demands of the fruit which is impatient to become ripe? No. It happens in its own good time. The ripening of the fruit depends on the roots of the tree, upon the soil and the season and the sun. Similarly, the ripening of the soul into its ultimate states of maturity depends on the roots of the religion, upon the season of the soul and upon the radiant light of the *satguru*. Thus, the wise hold firmly to the strong trunk of sectarianism, to traditionalism, to the principles lived from the time of the ṛishis who brought forth the *Vedas* and the *Āgamas*, the revealed scriptures of the timeless Sanātana Dharma.

Devotee: *It is sometimes taught that advanced souls need only follow the path of yoga to realize God. Are Vedānta philosophy and yoga disciplines sufficient to know God in this life, or are all the increments of religion needed?*
Gurudeva: Man has an instinctive, an intellectual and a superconscious phase of mind. Śaiva Siddhānta theology postulates the progressive path of *charyā,* kriyā, yoga and jñāna. *Charyā* is virtuous and moral living. Kriyā is temple worship and devotion. Yoga is internalized devotion and union with God Śiva. And jñāna is the awakened state of the matured yogī. The *charyā mārga* harnesses and controls the instinctive mind. The kriyā *mārga* harnesses and controls the intellectual mind. The yoga *mārga* releases man's individual awareness so that he is able to function superconsciously. And the jñāna *mārga,* after union with God, maintains that superconsciousness, as knowing bursts forth from within. It is from here that *śruti,* our great and lasting revealed scriptures, have come.

All of the increments of a religion control and culture the instinctive and intellectual mind. When a devotee sits in meditation and is plagued with instinctive desire through thoughts, feelings and fantasies, it is only because the instinctive mind has not been harnessed. He should first perform *charyā* more diligently, later to earn the right to practice yoga. When the devotee sits in meditation and the intellect plagues him, he has one thought dancing into another, ideas magnifying into images in an unstilled mind, it is kriyā that must be better performed as a divine antidote which harnesses the rash intellect through a deeply mystical process. Needless to say, Vedānta is the outgrowth and product of jñāna, and yoga is the result of *charyā* and kriyā, the great disciplinarians of the instinctive-intellectual mind. All of this is Śaiva Siddhānta. Similarly, each sect within the Hindu religion has its specific traditions, goals and path of attainment.

Why hide our religion under the cloak of an intellectual explanation of Vedānta and certain simple practices of yoga when they are the earned outgrowth of a truly religious life? It was fine to do so in the early days in North America, for it helped to break up Western thinking with the truths of reincarnation and karma and physical yoga practices; but those days are over. The Catholic and Protestant churches declare these ideas a threat to their very existence, especially the concept that God is everywhere and in all things. Thus they naturally rise up in a unified force against the swāmīs who entice members of Abrahamic congregations away, and I rise up when these same swāmīs refuse these sincere aspirants formal entrance into their sect of the Hindu religion. We deplore what has resulted in the lives of many in the Western world this last century who live in a state of limbo, apostate to their former religion but not accepted into their new faith by the Indian Hindu congregation of their community.

In conclusion, Vedānta is a profound and intriguing philosophy. It complements existentialism as an opposite point of view. Haṭha yoga is beneficial to the physical body of the peoples of all religions. But when those simple beginnings inevitably extend to the preaching of reincarnation and karma, it leads Christian-Judaic followers astray. On the other hand, Vedānta for the nonreligious intellectual is reduced to simply another subject to be processed through the mental gridwork. This is fine. The same applies to the physical culturist who stresses only yoga āsanas. It is only when the individual begins to believe the swāmī's own philosophy and slowly relinquishes the Christian-Judaic-Islamic faith by accepting Hindu beliefs that he becomes apostate to his religion. It then becomes the swāmī's moral obligation to help the devotee complete the conversion into the Hindu religion.

I myself listened to swāmīs from India in early years, even before I met my *satguru*, and believed most of what they were postulating about religion: that all religions lead to the same goal, that Vedānta will make Christians better Christians and Jews better Jews, that sectarianism is narrow-minded and divisive. Then a number of years later I discovered that I had been misled.

Westerners are wiser now as to who comes from Asia and what he has to offer. And the Catholic and Protestant churches are better informed now, too. This is why we call for established Hindu religionists, well-schooled in the Śaivite, Vaishṇavite, Smārta or Śākta sect, to come forward and work with and work for a new generation of half-converted Westerners and immigrant Indians and their foreign-born offspring living far from their religious homeland and thus prone to stray from the religion of their grandparents.

Devotee: *Do you have to be a Hindu to realize God?*
Gurudeva: The Christian-Judaic-Islamic religions, also known as the Abrahamic faiths, do not hold to the doctrine that God is everywhere and in all things. Their belief is that God is eternally separate from the world He created. The first *samādhi* of Satchidānanda, experiencing God in and through all things, postulated by Sanātana Dharma and other Eastern faiths, believed in and then attained by their followers, is in most cases unattainable through those religious paths that block the conscious and subconscious states of mind of their followers by negating and denying this mystical experience as apostasy. Extraterrestrial channels encased in the *sushumṇā* current in the spine of man are inherent in the fiber of the religions that know of and lead man's consciousness to God Realization. These inner channels of consciousness are available to its members, guiding them to their ultimate destiny on this planet. Still, there are rare souls who dive deeply into themselves despite their faith's beliefs, and penetrate into the states of Satchidānanda, sometimes becoming heretical members of the faith that claimed no such mystical experience was possible. But once

Satchidānanda is even briefly experienced, the inner knowledge of reincarnation, the subtle forces of the law of karma and the presence of God in all things are intuitively understood. Actually, one of the major problems of the Abrahamic religions is having within them undeclared apostates who have had these universal inner experiences and who, in turn, silently sway the minds of other followers, not by preaching alien philosophies but by sharing their own compelling mystical encounters.

Devotee: *Is it true that Hindu leaders sometimes make overt efforts to proselytize and convert Jews, Muslims and Christians?*
Gurudeva: Yes, this is true. Overt efforts are made to convert Jews, Christians and Muslims into one of the denominations of Hinduism, but only if they previously had a forced conversion from Hinduism through bribery, coercion or financial and educational rewards. Through ignorance and dire need, born Hindus have accepted "new religions" in order to have food on the table at the end of the day, to gain access to schools for their children or to a hospital for health care, to qualify for employment or a promotion, to protect their lands from confiscation or their families from harm. All this is a part of conversions brought about by political power or sheer cunning. This is not just a matter of history. It continues today, in the year 2000, and beyond. It is something all Hindus are concerned about.

It is the child of such force-converted families who will become a member of the religion through birth and belief; but it is only that child's child, the third generation, who can be regarded as a settled, born member of the new religion. It takes three generations for this process to be completed. Therefore, our proselytizing is focused on the first two generations, with a view to bringing them back to the Hindu religion. If we neglect them, we are not caring for our brothers and sisters. This kind of proselytizing among our own we consider our duty, for it is educating the young and re-educating their parents, and it is not infringing on the other faiths who imposed these unethical conversions.

Devotee: *Why do other religions sometimes use unscrupulous tactics to convert people away from Hinduism?*
Gurudeva: Conversion has often been a point of contention between religions. This need not be so, if only all the spiritual leaders would respect the other religions. Historically, the Christians and Muslims have sought to convert members away from Hinduism, away from all the sects—Śaivism, Vaishṇavism, Smārtism and Śaktism. The Jews, however, have never infringed in this way, and have shown a deep affinity and support for the Hindu faith. Christians and Muslims seek converts because they genuinely believe that theirs is the only true religion on the planet.

In November of 1999 Catholic Pope John Paul II dispelled all doubt as to his Church's dedication to world domination in New Delhi, India, on Dīpāvalī Day. Closing a three-year Asian Synod of Bishops, he issued the voluminious "Post-Synodal Apostolic Exhortation Ecclesia in Asia of the Holy Father John Paul II to the Bishops, Priests and Deacons, Men and Women in the Consecrated Life and All the Lay Faithful on Jesus Christ the Saviour and His Mission of Love and Service in Asia."

Many Hindus who believe that Catholics are friendly to their religion may be surprised upon reading excerpts from John Paul II's message to his missionaries in Asia: "Just as in the first millennium the Cross was planted on the soil of Europe, and in the second on that of the Americas and Africa, we can pray that in the Third Christian Millennium a great harvest of faith will be reaped in this vast and vital continent [of Asia]....If the Church in Asia is to fulfill its providential destiny, evangelization must be your absolute priority.... Christ is the one Mediator between God and man and the sole Redeemer of the world, to be clearly distinguished from the founders of other great religions....I pray to the Lord to send many more committed laborers to reap the harvest of souls which I see as ready and plentiful [in Asia]....The universal presence of the Holy Spirit cannot serve as an excuse for a failure to proclaim Jesus Christ explicitly as the one and only Saviour....Vatican II taught clearly that the entire Church is missionary, and that the work of evangelization is the duty of the whole People of God....Jesus Christ [is] the fulfillment of the yearnings expressed in the mythologies and folklore of the Asian peoples....The Synod therefore renewed the commitment of the Church in Asia to the task of improving both ecumenical relations and interreligious dialogue [as] essential to the Church's evangelizing mission on the continent....From the Christian point of view, interreligious dialogue is more than a way of fostering mutual knowledge and enrichment; it is a part of the Church's evangelizing mission....In many countries, Catholic schools play an important role in evangelization."

Asiaweek magazine, out of Hong Kong, commented in an editorial, "The pope's message threatens to alienate liberal Indians who previously dismissed the warnings of Hindu chauvinists as fanatical paranoia. But the pope's statements make clear the Vatican's expansionist agenda. And they lend credence to the longstanding complaint that Christianity's many good works in India are meant to give it a foothold on the nation's soul" (HINDUISM TODAY, Feb., 2000).

Hindus do not become angry at the Christians or the Muslims who seek out converts, knowing that predators always take the weakest prey. United Hindus of the world concur that religious education of the *harijan*, the śūdra, the truant youth and the adult gone astray is the dynamic key for moving Hinduism out of an agricultural era into the technological age. We feel our battle is not with the other religions. The battle and the challenge lie within Hinduism itself. What can one lose by learning the Sanātana Dharma? Ignorance. Only ignorance can be lost and personal realization of God gained. Those who are educated and think for themselves can only become strong and secure, well able to make the proper choice in their personal dharma.

Devotee: *What are the unscrupulous tactics used to convert Hindus away from their God and Gods?*

Gurudeva: Hindus who are still in the agricultural era are often simple, virtuous people, uneducated and believing. They work on the farms. They grow the crops and tend the herds. They are vulnerable to many tactics, and many are used. It's very sad, but true. One of the Śaiva swāmīs of our order visited India recently, and I will ask him to relate what was told to him. "During a pilgrimage to India years ago, we were approached by many devout Hindus who were deeply disturbed about the way their children and neighbors were being converted to Christianity. Of course, this is nothing new. It has been going on for centuries, but it is shocking to hear from those who are suffering that it is still happening. We were told, for instance, that a Christian feeding hall was opened in Chennai for undernourished and impoverished children. The children came for a few days, delighted to have a warm and healthy meal. Then they were told that it was getting difficult to keep track and that it would be necessary to identify which children were part of the program. The identification was completed on hundreds of young and hungry Hindu children. It was in the form of a small Christian cross tattooed on their chest!"

Another Chennai incident was related. A Catholic convent began a program of taking six-to eight-year-old Hindu children to a popular snake farm on weekends, including free snacks. About three or four buses were full each week. On the way to the snake farm at a given signal the driver would disengage the electrical wires and the engine would sputter to a stop on the roadside. He would try and try to start it, but of course could not. After some waiting, the nuns would say, "Well, we all want to get to the snake farm. The driver is having problems. Let's all pray for help. Now, how many of you worship Lord Gaṇeśa?" Several children would raise their hands. "Fine. Let's pray to Lord Gaṇeśa to help the bus driver." And all would pray for a few minutes. The driver would try again, and nothing would happen. Then the nuns would ask, "How many of you worship Lord Murugan?" This would go on as devotees of Śiva, Rāma, Kṛishṇa and others all failed.

Finally the nuns would say, "All your Gods have been unable to help. Let's try something new. Let's all pray to Jesus Christ. Get on your knees and pray to Jesus to start the bus." The children prayed, the bus driver reconnected the wiring, and the bus started. The children were told, "You see, Jesus is more powerful than all the Hindu Gods. Aren't you glad we prayed to Jesus? Now we can enjoy a day at the snake farm. Everyone say with me, 'Thank you, Jesus.'" The innocent children, only six or seven years old, did enjoy the day and were deeply impressed with the apparent helplessness of their Hindu Gods. These are two examples of what we were told by reliable elders.

Devotee: *Are Hindus who have entered the technological age equally affected by these deceptive means of conversion?*
Gurudeva: No, they are not. They are more profoundly influenced by a more sophisticated brand of conversion—not to Christianity or Islam, but to modern Western thought, Freudian psychology, Marxist Communism and the postulations of the existentialist Frenchman, Jean Paul Sartre, who declared that God does not exist. Existentialist thought has poisoned the minds of many good Hindus, turned them away from belief toward nonbelief. Existentialism offers—in the place of devotion and yoga and inner attainment—a

dark view of man and of the universe. It postulates that there is no inherent meaning in life, nor is there immortality of the soul. It tells its follower that he cannot know order or harmony, for he is essentially a troubled being who must rely only on himself. It is a self-centered system, whereas Hinduism is a selfless, evolutionary, God-centric system.

Devotee: *Are there ethics and scruples controlling conversion from one religion to another, such as corporations have in moving a top executive from one company to another?*
Gurudeva: Doctors and lawyers have ethical guidelines concerning their patients and clients. Corporate officers have codes of conduct, too. The best among them have a cultured protocol and respect for one another. This is not always true among religionists. They can and often do disdain one another. In the technological age, ethics exist among the white-collar workers, and disdain exists among blue-collar workers toward management. There is a stratum of humanity that will always work outside the boundaries of educated protocol, propelled by greed and by fear.

The religions and their leaders should not and must not be unscrupulous, for that will be harmful to their constituency in the future. Religious leaders should rise at least to the level of corporate managers. For our part, we can suggest this as a solution to the problems of conversion.

Why should someone be ripped away from his born and raised religion to another and "better one" like a piece of merchandise snatched from the supermarket shelf, sold, redistributed and wholesaled to a foreign market? In India today the problems of forced or deceitful conversions are so prevalent that the government is trying to pass a law to prohibit such tactics, like the laws that already exist in Nepal. We hope such legislation is passed, not only in India but wherever similar problems exist.

Ethics must be established among all the religionists of

the world. They must nurture an appreciation for each other, not merely a tolerance. Religious leaders, above all, must remain fair, despite their enthusiasm. We are not marketing a product. We are not competing for customers. The values and tenets we are offering must go into knowledgeable and willing hands. They cannot be forced upon the weak or foisted upon the unwary. A doctor would hate and then undermine another who stole his patients and slandered his name to effect the deed. An advocate would feel justifiably injured if clients were bribed to leave him for the services of a fellow attorney. The king of a country is riled at the loss of his lands, and religionists become antagonistic one to another when their fences are cut and their flocks taken elsewhere. Yes, a certain protocol must be established. Permission must be granted from one's religious leaders, making for a graceful exit from one and entrance into another, just as a citizen formally changes his loyalty from one nation to another, legally and ethically. When war commences, warlords gather, and their nations decide on the ethics of torture, cruelty and needless slaughter. How much more essential is it, then, for religious leaders to come to fair agreements and rules of conduct in their handling of souls?

All religions are not the same. There are eleven major ones, and a multitude of faiths form a twelfth. A oneness of ethics must exist among the religionists, priests, ministers, pandits, *aadheenakartars,* Śaṅkarāchāryas and others in the higher echelons, at the corporate level, for religion today is not unlike the great corporations which produce and distribute their products and services, supplying the world with food and plenty. Ethics must be established among the presidents and chairmen and executive directors of the religions. Then these holy personages will command the members to reach out and seek new members in a most enlightened way.

Hindudharme
Navāgatasya Sthānam?

हिन्दुधर्मे नवागतस्य स्थानम्?

Does Hinduism Accept Newcomers?

Does Hinduism Accept Newcomers?

OUR DISCUSSION OF BECOMING A HINDU naturally gives rise to the question of how Hinduism historically has looked at the matter. Here we answer that query and the related question: "What makes a person a Hindu?"

What Is Hinduism?

Hinduism is India's indigenous religious and cultural system, followed today by over one billion adherents, mostly in India but with large populations in many other countries. Also called Sanātana Dharma, "eternal religion," and Vaidika Dharma, "religion of the *Vedas,*" Hinduism encompasses a broad spectrum of philosophies ranging from pluralistic theism to absolute monism. It is a family of myriad faiths with four primary denominations: Śaivism, Vaishṇavism, Śāktism and Smārtism. These four hold such divergent beliefs that each is a complete and independent religion. Yet they share a vast heritage of culture and belief: karma, dharma, reincarnation, all-pervasive Divinity, temple worship, sacraments, manifold Deities, the many yogas, the guru-*śishya* tradition and a reliance on the *Vedas* as scriptural authority.

From the rich soil of Hinduism long ago sprang various other traditions. Among these were Jainism, Buddhism, Vīraśaivism and Sikhism, all of which rejected the *Vedas* and thus emerged as completely distinct religions, dissociated from Hinduism, while still sharing many philosophical insights and cultural values with their parent faith.

Not unlike all the other major religions of the world,

Hinduism has no central headquarters. Nor do the Christians, Jews, Muslims or Buddhists. They all have many who represent and function as secretariates for their various denominations. Hinduism is no different in today's world. It has had many exemplars in the past and will in the future of its denominations and the teaching lineages within them, each headed by a pontiff.

Critics have pointed out that Hinduism is not an organized religion. In truth, they are correct. For 1,200 years Islamic and Christian rule in India, Hinduism's central citadel, eroded greatly upon its perpetuation. Yet it survived. In today's world it may be accused of being a poorly organized religion, but it's getting better daily, as a few minutes on the World Wide Web will prove (see our listing at the end of this book). Its temples and active organizations encircle the world. Whatever its faults, it has kept the fires of *sādhana* and renunciation, of unabashed spiritual life and yoga disciplines alive. No other faith has done that to the same extent. No other major ancient faith has survived the assaults and the insults of the Abrahamic faiths. Hinduism's nearly three million swāmīs, gurus and sādhus work tirelessly within, upon and among themselves and then, when ready, serve others, leading them from darkness into light, from death to immortality.

What Makes One a Hindu?

Those who follow the Hindu way of life are Hindus. In the *Mahābhārata* the great King Yudhishṭhira was asked, "What makes a brahmin—birth, learning or conduct?" He replied, "It is conduct that makes a brahmin." Similarly, the modern Hindu may well state that it is conduct, based upon deep, practical understanding of dharma, karma and reincarnation, that makes a Hindu. After all, he might muse, is not a true devotee whose heart is filled with faith in and love for his Ishṭa Devatā and who lives the Hindu Dharma as much a Hindu as his agnostic neighbor, though the first was born in Indonesia or North America and the second in Andhra Pradesh?

Śrī K. Navaratnam of Sri Lanka, a devotee for some forty years of Satguru Śiva Yogaswāmī, in his *Studies in Hinduism* quotes from the book, *Introduction to the Study of the Hindu Doctrines:* "Hindus are those who adhere to the Hindu tradition, on the understanding that they are duly qualified to do so really effectively, and not simply in an exterior and illusory way; non-Hindus, on the contrary, are those who, for any reason whatsoever, do not participate in the tradition in question." Śrī K. Navaratnam enumerates a set of basic beliefs held by Hindus:

1. A belief in the existence of God.
2. A belief in the existence of a soul separate from the body.
3. A belief in the existence of the finitizing principle known as *avidyā* (lack of knowledge) or māyā (limiting principle of matter).
4. A belief in the principle of matter—*prakṛiti* or māyā.
5. A belief in the theory of karma and reincarnation.
6. A belief in the indispensable guidance of a guru to guide the spiritual aspirant towards God Realization.
7. A belief in *moksha*, liberation, as the goal of human existence.
8. A belief in the indispensable necessity of temple worship in religious life.
9. A belief in graded forms of religious practices, both internal and external, until one realizes God.
10. A belief in ahiṁsā as the greatest dharma or virtue.
11. A belief in mental and physical purity as indispensable factors for spiritual progress.

Śrī Śrī Śrī Jayendra Sarasvatī, 69th Śaṅkarāchārya of the Kamakoti Peetham, Kanchipuram, India, defines in one of his writings the basic features of Hinduism as follows:

1. The concept of idol worship and the worship of God in his Nirguṇa as well as Saguṇa form.
2. The wearing of sacred marks on the forehead.
3. Belief in the theory of past and future births in accordance with the theory of karma.
4. Cremation of ordinary men and burial of great men.

The periodical *Hindu Vishva* (Jan./Feb., 1986) cites the following definitions: "He who has perfect faith in the law of karma, the law of reincarnation, avatāra [divine incarnations], ancestor worship, *varṇāśrama dharma* [social duty], *Vedas* and existence of God; he who practices the instructions given in the *Vedas* with faith and earnestness; he who does *snāna* [ritual bathing], *sṛāddha* [death memorial], *pitṛitarpaṇa* [offerings to ancestors] and the *pañcha mahāyajñas* [five great sacrifices: to ṛishis, ancestors, Gods, creatures and men], he who follows the *varṇāśrama* dharmas, he who worships the avatāras and studies the *Vedas* is a Hindu.' "

The Vishva Hindu Parishad's official definition from its Memorandum of Association, Rules and Regulation (1966) states: "*Hindu* means a person believing in, following or respecting the eternal values of life, ethical and spiritual, which have sprung up in Bhāratkhand [India] and includes any person calling himself a Hindu."

In all definitions, the three pivotal beliefs for Hindus are karma, reincarnation and the belief in all-pervasive Divinity—forming as they do the crux of day-to-day religion, explaining our past existence, guiding our present life and determining our future union with God. It is apparent from the pervasiveness of these beliefs today that a large number of non-Hindus qualify as self-declared Hindus already, for many believe in karma, dharma and reincarnation, strive to see God everywhere, have some concept of māyā, recognize someone as their guru, respect temple worship and believe in the evolution of the soul. Many of these beliefs are heretical to most other religions, especially Christianity and the Jewish faith. Those who do believe in karma, reincarnation and union with the Divine have, indeed, evolved beyond the boundaries of Western religion.

The Indian Supreme Court, in 1966, formalized a judicial definition of Hindu beliefs to legally distinguish Hindu denominations from other religions in India. This seven-point list was affirmed by the Court in 1995 in judging cases regarding religious identity:

1. Acceptance of the *Vedas* with reverence as the highest authority in religious and philosophic matters and acceptance with reverence of *Vedas* by Hindu thinkers and philosophers as the sole foundation of Hindu philosophy.
2. Spirit of tolerance and willingness to understand and appreciate the opponent's point of view based on the realization that truth is many sided.
3. Acceptance of great world rhythm by all six systems of Hindu philosophy: vast periods of creation, maintenance and dissolution follow each other in endless succession;
4. Acceptance by all systems of Hindu philosophy of the belief in rebirth and pre-existence.
5. Recognition of the fact that the means or ways to salvation are many.
6. Realization of the truth that numbers of Gods to be worshiped may be large, yet there being Hindus who do not believe in the worshiping of idols.
7. Unlike other religions, or religious creeds, Hindu religion's not being tied down to any definite set of philosophic concepts, as such.

A Summary of What Most Hindus Believe

Three decades ago we crafted a simple summary of Hindu beliefs and distributed it in hundreds of thousands of pamphlets around the world. On August, 1995, these nine belief were published by the Religious News Service in Washington, DC, for hundreds of American newspapers. On February 8, 1993, the *Christianity Today* magazine printed them side by side with their Christian counterparts so Christians could better comprehend Hindus (See p. 248-250).

NINE BELIEFS OF HINDUISM

1. Hindus believe in the divinity of the *Vedas,* the world's most ancient scripture, and venerate the *Āgamas* as equally revealed. These primordial hymns are God's word and the bedrock of Sanātana Dharma, the eternal religion which has neither beginning nor end.
2. Hindus believe in a one, all-pervasive Supreme Being who is both immanent and transcendent, both Creator and Unmanifest Reality.
3. Hindus believe that the universe undergoes endless cycles of creation, preservation and dissolution.
4. Hindus believe in karma, the law of cause and effect by which each individual creates his own destiny by his thoughts, words and deeds.
5. Hindus believe that the soul reincarnates, evolving through many births until all karmas have been resolved, and *moksha,* spiritual knowledge and liberation from the cycle of rebirth, is attained. Not a single soul will be eternally deprived of this destiny.
6. Hindus believe that divine beings exist in unseen worlds and that temple worship, rituals and sacraments as well as personal devotionals create a communion with these devas and Gods.
7. Hindus believe that a spiritually awakened master, or *satguru,* is essential to know the Transcendent Absolute, as

are personal discipline, good conduct, purification, pilgrimage, self-inquiry and meditation.

8. Hindus believe that all life is sacred, to be loved and revered, and therefore practice ahiṁsā, "noninjury."
9. Hindus believe that no particular religion teaches the only way to salvation above all others, but that all genuine religious paths are facets of God's Pure Love and Light, deserving tolerance and understanding.

FIVE OBLIGATIONS OF ALL HINDUS

1. **WORSHIP, UPĀSANĀ:** Young Hindus are taught daily worship in the family shrine room—rituals, disciplines, chants, yogas and religious study. They learn to be secure through devotion in home and temple, wearing traditional dress, bringing forth love of the Divine and preparing the mind for serene meditation.
2. **HOLY DAYS, UTSAVA:** Young Hindus are taught to participate in Hindu festivals and holy days in the home and temple. They learn to be happy through sweet communion with God at such auspicious celebrations. *Utsava* includes fasting and attending the temple on Monday or Friday and other holy days.
3. **VIRTUOUS LIVING, DHARMA:** Young Hindus are taught to live a life of duty and good conduct. They learn to be selfless by thinking of others first, being respectful of parents, elders and swāmīs, following divine law, especially āhiṁsā, mental, emotional and physical noninjury to all beings. Thus they resolve karmas.
4. **PILGRIMAGE, TĪRTHAYĀTRĀ:** Young Hindus are taught the value of pilgrimage and are taken at least once a year for darśana of holy persons, temples and places, near or far. They learn to be detached by setting aside worldly affairs and making God, Gods and gurus life's singular focus during these journeys.
5. **RITES OF PASSAGE, SAṀSKĀRA:** Young Hindus are taught to

observe the many sacraments which mark and sanctify their passages through life. They learn to be traditional by celebrating the rites of birth, name-giving, head-shaving, first feeding, ear-piercing, first learning, coming of age, marriage and death.

Hinduism Has Always Accepted Adoptives and Converts

It is sometimes claimed that one must be born in a Hindu family to be a Hindu, that one cannot adopt it or convert from another faith. This is simply not true. The acceptance of outsiders into the Hindu fold has occurred for thousands of years. Groups as diverse as local aborigines and the invading Greeks of Alexander the Great have been brought in. Entering Hinduism has traditionally required little more than accepting and living the beliefs and codes of Hindus. This remains the basic factor in the process, although there are and always have been formal ceremonies recognizing entrance into the religion—particularly the *nāmakaraṇa saṁskāra*, or naming rite in the case of adoptives and converts, and the *vrātyastoma*, vow-taking rite, in the case of those returning to one sect or another of the Hindu religion.

The most compelling testimony to Hinduism's acceptance of non-Hindus into its fold is history. Possibly the most often quoted exposition of the subject appears in the *Complete Works of Swāmī Vivekānanda* (Vol. 5, p. 233), in an interview called "On the bounds of Hinduism," which first appeared in the *Prabuddha Bhārata* in April, 1899: "Having been directed by the Editor, writes our representative, to interview Swāmī Vivekānanda on the question of converts to Hinduism, I found an opportunity one evening on the roof of a Ganges houseboat. It was after nightfall, and we had stopped at the embankment of the Rāmakṛishṇa Maṭh, and there the swāmī came down to speak with me. Time and place were alike delightful. Overhead the stars, and around, the rolling Gaṅgā; and on one side stood the dimly lighted building, with its background of palms and lofty shade-trees. 'I want to see you, Swāmī,' I began, 'on this matter of receiving back into Hinduism those who have been perverted from it. Is it your opinion that they should be received?'

'Certainly,' said the swāmī, 'they can and ought to be taken.' He sat gravely for a moment, thinking, and then resumed. 'The vast majority of Hindu perverts to Islam and Christianity are perverts by the sword, or the descendants of these. It would be obviously unfair to subject these to disabilities of any kind. As to the case of born aliens, did you say? Why, born aliens have been converted in the past by crowds, and the process is still going on.'

'In my own opinion, this statement not only applies to aboriginal tribes, to outlying nations, and to almost all our conquerors before the Mohammedan conquest, but also to all those castes who find a special origin in the *Purāṇas*. I hold that they have been aliens thus adopted.'

'Ceremonies of expiation are no doubt suitable in the case of willing converts, returning to their Mother-Church, as it were; but on those who were alienated by conquest—as in Kashmir and Nepal—or on strangers wishing to join us, no penance should be imposed.'

'But of what caste would these people be, Swāmijī?' I ventured to ask. 'They must have some, or they can never be assimilated into the great body of Hindus. Where shall we look for their rightful place?'

'Returning converts,' said the swāmī quietly, 'will gain their own castes, of course. And new people will make theirs. You will remember,' he added, 'that this has already been done in the case of Vaishṇavism. Converts from different castes and aliens were all able to combine under that flag and form a caste by themselves—and a very respectable one, too. From Rāmānuja down to Chaitanya of Bengal, all great Vaishṇava teachers have done the same.'

'Then as to names,' I enquired, 'I suppose aliens and perverts who have adopted non-Hindu names should be named newly. Would you give them caste names, or what?' 'Certainly,' said the swāmī thoughtfully, 'there is a great deal in a name!' and on this question he would say no more."

Dr. S. Rādhākṛishṇan, eminent philosopher and former president of India, confirmed Swāmī Vivekānanda's views in his well-known book, *The Hindu View of Life* (p. 28-29): "In a sense, Hinduism may be regarded as the first example in the world of a missionary religion. Only its missionary spirit is different from that associated with the proselytizing creeds. It did not regard it as its mission to convert humanity to any one opinion. For what counts is conduct and not belief. Worshipers of different Gods and followers of different rites were taken into the Hindu fold. The ancient practice of *vrātyastoma,* described fully in the *Taṇḍya Brāhmaṇa,* shows that not only individuals but whole tribes were absorbed into Hinduism. Many modern sects accept outsiders. *Devala Smṛiti* lays down rules for the simple purification of people forcibly converted to other faiths, or of womenfolk defiled and confined for years, and even of people who, for worldly advantage, embrace other faiths."

In a recent article, writer Shreeram Tyambak Godbole of Bombay observes, "Hinduism . . . has been assimilating into itself all those who have been willing, without offending anybody. Whoever from other religions adopted even outwardly the customs and manners of the Hindus could, in course of time, hope to get his progeny easily assimilated in the Hindu society. This process has been going on for the last two or two and a half millenniums. The beginnings of this process can be seen in the sixty-fifth chapter of *Mahābhārata,* Śantiparva, where Indra is described to have ordered Mandhatru to give all access to all foreigners, like the Yavanas, into the Vedic religion."

He gives a historical example, "[The] Bactrian Greeks had soon to run down to India as refugees, driven headlong by U-echis, when they were all admitted to the Hindu fold. The same fate the U-echis, the Sakas, the Kushans and the Huns had to face. The Kushan emperor, Kadphasis II, took to Śiva worship so devoutly that on his coins he inscribed the image of the Lord Śiva and had himself mentioned as the devotee of Śiva. Huvishka and Vasudeva and their descendants also inscribed Lord Śiva and his Nandi on their coins.... While the Abhirs became Vaishṇavas, the Scythians and U-echis became Śaivas.... Huns again became Śaivas. The Hun King Mihirkula had inscribed on his silver coins 'Jayatu Vrshadhvajah' and 'Jayatu Vrshah' along with Śiva's Triśula and his Nandi and his umbrella.... All the Bactrian Greeks, the U-echis, the Sakas, the Kushans, and the Huns are now so well assimilated into the Hindu society that their separate identity cannot at all be traced."

Our friend and compatriate in promoting Sanātana Dharma, Sri Ram Swarup (1920-1998), had this to say about the power of those who have converted to or adopted the Hindu faith. "Hitherto, Hindus knew only two categories: Hindus born in India and Hindu emigrants who went overseas during the last few centuries, often under very adverse conditions. But now we have also a new, fast-growing third category of those who adopt Hinduism by free choice. This is an important category, and traditional Hinduism should become aware of them. Their contribution to Hinduism is notable. Hindu thought is changing the intellectual-religious contour of Europe and America and attracting their best minds. In this thought, they also find the principle of their own self-discovery and recovery. The new religion of these countries is now really the 'New Age,' which is greatly worrying the Christian establishment. The Pope sees 'Eastern influences' in this new development. Pat Robertson, an influential American evangelist, finds that 'the New Age and Hinduism—it is the same thing.' He complains, 'We are importing Hinduism into America.' "

Must One Be Born in India to Be a Hindu?

At this time certain deeply ingrained misconceptions must also be erased, such as the mistaken notion—postulated primarily by brahmin pandits and a few of the Śaṅkarāchāryas and parroted by Western academics—that one must be born in India to be a Hindu. Of course, the Hindus of Nepal and Sri Lanka, the Hindus born in Bali and Malaysia, the Mauritian-born and Bangladesh-born Hindus would find such a concept very strange indeed, and few in the world would question their Hinduness. But the issue is often raised in America and Europe. Italian-born Swāmī Yogānandagiri bravely tackled this issue in his nation, as reported in our international magazine, HINDUISM TODAY.

Swāmī explained, "We have to overcome a misunderstanding asserted by Italian scholars that one has to be born in India to be a Hindu. Our *saṅga* also hopes to spread the authentic Hindu culture among Italians who take yoga as just a sweet gymnastic."

His invitation to HINDUISM TODAY outlined plans for a June, 1997, international conference in Milan on the controversial subject of conversion to Hinduism, among other subjects. The problem is serious in Italy, for Hinduism is not officially recognized by the government. An individual's conversion and name change cannot be legalized. Tax-deductible status is not granted to Hindu organizations. HINDUISM TODAY accepted the invitation and sent representatives Āchārya Ceyonswāmī and Sannyāsin Skandanāthaswāmī to the conference.

It was in 1985 that Swāmī Yogānandagiri established the Gitānanda Āshram in Savona, perched in the hills a few miles from the Mediterranean Ligurian Sea above Corsica. He became a yogī in his teens and was trained in India by the late Swāmī Gitānanda of Pondicherry, among others. He learned Sanskrit, absorbed the South Indian Āgamic tradition, received sacraments making him a Hindu and was ultimately initiated as a renunciate monk.

Malaysian-born Skandanāthaswāmī reported later, "I couldn't believe my eyes when we reached Savona. Swāmī Yogānandagiri and a small band of dedicated Italian Hindus have established full, traditional Hinduism at his *āśrama*. Stepping into his Śri Chakra temple was like being in India. Other swāmīs teach yoga but often remain at a distance from Hinduism. But Yogānandagiri boldly declares his Hindu heritage, and that in Italy!"

The conference was the first organized by Swāmī's newly created Unione Induista Italiana (Italian Hindu Union), as an attempt to unify under a Hindu banner those Italians already immersed in Indian culture. The three days included workshops on Indian dance, yoga, āyurveda and astrology, all presented by leading Hindus.

But a pivotal debate was taking place at meetings that pitted Italian professors of religion against Hindu swāmīs and delegates on the issue of converting to Hinduism. Chief adversary Professor Mario Piantelli opined that conversion to Hinduism is impossible for those not born in India. He was unanimously countered by all the Hindu delegates, who cited Indian Supreme Court decisions and statements by Swāmī Vivekānanda and Dr. S. Rādhākṛishṇan, former president of India (See p. 160).

That might have been the end of the issue, but the day after the conference ended, a national Italian daily, *L'Unità* of Rome, published Piantelli's opinions in a major article. Swāmī Yogānandagiri flew to Rome to issue a rebuttal, and the debate entered the national forum.

Swāmī Yogānandagiri wrote in his rebuttal: "Contrary to Professor Piantelli's statements, the Italian Hindu Union comprises people who not only love India, but have received a religious formation in India with all sacraments and who identify themselves deeply and seriously with the Hindu faith. The statement that *Hinduism* is a neologism referring only to those born in India is a wrong interpretation. The word *Hindu* has evolved. Today in modern India Hindus are those following the principles of Sanātana Dharma. Its main characteristic is its universality. There are no decrees or scriptures which say only those born in India can be Hindu. What about the children of the Hindus born in America, Africa, Sri Lanka, Malaysia, Mauritius and Europe? They call themselves Hindu just like we Italian Hindus. So how can it be an exclusive religion only for those born in India? On the contrary, the Supreme Indian Court in 1966 codified the definition of Hinduism and in 1995 confirmed that: 'Hindus are those who accept the *Vedas* (sacred text) as the highest religious and philosophical authority and are tolerant and accept that truth can have many facets, who believe in cosmic cycles, rebirth and pre-existence and recognize that many paths lead to salvation.' Italian Hindus, among which there are also Indian citizens living in Italy, already exist and are recognized by Indian Hindus and Buddhists. Many governments have legally recognized Hinduism."

Swāmī had many allies. Dr. R. Gopalakṛishṇan, the Director of Rādhākṛishṇan Institute for Advanced Study in Philosophy, University of Madras said, "As an Indian and as a Hindu, I find there is no truth in this statement that those who are born in India alone are eligible to become Hindus." Dr. Atulchandra S. Thombare from Pune, India, noted, "A man can change his nationality, and even his sex, why not his religion?" Indian Ambassador to Italy, Mr. Fabian, a Catholic, said, "Faith is a matter of the heart and personal choice. If someone practices Hinduism and is accepted by Hindus, then he is one."

Swāmī is allying himself with the Buddhists, who are also pressing for official recognition in Italy. They are, according to Swāmī, two years ahead of the Hindus in the decade-long process of changing the complex Italian laws relating to conversion.

The Ceremony of Welcoming Back

The *vrātyastoma* ceremony ("vow pronouncement"), dating back to the *Taṇḍya Brāhmaṇa* of the *Ṛig Veda,* is performed for Hindus returning to India from abroad and for those who have embraced other faiths. One finds a wide range of converts in India, from communities such as the Syrian Malabar Christians, who adopted Christianity shortly after that religion's founding, to the Muslim converts of a thousand years ago, to Indians converted in the last few generations. Especially in the case of many recent converts, the conversion is often superficial, and the return to Hinduism is a simple matter of ceremonial recognition. In other cases, complete reeducation is required.

There are many organizations in India active in reconversion, some motivated by fears of non-Hindu dominance in regions once all Hindu. The Masurāśrama in Mumbai specializes in reconversions through the *śuddhi śraddha,* purification ceremony, bringing dozens of converts back into the Sanātana Dharma each month. Masurāśrama founder, Dharma Bhaskar Masurkar Maharāj, set a strong precedent in 1928 when he organized the purification rite for 1,150 devotees in Goa who had previously converted to Christianity. About the same time, Swāmī Āgamānandajī of the Rāmakṛishṇa Mission in Kerala reconverted hundreds to Hinduism, as did Nārāyaṇa Guru. More recently, two South Indian āśramas—Madurai Aadheenam and Kundrakuddi Aadheenam—have brought thousands of Indians back into Hinduism in mass conversion rites. Since the early 1960s, the Vishva Hindu Parishad has reportedly reconverted a half-million individuals through *śuddhi* ceremonies all over India. The VHP activities are extremely distressing to Christian missionaries who, according to an analysis published in HINDUISM TODAY (Feb. 1989), spent an average of $6,000 to win over each convert.

When such souls do return, it is the duty of established

Aum Gaṇeśa!

Vrātyastoma

व्रात्यस्तोम

விரத்தியாஸ்தோம

Purification Sacrament for Returning to the Eternal Faith

I, ______________________________,
Hindu Name of Devotee (Please Print)

having voluntarily declared my acceptance of the principles of the Sanātana Dharma, including a firm belief in all-pervasive Divinity, Satchidānanda, and the Vedic revelations of *karma, dharma* and *puṇarjanma,* and having severed all non-Hindu religious affiliations, attachments and commitments, hereby humbly beg to re-enter the ____________ sect of the Hindu religion through the traditional Vrātyastoma, the purificatory vow ceremony, also known as Śuddhi Śraddhā, and plead for gracious permission from the community to return to my cherished Hindu faith. I solemnly promise to live as an example for the next generation. Aum.

Signature of devotee: ______________________________

It is Hereby Certified

that this devotee, born in ____________________ on ____________________ was duly given the *vrātyastoma* ceremony on the auspicious day of ____________________ at the Hindu temple known as ____________________, in accordance with the traditions of the world's most ancient faith and vowed before the Deity, the Mahādevas and the *devas* faithfulness to the Sanātana Dharma. Thus, this devotee has been eternally and immutably bound to the Hindu religion and is now again recognized as a member of this and all of our communities worldwide with full rights of access to all public Hindu temples, shrines and institutions throughout the world from this day onward.

____
OFFICIATING PRIEST

WITNESSES:

____
ASSISTANT PRIEST

____
CITY & COUNTRY

Above is a vrātyastoma *certificate that can be photocopied (enlarged) to document the* śuddhi *ceremony held at a temple. This sacrament marks the formal reentrance into a particular sect of Hinduism, through the acceptance of established members and the blessings of Gods and devas invoked through rites performed by an authorized priest.*

followers to shepherd them, blend them in and assist at every opportunity to make them successful members of the international extended family of our venerable faith. It is vital that reconversion campaigns are followed up with continuing education, social improvement, community temple building and priest training to create fully self-sustaining groups. It is one of the duties of the Hindu priesthood to stand guard at the gates of Sanātana Dharma and perform the sacred ceremonies for worthy souls to allow them entrance for the first time or reentrance into the Hindu fold in case they strayed into an alien faith and now desire to return. The priesthoods of all four major denominations of Sanātana Dharma—Śaivism, Vaishṇavism, Smārtism and Śaktism—are performing the duty, empowered by the Gods, of bringing devotees back into the Hindu fold through a congregation of devotees.

Swāmī Tilak aptly noted the present trend in Hinduism: "Multitudes of serious and sincere seekers of Truth are knocking at our doors. We cannot disappoint them, keeping our doors closed. We will have to open our doors and accord a hearty welcome to our new visitors. Whoever comes to us is ours, and we have a duty to make him feel quite at home with us. We must not suffer from superiority complex. Nor should fear or suspicion mar our magnanimity. While in Indonesia, we were pleased to see that the local Hindus had started taking non-Hindus in. We shall have to do the same all over. ... Marriages of mixed nature are unavoidable. Whether we like it or not, we will have to make room for them. We cannot lose a person only because he or she has got married to a non-Hindu. We should rather try to bring a Hindu's non-Hindu spouse into our fold. In Trinidad, Guyana, Suriname and Jamaica, the pandits wisely do not perform the marriage of a mix-couple until the non-Hindu partner agrees to embrace Hinduism as his or her religion" *(Hindu Vishva,* July/August, 1985).

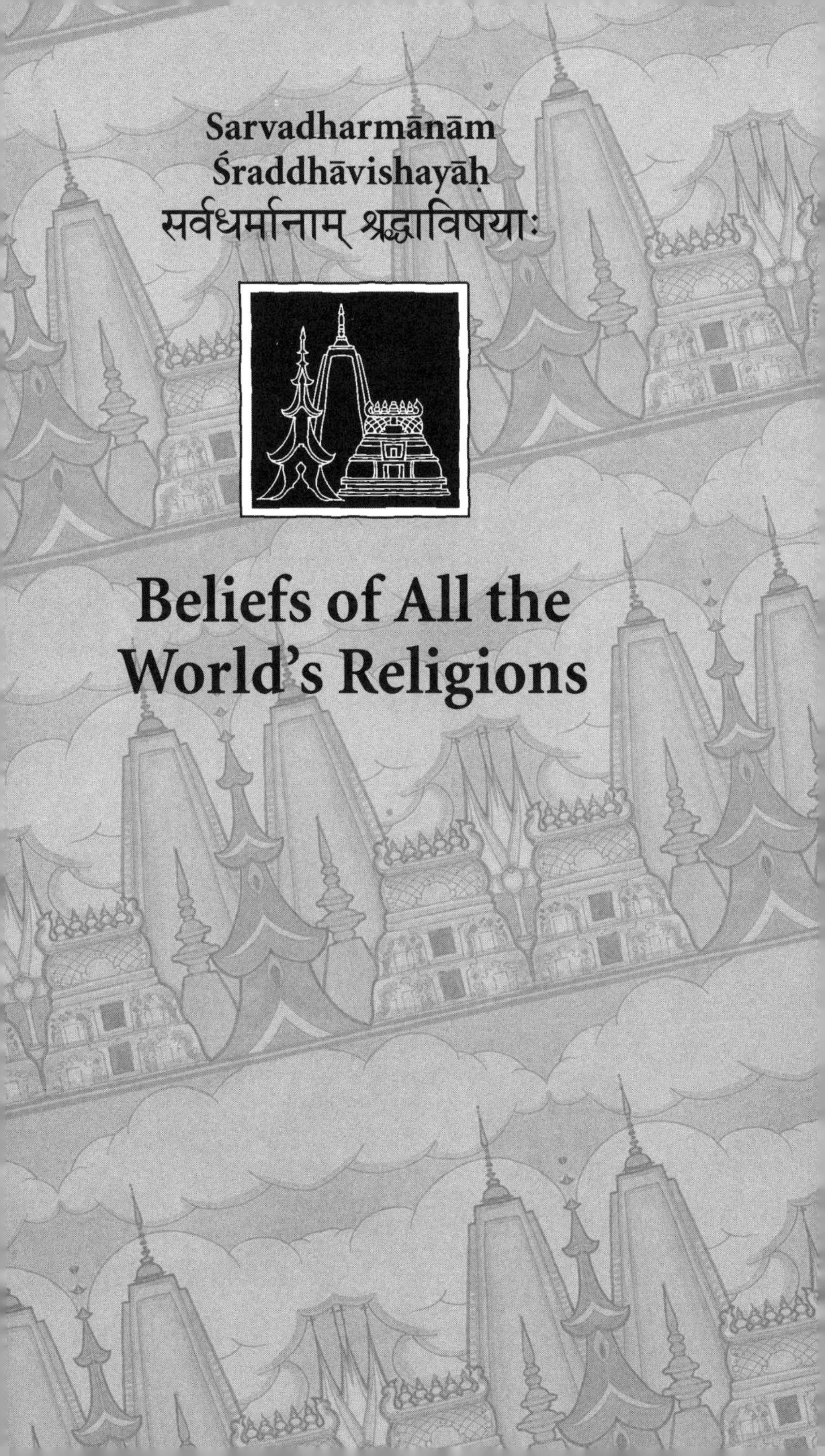

Sarvadharmānām
Śraddhāvishayāḥ
सर्वधर्मानाम् श्रद्धाविषयाः

Beliefs of All the World's Religions

Beliefs of All the World's Religions

IF RELIGIONS HAVE EVER CONFUSED AND confounded you, take heart! This next chapter, drawn from *Dancing with Śiva*, was written just for you. It is our humble attempt to gather from hundreds of sources a simple, in-a-nutshell summary of the world's major spiritual paths. The strength of this undertaking, brevity, is also its flaw. Complex and subtle distinctions, not to mention important exceptions, are consciously set aside for the sake of simplicity. There are hundreds of books addressing deeper matters, but none that we know of which have attempted a straightforward comparative summary. There is a need for no-nonsense reviews of religions, and this may hopefully begin to meet that need.

By juxtaposing a few of their major beliefs, we hope to highlight how other major world religions and important modern secular philosophies are similar to and differ from Hinduism. A leisurely hour with this section under a favorite tree will endow you with a good grasp of the essential truths of every major religion practiced today on the planet. It may also dispel the myth that all religions are one, that they all seek to lead adherents by the same means to the same Ultimate Reality. They don't, as a conscientious review will show.

As you read through the 171 beliefs in this study, put a check by the ones you believe. Why, you might find that you are a Buddhist-Christian-Existentialist or a Taoist-New Age-Materialist. Place yourself in the cosmology of the beliefs of the world. Many have found this self-inquiry satisfying, others awesomely revealing.

Pilgrim, pilgrimage and road—it was but myself toward my Self, and your arrival was but myself at my own door.
SUFI MYSTIC, JALAL AL-DIN RUMI (1207–73)

Once we have chosen and accepted our faith, it is then our spiritual duty to learn it well and live by it as a wholehearted, contributing member of a faith community so that we pass it on in a vibrant way to those who come after us, the next generation. This is carrying the traditions of the past forward, setting the patterns for our descendants, just as they were set for us by our elders. It is of the utmost importance that man's religious traditions be protected and preserved. It is our prayer that you come to know and live your religion and be fulfilled by it. The spiritual path lies before you. Study well the religions that follow. Having studied, you will be more confident in your choice of faiths from among the many that lead to the one truth within you.

It is most useful at this time that you become acquainted with religion from a broad perspective. Among these religions and the many faiths, which are potential new religions yet to be tried and proven through time, you will find your path. All of these religions and faiths are valid and serviceable to those on the spiritual path. It is not uncommon to change from one to another faith as you progress in your unfoldment. It is also not uncommon to change formally from one religion to another, even if you have been confirmed in that religion.

Religion is the foundation for all spiritual unfoldment, the basis for the practice of yoga, meditation, contemplation and inner transcendental states—itself the stable fortress for the mind to rest within when consciousness returns from ecstasy to its normal state. Once one's religion is carefully chosen, then understood and lived, that inner stability, that foundation, which seals off the lower abysses of the mind, is permanently there. The higher doors are open for the seeker. From our perspective, all religions are but God's Divine Law at work, and all worship the same God whom we, as Śaivites, call Śiva. Nevertheless, as stated earlier, religions are not all the same. Significant differences exist. It is up to each of us to evaluate those differences and determine the direction of our quest.

You will note that throughout this chapter, you are invited to write down your philosophical stance on each belief. Nine beliefs are listed for each of the world religions and faiths, and after each belief is a line for your evaluation. There are four choices. "Do believe" means that you now believe the statement given. "Do not believe" means that you have never believed the statement. "Once believed" means that you once held the belief but now do not. "Unfamiliar" means that you have never heard of or do not understand the statement. In making your evaluation, it is good to read through the all nine beliefs first before marking or checking any. When you are ready to mark your responses, check only those you are sure of first, then go back over the remaining beliefs a few times to make a final choice.

There are no right and wrong answers, for the purpose of the exercise is not to test your knowledge but to help you understand your beliefs. Therefore, be fully honest with yourself in marking your answers. When you are done with the entire section, you will know, perhaps for the first time, what you truly believe and what religion's beliefs are closest to your own.

"Why," you might ask, "is this important?" The reason is that it is from our beliefs that we form our attitudes. Here is an illustration. When you observe that people of one faith behave differently from those of another faith with different attitudes, you are really seeing a different set of beliefs at work. The person of a faith that denies reincarnation will look upon a child prodigy as "lucky," whereas the person of a faith that believes in the process of reincarnation will wonder how many lives that soul worked to achieve such mastery and who he was in his last life.

We are concerned with all of the great religions of the world. Though we are of the Saivite Hindu religion, we know no barriers or boundaries, and see only that the success of any person on the path is reliant upon the depth and strength of his roots, his religious roots. A great tree with roots well wrapped around boulders and sunk deep into the earth can withstand any storm. High winds are nothing more to it than the cleansing of its branches. The individual on the path must be as firm in his religious foundation as this tree that I use as an example, in order to withstand raging emotions, depression and elation, confusion and despair. To him, they will be nothing more than a cleansing of false concepts as he dives deeper into his religion and philosophy. We can clearly see that religion and tradition are interlocked in the annals of time back many thousands of years, and we can easily ascertain how tradition moves forward from one generation to the next, setting the patterns for humanity. Every time-honored tradition loyally serves mankind, and following it through the context of one of the great religions of the world, one cannot go astray.

Religion is the bringing together of the three worlds. This means that the ascended masters, angels, devas, Deities, saints, sages of the world's major religions, living without physical bodies in the inner worlds, still guide and govern, help and protect, shower forth blessings and inspiration to the members of their religious family, such as Taoism, Buddhism, Judaism, Christianity, Hinduism and so forth. This is why it is important to have a family name that proclaims your faith constantly in daily life. One cannot be all the religions of the world unless he truly adheres to the doctrines, to the dogma and philosophy of one of them. The tree will never grow strong enough to withstand high winds if it is planted in a bucket and carried here and there.

Hinduism

Hinduism

FOUNDED: Hinduism, the world's oldest religion, has no beginning—it predates recorded history.
FOUNDER: Hinduism has no human founder.
MAJOR SCRIPTURES: The *Vedas, Āgamas* and more.
ADHERENTS: Nearly one billion, mostly in India, Sri Lanka, Bangladesh, Bhutan, Nepal, Malaysia, Indonesia, Indian Ocean, Africa, Europe and North and South America.
SECTS: There are four main denominations: Śaivism, Śāktism, Vaishṇavism and Smārtism.

SYNOPSIS

Hinduism is a vast and profound religion. It worships one Supreme Reality (called by many names) and teaches that all souls ultimately realize Truth. There is no eternal hell, no damnation. It accepts all genuine spiritual paths—from pure monism ("God alone exists") to theistic dualism ("When shall I know His Grace?"). Each soul is free to find his own way, whether by devotion, austerity, meditation (yoga) or selfless service. Stress is placed on temple worship, scripture and the guru-disciple tradition. Festivals, pilgrimage, chanting of holy hymns and home worship are dynamic practices. Love, nonviolence, good conduct and the law of dharma define the Hindu path. Hinduism explains that the soul reincarnates until all karmas are resolved and God Realization is attained. The magnificent holy temples, the peaceful piety of the Hindu home, the subtle metaphysics and the science of yoga all play their part. Hinduism is a mystical religion, leading the devotee to personally experience the Truth within, finally reaching the pinnacle of consciousness where man and God are one.

GOALS OF THE FOUR MAJOR HINDU SECTS

ŚAIVISM: The primary goal of Śaivism is realizing one's identity with God Śiva, in perfect union and nondifferentiation. This is termed *nirvikalpa samādhi,* Self Realization, and may be attained in this life, granting *moksha,* permanent liberation from the cycles of birth and death. A secondary goal is *savikalpa samādhi,* the realization of Satchidānanda, a unitive experience within superconsciousness in which perfect Truth, knowledge and bliss are known. The soul's final destiny is *viśvagrāsa,* total merger in God Śiva.

ŚĀKTISM: The primary goal of Śāktism is *moksha,* defined as complete identification with God Śiva. A secondary goal for the Śāktas is to perform good works selflessly so that one may go, on death, to the heaven worlds and thereafter enjoy a good birth on earth, for heaven, too, is a transitory state. For Śāktas, God is both the formless Absolute (Śiva) and the manifest Divine (Śakti), worshiped as Pārvatī, Durgā, Kālī, Amman, Rājarājeśvarī, etc. Emphasis is given to the feminine manifest by which the masculine Unmanifest is ultimately reached.

VAISHṆAVISM: The primary goal of Vaishṇavites is *videha mukti,* liberation—attainable only after death—when the small self realizes union with God Vishṇu's body as a part of Him, yet maintains its pure individual personality. Lord Vishṇu—all-pervasive consciousness—is the soul of the universe, distinct from the world and from the *jīvas,* "embodied souls," which constitute His body. His transcendent Being is a celestial form residing in the city of Vaikuṇṭha, the home of all eternal values and perfection, where the soul joins Him upon *mukti,* liberation. A secondary goal—the experience of God's Grace—can be reached while yet embodied through taking refuge in Vishṇu's unbounded love. By loving and serving Vishṇu and meditating upon Him and His incarnations, our spiritual hunger grows and we experience His Grace flooding our whole being.

SMĀRTISM: The ultimate goal of Smārtas is *moksha,* to realize oneself as Brahman, the Absolute and only Reality, and become free from *saṁsāra,* the cycles of birth and death. For this, one must conquer the state of *avidyā,* ignorance, which causes the world to appear as real. All illusion has vanished for the realized being, *jīvanmukta,* even as he lives out life in the physical body. At death, his inner and outer bodies are extinguished. Brahman alone exists.

PATHS OF ATTAINMENT

ŚAIVISM: The path for Śaivites is divided into four progressive stages of belief and practice called *charyā,* kriyā, yoga and jñāna. The soul evolves through karma and reincarnation from the instinctive-intellectual sphere into virtuous and moral living, then into temple worship and devotion, followed by internalized worship or yoga and its meditative disciplines. Union with God Śiva comes through the grace of the *satguru* and culminates in the soul's maturity in the state of jñāna, or wisdom. Śaivism values both bhakti and yoga, devotional and contemplative *sādhanas.*

ŚĀKTISM: The spiritual practices in Śāktism are similar to those in Śaivism, though there is more emphasis in Śāktism on God's Power as opposed to Being, on mantras and *yantras,* and on embracing apparent opposites: male-female, absolute-relative, pleasure-pain, cause-effect, mind-body. Certain sects within Śāktism undertake "left-hand" *tantric* rites, consciously using the world of form to transmute and eventually transcend that world. The "left-hand" approach is somewhat occult in nature; it is considered a path for the few, not the many. The "right-hand" path is more conservative in nature.

VAISHṆAVISM: Most Vaishṇavites believe that religion is the performance of bhakti *sādhanas*, and that man can communicate with and receive the grace of the Gods and Goddesses through the *darśana* of their icons. The paths of karma yoga and jñāna yoga lead to bhakti yoga. Among the foremost practices of Vaishṇavites is chanting the holy names of the *avatāras*, Vishṇu's incarnations, especially Rāma and Kṛishṇa. Through total self-surrender, *prapatti*, to Vishṇu, to Kṛishṇa or to His beloved consort Rādhā Rāṇi, liberation from *saṁsāra* is attained.

SMĀRTISM: Smārtas, the most eclectic of Hindus, believe that *moksha* is achieved through jñāna yoga alone—defined as an intellectual and meditative but non-kuṇḍalinī-yoga path. Jñāna yoga's progressive stages are scriptural study *(śravaṇa)*, reflection *(manana)* and sustained meditation *(dhyāna)*. Guided by a realized guru and avowed to the unreality of the world, the initiate meditates on himself as Brahman to break through the illusion of māyā. Devotees may also choose from three other non-successive paths to cultivate devotion, accrue good karma and purify the mind. These are bhakti yoga, karma yoga and rāja yoga, which certain Smārtas teach can also bring enlightenment.

HINDU BELIEFS

1. I believe in the divinity of the *Vedas,* the world's most ancient scripture. These primordial hymns are God's word and the bedrock of Sanātana Dharma, the eternal religion.

   ❒ DO BELIEVE ❒ DO NOT BELIEVE ❒ ONCE BELIEVED ❒ UNFAMILIAR

2. I believe in a one, all-pervasive Supreme Being who is both immanent and transcendent, both Creator and Creation.

   ❒ DO BELIEVE ❒ DO NOT BELIEVE ❒ ONCE BELIEVED ❒ UNFAMILIAR

3. I believe that the universe undergoes endless cycles of creation, preservation and dissolution.

   ❒ DO BELIEVE ❒ DO NOT BELIEVE ❒ ONCE BELIEVED ❒ UNFAMILIAR

4. I believe in karma, the law of cause and effect by which each individual creates his own destiny by his thoughts, words and deeds.

   ❒ DO BELIEVE ❒ DO NOT BELIEVE ❒ ONCE BELIEVED ❒ UNFAMILIAR

5. I believe that all souls reincarnate, evolving through many births until all their karmas have been resolved and moksha, spiritual knowledge and liberation from the cycle of rebirth, is attained.

   ❒ DO BELIEVE ❒ DO NOT BELIEVE ❒ ONCE BELIEVED ❒ UNFAMILIAR

6. I believe that divine beings exist in unseen worlds and that temple worship, rituals, sacraments and yoga create a communion with these Gods, Goddesses and devas.

   ❒ DO BELIEVE ❒ DO NOT BELIEVE ❒ ONCE BELIEVED ❒ UNFAMILIAR

7. I believe that a spiritually awakened master, or *satguru,* is essential to know the Transcendent Absolute, as are personal discipline, good conduct, purification, pilgrimage, self-inquiry and meditation.

   ❒ DO BELIEVE ❒ DO NOT BELIEVE ❒ ONCE BELIEVED ❒ UNFAMILIAR

8. I believe that all life is sacred, to be loved and revered, and therefore practice ahiṁsā, noninjury in thought, word and deed.

   ❒ DO BELIEVE ❒ DO NOT BELIEVE ❒ ONCE BELIEVED ❒ UNFAMILIAR

9. I believe that no particular religion teaches the only way to salvation above all others, but that all faiths deserve tolerance and understanding.

   ❒ DO BELIEVE ❒ DO NOT BELIEVE ❒ ONCE BELIEVED ❒ UNFAMILIAR

Buddhism

Buddhism

FOUNDED: Buddhism began about 2,500 years ago in India.
FOUNDER: Gautama Siddhārtha, the Buddha, or "Enlightened One."
MAJOR SCRIPTURES: The *Tripitaka, Anguttara-Nikāya, Dhammapada, Sutta-Nipāta, Samyutta-Nikāya* and many others.
ADHERENTS: Over 300 million.
SECTS: Buddhism today is divided into three main sects: Theravāda, or Hinayāna (Sri Lanka, Thailand, Burma, Cambodia), Mahāyāna (China, Japan, Vietnam, Korea), and Vajrayāna (Tibet, Mongolia and Japan).

SYNOPSIS

Life's goal is *nirvāṇa.* Toward that end, Buddha's teachings are capsulized in the Four Noble Truths, *chatvāri ārya satyāni:*

1. THE TRUTH OF SUFFERING (DUḤKHA): Suffering is the central fact of life. Being born is pain, growing old is pain, sickness is pain, death is pain. Union with what we dislike is pain, separation from what we like is pain, not obtaining what we desire is pain.
2. THE TRUTH OF THE ORIGIN (SAMUDĀYA) OF SUFFERING: The cause of suffering is the desire *(icçhā),* craving *(tanhā)* or thirst *(trishnā)* for sensual pleasures, for existence and experience, for worldly possessions and power. This craving binds one to the wheel of rebirth, *saṁsāra.*
3. THE TRUTH OF THE CESSATION (NIRODHA) OF SUFFERING: Suffering can be brought to an end only by the complete cessation of desires—the forsaking, relinquishing and detaching of oneself from desire and craving.
4. THE TRUTH OF THE PATH (MĀRGA) TO ENDING SUFFERING: The means to the end of suffering is the Noble Eightfold Path *(ārya āshṭānga mārga),* right belief, right thought, right speech, right action, right livelihood, right effort, right mindfulness and right meditation.

GOALS OF BUDDHISM

The primary goal of the Buddhists is *nirvāṇa,* defined as the end of change, literally meaning "blowing out," as one blows out a candle. Theravāda tradition describes the indescribable as "peace and tranquility." The Mahāyāna and Vajrayāna traditions view it as "neither existence nor nonexistence," "emptiness and the unchanging essence of the Buddha" and "ultimate Reality." It is synonymous with release from the bonds of desire, ego, suffering and rebirth. Buddha never defined *nirvāṇa,* except to say, "There is an unborn, an unoriginated, an unmade, an uncompounded," and it lies beyond the experiences of the senses. *Nirvāṇa* is not a state of annihilation, but of peace and reality. As with Jainism, Buddhism has no creator God and thus no union with Him.

PATH OF ATTAINMENT

Buddhism takes followers through progressive stages of *dhyāna, samāpatti* and *samādhi. Dhyāna* is meditation, which leads to moral and intellectual purification, and to detachment which leads to pure consciousness. The *samāpattis,* or further *dhyānas,* lead through a progressive nullification of psychic, mental and emotional activity to a state which is perfect solitude, neither perception nor nonperception. This leads further to *samādhi,* supernatural consciousness and, finally, entrance into the ineffable *nirvāṇa.* Many Buddhists understand the ultimate destiny and goal to be a heaven of bliss where one can enjoy eternity with the Bodhisattvas. Mahāyāna places less value on monasticism than Theravāda and differs further in believing one can rely on the active help of other realized beings for salvation. Vajrayāna, also called Tantric or Mantrayāna Buddhism, stresses *tantric* rituals and yoga practices under the guidance of a guru. Its recognition of and involvement in the supernatural distinguishes it from other Buddhist schools.

BUDDHIST BELIEFS

1. I believe that the Supreme is completely transcendent and can be described as Sūnya, a void or state of nonbeing.

   ❒ DO BELIEVE ❒ DO NOT BELIEVE ❒ ONCE BELIEVED ❒ UNFAMILIAR

2. I believe in the Four Noble Truths: 1. that suffering is universal; 2. that desire is the cause of suffering; 3. that suffering may be ended by the annihilation of desire; 4. that to end desire one must follow the Eight-Fold Path.

   ❒ DO BELIEVE ❒ DO NOT BELIEVE ❒ ONCE BELIEVED ❒ UNFAMILIAR

3. I believe in the Eight-Fold Path of right belief, right aims, right speech, right actions, right occupation, right endeavor, right mindfulness and right meditation.

   ❒ DO BELIEVE ❒ DO NOT BELIEVE ❒ ONCE BELIEVED ❒ UNFAMILIAR

4. I believe that life's aim is to end suffering through the annihilation of individual existence and absorption into *nirvāṇa,* the Real.

   ❒ DO BELIEVE ❒ DO NOT BELIEVE ❒ ONCE BELIEVED ❒ UNFAMILIAR

5. I believe in the "Middle Path," living moderately, avoiding extremes of luxury and asceticism.

   ❒ DO BELIEVE ❒ DO NOT BELIEVE ❒ ONCE BELIEVED ❒ UNFAMILIAR

6. I believe in the greatness of self-giving love and compassion toward all creatures that live, for these contain merit exceeding the giving of offerings to the Gods.

   ❒ DO BELIEVE ❒ DO NOT BELIEVE ❒ ONCE BELIEVED ❒ UNFAMILIAR

7. I believe in the sanctity of the Buddha and in the sacred scriptures of Buddhism: the *Tripitaka* (Three Baskets of Wisdom) and/or the *Mahāyāna Sūtras.*

   ❒ DO BELIEVE ❒ DO NOT BELIEVE ❒ ONCE BELIEVED ❒ UNFAMILIAR

8. I believe that man's true nature is divine and eternal, yet his individuality is subject to the change that affects all forms and is therefore transient, dissolving at liberation into *nirvāṇa.*

   ❒ DO BELIEVE ❒ DO NOT BELIEVE ❒ ONCE BELIEVED ❒ UNFAMILIAR

9. I believe in dharma (the Way), karma (cause and effect), reincarnation, the *saṅga* (brotherhood of seekers) and the passage on Earth as an opportunity to end the cycle of birth and death.

   ❒ DO BELIEVE ❒ DO NOT BELIEVE ❒ ONCE BELIEVED ❒ UNFAMILIAR

Jainism

Jainism

FOUNDED: Jainism began about 2,500 years ago in India.
FOUNDER: Nataputra Vardhamāna, known as Mahāvīra, "Great Hero."
MAJOR SCRIPTURES: The *Jain Āgamas* and *Siddhāntas.*
ADHERENTS: About six million, almost exclusively in Central and South India, especially in Mumbai.
SECTS: There are two sects. The Digambara ("Sky-clad") sect holds that a saint should own nothing, not even clothes, thus their practice of wearing only a loincloth. They believe that salvation in this birth is not possible for women. The Svetambara ("White-robed") sect disagrees with these points.

SYNOPSIS

Jainism strives for the realization of the highest perfection of man, which in its original purity is free from all pain and the bondage of birth and death. The term *Jain* is derived from the Sanskrit *jina*, "conqueror," and implies conquest over this bondage imposed by the phenomenal world. Jainism does not consider it necessary to recognize a God or any being higher than the perfect man. Souls are beginningless and endless, eternally individual. It classes souls into three broad categories: those that are not yet evolved; those in the process of evolution and those that are liberated, free from rebirth. Jainism has strong monastic-ascetic leanings, even for householders. Its supreme ideal is ahiṁsā, equal kindness and reverence for all life. The *Jain Āgamas* teach great reverence for all forms of life, strict codes of vegetarianism, asceticism, nonviolence even in self-defense, and opposition to war. Jainism is, above all, a religion of love and compassion.

THE GOALS OF JAINISM

The primary goal of the Jains is becoming a Paramātman, a perfected soul. This is accomplished when all layers of karma, which is viewed as a substance, are removed, leading the soul to rise to the ceiling of the universe, from darkness to light, where, beyond the Gods and all currents of transmigration, the soul abides forever in the solitary bliss of *moksha. Moksha* is defined in Jainism as liberation, self-unity and integration, pure aloneness and endless calm, freedom from action and desire, freedom from karma and rebirth. *Moksha* is attainable in this world or at the time of death. When it is reached, man has fulfilled his destiny as the man-God. For the Jains there is no creator God and, therefore, no communion with Him. The nature of the soul is pure consciousness, power, bliss and omniscience.

PATH OF ATTAINMENT

The soul passes through various stages of spiritual development, called *guṇasthānas,* progressive manifestations of the innate faculties of knowledge and power accompanied by decreasing sinfulness and increasing purity. Souls attain better births according to the amount of personal karma they are able to eliminate during life. Between births, souls dwell in one of the seven hells, the sixteen heavens or fourteen celestial regions. Liberated souls abide at the top of the universe. All Jains take five vows, but it is the monk who practices celibacy and poverty. Jainism places great stress on ahiṁsā, asceticism, yoga and monasticism as the means of attainment. Temple pūjās are performed to the twenty-four Tīrthankaras or spiritual preceptors, literally "ford-crossers," those who take others across the ocean of *saṁsāra.*

JAIN BELIEFS

1. I believe in the spiritual lineage of the 24 Tīrthankaras ("ford-crossers") of whom the ascetic sage Mahāvīra was the last—that they should be revered and worshiped above all else.

   ❒ DO BELIEVE ❒ DO NOT BELIEVE ❒ ONCE BELIEVED ❒ UNFAMILIAR

2. I believe in the sacredness of all life, that one must cease injury to sentient creatures, large and small, and that even unintentional killing creates karma.

   ❒ DO BELIEVE ❒ DO NOT BELIEVE ❒ ONCE BELIEVED ❒ UNFAMILIAR

3. I believe that God is neither Creator, Father nor Friend. Such human conceptions are limited. All that may be said of Him is: He is.

   ❒ DO BELIEVE ❒ DO NOT BELIEVE ❒ ONCE BELIEVED ❒ UNFAMILIAR

4. I believe that each man's soul is eternal and individual and that each must conquer himself by his own efforts and subordinate the worldly to the heavenly in order to attain *moksha,* or release.

   ❒ DO BELIEVE ❒ DO NOT BELIEVE ❒ ONCE BELIEVED ❒ UNFAMILIAR

5. I believe the conquest of oneself can only be achieved in ascetic discipline and strict religious observance, and that nonascetics and women will have their salvation in another life.

   ❒ DO BELIEVE ❒ DO NOT BELIEVE ❒ ONCE BELIEVED ❒ UNFAMILIAR

6. I believe that the principle governing the successions of life is karma, that our actions, both good and bad, bind us and that karma may only be consumed by purification, penance and austerity.

   ❒ DO BELIEVE ❒ DO NOT BELIEVE ❒ ONCE BELIEVED ❒ UNFAMILIAR

7. I believe in the *Jain Āgamas* and *Siddhāntas* as the sacred scriptures that guide man's moral and spiritual life.

   ❒ DO BELIEVE ❒ DO NOT BELIEVE ❒ ONCE BELIEVED ❒ UNFAMILIAR

8. I believe in the Three Jewels: right knowledge, right faith and right conduct.

   ❒ DO BELIEVE ❒ DO NOT BELIEVE ❒ ONCE BELIEVED ❒ UNFAMILIAR

9. I believe the ultimate goal of *moksha* is eternal release from *saṁsāra,* the "wheel of birth and death," and the concomitant attainment of Supreme Knowledge.

   ❒ DO BELIEVE ❒ DO NOT BELIEVE ❒ ONCE BELIEVED ❒ UNFAMILIAR

Sikhism

Sikhism

FOUNDED: Sikhism began about 500 years ago in Northern India, now the country of Pakistan.
FOUNDER: Guru Nānak.
MAJOR SCRIPTURE: The *Ādi Granth,* revered as the present guru of the faith.
ADHERENTS: Estimated at nine million, mostly in India's state of Punjab.
SECTS: Besides the Khalsa, there are the Ram Raiyas in Uttar Pradesh and two groups that have living gurus—Mandharis and Nirankaris.

SYNOPSIS

The Muslims began their invasions of India some 1,200 years ago. As a result of Islam's struggle with Hindu religion and culture, leaders sought a reconciliation between the two faiths, a middle path that embraced both. Sikhism (from *śikka,* meaning "disciple") united Hindu *bhakti* and Sufi mysticism most successfully. Sikhism began as a peaceful religion and patiently bore much persecution from the Muslims, but with the tenth guru, Govind Singh, self-preservation forced a strong militarism aimed at protecting the faith and way of life against severe opposition. Sikhism stresses the importance of devotion, intense faith in the guru, the repetition of God's name *(nām)* as a means of salvation, opposition to the worship of idols, the brotherhood of all men and rejection of caste differences (though certain caste attitudes persist today). There have been no gurus in the main Sikh tradition since Guru Govind Singh, whose last instructions to followers were to honor and cherish the teachings of the ten gurus as embodied in the scripture, *Ādi Granth.*

THE GOALS OF SIKHISM

The goal of Sikhism lies in *moksha,* which is release and union with God, described as that of a lover with the beloved and resulting in self-transcendence, egolessness and enduring bliss, or ānanda. The Sikh is immersed in God, assimilated, identified with Him. It is the fulfillment of individuality in which man, freed of all limitations, becomes co-extensive and co-operant and co-present with God. In Sikhism, *moksha* means release into God's love. Man is not God, but is fulfilled in unitary, mystical consciousness with Him. God is the Personal Lord and Creator.

PATH OF ATTAINMENT

To lead man to the goal of *moksha,* Sikhism follows a path of japa and hymns. Through chanting of the Holy Names, Sat Nām, the soul is cleansed of its impurity, the ego is conquered and the wandering mind is stilled. This leads to a superconscious stillness. From here one enters into the divine light and thus attains the state of divine bliss. Once this highest goal is attained, the devotee must devote his awareness to the good of others. The highest goal can be realized only by God's grace, and this is obtained exclusively by following the *satguru* (or nowadays a *sant,* or saint, since there are no living gurus, by the edict of Govind Singh, the tenth and last guru) and by repeating the holy names of the Lord guided by the *Ādi Granth,* the scripture and sole repository of spiritual authority. For Sikhs there is no image worship, no symbol of Divinity.

SIKH BELIEFS

1. I believe in God as the sovereign One, the omnipotent, immortal and personal Creator, a being beyond time, who is called Sat Nām, for His name is Truth.

   ❐ DO BELIEVE ❐ DO NOT BELIEVE ❐ ONCE BELIEVED ❐ UNFAMILIAR

2. I believe that man grows spiritually by living truthfully, serving selflessly and by repetition of the Holy Name and Guru Nānak's Prayer, *Japaji.*

   ❐ DO BELIEVE ❐ DO NOT BELIEVE ❐ ONCE BELIEVED ❐ UNFAMILIAR

3. I believe that salvation lies in understanding the divine Truth and that man's surest path lies in faith, love, purity and devotion.

   ❐ DO BELIEVE ❐ DO NOT BELIEVE ❐ ONCE BELIEVED ❐ UNFAMILIAR

4. I believe in the scriptural and ethical authority of the *Ādi Granth* as God's revelation.

   ❐ DO BELIEVE ❐ DO NOT BELIEVE ❐ ONCE BELIEVED ❐ UNFAMILIAR

5. I believe that to know God the guru is essential as the guide who, himself absorbed in love of the Real, is able to awaken the soul to its true, divine nature.

   ❐ DO BELIEVE ❐ DO NOT BELIEVE ❐ ONCE BELIEVED ❐ UNFAMILIAR

6. I believe in the line of ten gurus: Guru Nānak, Guru Angad, Guru Amardas, Guru Rām Dās, Guru Arjun, Guru Har Govind, Guru Har Rai, Guru Har Kṛishṇan, Guru Tegh Bahadur and Guru Govind Singh—all these are my teachers.

   ❐ DO BELIEVE ❐ DO NOT BELIEVE ❐ ONCE BELIEVED ❐ UNFAMILIAR

7. I believe that the world is māya, a vain and transitory illusion; only God is true as all else passes away.

   ❐ DO BELIEVE ❐ DO NOT BELIEVE ❐ ONCE BELIEVED ❐ UNFAMILIAR

8. I believe in adopting the last name "Singh," meaning "lion" and signifying courage, and in the five symbols: 1) white dress (purity), 2) sword (bravery), 3) iron bracelet (morality), 4) uncut hair and beard (renunciation), and 5) comb (cleanliness).

   ❐ DO BELIEVE ❐ DO NOT BELIEVE ❐ ONCE BELIEVED ❐ UNFAMILIAR

9. I believe in the natural path and stand opposed to fasting, pilgrimage, caste, idolatry, celibacy and asceticism.

   ❐ DO BELIEVE ❐ DO NOT BELIEVE ❐ ONCE BELIEVED ❐ UNFAMILIAR

Taoism

Taoism

FOUNDED: Taoism began about 2,500 years ago in China.
FOUNDER: Lao-tzu, whom Confucius described as a dragon riding the wind and clouds.
MAJOR SCRIPTURE: The *Tao-te-Ching,* or "Book of Reason and Virtue," is among the shortest of all scriptures, containing only 5,000 words. Also central are the sacred writings of Chuang-tsu.
ADHERENTS: Estimated at 50 million, mostly in China and other parts of Asia.
SECTS: Taoism is a potently mystical tradition, so interpretations have been diverse and its sects are many.

SYNOPSIS

The Tao, or Way, has never been put down in words; rather it is left for the seeker to discover within. Lao-tzu himself wrote, "The Tao that can be named is not the eternal Tao." Taoism is concerned with man's spiritual level of being, and in the *Tao-te-Ching* the awakened man is compared to bamboo: upright, simple and useful outside—and hollow inside. Effulgent emptiness is the spirit of Tao, but no words will capture its spontaneity, its eternal newness. Adherents of the faith are taught to see the Tao everywhere, in all beings and in all things. Taoist shrines are the homes of divine beings who guide the religion, bless and protect worshipers. A uniquely Taoist concept is *wu-wei,* nonaction. This does not mean no action, but rather not exceeding spontaneous action that accords with needs as they naturally arise; not indulging in calculated action and not acting so as to exceed the very minimum required for effective results. If we keep still and listen to the inner promptings of the Tao, we shall act effortlessly, efficiently, hardly giving the matter a thought. We will be ourselves, as we are.

THE GOALS OF TAOISM

The primary goal of Taoism may be described as the mystical intuition of the Tao, which is the Way, the Primal Meaning, the Undivided Unity, the Ultimate Reality. Both immanent and transcendent, the Tao is the natural way of all beings, it is the nameless beginning of heaven and earth, and it is the mother of all things. All things depend upon the Tao, all things return to it. Yet it lies hidden, transmitting its power and perfection to all things. He who has realized the Tao has uncovered the layers of consciousness so that he arrives at pure consciousness and sees the inner truth of everything. Only one who is free of desire can apprehend the Tao, thereafter leading a life of "actionless activity." There is no Personal God in Taoism, and thus no union with Him. There are three worlds and beings within them, and worship is part of the path.

PATH OF ATTAINMENT

One who follows the Tao follows the natural order of things, not seeking to improve upon nature or to legislate virtue to others. The Taoist observes *wu-wei,* or nondoing, like water which without effort seeks and finds its proper level. This path includes purifying oneself through stilling the appetites and the emotions, accomplished in part through meditation, breath control and other forms of inner discipline, generally under a master. The foremost practice is goodness or naturalness, and detachment from the Ten Thousand Things of the world.

TAOIST BELIEFS

1. I believe that the Eternal may be understood as the Tao, or "Way," which embraces the moral and physical order of the universe, the path of virtue which Heaven itself follows, and the Absolute—yet so great is it that "the Tao that can be described is not the Eternal Tao."

❒ DO BELIEVE ❒ DO NOT BELIEVE ❒ ONCE BELIEVED ❒ UNFAMILIAR

2. I believe in the unique greatness of the sage Lao-tsu and in his disciple Chuang-tsu.

❒ DO BELIEVE ❒ DO NOT BELIEVE ❒ ONCE BELIEVED ❒ UNFAMILIAR

3. I believe in the scriptural insights and final authority of the *Tao-te-Ching* and in the sacredness of Chuang-tsu's writings.

❒ DO BELIEVE ❒ DO NOT BELIEVE ❒ ONCE BELIEVED ❒ UNFAMILIAR

4. I believe that man aligns himself with the Eternal when he observes humility, simplicity, gentle yielding, serenity and effortless action.

❒ DO BELIEVE ❒ DO NOT BELIEVE ❒ ONCE BELIEVED ❒ UNFAMILIAR

5. I believe that the goal and the path of life are essentially the same, and that the Tao can be known only to exalted beings who realize it themselves—reflections of the Beyond are of no avail.

❒ DO BELIEVE ❒ DO NOT BELIEVE ❒ ONCE BELIEVED ❒ UNFAMILIAR

6. I believe the omniscient and impersonal Supreme is implacable, beyond concern for human woe, but that there exist lesser Divinities—from the high Gods who endure for eons, to the nature spirits and demons.

❒ DO BELIEVE ❒ DO NOT BELIEVE ❒ ONCE BELIEVED ❒ UNFAMILIAR

7. I believe that all actions create their opposing forces, and the wise will seek inaction in action.

❒ DO BELIEVE ❒ DO NOT BELIEVE ❒ ONCE BELIEVED ❒ UNFAMILIAR

8. I believe that man is one of the Ten Thousand Things of manifestation, is finite and will pass; only the Tao endures forever.

❒ DO BELIEVE ❒ DO NOT BELIEVE ❒ ONCE BELIEVED ❒ UNFAMILIAR

9. I believe in the oneness of all creation, in the spirituality of the material realms and in the brotherhood of all men.

❒ DO BELIEVE ❒ DO NOT BELIEVE ❒ ONCE BELIEVED ❒ UNFAMILIAR

Confucianism

Confucianism

FOUNDED: Confucianism began about 2,500 years ago in China.
FOUNDER: Supreme Sage K'ung-fu-tsu (Confucius) and Second Sage Meng-tzu (Mencius).
MAJOR SCRIPTURES: The *Analects, Doctrine of the Mean, Great Learning* and *Mencius.*
ADHERENTS: Estimated at 350 million, mostly in China, Japan, Burma and Thailand.
SECTS: There are no formal sects within Confucianism. Followers are free to profess other religions yet still be Confucianists.

SYNOPSIS

Confucianism is, and has been for over 25 centuries, the dominant philosophical system in China and the guiding light in almost every aspect of Chinese life. Confucius and his followers traveled throughout the many feudal states of the Chinese empire, persuading rulers to adopt his social reforms. They did not offer a point-by-point program, but stressed instead the "Way," or "One Thread," Jen (also translated as "humanity or love"), that runs through all Confucius' teachings. They urged individuals to strive for perfect virtue, righteousness (called Yi) and improvement of character. They taught the importance of harmony in the family, order in the state and peace in the empire, which they saw as inherently interdependent. Teachings emphasize a code of conduct, self-cultivation and propriety—and thus the attainment of social and national order. Stress is more on human duty and the ideal of the "superior man" than on a divine or supramundane Reality. Still, Confucius fasted, worshiped the ancestors, attended sacrifices and sought to live in harmony with Heaven. Confucianism is now enjoying a renaissance in China.

THE GOALS OF CONFUCIANISM

The primary goal of Confucianism is to create a true nobility through proper education and the inculcation of all the virtues. It is described as the return to the way of one's ancestors, and the classics are studied to discover the ancient way of virtue. Spiritual nobility is attainable by all men; it is a moral achievement. Confucius accepted the Tao, but placed emphasis on this return to an idealized age and the cultivation of the superior man, on the pragmatic rather than the mystical. The superior man's greatest virtue is benevolent love. The other great virtues are duty, wisdom, truth and propriety. Salvation is seen as realizing and living one's natural goodness, which is endowed by heaven through education. The superior man always knows the right and follows his knowledge.

PATH OF ATTAINMENT

Besides virtue, the five relationships offer the follower of Confucianism the means for progressing. These five relationships are to his ruler, his father, his wife, his elder brother and his friend. Ancestors are revered in Confucianism, and it is assumed that their spirit survives death. With respect to a Deity, Confucius was himself an agnostic, preferring to place emphasis on the ethical life here rather than to speak of a spiritual life beyond earthly existence, guiding men's minds not to the future, but to the present and the past.

CONFUCIAN BELIEFS

1. I believe in the presence of the Supreme Ruler in all things, and in Heaven as the Ethical Principle whose law is order, impersonal and yet interested in mankind.

   ❒ DO BELIEVE ❒ DO NOT BELIEVE ❒ ONCE BELIEVED ❒ UNFAMILIAR

2. I believe that the purpose of life is to follow an orderly and reverent existence in accord with *Li*, propriety or virtue, so as to become the Superior Man.

   ❒ DO BELIEVE ❒ DO NOT BELIEVE ❒ ONCE BELIEVED ❒ UNFAMILIAR

3. I believe in the Golden Rule: "Never do to others what you would not like them to do to you."

   ❒ DO BELIEVE ❒ DO NOT BELIEVE ❒ ONCE BELIEVED ❒ UNFAMILIAR

4. I believe that Confucius, China's First Sage, is the Master of Life whose teachings embody the most profound understanding of Earth and Heaven, and that Mencius is China's Second Sage.

   ❒ DO BELIEVE ❒ DO NOT BELIEVE ❒ ONCE BELIEVED ❒ UNFAMILIAR

5. I believe in the writings of Confucius as scriptural truth and in the Four Sacred Books: The *Analects, Doctrine of the Mean, Great Learning,* and *Mencius.*

   ❒ DO BELIEVE ❒ DO NOT BELIEVE ❒ ONCE BELIEVED ❒ UNFAMILIAR

6. I believe that each man has five relationships, entailing five duties to his fellow man: to his ruler, to his father, to his wife, to his elder brother and to his friend—the foremost being his familial duties.

   ❒ DO BELIEVE ❒ DO NOT BELIEVE ❒ ONCE BELIEVED ❒ UNFAMILIAR

7. I believe that human nature is inherently good, and evil is an unnatural condition arising from inharmony.

   ❒ DO BELIEVE ❒ DO NOT BELIEVE ❒ ONCE BELIEVED ❒ UNFAMILIAR

8. I believe that man is master of his own life and fate, free to conduct himself as he will, and that he should cultivate qualities of benevolence, righteousness, propriety, wisdom and sincerity.

   ❒ DO BELIEVE ❒ DO NOT BELIEVE ❒ ONCE BELIEVED ❒ UNFAMILIAR

9. I believe that the family is the most essential institution among men, and that religion should support the family and the state.

   ❒ DO BELIEVE ❒ DO NOT BELIEVE ❒ ONCE BELIEVED ❒ UNFAMILIAR

Shintoism

Shintoism

FOUNDED: Shintoism began around 2,500–3,000 years ago in Japan.
FOUNDER: Each of the thirteen ancient sects has its own founder.
MAJOR SCRIPTURES: *Kojiki* (Record of Ancient Things), *Nihongi* (Chronicles of Japan), a later work, *Yengishiki* (Institutes of the period of Yengi), and the *Collection of 10,000 Leaves* are the primary works, but they are not regarded as revealed scripture.
ADHERENTS: Estimated at 30 million, mostly in Japan. Most are also Buddhists.

SYNOPSIS

There are two main divisions. One is the thirteen ancient sects, all very similar. The second is known as State Shinto, and is a later synthesis finding its highest expression in the worship of the Emperor and loyalty to the State and family. Shinto (from the Chinese characters *Shen* and *Tao,* signifying the "Way of the Spirits") is called Kami-no-michi in its native Japan. Kami are the many Gods or nature spirits. Shinto shrines are many—over 100,000 in Japan. In the shrines no images are worshiped, rather it is considered that the Kami themselves are there. Fresh foods, water, incense, etc., are offered daily upon the altar. There is an inward belief in the sacredness of the whole of the universe, that man can be in tune with this sacredness. Stress is placed on truthfulness and purification through which man may remove the "dust" which conceals his inherently divine nature and thus receive the guidance and blessings of Kami. The Shintoist's ardent love of the motherland has found unique expression in the loyalty and devotion of the Japanese people to their state institutions.

THE GOALS OF SHINTOISM

The primary goal of Shintoism is to achieve immortality among the ancestral beings, the Kami. Kami is understood by the Shintoist as a supernatural, holy power living in or connected to the world of the spirit. Shintoism is strongly animistic, as are most Eastern and Oriental faiths, believing that all living things possess a Kami nature. Man's nature is the highest, for he possesses the most Kami. Salvation is living in the spirit world with these divine beings, the Kami.

PATH OF ATTAINMENT

Salvation is achieved in Shinto through observance of all taboos and the avoidance of persons and objects which might cause impurity or pollution. Prayers are made and offerings brought to the temples of the Gods and Goddesses, of which there are said to be 800 myriad in the universe. Man has no Supreme God to obey, but needs only know how to adjust to Kami in its various manifestations. A person's Kami nature survives death, and a man naturally desires to be worthy of being remembered with approbation by his descendants. Therefore, fulfillment of duty is a most important aspect of Shinto.

SHINTO BELIEFS

1. I believe in the "Way of the Gods," Kami-no-michi, which asserts nature's sacredness and uniquely reveals the supernatural.
❒ DO BELIEVE ❒ DO NOT BELIEVE ❒ ONCE BELIEVED ❒ UNFAMILIAR

2. I believe there is not a single Supreme Being, but myriad Gods, superior beings, among all the wonders of the universe which is not inanimate but filled everywhere with sentient life.
❒ DO BELIEVE ❒ DO NOT BELIEVE ❒ ONCE BELIEVED ❒ UNFAMILIAR

3. I believe in the scriptural authority of the great books known as the *Record of Ancient Things, Chronicles of Japan, Institutes of the Period of Yengi* and *Collection of 10,000 Leaves.*
❒ DO BELIEVE ❒ DO NOT BELIEVE ❒ ONCE BELIEVED ❒ UNFAMILIAR

4. I believe in the sanctity of cleanliness and purity, of body and spirit, and that impurity is a religious transgression.
❒ DO BELIEVE ❒ DO NOT BELIEVE ❒ ONCE BELIEVED ❒ UNFAMILIAR

5. I believe that the State is a divine institution whose laws should not be transgressed and to which individuals must sacrifice their own needs.
❒ DO BELIEVE ❒ DO NOT BELIEVE ❒ ONCE BELIEVED ❒ UNFAMILIAR

6. I believe in moral and spiritual uprightness as the cornerstone of religious ethics and in the supreme value of loyalty.
❒ DO BELIEVE ❒ DO NOT BELIEVE ❒ ONCE BELIEVED ❒ UNFAMILIAR

7. I believe that the supernatural reveals itself through all that is natural and beautiful, and value these above philosophical or theological doctrine.
❒ DO BELIEVE ❒ DO NOT BELIEVE ❒ ONCE BELIEVED ❒ UNFAMILIAR

8. I believe that whatever is, is Divine Spirit, that the world is a one brotherhood, that all men are capable of deep affinity with the Divine and that there exists no evil in the world whatsoever.
❒ DO BELIEVE ❒ DO NOT BELIEVE ❒ ONCE BELIEVED ❒ UNFAMILIAR

9. I believe in the practical use of ceremony and ritual, and in the worship of the Deities that animate nature, including the Sun Goddess Amaterasu, the Moon God Tsuki-yomi, and the Storm God Sasa-no-wo.
❒ DO BELIEVE ❒ DO NOT BELIEVE ❒ ONCE BELIEVED ❒ UNFAMILIAR

Zoroastrianism

Zoroastrianism

FOUNDED: Zoroastrianism began 2,600 years ago in ancient Iran.
FOUNDER: Spenta Zarathustra (Zoroaster).
MAJOR SCRIPTURE: Portions of the *Zend Avesta* (Persian).
ADHERENTS: 125,000, mostly near Mumbai, where they are called Parsis.
SECTS: The present-day sects are three: Shahenshai, Kadmi and Fassali.

SYNOPSIS

Two principles form the basis of Zoroastrian ethics: the maintenance of life and the struggle against evil. In order to maintain life, one must till the soil, raise cattle, marry and have children. Asceticism and celibacy are condemned; purity and avoidance of defilement (from death, demons, etc.) are valued. In order to combat evil, one must at all times oppose the forces of evil and those who side with them. Zoroastrianism stresses monotheism, while recognizing the universal sway of two opposite forces (dualism). The powers of good are led by Ahura Mazda, or Ormazd (the Wise Lord), and the forces of evil by Angra Mainyu or Ahriman (the Evil Spirit). Each side has an array of warriors; bands of angels and archangels on one side and hosts of demons and archfiends on the other. Good will eventually triumph on Judgment Day, when a Messiah and Savior named Saoshyant will appear to punish the wicked and establish the righteous in a paradise on Earth. A central feature of the faith is the sacred fire that is constantly kept burning in every home, fueled by fragrant sandalwood. Fire is considered the only worshipful symbol, the great purifier and sustainer, of the nature of the sun itself.

THE GOALS OF ZOROASTRIANISM

The goal of Zoroastrianism is to be rewarded with a place in heaven where the soul will be with God, called Ahura Mazda, sharing His blessed existence forever.

PATH OF ATTAINMENT

Man's life, according to Zoroastrianism, is a moral struggle, not a search for knowledge or enlightenment. He is put on the earth to affirm and approve the world, not to deny it, not to escape from it. Salvation is found in obedience to the will of Ahura Mazda as revealed and taught by His prophet, Zoroaster. Man has but one life. He also has the freedom to choose between good and evil, the latter being embodied in Angra Mainyu who rebelled against God. At death, each is judged and consigned to his deserved abode.

Zoroastrians hold truth as the greatest virtue, followed by good thoughts, words and deeds. They value the ethical life most highly. Though there will be a resurrection of the dead, a judgment and a kingdom of heaven on Earth, followed by punishment of the wicked, all sins are eventually burned away and all of mankind exists forever with Ahura Mazda. Hell, for the Zoroastrian, is not eternal.

ZOROASTRIAN BELIEFS

1. I believe there are two Great Beings in the universe. One, Ahura Mazda, created man and all that is good, beautiful and true, while the other, Angra Mainyu, vivifies all that is evil, ugly and destructive.

   ❒ DO BELIEVE ❒ DO NOT BELIEVE ❒ ONCE BELIEVED ❒ UNFAMILIAR

2. I believe that man has free will to align himself with good or evil, and when all mankind is in harmony with the God Ahura Mazda, Angra Mainyu will be conquered.

   ❒ DO BELIEVE ❒ DO NOT BELIEVE ❒ ONCE BELIEVED ❒ UNFAMILIAR

3. I believe the soul is immortal and upon death crosses over Hell by a narrow bridge—the good crossing safely to Heaven and the evil falling into Hell.

   ❒ DO BELIEVE ❒ DO NOT BELIEVE ❒ ONCE BELIEVED ❒ UNFAMILIAR

4. I believe that a savior named Saoshyant will appear at the end of time, born of a virgin, reviving the dead, rewarding the good and punishing the evil, and thereafter Ahura Mazda will reign.

   ❒ DO BELIEVE ❒ DO NOT BELIEVE ❒ ONCE BELIEVED ❒ UNFAMILIAR

5. I believe that Zoroaster, also known as Zarathustra, is the foremost Prophet of God.

   ❒ DO BELIEVE ❒ DO NOT BELIEVE ❒ ONCE BELIEVED ❒ UNFAMILIAR

6. I believe in the scriptural authority of the *Zend Avesta.*

   ❒ DO BELIEVE ❒ DO NOT BELIEVE ❒ ONCE BELIEVED ❒ UNFAMILIAR

7. I believe that purity is the first virtue, truth the second and charity the third—and that man must discipline himself by good thoughts, words and deeds.

   ❒ DO BELIEVE ❒ DO NOT BELIEVE ❒ ONCE BELIEVED ❒ UNFAMILIAR

8. I believe that marriage excels continence, action excels contemplation and forgiveness excels revenge.

   ❒ DO BELIEVE ❒ DO NOT BELIEVE ❒ ONCE BELIEVED ❒ UNFAMILIAR

9. I believe in God as Seven Persons: Eternal Light; Right and Justice; Goodness and Love; Strength of Spirit; Piety and Faith; Health and Perfection; and Immortality—and that He may best be worshiped through the representation of fire.

   ❒ DO BELIEVE ❒ DO NOT BELIEVE ❒ ONCE BELIEVED ❒ UNFAMILIAR

Judaism

Judaism

FOUNDED: Judaism began about 3,700 years ago in the Near East, chiefly Canaan (now Israel) and Egypt.
FOUNDERS: Abraham, who started the lineage, and Moses, who emancipated the enslaved Jewish tribes from Egypt.
MAJOR SCRIPTURE: The *Torah* (the *Old Testament* and the *Talmud).*
ADHERENTS: About 12 million worldwide, over half in the United States.
SECTS: Jews are divided into Orthodox, Conservative and Reform sects, with other regional and ethnic divisions.

SYNOPSIS

The religion of the Jews is inseparable from their history as a people. Much of the *Torah* traces the ancestry of Abraham through Isaac, Jacob, Joseph and finally to Moses, the foremost of God's prophets in Hebrew history. It was Moses who conveyed to Judaism the Ten Commandments given by God and established the religious laws and traditions.

The *Torah* (literally, "doctrine, teaching, law") consists primarily of the written *Torah,* i.e. the Hebrew *Bible,* or the *Old Testament;* and secondarily of oral Torah, ultimately codified as *Talmud* (literally, "instruction"), in two reductions, Jerusalem *Talmud* and the more authoritative Babylonian *Talmud.* In the narrower sense, *Torah* denotes only the *Pentateuch,* i.e., the first five books of the *Old Testament.* But in extended usage, *Torah* as scripture is somewhat analogous to the Hindu *Veda,* which beyond the four *Saṁhitās* may also apply to their extensions, the *Brāhmaṇas, Āraṇyakas* and *Upanishads.* As a term for moral and religious principles, Jewish *Torah* has as comprehensive an application as Hindu Dharma.

By far the most profound characteristic of Judaism is its strict monotheism. The Jews hold an unshakable belief in one God and one God only, known as Yahweh, "whose name cannot be taken in vain," and from whom all creation flows. The Jewish people consider themselves a chosen people, apart from all the other peoples of the Earth, by virtue of their covenant with Yahweh.

Much stress is placed on the hallowing of daily existence, worship in the synagogue, prayer and reading of the scriptures. Few religions can boast of such a close-knit family tradition as Judaism, making the home a great strength to the religion and a constant refuge to the faithful. Each day, morning and evening, every devout Jew affirms his faith by repeating Moses' prayer: "Hear, O Israel, the Lord our God, the Lord is One."

THE GOALS OF JUDAISM

The goal of Judaism lies in the strict obedience to the *Torah,* Jewish scripture, which can alleviate the plight of the individual and of society. Obeying God's law brings rewards in the future life when the Messiah will come to overthrow evil and reward the righteous in God's kingdom on the earth, the Day of the Lord. The soul thereafter will enjoy God's presence and love.

PATH OF ATTAINMENT

Man has two impulses: good and evil. He can either follow God's law or rebel and be influenced by Satan, who caused God's creation to go astray. Following God's law is the highest morality, possible through obedience to the *Torah,* which pleases God. One must follow justice, charity, ethics and honesty, being true to the one true God, Yahweh.

JUDAIC BELIEFS

1. I believe in the One God and Creator who is incorporeal and transcendent, beyond the limitation of form, yet who cares for the world and its creatures, rewarding the good and punishing the evil.
❒ DO BELIEVE ❒ DO NOT BELIEVE ❒ ONCE BELIEVED ❒ UNFAMILIAR

2. I believe in the Prophets, of whom Moses was God's foremost, and in the Commandments revealed to him by God on Mount Sinai as man's highest law.
❒ DO BELIEVE ❒ DO NOT BELIEVE ❒ ONCE BELIEVED ❒ UNFAMILIAR

3. I believe in the *Torah* as God's word and scripture, composed of all the *Old Testament* books (the Hebrew *Bible)* and the *Talmud.* They are God's only immutable law.
❒ DO BELIEVE ❒ DO NOT BELIEVE ❒ ONCE BELIEVED ❒ UNFAMILIAR

4. I believe that upon death the soul goes to Heaven (or to Hell first if it has been sinful), that one day the Messiah will appear on Earth and there will be a Day of Judgment, and the dead shall physically arise to Life Everlasting.
❒ DO BELIEVE ❒ DO NOT BELIEVE ❒ ONCE BELIEVED ❒ UNFAMILIAR

5. I believe that the universe is not eternal, but was created by and will be destroyed by God.
❒ DO BELIEVE ❒ DO NOT BELIEVE ❒ ONCE BELIEVED ❒ UNFAMILIAR

6. I believe that no priest should intervene in the relationship of man and God, nor should God be represented in any form, nor should any being be worshiped other than the One God, Yahweh.
❒ DO BELIEVE ❒ DO NOT BELIEVE ❒ ONCE BELIEVED ❒ UNFAMILIAR

7. I believe in man's spiritualization through adherence to the law, justice, charity and honesty.
❒ DO BELIEVE ❒ DO NOT BELIEVE ❒ ONCE BELIEVED ❒ UNFAMILIAR

8. I believe that God has established a unique spiritual covenant with the Hebrew people to uphold for mankind the highest standards of monotheism and piety.
❒ DO BELIEVE ❒ DO NOT BELIEVE ❒ ONCE BELIEVED ❒ UNFAMILIAR

9. I believe in the duty of the family to make the home a House of God through devotions and ritual, prayers, sacred festivals and observation of the Holy Sabbath Day.
❒ DO BELIEVE ❒ DO NOT BELIEVE ❒ ONCE BELIEVED ❒ UNFAMILIAR

Christianity

Christianity

FOUNDED: Christianity began about 2,000 years ago in what is now Israel.
FOUNDER: Jesus of Nazareth, or Jesus Christ, "Anointed One," "the Messiah."
MAJOR SCRIPTURE: The *Bible—Old* and *New Testaments.*
ADHERENTS: Estimated at 1.5 billion.
SECTS: Christianity is divided into three main sects: Roman Catholic, Eastern Orthodox and Protestant. Among Protestants there are over 20,000 denominations.

SYNOPSIS

The majority of Christians adhere to the Apostles' Creed: "I believe in God, the Father Almighty, Maker of Heaven and Earth, and Jesus Christ, His only Son, our Lord, Who was conceived by the Holy Ghost, born of the Virgin Mary, suffered under Pontius Pilate, was crucified, dead and buried. He descended into Hell. The third day He rose again from the dead. He ascended unto Heaven and sitteth on the right hand of God, the Father Almighty. From thence He shall come to judge the quick and the dead. I believe in the Holy Ghost,...the communion of saints, the forgiveness of sins, the resurrection of the body and the life everlasting." Most Christian faith revolves around the basic principles of this creed, but with important exceptions to its various beliefs. Christianity has an unswerving conviction that it is the only true religion, the only path to salvation. This engenders a missionary zeal, an urgency to evangelize around the world.

Stress is placed on acceptance of Jesus as God incarnate and Savior, on good conduct, compassion, service to mankind, faith and preparation for the Final Judgment. Only good Christians will be saved and accepted into heaven. Today over half of all Christians are black. Membership is diminishing in developed nations but increasing in undeveloped nations.

THE GOALS OF CHRISTIANITY

The goal of Christianity is eternal life with God in heaven, a perfect existence in which God's glory and bliss are shared. It is also a personal life, enjoyed differently by souls according to the amount of grace achieved in life.

PATH OF ATTAINMENT

Man's plight is caused by disobedience to God's will. Man needs redemption from the forces which would enslave and destroy him—fear, selfishness, hopelessness, desire and the supernatural forces of the Devil, sin and death against which he is powerless. His salvation comes only through faith in Jesus Christ, that is, in acceptance of Jesus' resurrection from the dead as proof of God's power over the forces of sin and death. The good Christian lives a life of virtue and obedience to God out of gratitude to God for sacrificing Jesus for the sins of all who come to accept Jesus Christ as personal Savior and Lord. Jesus is to return again to judge the world and bring God's rule to the earth. Through following the law of God as found in the *Holy Bible* and through God's grace, man attains salvation. Those who do not achieve this blessedness are, after death, consigned to a hell of eternal suffering and damnation.

CHRISTIAN BELIEFS

1. I believe in God the Father, Creator of the universe, reigning forever distinct over man, His beloved creation.
❐ DO BELIEVE ❐ DO NOT BELIEVE ❐ ONCE BELIEVED ❐ UNFAMILIAR

2. I believe man is born a sinner, and that he may know salvation only through the Savior, Jesus Christ, God's only begotten Son.
❐ DO BELIEVE ❐ DO NOT BELIEVE ❐ ONCE BELIEVED ❐ UNFAMILIAR

3. I believe that Jesus Christ was born of Mary, a virgin.
❐ DO BELIEVE ❐ DO NOT BELIEVE ❐ ONCE BELIEVED ❐ UNFAMILIAR

4. I believe that Jesus Christ was crucified on the cross, then resurrected from the dead and now sits at the right hand of the Father as the final judge of the dead, and that He will return again as prophesied.
❐ DO BELIEVE ❐ DO NOT BELIEVE ❐ ONCE BELIEVED ❐ UNFAMILIAR

5. I believe that the soul is embodied for a single lifetime, but is immortal and accountable to God for all thoughts and actions.
❐ DO BELIEVE ❐ DO NOT BELIEVE ❐ ONCE BELIEVED ❐ UNFAMILIAR

6. I believe in the historical truth of the *Holy Bible*, that it is sacred scripture of the highest authority and the only word of God.
❐ DO BELIEVE ❐ DO NOT BELIEVE ❐ ONCE BELIEVED ❐ UNFAMILIAR

7. I believe that upon death and according to its earthly deeds and its acceptance of the Christian faith, the soul enters Heaven, Purgatory or Hell. There it awaits the Last Judgment when the dead shall rise again, the redeemed to enjoy life everlasting and the unsaved to suffer eternally.
❐ DO BELIEVE ❐ DO NOT BELIEVE ❐ ONCE BELIEVED ❐ UNFAMILIAR

8. I believe in the intrinsic goodness of mankind and the affirmative nature of life, and in the priceless value of love, charity and faith.
❐ DO BELIEVE ❐ DO NOT BELIEVE ❐ ONCE BELIEVED ❐ UNFAMILIAR

9. I believe in the Holy Trinity of God who reveals Himself as Father, Son and Holy Ghost, and in the existence of Satan, the personification of evil, deception and darkness.
❐ DO BELIEVE ❐ DO NOT BELIEVE ❐ ONCE BELIEVED ❐ UNFAMILIAR

Islam

Islam

FOUNDED: Islam began about 1,400 years ago in present-day Saudi Arabia.
FOUNDER: Prophet Mohammed.
MAJOR SCRIPTURES: The *Koran,* Islam's revealed scripture, and the *Hadith,* the teachings, sayings and life of the Prophet Mohammed.
ADHERENTS: One billion, mostly in the Middle East, Indonesia, Pakistan, Bangladesh, Africa, China and Eastern Europe.
SECTS: There are two main divisions within Islam. The Sunnis are followers of the political successors of Mohammed. The Shiites are followers of Mohammed's family successors, all martyred at an early age.

SYNOPSIS

Islam means "submission," surrender to the will of God, called Allah. Those who submit are called Muslims. Islam is based upon five "pillars," or principal acts of faith to which every Muslim in the world adheres. These are: 1) Faith in Allah: "There is no God but Allah, and Mohammed is His Prophet." 2) Praying five times daily: kneeling in the direction of Mecca, the holy city. 3) Giving of alms: a share of each Muslim's income is given to support the mosque and the poor. 4) Fasting: throughout Ramadan, the ninth month of the Muslim calendar, the faithful fast from sunrise to sunset. 5) Pilgrimage: the binding force of the peoples who have embraced Islam. At least once in life every believer, physically and materially able to do so, must go to Mecca, the holy city. They go dressed in simple, seamless white garments.

Islam teaches absolute monotheism and Mohammed's primacy as God's last Prophet on Earth. Stress is on the brotherhood of believers, nondifference of religious and secular life, obedience to God's Law, abstinence from alcohol, good conduct and the limitation of all except Allah. Today Islam is the world's fastest-growing religion.

THE GOALS OF ISLAM

The primary goal of Islam is to enjoy eternal life, both physical and spiritual, in heaven with Allah. Heaven is a paradise in which all the joys and pleasures abound, in which one lives amid beautiful gardens and fountains, enjoying the choicest foods served by sweet maidens. Man is the noblest creation of God, ranking above the angels. It is the sacred duty of Muslims to convert others to the Islamic faith. Islam has an ardent conviction that it is the only true religion, the only path to salvation. From this belief arises an extraordinary zeal, to share the faith and to convert others. The ideal human society is an Islamic theocracy.

PATH OF ATTAINMENT

Total submission to Allah is the single path to salvation, and even that is no guarantee, for Allah may desire even a faithful soul to experience misery. The good Muslim surrenders all pride, the chief among sins, and follows explicitly the will of Allah as revealed in the *Koran* by His last and greatest prophet, Mohammed. This and this alone brings a full and meaningful life and avoids the terrors of Hell which befall sinners and infidels. He believes in the Five Doctrines and observes the Five Pillars. The virtues of truthfulness, temperance and humility before God are foremost for Islam, and the practices of fasting, pilgrimage, prayer and charity to the Muslim community are most necessary to please Allah. The five doctrines are: 1) There is only one true God, Allah. 2) There are angels, chief of whom is Gabriel. 3) There are four inspired books: the *Torah* of Moses, the *Zabur* (Psalms) of David, the *Injil* (Evangel) of Jesus, and the *Koran,* Allah's final message, which supersedes all other scriptures. 4) There have been numerous prophets of Allah, culminating in Mohammed, the Last Prophet. 5) There will be a final Day of Judgment and Resurrection. A sixth, but optional, doctrine is belief in *kismet,* "fate" or "destiny."

ISLAMIC BELIEFS

1. I believe that Allah is the Supreme Creator and Sustainer, all-knowing and transcendent and yet the arbiter of good and evil, the final judge of men.

❐ DO BELIEVE ❐ DO NOT BELIEVE ❐ ONCE BELIEVED ❐ UNFAMILIAR

2. I believe in the Five Pillars of Faith: 1) praying five times daily, 2) charity through alms-giving, 3) fasting during the ninth month, 4) pilgrimage to Holy Mecca, Saudi Arabia, and 5) profession of faith by acknowledging, "There is no God but Allah, and Mohammed is His Prophet."

❐ DO BELIEVE ❐ DO NOT BELIEVE ❐ ONCE BELIEVED ❐ UNFAMILIAR

3. I believe in the *Koran* as the Word of God and sacred scripture mediated through the Angel Gabriel to Mohammed.

❐ DO BELIEVE ❐ DO NOT BELIEVE ❐ ONCE BELIEVED ❐ UNFAMILIAR

4. I believe in the direct communion of each man with God, that all are equal in the eyes of God and therefore priests or other intercessors are unneeded.

❐ DO BELIEVE ❐ DO NOT BELIEVE ❐ ONCE BELIEVED ❐ UNFAMILIAR

5. I believe in the pure transcendence of God, great beyond imagining—no form or idol can be worshiped in His Name.

❐ DO BELIEVE ❐ DO NOT BELIEVE ❐ ONCE BELIEVED ❐ UNFAMILIAR

6. I believe that the soul of man is immortal, embodied once on earth, then entering Heaven or Hell upon death according to its conduct and faith on earth.

❐ DO BELIEVE ❐ DO NOT BELIEVE ❐ ONCE BELIEVED ❐ UNFAMILIAR

7. I believe in the Last Judgment and that man should stand in humble awe and fear of God's wrathful and vengeful power.

❐ DO BELIEVE ❐ DO NOT BELIEVE ❐ ONCE BELIEVED ❐ UNFAMILIAR

8. I believe that truthfulness should be observed in all circumstances, even though it may bring injury or pain.

❐ DO BELIEVE ❐ DO NOT BELIEVE ❐ ONCE BELIEVED ❐ UNFAMILIAR

9. I believe that salvation is only obtained through God's grace and not through man's efforts, yet man should do good and avoid all sins, especially drunkenness, usury and gambling.

❐ DO BELIEVE ❐ DO NOT BELIEVE ❐ ONCE BELIEVED ❐ UNFAMILIAR

Faiths

Faiths

In his search of the Divine, man has created innumerable smaller "faiths." These spiritual paths are often charismatic or mystical in source or nature and have a powerful spiritual presence despite being numerically small. A few examples:

SPIRITUALISM: Spiritualism holds that there is another, perhaps deeper, reality on "the other side" which can be contacted by mediums or psychics who have sufficient sensitivity. It is one of the oldest forms of communion.

SHAMANISM: This broad term includes the thousands of tribal faiths which have existed on every continent since long before recorded history. Beliefs include a deep sense of the sacredness of life and of the earth, communion with spirit guides and in the ability of man to live in harmony with and influence nature.

THEOSOPHY: Inspired by Hinduism and Buddhism and founded in 1875 by Madame Blavatsky and Colonel H.S. Olcott, Theosophy emphasizes mystical experience, esoteric doctrines and monism. Theosophists seek universal brotherhood, exploring the unexplained laws of nature and the psychic powers latent in man.

UNIVERSALISM: Many faiths are based on universalist principles, often as a conscious effort to avoid certain doctrines which are seen as narrow or sectarian. Universalism arises in all religions, whether Christian (Unitarianism), Islam (Baha'i), Jain (Rajneeshism) or Hindu (dozens of integrating-all-religions movements, such as those of Satya Sāī Bāba, Kṛishṇamūrti and Mahārshi Mahesh Yogī).

OTHER FAITHS

Among thousands of other faiths are: indigenous people's tribal religions, humanitarianism, neo-Indian religion, shamanism, Anthroposophy, Swedenborgianism, Gnosticism, Neoplatonism, Scientology, Eckankar, channeling, witchcraft, Paganism, occultism, Subud, mysticism, Freemasonry, Satan worship, Huna, Voodoo, Santaria, Sufism, Baha'i, Rosicrucianism, Christian Science and Religious Science.

A SAMPLING OF BELIEFS OF FAITHS

1. I believe in the fundamental unity and common source of all religions (Baha'i and Universalism).

   ❒ DO BELIEVE ❒ DO NOT BELIEVE ❒ ONCE BELIEVED ❒ UNFAMILIAR

2. I believe man's natural spirituality is best expressed in loving and practical aid to his fellow man, rather than metaphysical inquiry (Humanitarianism).

   ❒ DO BELIEVE ❒ DO NOT BELIEVE ❒ ONCE BELIEVED ❒ UNFAMILIAR

3. I believe in the unity of religions, the efficacy of devotion, *sādhana* and service and in Satya Sāī Bāba as the living Incarnation of God (Saiism).

   ❒ DO BELIEVE ❒ DO NOT BELIEVE ❒ ONCE BELIEVED ❒ UNFAMILIAR

4. I believe that spiritual progress comes through analysis of current and past life experiences which resolve past karma most directly (Scientology).

   ❒ DO BELIEVE ❒ DO NOT BELIEVE ❒ ONCE BELIEVED ❒ UNFAMILIAR

5. I believe that there is no God beyond the Divine within man and no truth beyond existential freedom, that all religions imprison man, causing repression, fear and poverty (Rajneeshism).

   ❒ DO BELIEVE ❒ DO NOT BELIEVE ❒ ONCE BELIEVED ❒ UNFAMILIAR

6. I believe man's sense of the sacred can be fulfilled naturally, without formal worship, houses of God, ceremony, creeds or theology (various faiths).

   ❒ DO BELIEVE ❒ DO NOT BELIEVE ❒ ONCE BELIEVED ❒ UNFAMILIAR

7. I believe religion consists of unitive and direct mystical experience which should be the objective of every religious aspirant (mysticism).

   ❒ DO BELIEVE ❒ DO NOT BELIEVE ❒ ONCE BELIEVED ❒ UNFAMILIAR

8. I believe that the cultivation of occult powers including ESP, astral travel, past life readings, etc., is the highest pursuit of that which is spiritual (occultism).

❒ DO BELIEVE ❒ DO NOT BELIEVE ❒ ONCE BELIEVED ❒ UNFAMILIAR

9. I believe in the intimate relationship of man, Spirit and the earth—which is a living, sacred being—and in the brotherhood of all creatures (indigenous tribalism).

❒ DO BELIEVE ❒ DO NOT BELIEVE ❒ ONCE BELIEVED ❒ UNFAMILIAR

Movements

Here we explore some of the larger movements, which are not necessarily spiritual in nature, but are important currents of thought and belief which shape modern politics and society. Others that we have not delved into include Human Rights, Gay Liberation, Women's Equality, Anti-Abortion, Anti-Child-Abuse, Interfaith, Native Rights, Extraterrestrialism and more.

DRUG CULTURE

"Drug culture" refers to the fluid ideas and unrestrained way of life developed in Western societies during the 1960s. Its adherents affect a lifestyle based on the use of various natural and man-made drugs such as marijuana, hashish, peyote, mescaline, cocaine, LSD and chemical designer drugs.

DRUG CULTURE BELIEFS

1. I believe that one can achieve the ultimate goal of enlightenment, as understood by any religion, through the use of drugs.

❒ DO BELIEVE ❒ DO NOT BELIEVE ❒ ONCE BELIEVED ❒ UNFAMILIAR

2. I believe that the psychedelic drug experience, properly handled, fulfills the role of a spiritual teacher or guru.

❒ DO BELIEVE ❒ DO NOT BELIEVE ❒ ONCE BELIEVED ❒ UNFAMILIAR

3. I believe that drugs give mystical experiences of various types

identical to and therefore equally as valid as those achieved through yoga, penance, grace, etc.

❒ DO BELIEVE ❒ DO NOT BELIEVE ❒ ONCE BELIEVED ❒ UNFAMILIAR

4. I believe that the knowledge gained on drugs is more valid than the traditional knowledge given by society or religion because it is direct, personal experience of a higher order.

❒ DO BELIEVE ❒ DO NOT BELIEVE ❒ ONCE BELIEVED ❒ UNFAMILIAR

5. I believe that people who take drugs are more "aware" or "enlightened" than those who do not.

❒ DO BELIEVE ❒ DO NOT BELIEVE ❒ ONCE BELIEVED ❒ UNFAMILIAR

6. I believe that one can solve his personal psychological problems or "hangups" by taking drugs.

❒ DO BELIEVE ❒ DO NOT BELIEVE ❒ ONCE BELIEVED ❒ UNFAMILIAR

7. I believe in living simply, close to nature and in harmony with others and that sexual relationships need not be restricted by the traditional morals imposed by society.

❒ DO BELIEVE ❒ DO NOT BELIEVE ❒ ONCE BELIEVED ❒ UNFAMILIAR

8. I believe that the ideal life is to completely drop out of society, becoming self-sufficient and associating with others of a like mind, and that those who do not drop out of society but continue to involve themselves in mundane materialism are living in a lower consciousness.

❒ DO BELIEVE ❒ DO NOT BELIEVE ❒ ONCE BELIEVED ❒ UNFAMILIAR

9. I believe that the meaning of life is found in intense self-revelatory experiences, which can be attained through drugs that open the doors of perception to higher consciousness.

❒ DO BELIEVE ❒ DO NOT BELIEVE ❒ ONCE BELIEVED ❒ UNFAMILIAR

NEW AGE

The term *new age* was coined in the 1970s to denote an awakening of the mass consciousness to deeper realities and the need for individual attunement with universal, higher consciousness and creative transformation. In practice, new-age thinking embraces myriad enlightenment teachings (mostly of Eastern origin)—from crystalography to Zen, parapsychology to holistic medicine.

NEW AGE BELIEFS

1. I believe in the one Eternal Source or Ultimate Reality, called by many names, which flows through all forms of nature and can be known through spiritual realization and experience.

   ❒ DO BELIEVE ❒ DO NOT BELIEVE ❒ ONCE BELIEVED ❒ UNFAMILIAR

2. I believe in unseen worlds and beings who may interact with our world, and that some are benevolent and help guide and protect us, while others are malevolent, and that channeling, or mediumship, is a means of contacting such souls.

   ❒ DO BELIEVE ❒ DO NOT BELIEVE ❒ ONCE BELIEVED ❒ UNFAMILIAR

3. I believe that the world is a dynamic, conscious entity; that mankind is but one part of the cosmic ecology and that, as stewards, we must treat the world responsibly, with love, respect and reverence.

   ❒ DO BELIEVE ❒ DO NOT BELIEVE ❒ ONCE BELIEVED ❒ UNFAMILIAR

4. I believe that consciousness is present in and conveyed through some structures more than others. Thus, for example, crystals are powerful sources or channels of knowledge and spiritual strength.

   ❒ DO BELIEVE ❒ DO NOT BELIEVE ❒ ONCE BELIEVED ❒ UNFAMILIAR

5. I believe in meditation, trance, rebirthing, self-healing, channeling, past-life regression, crystals, sexual *tantras,* drugs and more as effective tools in the quest for wholeness and oneness with the sacred, and that one should continue to explore alternatives and not feel restricted to the disciplines of any one system of thought.

   ❒ DO BELIEVE ❒ DO NOT BELIEVE ❒ ONCE BELIEVED ❒ UNFAMILIAR

6. I believe the world has entered the New Age, the age of Aquarius, awakening to the consciousness of love, selflessness, compassion and creativity, from the old age of hatred, war, ignorance and greed. Those who perceive this vision should share it with others to uplift society.

   ❒ DO BELIEVE ❒ DO NOT BELIEVE ❒ ONCE BELIEVED ❒ UNFAMILIAR

7. I believe that traditional religions are outmoded and that we are moving toward a universal brotherhood; yet, the Eastern religions and so-called primitive faiths are rich reservoirs of truth and spiritual practice.

   ❒ DO BELIEVE ❒ DO NOT BELIEVE ❒ ONCE BELIEVED ❒ UNFAMILIAR

8. I believe in nonconformity and noncommitment: that each person is responsible to his-her own conscience only and not to the dictates of society which often unduly hamper freedom of expression, and that even spiritual gurus are to be approached with circumspection.

❒ DO BELIEVE ❒ DO NOT BELIEVE ❒ ONCE BELIEVED ❒ UNFAMILIAR

9. I believe that many of society's traditional economic and social structures are outmoded and should be abandoned for ones which reflect new-age consciousness, and that dropping out of society is a valid new-age alternative.

❒ DO BELIEVE ❒ DO NOT BELIEVE ❒ ONCE BELIEVED ❒ UNFAMILIAR

ECOLOGY MOVEMENT

In the 1980s there arose an Earth-ethics movement complete with philosophy, an immense following and compelling missionary zeal. It deemed the present global environmental imbalance so severe as to threaten future generations' quality of life, perhaps even leading to the extinction of the human race. There is a wide philosophical range among adherents: 1) man-centered conservationists seek to preserve natural resources for human enjoyment, 2) environmentalists work to preserve ecosystems and species and 3) "deep ecologists" call for spiritualization of human life in consonance with a sacred nature. In the 1990s this movement brought together organizational, tribal, religious and political leaders from hundreds of nations to focus on global concerns at international conferences. Adherents believe the world must act speedily to protect nature and humanity from disaster.

BELIEFS OF THE ECOLOGY MOVEMENT

1. I believe that all nature is sacred and One and that each life form has intrinsic value in a cosmos where elements, plants, animals and humans are intimately interconnected, essential to and dependent on the whole.

❒ DO BELIEVE ❒ DO NOT BELIEVE ❒ ONCE BELIEVED ❒ UNFAMILIAR

2. I believe that every human being has the right to a healthy, pristine, undiminished environment, and that we are morally obliged to work toward assuring this right for future generations.

❒ DO BELIEVE ❒ DO NOT BELIEVE ❒ ONCE BELIEVED ❒ UNFAMILIAR

3. I believe that all living beings have an inalienable right to exist, and that through our ignorance, assisted by science, we have disrupted life's balance and brought about the extinction of vast numbers of plant and animal species.

❒ DO BELIEVE ❒ DO NOT BELIEVE ❒ ONCE BELIEVED ❒ UNFAMILIAR

4. I believe that the sacredness of life demands the practice of nonviolence, that differences must be resolved by consultation rather than conflict. Nations must work toward complete disarmament.

❒ DO BELIEVE ❒ DO NOT BELIEVE ❒ ONCE BELIEVED ❒ UNFAMILIAR

5. I believe we must change our system of values away from materialism and consumerism, transform our hearts and minds, make simple and concrete changes in our way of life and renew our deepest religious impulses as we create a global society.

❒ DO BELIEVE ❒ DO NOT BELIEVE ❒ ONCE BELIEVED ❒ UNFAMILIAR

6. I believe mankind must rediscover the value of frugality, avoid waste, implement sustainable systems of nonpolluting farming, manufacturing and energy production to enable future generations to meet their needs. Simplicity of life fosters inner freedom and outer sustainability.

❒ DO BELIEVE ❒ DO NOT BELIEVE ❒ ONCE BELIEVED ❒ UNFAMILIAR

7. I believe that biological, cultural and religious diversity are essential to life's purpose, and that all species and human traditions, especially indigenous faiths, must be preserved through peaceful co-existence, protection of habitats through wilderness preservation.

❒ DO BELIEVE ❒ DO NOT BELIEVE ❒ ONCE BELIEVED ❒ UNFAMILIAR

8. I believe that the present ecological crisis is, at its heart, a spiritual crisis for the human race and affirm the importance of respecting all spiritual traditions, promoting those that foster concern and responsibility for the environment and vigorously challenging those that do not.

❒ DO BELIEVE ❒ DO NOT BELIEVE ❒ ONCE BELIEVED ❒ UNFAMILIAR

9. I believe that overpopulation poses one of the greatest threats to the natural environment and to the quality of human life, and that to establish a sustainable earth community we must promote the extended family and make greater efforts to educate women and children.

❒ DO BELIEVE ❒ DO NOT BELIEVE ❒ ONCE BELIEVED ❒ UNFAMILIAR

FUNDAMENTALISM

Fundamentalism describes any religious creed or philosophical persuasion marked by extreme dogmatism and intolerance. There are fundamentalist denominations within virtually every religion and faith—including Christianity, Judaism, Islam, Buddhism, Sikhism and Hinduism—all believing in a literal interpretation of their scripture as *the* exclusive truth, the one and only way which all souls must follow to attain salvation. Historically, fundamentalism, especially when coupled with evangelical zeal, has led to aggression and violence against nonbelievers.

FUNDAMENTALIST BELIEFS

1. I believe that there is only one acceptable perception of truth, and it is stated in our scriptures; and all who do not accept this doctrine are following false paths and are destined to eternal damnation.

   ❒ DO BELIEVE ❒ DO NOT BELIEVE ❒ ONCE BELIEVED ❒ UNFAMILIAR

2. I believe that the gospel was spoken at one point in time by our messiah, the one and only true representative of God, and is not subject to or in need of adaptation through time or circumstance.

   ❒ DO BELIEVE ❒ DO NOT BELIEVE ❒ ONCE BELIEVED ❒ UNFAMILIAR

3. I believe that the members of our faith have been divinely commissioned by God and are duty-bound to spread His holy word throughout the world.

   ❒ DO BELIEVE ❒ DO NOT BELIEVE ❒ ONCE BELIEVED ❒ UNFAMILIAR

4. I believe that government should reflect and embody the beliefs of my faith, and that even nonbelievers should abide by our religious law as the law of the land.

   ❒ DO BELIEVE ❒ DO NOT BELIEVE ❒ ONCE BELIEVED ❒ UNFAMILIAR

5. I believe that there is in this world a battle between the believers, representing the forces of light, and the nonbelievers, representing the forces of darkness, and that ultimately good will conquer evil.
   ❒ DO BELIEVE ❒ DO NOT BELIEVE ❒ ONCE BELIEVED ❒ UNFAMILIAR
6. I believe that, if necessary, force and violence should be used to bring nonbelievers and dissidents to accept the truth of our religious doctrine, and that the use of such force is justifiable in the name of God.
   ❒ DO BELIEVE ❒ DO NOT BELIEVE ❒ ONCE BELIEVED ❒ UNFAMILIAR
7. I believe that free inquiry and the questioning of our religious doctrine is the first step to heresy and should be guarded against, and that modern liberties are forms of self-indulgence and sin.
   ❒ DO BELIEVE ❒ DO NOT BELIEVE ❒ ONCE BELIEVED ❒ UNFAMILIAR
8. I believe that our codes of morality are God's absolute commandments and are not subject to change, revision or reinterpretation.
   ❒ DO BELIEVE ❒ DO NOT BELIEVE ❒ ONCE BELIEVED ❒ UNFAMILIAR
9. I believe that education for children should consist of strict and exclusive learning of our teachings and careful censorship of other forms of thought and belief.
   ❒ DO BELIEVE ❒ DO NOT BELIEVE ❒ ONCE BELIEVED ❒ UNFAMILIAR

Atheistic Philosophies

Atheistic Philosophies

In this section we will examine the beliefs of four philosophies or world views that exclude God: materialism, Communism, existentialism, and secular humanism. Of course, there are many smaller isms that could be listed here, but these are among the most prevalent. Their ideas and teachings have great influence throughout the world, especially through Western universities and the Western news media.

MATERIALISM

Materialism is the opinion that "nothing exists except matter and its movements and modifications." In practice it is "devotion to material needs or desires to the neglect of spiritual matters; a way of life, opinion or tendency based entirely upon material interests" *(Oxford Eng. Dict.)*. There is a vast range of philosophies based on materialism, often embracing the philosophy of Western science, including determinism, or predetermination, the view that events occur by natural law and the results can be the only ones possible.

MATERIALIST BELIEFS

1. I believe that all religious endeavor is a waste of time and energy, that there is no God, and all so-called paranormal or psychic phenomena are quackery and superstition.

   ❒ DO BELIEVE ❒ DO NOT BELIEVE ❒ ONCE BELIEVED ❒ UNFAMILIAR

2. I believe that there is no such thing as the soul; death of the body is death of the mind, and there is no reincarnation or afterlife.

   ❒ DO BELIEVE ❒ DO NOT BELIEVE ❒ ONCE BELIEVED ❒ UNFAMILIAR

3. I believe that the material universe, governed by natural laws and chance, is the ultimate and only reality and that all apparently nonmaterial substances, such as mind, are explicable as modifications of matter.

   ❒ DO BELIEVE ❒ DO NOT BELIEVE ❒ ONCE BELIEVED ❒ UNFAMILIAR

4. I believe that science is the means of understanding all the secrets of the universe, for all phenomena are the result of material pro-

cesses which are governed by predictable, natural laws.

❒ DO BELIEVE ❒ DO NOT BELIEVE ❒ ONCE BELIEVED ❒ UNFAMILIAR

5. I believe that free will is an illusion; that each event, being a fortuitous combination of particles and forces, can only happen in one way and is thus predetermined (deterministic materialism).

❒ DO BELIEVE ❒ DO NOT BELIEVE ❒ ONCE BELIEVED ❒ UNFAMILIAR

6. I believe that there is no objective "higher purpose" in life, no absolute basis for ethics or morality and no retribution for sin or reward for virtue. Seeking pleasure and avoiding pain are the only two goals rational men will pursue—what pleases me is good, what pains me is bad (hedonistic materialism).

❒ DO BELIEVE ❒ DO NOT BELIEVE ❒ ONCE BELIEVED ❒ UNFAMILIAR

7. I believe that all novel qualities of existence can be derived from changing material conditions—that men's mental and spiritual life, their ideas and aims, reflect their material conditions of existence (dialectical materialism).

❒ DO BELIEVE ❒ DO NOT BELIEVE ❒ ONCE BELIEVED ❒ UNFAMILIAR

8. I believe that though not all things consist of matter or its modifications, whatever exists can be satisfactorily explained in natural terms (modified or naturalistic materialism).

❒ DO BELIEVE ❒ DO NOT BELIEVE ❒ ONCE BELIEVED ❒ UNFAMILIAR

9. I believe that man, the highest and most complex of the evolutionary process prevailing throughout the universe, may continue to evolve into an even more perfect being or higher species (utopian materialism).

❒ DO BELIEVE ❒ DO NOT BELIEVE ❒ ONCE BELIEVED ❒ UNFAMILIAR

COMMUNISM

Communism emerged around the turn of the twentieth century in present-day Russia as "a hypothetical stage of socialism, as formulated by Marx, Engels, Lenin and others, to be characterized by a classless and stateless society and the equal distribution of economic goods and to be achieved by revolutionary and dictatorial, rather than gradualistic, means" *(Webster's New World Dictionary)*. Communism is proudly atheistic and seeks to liberate mankind from superstition and "spiritual bondage."

COMMUNIST BELIEFS

1. I believe there is no God and no knowable providential order, that this physical world is the only reality, physical beings are the only real beings, and reason is man's highest faculty.

   ❒ DO BELIEVE ❒ DO NOT BELIEVE ❒ ONCE BELIEVED ❒ UNFAMILIAR

2. I believe religion is "the opiate of the people," an exploiters' tool of oppression that should be eliminated and its resources redirected to improving world conditions to lift mankind from misery.

   ❒ DO BELIEVE ❒ DO NOT BELIEVE ❒ ONCE BELIEVED ❒ UNFAMILIAR

3. I believe mysticism and religion are primitive and fraught with error, prejudice and superstition, and that modern science, based on materialism and empirical evidence, is the only respectable avenue to useful knowledge.

   ❒ DO BELIEVE ❒ DO NOT BELIEVE ❒ ONCE BELIEVED ❒ UNFAMILIAR

4. I believe that each person has but a single life and that death is final. Therefore, in this life we are to attain all that is deemed worthwhile and express our finer qualities in service to the greater social good.

   ❒ DO BELIEVE ❒ DO NOT BELIEVE ❒ ONCE BELIEVED ❒ UNFAMILIAR

5. I believe that as in the case of nature, history evolves in a continuous line from lower to higher forms, from tribalism, feudalism and capitalism to its final maturity in socialism, and that the collapse of capitalism and the establishment of socialism will usher in an age of peace and plenty, when state control will no longer be needed.

   ❒ DO BELIEVE ❒ DO NOT BELIEVE ❒ ONCE BELIEVED ❒ UNFAMILIAR

6. I believe that all men are created equal and are inherently good, and that distinctive attitudes, personalities and experiences are determined solely by one's environment; therefore, to uplift mankind, improve the environment.

   ❒ DO BELIEVE ❒ DO NOT BELIEVE ❒ ONCE BELIEVED ❒ UNFAMILIAR

7. I believe that the views expressed by our great Marxist revolutionaries represent the one and only correct world outlook, and

that it is imperative to overthrow the capitalist regimes, through violent revolution if necessary, to usher in a new order.

❒ DO BELIEVE ❒ DO NOT BELIEVE ❒ ONCE BELIEVED ❒ UNFAMILIAR

8. I believe that the world's wealth should be shared equally, and that unequal distribution caused by class distinctions, is the root of all social evils, driving men to greed, selfishness and exploitation. Economic necessity is the basic moving force in society.

❒ DO BELIEVE ❒ DO NOT BELIEVE ❒ ONCE BELIEVED ❒ UNFAMILIAR

9. I believe there is no knowable providential order, that death is permanent, that God does not exist and that the highest life is one of intense consciousness.

❒ DO BELIEVE ❒ DO NOT BELIEVE ❒ ONCE BELIEVED ❒ UNFAMILIAR

EXISTENTIALISM

Existentialism arose in Europe in the mid-nineteenth century. It teaches that God does not exist, or cannot be known, and affirms individuality and freedom. Stress is on transcendence of the mundane world through exaltation of will, the meaninglessness of existence and the absence of a substratum upon which to base truths or values. Man simply exists, free to create his own meaning in life. It is, however, impotant to bear in mind that there is a vital strain of religious, or quasi-religious, existentialism as well.

EXISTENTIALIST BELIEFS

1. I believe that there is no knowable providential order in nature or in the larger realm of existence or cosmos.

❒ DO BELIEVE ❒ DO NOT BELIEVE ❒ ONCE BELIEVED ❒ UNFAMILIAR

2. I believe that the being of man is ultimately meaningless, which is to say that man knows not why he exists and cannot rise to the knowledge of his destiny.

❒ DO BELIEVE ❒ DO NOT BELIEVE ❒ ONCE BELIEVED ❒ UNFAMILIAR

3. I believe that each man is an individual and should break his dependence on society and rely solely upon his own individual life, spirit, personality and thought.

❒ DO BELIEVE ❒ DO NOT BELIEVE ❒ ONCE BELIEVED ❒ UNFAMILIAR

4. I believe that immortality is not a condition of man. Death is quite realistically seen as an ultimate end and radical fact which cannot be overcome. Man should not tolerate even an anguished hope of personal survival.

❒ DO BELIEVE ❒ DO NOT BELIEVE ❒ ONCE BELIEVED ❒ UNFAMILIAR

5. I believe that harmony and security in human relationships are impossible to achieve, and the only satisfactory attitude toward others is based upon explicit recognition of this fact.

❒ DO BELIEVE ❒ DO NOT BELIEVE ❒ ONCE BELIEVED ❒ UNFAMILIAR

6. I believe that "Evil is not an illusion. It is not the effect of passions which might be cured, or a fear which might be overcome. It is not an ignorance which might be enlightened. Evil cannot be redeemed" (Sartre).

❒ DO BELIEVE ❒ DO NOT BELIEVE ❒ ONCE BELIEVED ❒ UNFAMILIAR

7. I believe that God does not exist.

❒ DO BELIEVE ❒ DO NOT BELIEVE ❒ ONCE BELIEVED ❒ UNFAMILIAR

8. I believe that the highest and best life is lived in the intensity of being fully conscious of the life experience. This experience necessarily contains problems, struggle, suffering and conflict. This is man's unalterable reality within which his free creative action and choice gives birth to the fullness of consciousness which would otherwise be deadened by security and contentment.

❒ DO BELIEVE ❒ DO NOT BELIEVE ❒ ONCE BELIEVED ❒ UNFAMILIAR

9. I believe that the soul of man is not whole without such unpleasant things as death, anxiety, guilt, fear and trembling, and despair. It would be the final error of reason to deny that these emotions exist, or to strive to manipulate them out of existence. Therefore, it can be said that nothing can be accomplished by denying that man is essentially a troubled being, except to make more trouble.

❒ DO BELIEVE ❒ DO NOT BELIEVE ❒ ONCE BELIEVED ❒ UNFAMILIAR

SECULAR HUMANISM

Humanism is "a modern, nontheistic, rationalist movement that holds that man is capable of self-fulfillment, ethical conduct, etc., without recourse to supernaturalism" *(Webster's New World Dictionary)*. By the term *secular* this stream distinguishes itself from theistic (Christian) humanism. Secular humanism evolved out of 18th-century rejection of revealed Christianity and the emergence of modern science and free thought. Modern secular humanists condemn and refute all assertions of divine or paranormal phenomena.

SECULAR HUMANIST BELIEFS

1. I believe in nontheism, as there is no rational proof for the existence of God, and do not delude myself with thoughts of a Supreme Being.

   ❐ DO BELIEVE ❐ DO NOT BELIEVE ❐ ONCE BELIEVED ❐ UNFAMILIAR

2. I believe that traditional religions and faiths preach false doctrines, are oppressive and lead their followers toward ignorance, bigotry and dogmatism, and that it is my duty to be actively skeptical of, and challenge the illusions of orthodox religions and all attempts to explain the world in supernatural terms.

   ❐ DO BELIEVE ❐ DO NOT BELIEVE ❐ ONCE BELIEVED ❐ UNFAMILIAR

3. I believe in the preservation and enhancement of the human species as my ultimate concern, and in the global human family, which must preserve the Earth for future generations through developing a secular, planetary morality and system of law.

   ❐ DO BELIEVE ❐ DO NOT BELIEVE ❐ ONCE BELIEVED ❐ UNFAMILIAR

4. I believe that living a good, moral life is the best means for individual and collective happiness and that morality has a rational, secular basis.

   ❐ DO BELIEVE ❐ DO NOT BELIEVE ❐ ONCE BELIEVED ❐ UNFAMILIAR

5. I believe in expanding human rights and intellectual and moral freedom, and in secular democracy, with strict separation of church and state, as the means of eliminating discrimination and attaining equality and justice for all.

   ❐ DO BELIEVE ❐ DO NOT BELIEVE ❐ ONCE BELIEVED ❐ UNFAMILIAR

6. I believe in the development of the creative human potential through education in the arts and sciences, and in the paramount importance of free inquiry in an open, pluralistic, universalist society.

   ❐ DO BELIEVE ❐ DO NOT BELIEVE ❐ ONCE BELIEVED ❐ UNFAMILIAR

7. I believe in the application and development of reason and modern science as the highest means to understanding the universe, solving human problems and enabling each individual to realize his greatest potential.

   ❒ DO BELIEVE ❒ DO NOT BELIEVE ❒ ONCE BELIEVED ❒ UNFAMILIAR

8. I believe in striving for fulfillment and happiness in this life and reject all notions of reincarnation and afterlife as false and baseless, seeking my fullest capacity as a human being here and now, serving others and creating a better, more just world.

   ❒ DO BELIEVE ❒ DO NOT BELIEVE ❒ ONCE BELIEVED ❒ UNFAMILIAR

9. I believe in Darwin's theory of evolution as scientific fact, and in naturalism, holding that the known world is all that exists, and that it has no supernatural or spiritual creation, control or significance.

   ❒ DO BELIEVE ❒ DO NOT BELIEVE ❒ ONCE BELIEVED ❒ UNFAMILIAR

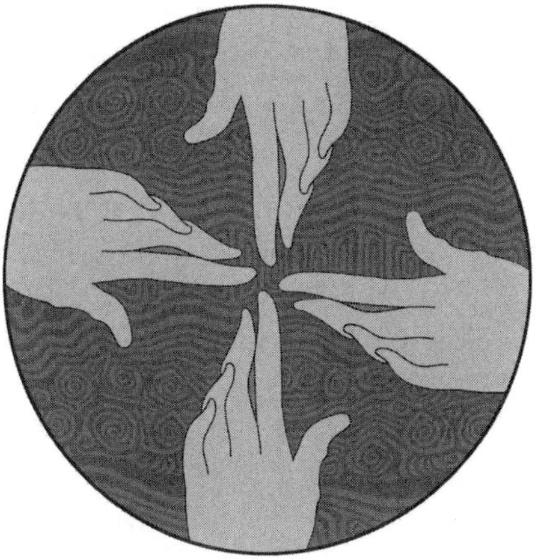

Religious Comparisons

Comparing Eastern and Western Views

In the following analysis, using one of several common religious categorizations, we compare the Eastern religions with the Western ones on many points of belief. The Eastern religions are Hinduism, Jainism, Buddhism and Sikhism. The Western religions are Judaism, Zoroastrianism, Christianity and Islam. We can see immediately that there is a vast difference between Eastern and Western religions, with the Eastern goals being unitive and introspective and the Western goals being dualistic, extroverted. The Eastern mind tends to see God everywhere, in all things, and to see everything as sacred. The Western mind considers it heresy to believe that God pervades all things, and makes a strong difference between what is sacred and what is profane. In general we notice the Eastern holding to karma, reincarnation and liberation, the Western postulating a single life for the soul, followed by reward or punishment.

Keep in mind that this is not a comprehensive comparison, as it does not take into account the East Asia religions—Taoism, Confucianism and Shinto.

To discover your own belief patterns, take a pencil and put a check mark next to the view—Eastern or Western—which is closest to your own belief on each of the subjects.

We might note here that the Eastern religions described here all originated in India, and that Jainism, Buddhism and Sikhism were offshoots of Hinduism. Among the Western faiths, Judaism, Christianity and Islam all share a common root in Abraham, and in recent times the term *Abrahamic* has been coined to denote these three world religions. Naturally there are important exceptions to the views expressed (for example, Buddhism does not believe in a Personal God). Nevertheless these broad generalities are useful, as they give a scholarly window into the East and the West.

DIFFERENCES

On Creation

EASTERN VIEW: The universe exists in endless cycles of creation, preservation and destruction. There is no absolute end to the world, neither is there a duality of God and world, but a unity.

WESTERN VIEW: The world was created by God and at some point in the future will be forever destroyed by Him. He is distinct from it, and rules it from above. Stresses a dualistic nature of the world.

On the True God

EASTERN VIEW: There is but one true and absolute God. All religions speak of Him. All souls are destined to receive God's grace through a process that takes them through diverse experiences on many paths according to their understanding, temperament and maturity of soul. God is pure Love and Consciousness but may be terrifying as well.

WESTERN VIEW: There is but one true God and one true religion. Those who accept it will enjoy God's grace; all others, unless they repent and come to my God, will suffer eternally in hell. God is loving as well as wrathful.

On Proof of God's Existence

EASTERN VIEW: Proof of God's existence and love lies in direct communion, and indirectly through enlightened gurus, the God-Realized men of all ages, and the revealed scriptures they bring forth in every age.

WESTERN VIEW: Proof of God's love and promise for man is in the person of His Prophet and in His unchanging and unique revealed scripture.

On Personal Experience of God

EASTERN VIEW: Personal, inner and often mystical experience of God is the crux of religion. Man can and ultimately must know God during earthly life. Individually oriented and introspective.

WESTERN VIEW: It is presumptuous for man to seek personal knowledge of God. The linchpin of religion is not experience but belief and faith, coupled with a virtuous life. Socially oriented and extroverted.

On the Path to God, and Divine Judgment

EASTERN VIEW: Man is free to choose his form of worship, for all paths lead ultimately to God. Sin is only of the mind, not of the soul, which is pure. There is no Judgment Day for God does not judge or punish. He lovingly guides all souls back to Himself.

WESTERN VIEW: Only one path leads to God, others are false and futile. Everyone must convert to the one true religion. Failing that, the soul, laden with sin, will be damned on Judgment Day.

On Man's Plight

EASTERN VIEW: Man's plight is but his soul's immaturity. He is ever on a progressive path which leads from ignorance to knowledge, from death to immortality.

WESTERN VIEW: Man's plight is due to disobedience to God's will, to nonbelief and nonacceptance of His law.

On Hell

EASTERN VIEW: God is Love and is inextricably one with the soul, guiding it through karmas into the fulfillment of dharma and finally to *moksha,* liberation. Hell is a lower astral realm, not a physical place; nor is it eternal. Hell exists as a period of karmic intensity or suffering, a state of mind in life or between lives.

WESTERN VIEW: On Judgment Day the physical body of every soul that ever lived is brought to life, and God consigns pure souls to heaven and sinners to hell, a physical place where the body burns without being consumed and one suffers the anguish of knowing he will never be with God.

On Evil

EASTERN VIEW: There is no intrinsic evil. All is good. All is God. No force in the world or in man opposes God, though the veiling instinctive-intellectual mind keeps us from knowledge of Him.

WESTERN VIEW: There is indeed genuine evil in the world, a living force which opposes the will of God. This evil is embodied in Satan and his demons, and partially in man as one of his tendencies.

On Virtue and Salvation

EASTERN VIEW: Virtuous conduct and right belief are the foundation stones of religious life, the first step toward higher mystical communion. Liberation requires knowledge and personal attainment, not mere belief.

WESTERN VIEW: If one obeys God's commands for a moral and ethical life and believes in Him and in His Prophet—for example, Moses, Jesus, Mohammed or Zoroaster—salvation is assured.

On the Origin of Religion

EASTERN VIEW: Religion is cosmic, eternal, transcending human history, which is cyclical. Stress is placed on revelation of God's presence in the here and now.

WESTERN VIEW: Religion is historical, beginning with a prophet or event. Stress is placed on the past and on the rewards or punishments of the future. History is linear, never to be repeated.

Nature of Doctrines

EASTERN VIEW: Doctrines tend to be subtle, complex and

even paradoxical. Freedom to worship and to believe in a variety of ways is predominant. Other paths are accepted as God's divine will at work. Universal and tolerant.

WESTERN VIEW: Doctrines tend to be simple, clear and rational. Worship and belief are formalized, exacting and required. Other paths are endured, but not honored. Exclusivist and dogmatic.

On Liberation and Enlightenment

EASTERN VIEW: The goals of enlightenment and liberation are to be found in this life, within the context of time, within man himself. Doctrines may be dual or nondual, *dvaitic* or *advaitic.*

WESTERN VIEW: Salvation comes at the end of the world, the end of time, and has nothing to do with enlightenment. Strictly dualistic, *dvaitic.* Mystical sects, though minor, provide exceptions.

On the Path to Sainthood

EASTERN VIEW: Path to saintliness is through self-discipline, purification, concentration and contemplation. Value is placed on ascetic ideals, individual *sādhana,* yoga and superconscious awakening.

WESTERN VIEW: Path to saintliness is through self-sacrifice, submission to God and concern for the welfare of others. Value is placed on good works, social concerns and scriptural study, with little emphasis on yoga or asceticism.

On the Nature of Worship

EASTERN VIEW: Worship is individual, highly ritualistic and meditative, centering around the holy temple and the home shrine all days of the week.

WESTERN VIEW: Worship is congregational, simple in its rituals, centering around the church, synagogue or mosque, mostly on a Sabbath day.

SIMILARITIES

On God and Devas

EASTERN VIEW: Belief in a Supreme Deity, maker of all souls and all things, and in lesser Deities and Mahādevas.

WESTERN VIEW: Belief in a Supreme Deity, maker of all souls and all things, and in the angels and celestial hosts.

On Salvation and God's Will

EASTERN VIEW: Salvation is through strict obedience to God's will and the descent of His grace through the enlightened spiritual preceptor.

WESTERN VIEW: Salvation is through strict obedience to God's will, usually through a messiah, prophet or priest.

On Good Conduct

EASTERN VIEW: To live a virtuous and moral life is essential to further spiritual progress, for *adharmic* thoughts, deeds and words keep us from knowledge of God's closeness.

WESTERN VIEW: Religion must be based on ethical and moral conduct, for their opposite leads us away from God.

On the Destiny of the Soul

EASTERN VIEW: The purpose of life is to evolve, through experience, into our spiritual destiny. Things of the world are not the purpose of the world.

WESTERN VIEW: Man's destiny lies beyond this world, which is but an opportunity for earning eternal joy or suffering.

On the Nature of Reality

EASTERN VIEW: There is more to reality than we experience with the five senses. The soul is immortal, deathless and eternal, ultimately merging in God.

WESTERN VIEW: There is more to reality than the things of this world. The soul is immortal, deathless and eternal, living forever in God's presence or separated from Him.

Comparing Judaism, Christianity and Islam

The similarities between these three Abrahamic religions are stronger than their differences, though historically it is the differences that have been stressed. They each believe in a single life, followed by heaven or hell. They agree that God is opposed by evil, by Satan, who tempts and destroys sinners by causing disobedience to God's law. They are all prophet-oriented, though Christianity is the only one to make the prophet divine. They believe in their religion as the one and only true religion, and that nonbelievers are condemned, though Judaism is somewhat more tolerant or universal, believing God judges all men of all religions by their actions. These three Biblical religions are strongly monotheistic and dualistic, believing man is eternally separate from God and that man's highest destiny is in heaven. Together they rely not so much on inner experience or mystical contact and guidance, as on sacred rites, on faith and belief, and on good works to guide man Godward. Each believes that God has a special covenant with its members, though the terms differ. They each bury their dead, anticipating that the physical body will one day be resurrected on the earth, rising from the grave on Judgment Day.

On the True Religion

JUDAISM: There is but one true religion, Judaism, and one revealed scripture, the *Torah,* which includes the *Old Testament* and the *Talmud.*

CHRISTIANITY: There is but one true religion, Christianity, and one scripture—the *Holy Bible, Old* and *New Testaments.*

ISLAM: The one true faith is Islam, and the *Koran* is the highest revealed scripture, but other books are honored as revealed too, including the *Bible* and certain Hindu scriptures.

On Genesis and Original Sin

JUDAISM: Example of Adam, his temptation and fall from grace and in original sin. Some early and more of modern religious thinks tend to interpret this narrative as an allegory of human condition.

CHRISTIANITY: The same, but taking Adam's story literally.

ISLAM: Same, but Allah forgave Adam. Therefore, there is no original sin.

On the Proof of God's Power

JUDAISM: Such proof can be seen in the historic Exodus.

CHRISTIANITY: Proof of God's power lies in Christ's resurrection.

ISLAM: Proof of God's power is in the *Koran* itself.

On Man's Obligation to God

JUDAISM: Jews are obligated exclusively to Yahweh, since He delivered them out of Egypt.

CHRISTIANITY: Man is obligated to God since He sacrificed His Son for man's sins.

ISLAM: There exists no special obligation; avoidance of hell is man's motivation.

On the Means to Salvation

JUDAISM: Salvation is through strict adherence to the Law as stated in the *Torah.*

CHRISTIANITY: Salvation is through acceptance of Christ as Lord and Savior.

ISLAM: Salvation is through total submission to Allah.

Comparing Hinduism and Christianity

In 1993, our editors of HINDUISM TODAY were contacted by *Christianity Today* magazine to be interviewed for a major story called Hindus in America. Thus began a series of dialogs that added to their article crucial and often corrective insights to dispel common myths and misinformation about the world's oldest religion. Perhaps most significantly, they agreed to publish our own nine fundamental Hindu beliefs. The editors of *Christianity Today* counter-composed nine parallel Christian convictions, written just before press time in a series of grueling sessions by the best theologians they could assemble. The resulting point-counterpoint—whose brevity is both its strength and its weakness—summarizes the cosmic perspective of two of the world's largest faiths.

1. On the Word of God

HINDUS believe in the divinity of the *Vedas*, the world's most ancient scripture, and venerate the *Āgamas* as equally revealed. These primordial hymns are God's word and the bedrock of Sanātana Dharma, the eternal religion which has neither beginning nor end.

CHRISTIANS believe that the *Bible* is the uniquely inspired and fully trustworthy word of God. It is the final authority for Christians in matters of belief and practice, and though it was written long ago, it continues to speak to believers today.

2. On the Nature of God

HINDUS believe in a one, all-pervasive Supreme Being who is both immanent and transcendent, both Creator and Unmanifest Reality.

CHRISTIANS believe in one God in three persons. He is distinct from his creation, yet intimately involved with it as its sustainer and redeemer.

3. On Creation

HINDUS believe that the universe undergoes endless cycles of creation, preservation and dissolution.

CHRISTIANS believe that the world was created once by the divine will, was corrupted by sin, yet under God's providence moves toward final perfection.

4. On the Consequence of Deeds

HINDUS believe in karma, the law of cause and effect by which each individual creates his own destiny by his thoughts, words and deeds.

CHRISTIANS believe that, through God's grace and favor, lost sinners are rescued from the guilt, power and eternal consequences of their evil thoughts, words and deeds.

5. On Reincarnation and Eternal Life

HINDUS believe that the soul reincarnates, evolving through many births until all karmas have been resolved, and *moksha*, spiritual knowledge and liberation from the cycle of rebirth, is attained. Not a single soul will be eternally deprived of this destiny.

CHRISTIANS believe that it is appointed for human beings to die once and after that face judgment. In Adam's sin, the human race was spiritually alienated from God, and that those who are called by God and respond to his grace will have eternal life. Those who persist in rebellion will be lost eternally.

6. On the Spirit Worlds

HINDUS believe that divine beings exist in unseen worlds and that temple worship, rituals, sacraments as well as personal devotionals create a communion with these devas and Gods.

CHRISTIANS believe that spirit beings inhabit the universe, some good and some evil, but worship is due to God alone.

7. On Religious Preceptors

HINDUS believe that a spiritually awakened master, or *satguru,* is essential to know the Transcendent Absolute, as are personal discipline, good conduct, purification, pilgrimage, self-inquiry and meditation.

CHRISTIANS believe that God has given us a clear revelation of Himself in Jesus and the sacred Scriptures. He has empowered by his Spirit prophets, apostles, evangelists, and pastors who are teachers charged to guide us into faith and holiness in accordance with his Word.

8. On Reverence for Life

HINDUS believe that all life is sacred, to be loved and revered, and therefore practice ahiṁsā, "noninjury."

CHRISTIANS believe that life is to be highly esteemed but that it must be subordinated in the service of Biblical love and justice.

9. On the Path to Salvation

HINDUS believe that no particular religion teaches the only way to salvation above all others, but that all genuine religious paths are facets of God's Pure Love and Light, deserving tolerance and understanding.

CHRISTIANS believe that Jesus is God incarnate and, therefore, the only sure path to salvation. Many religions may offer ethical and spiritual insights, but only Jesus is the Way, the Truth and the Life.

Comparing the Four Hindu Denominations

The spectrum of Hindu religiousness is found within four major sects or denominations: Śaivism, Śāktism, Vaishṇavism and Smārtism. Among these four streams there are certainly more similarities than differences. All four believe in karma and reincarnation and in a Supreme Being who is both form and pervades form, who creates, sustains and destroys the universe, only to create it again in unending cycles. They strongly declare the validity and importance of temple worship, in the three worlds of existence and the myriad Gods and devas residing in them. They concur that there is no intrinsic evil, that the cosmos is created out of God and is permeated by Him. They each believe in māyā (though their definitions differ somewhat), and in the liberation of the soul from rebirth, called *moksha*, as the goal of human existence. They believe in dharma and in ahiṁsā, noninjury, and in the need for a *satguru* to lead the soul toward Self Realization. They wear the sacred marks, *tilaka,* on their foreheads as sacred symbols, though each wears a distinct mark. Finally, they prefer cremation of the body upon death, believing that the soul will inhabit another body in the next life. While Hinduism has many sacred scriptures, all sects ascribe the highest authority to the *Vedas* and *Āgamas*, though their *Āgamas* differ somewhat. Here, now, is a brief comparison of these four denominations.

On the Personal God/Goddess

ŚAIVISM: Personal God and temple Deity is Śiva, neither male nor female. Lords Gaṇeśa and Kārttikeya are also worshiped.

ŚĀKTISM: Personal Goddess and temple Deity is Śrī Devī or Śakti, female, worshiped as Rājarājeśvarī, Pārvatī, Lakshmī, Sarasvatī, Kālī, Amman, etc. —the Divine Mother.

VAISHṆAVISM: Personal God and temple Deity is Vishṇu, male. His incarnations as Rāma and Kṛishṇa are also worshiped, as well as His divine consort, Rādhā Rāṇī.

SMĀRTISM: Personal God and temple Deity is Īśvara, male or female, worshiped as Vishṇu, Śiva, Śakti, Gaṇeśa and Sūrya or any Deity of devotee's choice, e.g., Kumāra or Kṛishṇa.

On the Nature of Śakti

ŚAIVISM: Śakti is God Śiva's inseparable power and manifest will, energy or mind.

ŚĀKTISM: Śakti is an active, immanent Being, separate from a quiescent and remote Śiva.

VAISHṆAVISM: No special importance is given to Śakti. However, there are parallels wherein the divine consorts are conceived as the inseparable powers of Vishṇu and His incarnations: e.g., Kṛishṇa's Rādhā Rāṇī and Rāma's Sitā.

SMĀRTISM: Śakti is a divine form of Īśvara. It is God's manifesting power.

On the Nature of Personal God

ŚAIVISM: God Śiva is pure love and compassion, immanent and transcendent, pleased by our purity and *sādhana.*

ŚĀKTISM: The Goddess Śakti is both compassionate and terrifying, pleasing and wrathful, assuaged by sacrifice and submission.

VAISHṆAVISM: God Vishṇu is loving and beautiful, the object of man's devotion, pleased by our service and surrender.

SMĀRTISM: Īśvara appears as a human-like Deity according to devotees' loving worship, which is sometimes considered a rudimentary self-purifying practice.

On the Doctrine of Avatāra

ŚAIVISM: There are no divine earthly incarnations.

ŚĀKTISM: The Divine Mother does incarnate in this world.

VAISHṆAVISM: Vishṇu has ten or more incarnations.

SMĀRTISM: All Deities may assume earthly incarnations.

On the Soul and God

ŚAIVISM: God Śiva is one with the soul. The soul must realize this *advaitic* Truth by God Śiva's grace.

ŚĀKTISM: The Divine Mother, Śakti, is mediatrix, bestowing *advaitic moksha* on those who worship Her.

VAISHṆAVISM: God and soul are eternally distinct. Through Lord Vishṇu's grace, the soul's destiny is to worship and enjoy God.

SMĀRTISM: Īśvara and man are in reality Absolute Brahman. Within māyā, the soul and Īśvara appear as two. Jñāna dispels the illusion.

Spiritual Practice

ŚAIVISM: With bhakti as a base, emphasis is placed on *sādhana, tapas* and yoga. Ascetic.

ŚĀKTISM: Emphasis is on bhakti and tantra, sometimes occult, practices. Ascetic-occult.

VAISHṆAVISM: Emphasis is on supreme bhakti or surrender, called *prapatti*. Generally devotional and nonascetic.

SMĀRTISM: Preparatory *sādhanas* are bhakti, karma, rāja yoga. Highest path is through knowledge, leading to jñāna.

Major Scriptures

ŚAIVISM: *Vedas, Śaiva Āgamas* and *Śaiva Purāṇas.*

ŚĀKTISM: *Vedas, Śākta Āgamas (Tantras)* and *Purāṇas.*

VAISHṆAVISM: *Vedas, Vaishṇava Āgamas, Purāṇas* and the *Itihāsas (Rāmāyaṇa* and *Mahābhārata,* especially the *Bhagavad Gītā).*

SMĀRTISM: *Vedas, Āgamas* and classical *smṛiti—Purāṇas, Itihāsas,* especially the *Bhagavad Gītā,* etc.

Regions of Influence

ŚAIVISM: Geographically widespread, strongest in South and North India, Nepal and Sri Lanka.

ŚĀKTISM: Geographically widespread, most prominent in North India, especially Bengal and Assam.

VAISHṆAVISM: Geographically widespread, especially strong throughout India, North and South.

SMĀRTISM: Geographically widespread, most prominent in North and South India.

CONCLUSION

This concludes our comparison of Hinduism's four prominent denominations, and of other religions, faiths and philosophies. There are many more indigenous, tribal groups who follow similar paths with unique names, and there are many more paths yet to be discovered in the future. This chapter can be considered an outline, affording to careful readers a simple overview of those intangible human beliefs which, in all their variety, are at the root of attitudes and behavior which, over time, create culture. Hopefully it could do more; perhaps mark the beginning of discovering your own place in this grand scheme. Conversion is easy into any one of these forms of worship, practice and attainment. It is happening all the time. All souls on the path to perfection eventually commit themselves by choosing a preceptor, one who has gone before. Journeying through life without a preceptor is like traversing the ocean without a map or a compass. Even climbing the slopes of the Himalayas, a Sherpa is needed to safely guide. Compare your beliefs, as they are today, with all those cataloged in this synopsis, and come to terms with the supreme dedication that each of these paths demands of its followers. Having done this, declare boldly who you are to your own self. Claim your spiritual identity,

your preceptor and the religious faith to which you find you belong. Then follow your chosen path with all your heart. Give it your full devotion, energy and loyalty in fullfilling its goals. True seekers on the path hoping for genuine attainment do not wander from path to path, school to school, preceptor to preceptor, because it is known that indecision inhibits all spiritual growth.

Dharmāntarasya Shaṭpadī

धर्मान्तरस्य षट्पदी

Six Steps Toward Conversion

Six Steps Toward Conversion

TO GAIN CLEAR SUBCONSCIOUS MEMORY patterns of the past for his future religious life, the individual seeking to enter Hinduism must examine and reject those beliefs of his previous religion or philosophy which differ from those of the Hindu sect he wishes to join. Then he must examine and accept the Hindu beliefs which are new to him.

If he was confirmed or otherwise initiated in another religion or ideology, he must effect formal severance from his previous religion or faith before formally entering the Hindu religion through the the name-giving sacrament. Full religious conversion includes informing one's former religious or philosophical leader, preferably through a personal meeting, that the individual is entering a new religion.

Further, ethical conversion means that the parents and relatives, too, understand the momentous change that has taken place. This societal recognition, along with initiation, vow-taking and legal change of name on passport and all documents, signifies true conversion on all levels of being. Nothing less will suffice. Even within Hinduism itself there are formal ceremonies and soul-searching requirements for Hindus converting from one denomination to another, as when a Śaivite becomes a Vaishṇavite or a Smārta becomes a Śākta, accomplished, in part, in some communities by writing with a golden needle the divine mantras on the convert's tongue.

Before explaining the steps of conversion, we want to advise Hindu societies worldwide to make close inquiries of adoptives and converts as to their fulfilling the six steps of conversion to open the doors to the *ardha*-Hindu into the fullness of the sectarian faith of his or her choice. Detailed below are the procedures for religious reconciliation that we have practiced for several decades in our own fellowship, guiding sincere souls who have initiated a process of self-conversion which leads from a severance from their former faith into Śaivite Hinduism.

1. JOINING A HINDU COMMUNITY

First and most importantly, the devotee mixes socially and earns acceptance into an established Hindu community. The devotee should be worshiping regularly at the community's *satsaṅgas* or temples, making yearly pilgrimages, performing daily pūjā and *sādhanas* within the home and seriously striving to live up to the culture defined in the 365 Nandinātha Sūtras of *Living with Śiva*, which is a complete statement of Hindu values and culture.

2. POINT-COUNTERPOINT

The devotee undertakes certain assigned Hindu studies and a formal analysis of former religions, denominations, *sampradāyas* or philosophical systems. He or she writes a point-counterpoint comparing Hinduism with each such school of thought to demonstrate a thorough grasp of the similarities and differences. Part two of this assignment is to complete a written analysis of all former pledges or vows, indicating when and why each point mentioned in those vows was abandoned. This point-counterpoint is then presented to a Hindu elder for his review and comment.

3. SEVERING FROM FORMER MENTORS

If formal severance is required, the devotee returns to the former institution and attends services or lectures for a few weeks. Then, accompanied by a relative or friend as a witness, he or she meets personally with the former mentor. In the case of a married person, the spouse is preferred as a witness. The devotee explains that he will be joining the Hindu religion and wishes to sever ties with this church or institution. For an intimate understanding of severance, I would like to share with you a letter that one of my family counselors wrote to a potential convert from Catholicism: "Your point-counterpoint will do much for you in preparing you to meet your former priest to convince him that an inner transformation has occurred and you are indeed a Hindu soul, not a Catholic. This is a face-to-face meeting with the religious leader of your former faith or his successor. This step is done on a very personal level, as the fire of severance takes place during this confrontation. It cannot be done through the mail or on the telephone.

"During this meeting, your conviction and clear understanding of both religions will allow your priest to see the thoughtfulness and sincerity of the decision you have made. A letter of release can, many times, be obtained before you leave his office when he sees clearly that you have completely abandoned the Catholic faith. This letter validates your personal release and clears the way for your formal entrance into Hinduism in all three worlds. It is an essential experience and document necessary for your *nāmakaraṇa saṁskāra.*"

We have many letters from Catholic priests, even archbishops, attesting to full conversion to Hinduism on the part of their former parishioners. In the case of formal religions, the devotee requests a letter of release, as an apostate (such as with the Catholic Church) or as an inactive (as in most Protestant Christian denominations). If the religious leader grants a verbal severance but will not convey it in writing, the witness to the interview writes a letter stating what took place. This letter is later given to the guiding elder of the Hindu community which the devotee seeks to fully join.

Even if there is no granting of severance, verbally or in writing, the conversion is still considered complete, based on the canon law of the Catholic church (and which applies to other faiths in principle, such as Judaism) that someone who adopts another religion is, *ipso facto,* an apostate. In cases where there has been no formal commitment, such as in nonreligious schools of thought, an inner severance may be effected through heartfelt conversation with former mentors of that school in which the devotee shares his or her true convictions.

4. ADOPTING A HINDU NAME

The devotee then proceeds to have a legal change of name. The new name is placed on his or her passport, driver's license and all important financial and legal instruments, including credit cards, library cards and bank accounts. Even before formal entrance to Hinduism, devotees are encouraged to begin using their Hindu names at all times.

5. THE NĀMAKARAṆA SAṂSKĀRA

The name-giving sacrament can be held at nearly any Hindu temple. Before the *nāmakaraṇa saṁskāra,* the devotee informs family, relatives and close friends of his or her name change and intended entrance into Hinduism. At the sacred name-giving rite, the Hindu name is received, vows are taken and a certificate is signed, documenting the former name and the new name, place of ceremony and signature of the priest and at least three witnesses. This sacrament marks the formal entrance into a particular sect of Hinduism, through the acceptance and blessings of established members and the blessings of Gods and devas invoked through rites performed by an authorized Hindu priest.

When seeking out a priest who will perform the name-giving rite, it is necessary to approach someone from within the sect that you wish to enter. Most priests will be familiar with how to perform the ritual; but if not, here are a few guidelines. More information will be posted on our Website at www.himalayanacademy.com/basics/conversion/.

Arrangements must be made ahead of time. In summary, a *homa* (fire ceremony) is begun, with the supplicant sitting near the fire. He tells his old name and new name to the priest, along with his birthstar, *nakshatra*. When reciting the *saṅkalpa* (pronouncement of purpose), the priest intones the new name. A large tray of uncooked rice has been prepared. At an auspicious point in the ritual, the priest asks the participant to read aloud his declaration of loyalty to Hinduism. Then he is asked to recite his new name three times. After each recitation, the priest and the congregation proclaim, *Tatha astu*, meaning, "Be it so." Finally, the devotee is directed to write his new name in the tray of rice. The certificate is then signed by the devotee and witnesses.

On the day of this sacred occasion, the devotee should bring an offering basket of incense, fruits, a husked coconut, rock sugar, loose flowers and a beautiful flower garland for Lord Gaṇeśa. *Dakshiṇā*, a love offering for the priest, is a traditional appreciation of his services in bringing the seeker into the religion. A generous *dakshiṇā*, a sum of US$900 or more, is appropriate by year-2000 standards in the US, depending upon the number of priests attending. It is estimated that such a Vedic ceremony will take one to four hours and require many more hours of strict preparations. The presiding priest would be given $301 or more, his second helper $201 and other helpers $101. Traditionally, cash is wrapped in a betel leaf or its equivalent and handed personally to the priests right after the ceremony.

Since this is a once-in-a-lifetime happening, the cost of the giving should not be a consideration. Of course, when the rite is performed in a temple, the management should also be given $201 to $501 for the use of their facilities, which would be arranged with them in advance and could be paid by check. In general, generosity is preferred to miserliness when it comes to rewarding our priests for these enormously important sacred ceremonies and passages. Such appreciation in the form of equitable payment ensures the gratitude and good feelings of the priests for the life ahead. If more than one family member is receiving the *nāmakaraṇa saṁskāra,* the amount paid to the priests and the temple would not necessarily be increased. This depends on the protocol of the particular temple. Any reception held afterwards would, of course, involve additional costs. One may elect to give gifts to the temple, such as a picture of your guru and his books and other publications, in thanks for the assistance and services.

THE NĀMAKARAṆA CERTIFICATE

A sample *nāmakaraṇa* certificate is provided on the opposite page which can be photocopied (enlarged) to document a *nāmakaraṇa* held at any temple. Four originals of the certificate should be signed: one for the temple management to display, one for the devotee's records, one for one's guru and one for legal matters, such as immigration and travel. Each original is signed by the devotee, the priest, his assistant and at least three witnesses who are established members of the faith. From his original, the devotees should send photocopies to all friends and relatives. A copy of this significant document proving membership in the Hindu faith should always be kept with one's passport to respond to institutions that ask for proof of Hindu identity before allowing entrance to their premises, such as orthodox temples in India.

The *nāmakaraṇa* certificate is a legal document giving the name of the temple, home or hall where the ceremony was performed. It is proof of one's Hindu name that can be used for name changes on other documents, though ideally the name change should be legalized before the ceremony. In the United States a legal name change by court order is required to obtain a passport, and in some states it must be signed by a secretary of state. Each country has its own rules, so for these matters it is best to consult the proper authorities. For strength of character, commitment, loyalty and integrity, a double standard should be avoided at all costs, such as being a Hindu in the home and a non-Hindu to others by using the former name, or using a Hindu name on your driver's license but a non-Hindu name on your passport for international travel. This type of behavior reaps no spiritual benefits, but could reap harm to one's integrity.

Aum Gaṇeśa!

Nāmakaraṇa Saṁskāra

नामकरण संस्कार   நாமகரண சம்ஸ்காரம்

Hindu Name-Giving Sacrament

I, ______________________________,
Hindu Name of Devotee (Please Print)

formerly known as ______________________, having declared of my own volition acceptance of the principles of the Sanātana Dharma, and having formally severed all previous non-Hindu religious affiliations, attachments and commitments, hereby humbly petition entrance into the (❑ Śaiva ❑ Vaishṇava ❑ Śākta ❑ Smārta ❑ other) ______________ sect of the Hindu religion through the traditional *nāmakaraṇa saṁskāra* and plead for recognition by the community of devotees witnessing this sacred rite of this irrevocable adoption of or conversion to Hinduism. I have completed a study of the Hindu teachings and hereby proclaim my acceptance of the following nine beliefs of Hinduism and my promise to fulfill to the best of my ability the *pañcha nitya karmas:* worship, *upāsanā;* holy days, *utsava,* virtuous living, *dharma;* pilgrimage, *tīrthayātrā;* and rites of passage, *saṁskāra.* I now avow to the nine beliefs by reading them aloud. Aum.

1. I believe in the divinity of the *Vedas,* the world's most ancient scripture, and venerate the *Āgamas* as equally revealed. These primordial hymns are God's word and the bedrock of Sanātana Dharma, the eternal religion which has neither beginning nor end.
2. I believe in a one, all-pervasive Supreme Being who is both immanent and transcendent, both Creator and Unmanifest Reality.
3. I believe that the universe undergoes endless cycles of creation, preservation and dissolution.
4. I believe in *karma,* the law of cause and effect by which each individual creates his own destiny by his thoughts, words and deeds.
5. I believe that the soul reincarnates, evolving through many births until all *karmas* have been resolved, and *moksha,* spiritual knowledge and liberation from the cycle of rebirth, is attained. Not a single soul will be eternally deprived of this destiny.
6. I believe that divine beings exist in unseen worlds and that temple worship, rituals, sacraments as well as personal devotionals create a communion with these *devas* and Gods.
7. I believe that a spiritually awakened master, or *satguru,* is essential to know the Transcendent Absolute, as are personal discipline, good conduct, purification, pilgrimage, self-inquiry and meditation.
8. I believe that all life is sacred, to be loved and revered, and therefore practice *ahiṁsā,* "noninjury."
9. I believe that no particular religion teaches the only way to salvation above all others, but that all genuine religious paths are facets of God's Pure Love and Light, deserving tolerance and understanding.

Signature: former name: ____________________ *Hindu name:* ____________________

It is Hereby Certified

that this devotee, born in ______________________ on ____________, and now residing at______________________________, was at a *nāmakaraṇa samskāra* held at the temple known as ____________________, located in ____________________, on the auspicious day of ______________ duly given a Hindu name in accordance with the traditions of Sanātana Dharma before the Deity, the Mahādevas and the *devas* and the congregation of devotees. This person is thus bound eternally and immutably to the Hindu religion as a member of this most ancient faith with full rights of access to all public Hindu temples, shrines and institutions throughout the world from this day onward. Through this magical Vedic ceremony guardian *devas* have been invoked from the Antarloka to protect, guide and defend this devotee.

____________________ OFFICIATING PRIEST

____________________ ELDER WITNESS

____________________ ASSISTANT PRIEST

____________________ ELDER WITNESS

____________________ ELDER WITNESS

6. ANNOUNCING THE SEVERANCE AND NAME-GIVING

After the severance and name-giving, the devotee publishes a three-day announcement in a local newspaper stating that the name-change has been completed and that he or she has entered the Hindu religion through the *nāmakaraṇa saṁskāra.* The devotee should keep a copy of these announcements and all other documents related to the conversion (such as letters from attorneys and elders) as part of a dossier verifying the name-giving, which may be needed in the future, such as when seeking acceptance into a conservative Hindu organization, seeking permanent residency or citizenship in a foreign country or in other cases when the Hindu name may come into question. Similarly, many temples in India and other countries will ask to see the passport, name-giving certificate or other appropriate proof of Hindu identity before admitting devotees of non-Indian origin.

Real-Life Severance Letters And Other Personal Documents

ARCHDIOCESE OF CHICAGO

POST OFFICE BOX 1979

CHICAGO, ILLINOIS 60690

Office of the Chancellor
312/751-8220

January 12, 1979

Mr. Donald Charles Wharton, M.D.
601 East 32nd Street
Chicago, Illinois 60616

Dear Doctor Wharton:

In reply to your letter of December 31, 1978, I wish to inform you that the excommunication of which you speak in Canon 2314 of the Code of Canon Law is incurred ipso facto.

This means the excommunication is incurred by the very fact of apostasy and does not need the intervention of a bishop.

Sincerely,

Richard A. Rosemeyer

Rev. Msgr. Richard A. Rosemeyer
CHANCELLOR

RAR/bu

THE CHURCH OF JESUS CHRIST OF LATTER-DAY SAINTS
NOVATO FIRST WARD
MARIN STAKE
NOVATO, CALIFORNIA 94947

March 12, 1980

Nale Orta
P.O. Box 492
Novato, Ca. 94947

Dear Brother Orta:

In accordance with your wishes and the wishes of your Mother, a Bishop's Court was held March 5th, 1980. The decision of the court was to excommunicate you from the Church of Jesus Christ of Latter-Day Saints. All of the necessary paper work, including your membership records have been transferred to church headquarters in Salt Lake City.

Sincerely,

David W. Cox

Bishop David W. Cox

December 18, 1978

Dear Bob and Nancy,

Your letters seeking dismission from the Mendocino Presbyterian Church were read by the Session on December 12, 1978. They were received with much sadness, and much of the meeting was spent rereading and contemplating your words.

The Session appreciated the heartfelt and courteous presentations that must have been very painful for you to write.

By the authority stated in Article 82.18 of the Book of Discipline, with the Book of Order, the Session of the Mendocino Presbyterian Church does on December 12, 1978 release Robert Danz and Nancy Danz (nee Van Kuyl) from the Roll of Communicant Members of the Mendocino Presbyterian Church.

Although the Session was able to release you from the formal Roll of this church, it could not satisfy some of your other requests. The jurisdiction of the ruling body of this church ends with deletion of names from the Roll. The Session cannot alter the eternal sanctity of the Sacrament of Christian Baptism or nullify the claim of Jesus Christ upon His own chosen people. Nor can the Session provide particular rights to receive the Hindu sacraments that you desire.

Your reference to "heavenly overlords" and their jurisdiction over your religious life was not altogether understood, for the Christian Church regards Jesus Christ as the Only Savior and Lord over all creation.

Much of the Session's heartache had to do with its own sense of guilt at having somehow failed to meet your real needs. For those shortcomings, it asks your forgiveness. You have inspired some new thoughts and probably some new directions for the church, concerning the provision within the program for more opportunities for creative and private worship.

Your promise of continued prayer for this congregation was a comfort. Ours will, likewise, be faithfully with you and yours. You will be sorely missed, and your places among this church family will remain vacant, awaiting your return.

In Christ's service,

Lois B. Raymond, Clerk

Ronald R. Garton, Pastor

Mendocino Presbyterian Church

RONN GARTON, PASTOR BOX 105 MENDOCINO, CA 95460 707-937-5441

Zion Evangelical Church
3617 Fifth Avenue
Scottsbluff, Nebraska 69361

Rev. Nevin A. Haines, Pastor
Telephones: Church 632-8125
Parsonage 635-3343

March 15, 1979

TO: Sundari Peruman.

SUBJECT: Release from all church attachments.

Dear Sundari Peruman:

This letter releases you, who were formerly Kathrina Bauer, from all bonds and ties with this church and its Christian faith and doctrine, assumed through vows which you might have taken either verbally or written, or by parental vows and indoctrination through baptism, instruction in the home and confirmation.

The reason for this letter: (1) your own request, (2) your being unactive for a period of 46 years, and (3) your acceptance of and allegiance to faiths other than Christian.

Sincerely yours,

Nevin A. Haines
Rev. Nevin A. Haines,
by the authority vested in me as the pastor of Zion Evangelical Church, Scottsbluff, Nebraska, and as a minister of the Faith in the Gospel of our Lord and Saviour, Jesus Christ.

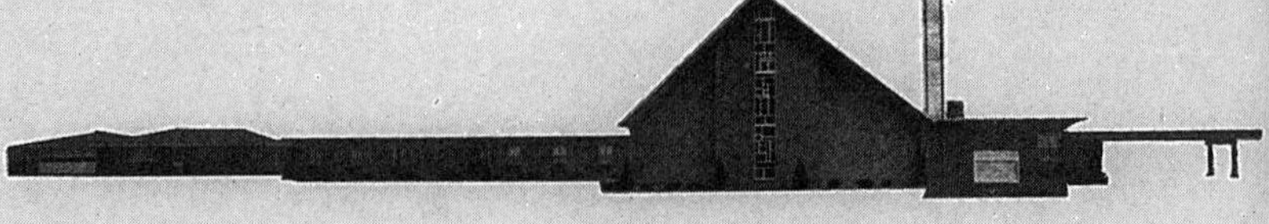

FIRST UNITED METHODIST CHURCH

325 EAST FRANKLIN STREET • APPLETON, WISCONSIN 54911 • MINISTERS: GORDON R. BENDER
TELEPHONE (414) 734-2677 DAVID H. BRICE

December 15, 1980

TO WHOM IT MAY CONCERN

This is to certify that Lucille Grobe was removed from membership in First United Methodist Church of Appleton, Wisconsin on November 9, 1970.

Gordon R. Bender
Pastor

LUTHERAN CHURCH OF THE GOOD SHEPHERD

501 CALIFORNIA AVENUE - RENO, NEVADA 89509

CHURCH OFFICE 329-0696
PASTOR'S HOME 329-4574

THE REV. JACK L. ERICSON . . . . Pastor
THE REV. RAYMOND L. STIFFLER . . . . . . Associate
THE REV. RAY CUNNINGHAM . . Missionary, Tanzania

THE LORD IS MY SHEPHERD

May 21, 1979

To Whom It May Concern:

Lloyd Harrison Jr. by his own request asked to be released from his membership in the Lutheran Church of the Good Shepherd and from any responsibilities or obligations to the Lutheran Church due to his baptism and confirmation in said church.

This request was so granted by an official vote of the Church Council of the Lutheran Church of the Good Shepherd following the appropriate precedures and a vote of 8 to 0 on Tuesday December 19, 1978.

The request is officially granted and made known to those who are concerned by this letter.

Sincerely,

Rev. Jack L. Ericson

Rev. Jack L. Ericson

RJLE/la

our lady of mt. carmel

July 15, 1980

Miss Stephanie Cunniff
1358 Danielson Road
Santa Barbara, CA 93108

Dear Stephanie:

In response to your request for a letter of excommunication from the Roman Catholic Church, I wish to remind you that apostasy automatically causes excommunication. Canon 2314, paragraph 1, reads as follows:

"All apostates from the Christian faith and each and every heretic or schismatic incurs ipso facto excommunication."

Since apostasy is a voluntary act of an individual, Canon Law declares an automatic penalty of excommunication, a penalty which the individual imposes upon himself/herself as a result of his/her free act, rather than a penalty imposed by a bishop or other ecclesiastical authority.

May I remind you that if you should change your mind, you may seek re-admission to the Catholic Church by confession and repentance of this grievous sin of apostasy.

Sincerely yours,

Fr. Henry A. Van Son
Pastor

1300 East Valley Road, in Montecito, Santa Barbara, California 93108

Reverent and Dear Sirs:

In accordance with canon 2314 of the Code Of Canon Laws of the Catholic Church, which states: "All apostates from the Christian Faith are ipso facto excommunicated," it is my insistance to be openly denounced of the Catholic Church, (in which I was baptised and confirmed and was a communicant) and cut off from the community of that church and excommunicated.

And I request that the Catholic authority record as soon as possible such open denouncing, rightful cutting off and excommunicating in my church records at the following church:

By this document I wish it to be known that I have embraced a non-Christian religion and do declare myself consciously apostate from the Catholic Church.

Signed by me Leonard Santana
this 8 day of Dec., 1978.

Witnessed by ______________

In the presence of George E. Stavis
Notory Public

GEORGE E. STAVIS
NOTARY PUBLIC, State of New York
No. 41-9160150
Qualified in Queens County
Commission Expires March 30, 1980

ATTORNEY OR PARTY WITHOUT ATTORNEY (Name and Address): TELEPHONE NO: 619 693 8823

MARY JUDITH HUNTER
10930 SUMMERDALE WAY #329
SAN DIEGO CA 92126

ATTORNEY FOR (Name): BAR#

COURT USE ONLY

COPY
KENNETH E. MARTONE
Clerk of the Superior Court
JUN 18 1992
By: LANI E. MARTIN Deputy
BUSINESS

SUPERIOR COURT OF CALIFORNIA, COUNTY OF SAN DIEGO

☑ 220 W. BROADWAY SAN DIEGO, CA 92101-3409 ☐ 325 S. MELROSE VISTA, CA 92083-6627 ☐ 250 E. MAIN EL CAJON, CA 92020-3913 ☐ 500 THIRD CHULA VISTA, CA 91910-5694

IN THE MATTER OF THE APPLICATION OF (Name(s)):
MARY JUDITH HUNTER
FOR CHANGE OF NAME(S)

HEARING DATE: ____
DEPT: ____ TIME: ____

PETITION FOR CHANGE OF NAME

CASE NUMBER 653149

Petitioner (Name): MARY JUDITH HUNTER respectfully alleges that:

1. Petitioner (Applicant) is:
   a. ☑ over 18 years of age.
   b. ☐ under 18 years of age.

   Date of Birth: JUNE 30, 1946
2. Petitioner's (Applicant's) place of birth:
   SAN DIEGO CA
3. Petitioner's (Applicant's) present address:
   10930 SUMMERDALE WAY UNIT 329 SAN DIEGO CA 92126
4. Petitioner's (Applicant's) present name:
   MARY JUDITH HUNTER
5. Petitioner's (Applicant's) proposed name:
   DAMARA SHANMUGAN
6. Reason for proposed change of name:
   RELIGION
7. Name, address and relationship of nearest living relative:
   (In case of a minor, and petition is signed by only one parent although both are living, the petition must state the address of the non-joining parent, if known.)
   MARY D VEATCH 8460 DALLAS LA MESA CA 92042

Wherefore Petitioner(s) request that the Court order a name change from MARY JUDITH HUNTER to DAMARA SHANMUGAN.

I declare under penalty of perjury under the laws of the State of California that the foregoing is true and correct.

Dated: 6-18-92 Mary Judith Hunter
(Signature of Petitioner(s))

____
(Signature of Attorney for Petitioner(s))

PETITION FOR CHANGE OF NAME

SUPCT 82(New 1-92)

SUPERIOR COURT OF CALIFORNIA, COUNTY OF SAN DIEGO

CALENDAR NO. 9

NUMBER	CLERK	REPORTER	CSR #
653149	BURKE-JENNINGS	Linda Schaffer CSR 2770	

DATE OF HEARING	TIME OF HEARING	DATE COMPLAINT FILED	JUDGE	DEPT
08/17/92	08:30AM	06-18-92	ARTHUR W. JONES	31

PLAINTIFF/PETITIONER	DEFENDANT/RESPONDENT
MARY JUDITH HUNTER	PETITION FOR CHANGE OF NAME

ATTORNEY FOR PLAINTIFF/PETITIONER	ATTORNEY FOR DEFENDANT/RESPONDENT
MARY JUDITH HUNTER (1) ☐P ☑NP	

1. PLAINTIFF CHANGE OF NAME

THIS MATTER HAVING COME BEFORE THE COURT THIS DATE, THE COURT ORDERS:

☐ PRIOR TO CALENDAR CALL ☐ OFF-CALENDAR ☑ GRANTED ☐ BOND$ ______ ☐ DENIED ☐ WITH/WITHOUT PREJUDICE

☐ PRIOR TO CALENDAR CALL ☐ CONTINUE TO ______ IN DEPT ______ AT ______ ☐ TRO ☐ CONTINUED ☐ VACATED

☐ ALL PREVIOUS ORDERS REMAIN IN FULL FORCE AND EFFECT.

☐ TAKEN UNDER SUBMISSION.

☐ JUDGMENT DEBTOR ______ ☐ SWORN AND EXAMINED ☐ NOT PRESENT

☐ WARRANT OF ATTACHMENT TO ISSUE WITH BAIL SET AT $ ______

☐ DEMURRER ☐ GENERAL ☐ SPECIAL ☐ OVERRULED ☐ ___ DAYS TO ANSWER

CAUSES ______, ______, ______, ______, ______, ______, ______, ______, ______

☐ DEMURRER ☐ GENERAL ☐ SPECIAL ☐ SUSTAINED ☐ ___ DAYS TO AMEND OR COURT WILL DEEM DISMISSED ☐ WITHOUT LEAVE

CAUSES ______, ______, ______, ______, ______, ______, ______, ______, ______

GROUNDS ______ ☐ PER MOVING POINTS AND AUTHORITIES

☐ SUMMARY ADJUDICATION OF ISSUES:

______ ARE GRANTED. ______ ARE DENIED.

☐ SANCTIONS AWARDED $ ______ AGAINST: ______ JOINTLY & SEVERALLY

PAYABLE ON OR BEFORE ______ TO: ______ ☐ SANCTIONS DENIED ☐ SANCTIONS SUSPENDED

☐ NOTICE WAIVED ☐ DISPOSES OF ENTIRE ACTION ☐ DOES NOT DISPOSE OF ENTIRE ACTION

☐ OTHER

SUPCT 718(Rev. 01-92) MOT-MINUTES/ORDER OF THE COURT

F I L E D
KENNETH E. MARTONE
Clerk of the Superior Court

JUL 24 1992

By: J. ALOSI, Deputy

IN THE SUPERIOR COURT OF THE STATE OF CALIFORNIA
IN AND FOR THE COUNTY OF SAN DIEGO
CERTIFICATE OF PUBLICATION

Case No: 653149

Mary Judith Hunter
10930 Summerdale Way #329
San Diego, CA. 92126-

Affidavit of Publication
Heartland News Legal Transcript
10010 Campo Rd. (P.O. Box 188)
Spring Valley, CA 91977
(619) 670-6194

I, Susan J. Meyers hereby certify that The Heartland News is a weekly newspaper of general circulation within the provisions of the Government Code of the State of California, printed and published in the County of San Diego, State of California, and the

ORDER TO SHOW CAUSE
FOR CHANGE OF NAME

SUPERIOR COURT
OF CALIFORNIA
COUNTY OF SAN DIEGO
220 W. Broadway
San Diego, CA 92101-3409
ORDER TO SHOW CAUSE
FOR CHANGE OF NAME
Case Number 653149

In the matter of the application of: MARY JUDITH HUNTER for change of name(s). Petitioner(s) MARY JUDITH HUNTER has/have filed a petition for an order to change names from MARY JUDITH HUNTER to DAMARA SHANMUGAN.
It is hereby ordered that all persons interested in this matter appear before this Court in Department SUP. CT. D-2 of the San Diego County Superior Court at the address shown above on Aug. 17, 1992, at 8:30 A.M., and show cause, if any they have, why this application for change of name should not be granted.
It is further ordered that a copy of this ORDER TO SHOW CAUSE be published in Heartland News, a newspaper of general circulation published in this county, at least once a week for four successive weeks prior to the day of the hearing. Date: Jun. 18, 1992. Arthur W. Jones, Judge of the Superior Court.
Attorney or party without attorney: Mary Judith Hunter 10930 Summerdale Way #329 San Diego, CA. 92126- (619)693-8823. . Jul. 2, 9, 16, 23, 1992.

the day of the hearing. Date: Jun. 18, 1992. Arthur W. Jones, Judge of the Superior Court.
Attorney or party without attorney: Mary Judith Hunter 10930 Summerdale Way #329 San Diego, CA. 92126- (619)693-8823. . Jul. 2, 9, 16, 23, 1992.

to which this certificate is annexed is a true and correct copy published in said newspaper on

Jul. 2, 9, 16, 23, 1992

I certify under penalty of perjury that the foregoing is true and correct, at Spring Valley, California, on

Jul. 23, 1992

Susan J. Meyers
Signature

Case No: 653149

Aum Ganesha!

SAIVA SIDDHANTA CHURCH
Namakarana Samskara
Hindu Name-Giving Sacrament

Damara Shanmugan,
*formerly known as Judy Hunter, having
declared of her own volition acceptance of the principles of the
Sanatana Dharma, and having severed all previous non-Hindu
religious affiliations, attachments and commitments, hereby
humbly petitions entrance into the Saivite Hindu religion
through the traditional Namakarana Samskara and pleads for
recognition of this irrevocable conversion to Hinduism.*

Damara Shanmugan
Hindu Name

Judy Hunter
Former Name

It is Hereby Certified That
Damara Shanmugan,

born in San Diego, California, at 6:00 AM on June 30, 1946, and now residing at
10930 Summerdale Way #329, San Diego, California 92126-5444, at a Namakarana
Samskara held at her request on this auspicious Satguru Purnima day, July 12, 1992, at
Kadavul Hindu Temple on the Garden Island of Kauai, Hawaii, was duly given her
Hindu name in accordance with the traditions of Saivite Hinduism and vowed before
the Deity, the Mahadevas and the devas her faithfulness to the Sanatana Dharma.
Thus, she has bound herself eternally and immutably to the Hindu religion and is
recognized as a member of this most ancient faith with full rights of access to all
public Hindu temples, shrines and institutions throughout the world from this day onward.

WITNESSES: SAIVA SIDDHANTA CHURCH

Ceyonswami
Jara Katir
Arya Sivadas Nilani Sivadas

Deva Seyn

Sivaya Subramuniyaswami

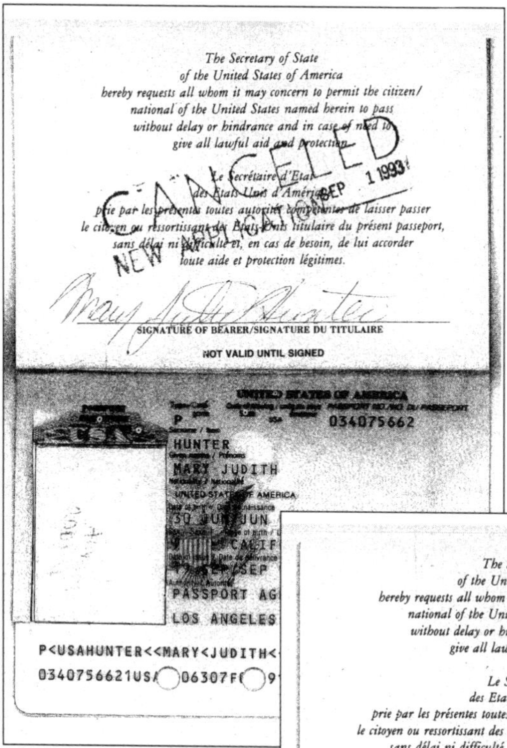

The Secretary of State
of the United States of America
hereby requests all whom it may concern to permit the citizen/
national of the United States named herein to pass
without delay or hindrance and in case of need to
give all lawful aid and protection.

Le Secrétaire d'Etat
des Etats-Unis d'Amérique
prie par les présentes toutes autorités compétentes de laisser passer
le citoyen ou ressortissant des Etats-Unis titulaire du présent passeport,
sans délai ni difficulté et, en cas de besoin, de lui accorder
toute aide et protection légitimes.

CANCELED
NEW APPLICATION SEP 1 1993

Mary Judith Hunter
SIGNATURE OF BEARER/SIGNATURE DU TITULAIRE
NOT VALID UNTIL SIGNED

UNITED STATES OF AMERICA
P
034075662
HUNTER
MARY JUDITH
UNITED STATES OF AMERICA
30 JUN/JUN
CALIF
SEP/SEP
PASSPORT AG
LOS ANGELES
P<USAHUNTER<<MARY<JUDITH<
0340756621US 06307F 9

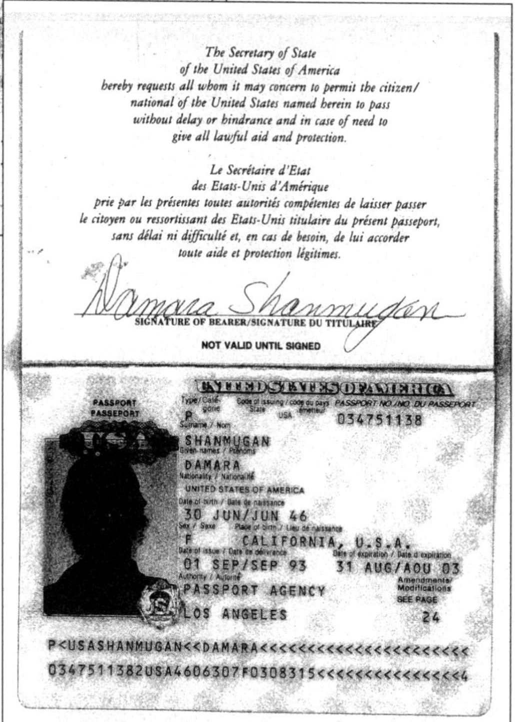

The Secretary of State
of the United States of America
hereby requests all whom it may concern to permit the citizen/
national of the United States named herein to pass
without delay or hindrance and in case of need to
give all lawful aid and protection.

Le Secrétaire d'Etat
des Etats-Unis d'Amérique
prie par les présentes toutes autorités compétentes de laisser passer
le citoyen ou ressortissant des Etats-Unis titulaire du présent passeport,
sans délai ni difficulté et, en cas de besoin, de lui accorder
toute aide et protection légitimes.

Damara Shanmugan
SIGNATURE OF BEARER/SIGNATURE DU TITULAIRE
NOT VALID UNTIL SIGNED

UNITED STATES OF AMERICA
PASSPORT
PASSEPORT
Type/Catégorie: P
Code of issuing State/Code du pays émetteur: USA
Passport No./No. du Passeport: 034751138
Surname/Nom: SHANMUGAN
Given names/Prénoms: DAMARA
Nationality/Nationalité: UNITED STATES OF AMERICA
Date of birth/Date de naissance: 30 JUN/JUN 46
Sex/Sexe: F
Place of birth/Lieu de naissance: CALIFORNIA, U.S.A.
Date of issue/Date de délivrance: 01 SEP/SEP 93
Date of expiration/Date d'expiration: 31 AUG/AOU 03
Authority/Autorité: PASSPORT AGENCY LOS ANGELES
Amendments/Modifications SEE PAGE 24
P<USASHANMUGAN<<DAMARA<<<<<<<<<<<<<<<<<<<<<<<
0347511382USA4606307F0308315<<<<<<<<<<<<<<<4

Hindudharmānusāreṇa
Nāmasvīkāraḥ

हिन्दुधर्मानुसारेण नामस्वीकारः

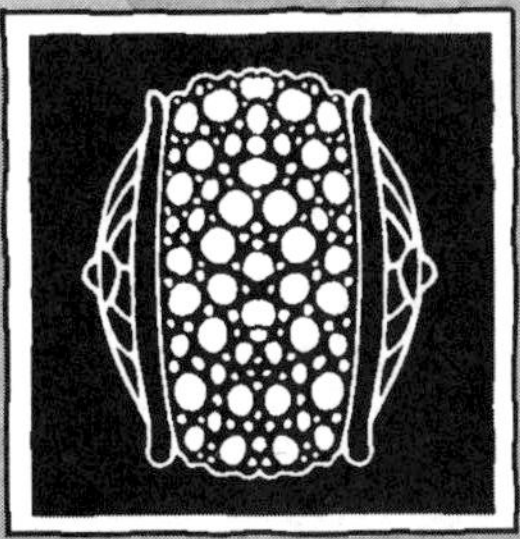

Choosing a Hindu Name

Anjali

Choosing a Hindu Name

OF ALL THE ASPECTS OF FULLY EMBRACING the Hindu religion, the legal changing of one's name is certainly the most public, requiring adjustment on the part of friends, relatives, neighbors and even business acquaintances. A few approach this with trepidation, but the expected negative reaction—particularly from personal and business acquaintances—seldom materializes. If the family becomes genuinely concerned, this will be overcome by the obvious love, sincerity and depth of conviction of the individual. Legally changing one's name is not unusual. Women do it all the time at marriage. Movie stars rarely use their birth name. Name changes for religious reasons are almost as common. Heavyweight boxer Cassius Clay startled the world in 1967 by proclaiming his conversion to Islam and changing his name to Muhammed Ali. But anyone who has gone through the experience of a religious name-change knows there are real obstacles. Here are a few:

1. Grandma's fears that you are rejecting the family traditions.
2. Your fears of what business associates might think.
3. The tendency to use the old name when you are among your non-Hindu friends.
4. The tendency to use the new first name and the old last name, or to modify the new Hindu name—Deva becomes Dave at work.
5. Using the name but not having it made legal.
6. Using the Hindu name with one group and former name with another, a practice of double standard that erodes one's self-image and encourages others to not take you seriously.

At my Himālayan Academy, we have been involved with hundreds of such name changes since 1957, and our advice is, be strong! Take on the responsibilities of your new way of thinking and accept the karma and dharma of the Hindu community. Yes, there is a gentle departure, a break to a certain degree with your family and non-Hindu friends. But you will also be surprised how well most will understand. Some will even be influenced and encouraged by your strength. You may find that they actually share many of your convictions and that you have more in common in these areas than you had suspected.

There is probably not a single major religion in the world which does not have a unique system of names for its members, names which identify them as adherents of that particular heritage. This is well known, and there is nothing unusual about changing your name for religious reasons. In fact, it is expected and respected as a sign of genuine conviction and identity. When my monks become US citizens, the INS gives them the boon to take any name they wish, without further court proceedings—yet another example of the fluidity of names in the wider world.

Naming Customs of the World

People so often change their names in North America, for reasons running from marriage to difficult pronunciation, that a change of name is readily accepted. Society wisely recognizes that there are perfectly good reasons to change one's name. As I just noted, they occur with every marriage. Most women have to go through all the processes of changing their bank accounts, driver's license, income tax records, and so on. In eastern Europe, where legislation has changed the basic assumptions concerning the family name, a different and unusual situation has developed. When a Czech woman, Anna Klimova, for instance, marries Josef Novak, both may retain their original family names, or the wife may become

Anna Novakova or, more remarkably, the husband may become Josef Klima, accepting his wife's family name. This is decided by mutual agreement, and their children's names are decided in the same manner.

Customs and patterns of names are different all over the world. Names have historically been changed in North America to give a more English-sounding name to one that may sound foreign or be difficult to pronounce. Thus, Michael Igor Peschkowski becomes Mike Nichols or Josef Nejezchleba becomes Joe Neez. Name changing is common among actors, singers and performers. Judy Garland was born Frances Gumm, James Garner was James Baumgardner and Arlene Francis was Arlene Kazañjian. Of all the nations in the world, Great Britain and the United States most closely follow the principle of Roman law that a person has the right to use and change his name as he pleases, except for fraudulent purposes.

Changing one's name upon changing one's religion is a common custom. So recognized is it that in the West given names are actually called "Christian names," referring back to a time when conversion to Christianity was widespread, accompanied by the adoption of Biblical names such as Ruth, Mary, Peter, Paul, Mark, Luke and so forth. A few decades ago in America, the Black Muslims had their members adopt Muslim names. It is quite natural that members of a religion wish to be recognized as a part of that heritage, and the name is one of the most obvious and important signs of their association. The venerable Madurai Aadheenam, a Śaivite religious institution founded in South India more than a thousand years ago, brings Indian Christians and Muslims back into Hinduism, giving them a Hindu name which they legally adopt after publishing it in the local newspaper.

Most American names are of English origin and are the result of a flurry of name changing and new customs regarding names—such as having two of them—which occurred in the eleventh to thirteenth centuries. Before the Norman conquest of England in 1066, everyone had a single name like Cuthbeorht, Leofwine, Ethelnoth, Aethelbeorht and Aethelthryth. All are true English names. After the conquest, those names were replaced by Norman names—William and Richard and John. Before 1066 only one percent of the English had a Biblical name, although they were Christians. Two and a half centuries later, nearly everyone boasted a Christian name, again following Norman custom.

Later in history, an increased social and political organization—particularly with regard to taxes and inheritance—required the addition of last names. That was when William the smith became William Smith. His son was called John Smith even if he was a farmer and not a smith. Or short Albert became Albert Short and his son was named Thomas Short, no matter what his height. Last names, then, are a fairly recent innovation, arising from the need to identify each John or Henry—the one by the bridge, the one in the woods, the short one or the one who owns the mill. The final tally for names of English origin shows one-third to be from localities, such as Brook, Wood, Ford, Lane and Bridges; another third derive from the father's name, such as Johnson (the son of John), Davidson, Richardson and less obviously Jennings, Hawkin and Hancock—all derivations from John; and the balance can be traced to occupations such as Smith, Taylor and Miller and less obviously Fletcher (arrow featherer), Mylne (variation of Miller) and Sawyer (one who saws). Finally, there are a series which come from nicknames such as Young, Gray, Armstrong and Smart.

In other parts of the world the use of names is different. Among the Chinese and Hungarians, the family name comes first, followed by the given or forename, for example, Mao Tse-tung, whose family name is Mao, not Tse-tung. The Russians and Icelanders add a patronymic, a name derived from the father, between the given name and the family name. Thus, in Russia if the father's name is Ivan Krylov, then the son's name, for example, will be Pyotr (given) Ivanovich (patronymic) Kyrlov (family), and the daughter's name will be, for example, Varvara Ivanovna Kyrlova. The usual form of address in Russian among acquaintances, neighbors and colleagues at work is by the given name and the patronymic, without the family name, i.e., Pyotr Ivanovich, without the Kyrlov.

In Africa, one might be named Ayondela, meaning "a little tree that bends and bends as we all bend toward death." The American Indian name Taipa means, "valley quail spreading its wings as it alights" and Onida means, "the looked-for one." Alaska's Eskimos give the name of a recently departed member, as they believe this newborn to be a reincarnation of the recently departed friend or family member. The Muslims make things very simple and religious by adding Mohammed to most male names. The Chinese make up new names for everyone. They also join first and second names in a nice meaning which might carry through the family—Precious Jade's sisters might be named Precious Jewel and Precious Peace. They also have a tradition of repulsive names, such as "cat vomit," which are intended to fool the evil spirits into thinking the child is unloved so they will leave him or her alone.

The Hawaiians use descriptive names now coupled with Christian given names such as David Kekoalauliionapalihauliuliokekoolau Kaapuava-kamehameha (Kekoa Kuapu for short), meaning, "the fine-leafed Koa tree on the beautiful green ridges of the Koolau Mountains." The Japanese use beautiful names like Umiko, "plum blossom child," and functional ones such as Taro, "first male," and Jiro "second male". German Jews used to have only one name but added surnames in the 19th century. Scandanavians began using surnames at the beginning of this century.

Hindu Names

The most ancient and common source of Hindu names is from the names of God and the Gods. Each child receives a name selected from those of the family's Ishṭa Devatā, chosen Deity. Such names are called theophoric. The custom of choosing a name from the Gods is among the most ancient, with examples in Persia, Greece, India and the early Indo-European civilizations. In Vedic times there was a Sanskṛit convention for forming patronymics: if Garga was the father, then Gargi was the son, Gargya the grandson and Gargyāyana the great-grandson.

Hindu names often indicate caste and sect. Iyer is for a certain caste of South Indian Śaivite brahmins. Sharma is for a caste of North Indian brahmins. The God names Venkateśvara or Kṛishṇa indicate a follower of Vishṇu. Common names of Śaivites are Naṭarāja, Mahādevan, Śivaliṅga, Nīlakaṇṭha, Subramaniam, Kandiah and Kumāra. Dās or Dāsa is a frequently used suffix meaning "slave" used by many denominations—hence Śivadas, Kālīdās, Haridās. Often the first name is chosen according to the syllable mystically related to the individual's *nakshatra,* birth star. There are 108 such sounds used to begin a name: four for each of the twenty-seven *nakshatras.*

Hindus sometimes change their name during their life as a result of a blessing at a temple or when a holy man initiates them. Swāmī Vivekānanda—who said, "Certainly, there is a great deal in a name!"—was originally named Narendranāth Dutt and had several names as a monk. The Tamil Saint Manikkavasagar was originally named Vathavooran. My own beloved Satguru, Śiva Yogaswāmī, was given the name Sadasivan at birth, then the Christian name John when he was sent to Catholic school as a child, then renamed Yoganāthan by the village headman who did not appreciate the Christian influence. Later in his life, Yoganāthan was given the title Yogaswāmī—"Master of Yoga"—and devotees used it so often that it became his name to this day.

Similarly, Kadaitswāmī, the name of Yogaswāmī's guru's guru, simply means the swāmī who frequented the *kadai* or marketplace. Yogaswāmī gave new names to many of his devotees, and many of those names were made legal. A good example is myself. Yogaswāmī gave me the name Subramuniya in 1949. Returning to the United States, I had it made legal in the courts in 1950. Such changes of name in Hinduism are considered sacred moments, indicative of spiritual changes taking place on the inside. In following this tradition of the Guru Paramparāi, we at Himālayan Academy require adoptives, converts and born Hindus with non-Śaivite names, such as those named in Vaishṇavite traditions, to adopt a Śaivite name, first and last, and have it made legal before entering our Śaiva Siddhānta Church.

A Sign of Commitment

The change of name, and using it under all circumstances, and this means *all* circumstances, is an important sign of religious sincerity to the Hindu community. It shows the willingness of the newcomer to stand up and be counted as a Hindu. So significant is the change of name to the Hindu community that an adoptive with a Hindu name on his passport can gain entry to many temples which categorically deny entrance to Westerners on the grounds that they are assumed to be non-Hindus. Proceed with confidence. Be a hundred-percenter. Don't sit on the fence. It is risky to walk down the middle of the road. Stand up boldly and declare who you are.

Western Hindus have been criticized in India for bearing Hindu names when it suits them in day-to-day circumstances, but maintaining a Christian or Jewish name on their passport, among relatives and for legal matters. Mature Hindus consider such deception noncommittal, immature and unacceptable. Legal name-change on all personal documents is one of the clearest indications of full and honest conversion. In the spring of 1988, after 20 years of dual identity, members of the ISKCON (International Society for Kṛishṇa Consciousness) community began a call for "non-Indian" devotees to adopt Vaishṇava names. Ashok Sarkar voiced the concern well in a letter to the editor published in *ISKCON World Review* (May 1988): "I would like to bring forth an important issue regarding the name registration of *Vaishṇava* devotees, an issue which has been overlooked by the ISKCON administration.

"The non-Indian Vaishṇavas or Neo-Vaishṇavas around the world have not officially changed their *'karmic'* names yet. Can you imagine that after 22 years of ISKCON's successful movement, suddenly you find out that officially there are no Vaishṇavas! Therefore, I strongly suggest all Vaishṇavas of ISKCON change their names officially as soon as possible. It is time for the Vaishṇavas to stand up and be counted in the political world and thus have a voice in the administration of every land we live in. Let the phone books show long listings of Vaishṇava names under *Das* and *Dasi.*" Unfortunately, this stage of commitment never happened. In fact, ISKCON later officially and ardently declared that they, as an organization and as individuals, are not Hindu and do not align themselves with Hinduism.

Sadly, today many Hindus relinquish their beautiful Hindu names when then come to the West or alter them to fit into Western society. Thus, *Sanmugasundaram* may become *Sam* or *Daram.* Taking a further step away from the Hindu dharma, parents may even begin giving Christian names to their Hindu children. Alarmed at this trend, the late Swāmī Tilak of the Vishva Hindu Parishad noted, "Westernization is rapidly penetrating the well-to-do urban Hindu families everywhere. Although they assert that Westernization does not mean in any way the acceptance of the non-Hindu values, they are drifting away more and more from their traditional way of life. First, they change their names: *Gyani* becomes *Johney* and *Mira* becomes *Mary*, on the pretext that non-Hindus find it difficult to follow Hindu names. This contagious disease is not limited to Trinidad or Guyana alone; Hindus all over out of *Bharat* [India] have begun to follow this obnoxious trend. To some it may look to be simply a business trick, but it is fraught with dire consequences. Lack of self-confidence works in its base way, which may lead one to demoralization. All caution must be taken against this awful tendency" (*Hindu Vishva*, July/August, 1985).

Sanskrit Birthstar Syllables

According to traditional *jyotishīs* (Indian astrologers), among the most auspicious Hindu first names begin the syllables that corresponds to one's birthstar, called *nakshatra*, which is the constellation with which the moon was aligned at the moment of birth. Below is a list of the twenty-seven *nakshatras* and the distinct Sanskrit syllables that correspond to each. To choose a *nakshatra* name (*nāma-nakshatra),* first determine the birthstar of the child or adult, then look for the star in the list below to determine the syllable(s) with which the name should begin. There are four sounds for each *nakshatra*, corresponding to the four quarters *(pādas)* of each constellation. If you know the *pāda* under which the child or adult was born, it is best to choose the syllable of that *pāda*. Several of the *nāma-nakshatra* syllables are quite rare in actual usage in the Sanskrit language. For example, someone born under the fourth *pāda* of Pūrvāshādhā *nakshatra* may not find more than two or three qualifying names beginning with the syllable *ḍha*, even in extensive name lists, so it is common practice to choose a name starting with a similar syllable. In this case the syllable *dhā* might be used, such as in the name *Dhārana*, or *dha* as in

Dharma. It is also common to resort to the syllable of another *pāda* within the same *nakshatra* if too few names are available.

Why chose a name based on *nakshatra*? The first reason is that it vibrates in harmony with the nature of the individual in this particular incarnation, by virtue of its unique relation to the moon at the moment of birth, which has a significant impact on the inner, emotional nature. Secondly, by simply hearing the name, an astute *jyotisha śāstrī*, priest, swāmī or *satguru* would immediately know the nature of the person, cognizing that he was born under, say, the *śravaṇā nakshatra.* He would thus be able to wisely counsel or console, advise and encourage accordingly. In ancient days, as today, this first sound of the first name was extremely important to knowledgeable preceptors.

Aśvinī Nakshatra

Chu	चु	(as in Fu-Manchu)
Che	चे	(as in chase)
Cho	चो	(as in choke)
Lā	ला	(as in lava)

Bharaṇī Nakshatra

Li	लि	(as in lilt)
Lu	लु	(as in lute)
Le	ले	(as in leg)
Lo	लो	(as in local)

Kṛittikā Nakshatra

Ā	आ	(as in ānanda)
I	इ	(as in iridescent)
U	उ	(as in uvula)
E	ए	(as in egg)

Rohiṇī Nakshatra

O	ओ	(as in odor)
Va	व	(as in vanilla)
Vī	वी	(as in Vīṇā)
Vo	वो	(as in vote)

Mṛigaśira Nakshatra

Ve	वे	(as in Veda)
Vo	वो	(as in votary)
Kā	का	(as in Kanji)
Ke	के	(as in Kenya)

Ārdrā Nakshatra

Ku	कु	(as in Kuwait)
Ghā	घा	(as in Ghana)
Ng	ङ	(pronounced "ng")
Çha	छ	(as in Churchill)

Punarvasu Nakshatra

Ke	के	(as in Kenya)
Ko	को	(as in kodiac)
Hā	हा	(as in hardy)
Hī	ही	(as in hither)

Pushya Nakshatra

Hū	हू	(as in hurrah)
He	हे	(as in heyday)
Ho	हो	(as in homogenous)
Ḍā	डा	(no English equiv.)

Aślesha Nakshatra

Ḍī	डी	(no English equiv.)
Ḍu	डु	(no English equiv.)
Ḍe	डे	(no English equiv.)
Ḍo	डो	(no English equiv.)

Maghā Nakshatra

Mā	मा	(as in māyā)
Mī	मी	(as in miracle)
Mū	मू	(as in mudra)
Me	मे	(as in megabyte)

Purvaphalguni Nakshatra

Mo	मो	(as in motion)
Ṭā	टा	(no English equiv.)
Ṭī	टी	(no English equiv.)
Ṭū	टू	(no English equiv.)

Uttaraphalguni Nakshatra

Ṭe	टे	(no English equiv.)
Ṭo	टो	(no English equiv.)
Pā	पा	(no English equiv.)
Pī	पी	(no English equiv.)

Hasta Nakshatra

Pu	पु	(as in purusha)
Shā	षा	(as in shanti)
Ṇā	णा	(no English equiv.)
Ṭhā	ठा	(no English equiv.)

Chitra Nakshatra

Pe	पे	(as in Peru)
Po	पो	(as in pole)
Rā	रा	(as in Rāma)
Rī	री	(as in Rio de Janeiro)

Svātī Nakshatra

Ru	रु	(as in rumor)
Re	रे	(as in regulate)
Rā	रा	(as in Rāma)
Tā	ता	(as in Tahiti)

Viśākhā Nakshatra

Tī	ती	(as in East Timor
Tū	तू	(as in tune)
Te	ते	(as in terrace)
To	तो	(as in total)

Anurādhā Nakshatra

Nā	ना	(as in Nagasaki)
Nī	नी	(as in Nicaragua)
Nū	नू	(as in numeral)
Ne	ने	(as in Nepal)

Jyeshṭā Nakshatra

No	नो	(as in noble)
Yā	या	(as in Yama)
Yī	यी	(as in yield)
Yū	यू	(as in Yukon)

Mūla Nakshatra

Ye	ये	(as in Yemen)
Yo	यो	(as in yo-yo)
Bā	बा	(as in ball)
Bī	बी	(as in Bini)

Pūrvāshādhā Nakshatra

Bu	बु	(as in Buddha)
Dhā	धा	(as in dharma)
Bha	भ	(as in bhakti)
Ḍhā	ढा	(no English equiv.)

Uttarāshādhā Nakshatra

Be	बे	(as in beta)
Bo	बो	(as in Bohemian)
Jā	जा	(as in jar)
Jī	जी	(as in jīva)

Śravaṇa Nakshatra

Ju	जु	(as in Jupiter)
Je	जे	(ay as in hay)
Jo	जो	(as in joke)
Gha	घ	(as in Ghana)

Dhanishṭā Nakshatra

Gā	गा	(as in garden)
Gī	गी	(ee as in keep)
Gū	गू	(as in guru)
Ge	गे	(as in Gestault)

Śatabhīshā Nakshatra

Go	गो	(as in go)
Sā	सा	(as in Sahara)
Sī	सी	(as in Sita)
Sū	सू	(as in Sūrya)

Pūrvabhādhrapada Nakshatra

Se	से	(as in Seoul)
So	सो	(as in sonar)
Dā	दा	(as in Dante)
Dī	दी	(as in dīpa)

Uttarabhādhrapada Nakshatra

Du	दु	(as in duty)
Tha	थ	(as in Thar Desert)
Jña	ज्ञ	(as in Jnana)
Da	द	(as in Tahiti)

Revatī Nakshatra

De	दे	(as in deva)
Do	दो	(as in donut)
Chā	चा	(as in chakra)
Chī	ची	(as in chief)

A Collection of Hindu Names

For individuals seeking to choose a Hindu name, we have humbly assembled here a list of names primarily from the South Indian Śaivite tradition, favoring shorter names which would be most easily pronounced in the West. Other very good sources are 1) *The Penguin Book of Hindu Names*, by Maneka Gandhi, and 2) *Pick a Pretty Indian Name for Your Baby*, by Meenal Pandya and Rashmee Pandya-Bhanot. Each book contains thousands of names from many of Hinduism's rich traditions. There are also several wonderful websites (listed on p. 428) with extensive lists of Hindu names.

As there is variety in traditions, there is variety in the pronunciation and spelling of names. For example, Shiva in the North of India may become Sivan in the South. For this purpose, we have listed a number of alternatives when multiple spellings and pronunciations exist. Names marked with an (M) are masculine, and those marked with an (F) are feminine. Names marked (M-F) are suitable for both genders.

If you are adopting or converting to Hinduism, we suggest that you select a first name and a last name, and proceed with confidence. Confirm the proper pronunciation with Hindus in the community you are joining. Begin using your new name. Later it can be made legal.

A

Abhisheka (M): inauguration; sacred oblation
Acharya (M): teacher, scholar
Adhyaksha (M): the great presider; Gaṇeśa
Adi (M): Primal Source; a name of Śiva
Aditi (F): freedom; security; Earth
Aditya (M): name of seven Dieties of the heavenly sphere; a constallation; the seventh lunar mansion; the plant *Calotropis Gigantea*
Adiyan, Adiyen (M): devotee, servant, slave
Agama (M-F): coming forth; arrival; birth; knowledge; wisdom
Agastya (M): thrower of mountains; one who humbles even the mountain; name of a ṛishi; Śiva

Agni (M): fire; gold; God of fire
Agnikumar (M): son of Agni; a name of Murugan
Agranya (M): first born; Gaṇeśa
Aja (M-F): unborn; Gaṇeśa
Ajita (F): invincible; irresistible; Śiva and Vishṇu
Alahan (M): beautiful one; Murugan
Amala (M-F): spotless; pure; shining; Lakshmī and Nārāyana; plant *Hibiscus Cannabinus* and tree *Emblica Officianalis*
Amara (M): immortal; a God; the Rudrāksha tree
Amba (F): mother; a good woman; Durgā
Ambara (M): circumference; sky; saffron; a kind of perfume
Ambika (F): mother; sensitive; compassionate; loving; Pārvatī
Ambikanatha (M): Ambikā's lord; Śiva
Ambu (M): water
Ambuja (M): produced in water; lotus; conch; the moon
Amiya (F): full of tenderness; nectar
Amrita (M-F): undying; immortal; imperishable; heaven; first kālā of the moon; beautiful; beloved; divine nectar
Anadi (M): eternal; immortal; Śiva
Anamaya (M-F): the savior of all ills; Murugan
Anand, Ananda, Anandan (M): happiness; joy; blissful one; Śiva and Gaurī
Anandapriya (M): dear one who gives joy
Anandi (F): bestower of pleasure; Gaurī
Anant, Ananta (M): unending, eternal; the Earth; Pārvatī
Anantamurti (M): of endless forms; Murugan
Anantashakti (M-F): the potent lord; Murugan
Anekatman (M): the plurality of souls; Śiva
Anil Kumar (M): son of the wind; Hanuman
Anishvara (M): having no superior; Śiva and Murugan
Anjali (F): prayerful
Appar (M): father; a famous Śaivite saint
Aran (M): forest dweller; Śiva
Arati (F): offering of fire; worship
Arul (M): grace
Arumuga, Arumugam (M): six-faced one; Murugan
Arun (M), Aruna (F): red; passionate; life-giving; dawn; Sūrya
Asha (F): hope; space; a quarter of the heavens
Ashok, Ashoka (M): without sorrow
Ashrita (F): the refuge; Gaṇeśa
Ashtamurti (M): lord of eight forms; Śiva
Asita (F): at rest; tranquil; at peace; Pārvatī
Atmabhuvi (M-F): the unborn Self; Murugan
Avyakta (M-F): the unmanifest; Śiva

B

Babhravi (F): fire-clad; victorious; omnipresent; descendent of sage Babhru; Dūrgā
Badarayani (F): new; young; pure; perfume
Bageshri (F): prosperity; beauty; a rāga
Bahubhuja (F): many-armed; Dūrgā
Bahudama (F): strong; powerful; a

mother of Skanda's retinue
Bahugandha (F): strong-scented, very fragrant; jasmine; sandalwood; musk
Bahulika (F): manifold, magnified, multiplied, multifaceted personality, the Pleiades
Bahumati (F): extremely knowledgeable; a scholar
Bahupushpa (F): decorated with flowers; respected, venerated
Bakavati (F): having the qualities of a heron: attentive, patient, watchful, cautious
Bakul (F): a flower
Bakula (M), Bakuli (F): a kind of tree; the fragrant flower of *Mimusops Elengi*
Bala (M-F), Balan (M): young boy or girl; newly risen; simple; pure; jasmine
Balaganapati (M): infant Gaṇeśa
Balaja (M-F): born of power; Arabian jasmine; grain; the Earth
Balakunda (F): young flower; jasmine
Balasarasvati (F): Goddess of knowledge
Balavati (F): powerful, strong; a daughter
Banashri (F): beauty of the forest
Bandhupriya (F): dear to friends and relations
Bandhura (F): rounded; lovely, charming
Banita (F): woman
Banshi (M): a flute; sweet-voiced; melodious
Barhayita (F): as beautiful as the eye on a peacock feather
Barhisha (F): *kusha* grass; ether; water; fire; sacrifice; light; splendor
Baruna, Baruni (F): wife of lord of the Sea; Dūrgā
Basanti (F): of the spring; the yellow color associated with spring
Basantika (F): spring
Batika (F): flower
Beanta (M): without end, eternal
Bekuri (F): playing a musical instrument; an *apsarā*
Bela (F): jasmine; wave; time
Beman (M): detached
Beni (M): plait of hair
Beniprasada (M): flowers sacred enough for offering
Bhadra (M-F): fair, auspicious, beautiful; fortunate, prosperous; happy; gentle; Śiva
Bhadrarupa (F): of beautiful form
Bhadrashashti (F): form of Dūrgā
Bhadrasoma (F): as noble and beautiful as the moon
Bhadravalli (F): beautiful vine; Arabian jasmine
Bhadrikā (F), Bhadrika (M): noble; beautiful, virtuous; auspicious
Bhagada (F): bestower of wealth and happiness; an attendant of Skanda
Bhagavat (M-F): possessing fortune; happy; divine; venerable
Bhagavati (F): God and nature conjoined; the Creator
Bhakta, Bhaktar (M): devotee
Bhaktavatsala (M-F): lover of devotees; Murugan
Bhakti (F): devotion, homage, piety
Bhalla (M-F): auspicious; Śiva
Bhallaka (M): a bear
Bhalli (F): arrow
Bhamini (F): shining, radiant, glorious; passionate
Bhanavi (F): descendant of the sun; shining like the sun; sacred; glorious, enlightening

Bhandila (F): fortune
Bhanuja (F): daughter of the sun; the Yamunā river
Bhanupriya (F): beloved of the sun
Bhanushri (F): glorious as the sun
Bharanda (M): one who fulfills; master; lord
Bharanyu (M): protector, master; fire, sun; friend
Bharatha (M): world protector
Bharati (F): descendant of Bharata; articulate; meritorious, virtuous
Bharga (M-F): the effulgent one; Śiva
Bharita (M-F): green
Bhashat (M): the heart
Bhasmapriya (M): a friend of the holy ash; a name of Śiva
Bhati (F): lovely, liked by all; perceptible; luminous; splendour
Bhatta, Bhattara, Bhatti (M): noble lord; prince; king
Bhattini (F): noble lady; a famous poet
Bhava (M-F), Bhavan (M): existence itself; Śiva
Bhavabhuti (M-F): prosperity; the ashes of Śiva
Bhavada (M-F): giving life; cause of existence
Bhavaja (F): born of the heart; beautiful; compassionate
Bhavanatha (M): lord of creation
Bhavani (F): noble, beautiful; Pārvatī
Bhavanikanta (M): Bhavani's husband
Bhavanti (F): charming; new; virtuous wife
Bhavarupa (M-F): handsome or beautiful
Bhavayana (M), Bhavayani (F): coming from Śiva; Gaṅgā
Bhavesha (M): Śiva, lord of wordly existence
Bhavyakirti (F): of great fame; wise
Bhima (M-F): of awesome strength; Śiva
Bija (F): germ, seed; element, source; the mystical root letter of a mantra
Bijakshara (F): the seed alphabet, Aum, the first syllable of a mantra; the atomic alphabet; profound, omnipotent
Bijamati (F): a mind good at comprehending causes
Bijanjali (F): a handful of seeds; lifegiving
Bijapushpa (F): a flower, maruvaka
Bijli (F): lightning, bright, illuminating, enlightening
Bijya (F): born of good parents
Bina (F): intelligence; lute, harmonious, melodious
Boddhri (M): a seer, one who knows, a preceptor
Bodha (M), Bodhana (M-F), Bodhi (F): knowledge, awakening; sermon; perception; Bṛihaspati
Bodhendra (M): lord of intelligence;
Brahmani (F): Brahmā's beloved
Buddhi (F): intellect; Gaṇeśa's consort
Buddhipriya (M-F): lover of intelligence; Gaṇeśa

C

Ceyon (M): ancient Tamil name of Lord Murugan
Chachari (M): moving quickly, restless
Chaha (M): desire, desired, charming, loving
Chaidya (M): intelligent; an administrator

Chaitra (M): absorbed in pleasure; as pleasant as the spring
Chaitraratha (M): chariot of intelligence; Sūrya
Chaitrasakha (M): friend of the spring; one who incites love
Chakora (M): shining; content
Chakrin (M): Kṛishṇa and Śiva
Chakroddhata (M): the Supreme
Chaksana (M): soothing to the eyes; appearance
Chaksas (M): look, sight; radiance; teacher
Chaksu (M): eye; Sun God, Sūrya
Chaksusa (M): preceptor, seer
Chala (M): ever-moving; Supreme Being
Chalaka (M): directing, driving; Supreme Soul
Chalameshvara (M): Śiva
Chaman (M): garden
Chamar (M): a rod with a large tuft of hair used for fanning
Chamaraja (M): leader of an army
Chamasa (M): cup; vessel used for drinking *soma* at sacrifices
Chamikara (M): gold, golden color; the thorn apple
Champa (M): soothing
Champaka (M): Champaka tree
Chamundi (F): Dūrgā as one of the seven mothers who destroyed the demons Chanda and Munda
Chandana (M): sandalwood
Chandanin (M): anointed with sandalwood; Śiva
Chandansu (M): hot-rayed, the sun
Chandesvara (M): attendant of Śiva
Chandi (F): silver; fair, precious; cooling
Chandipati (M): lord of Chandi; Śiva
Chandodeva (M): lord of the hymns
Chandra (F), Chandran (M): shining, radiant; the moon
Chandrabhala (M): bearing the moon on his forehead; Śiva
Chandradeva (M): the moon personified as Deity
Chandrakin (M): wearer of the moon; the peacock, with moon-like eyes on its tail
Chandrakumar (M): youthful moon; Murugan
Chandramani (M): moonstone
Chandramohan (M): as attractive as the moon
Chandranatha (M): lord of the moon; Śiva
Chandrapada (M): the feet of the moon; moonbeam
Chandraraja (M): born of the moon; the planet Mercury
Chandravarna (M): the moon's radiance; Murugan
Chandresa (M): lord of the moon; Śiva
Chandrika (F): moonlight
Chandrila (M): possessing the moon; Śiva
Charuvikrama (M): handsome hero; Śiva
Chatresa (M): lord of the umbrella; Śiva
Chaturbahu (M): Vishṇu and Śiva
Chaturveda (M): the four *Vedas*; the widsom of dharma, *artha*, kāma and *moksha*
Chayana (M): moon
Chechanna (M): vivacious
Chedi (M): intelligent; pleasant, likeable
Chedipati (M): king of the Chedis; master of bliss; honorific of Shishupala
Chediraja (M): king of Chedi
Chekitana (M): intelligent; Śiva

Chetana, Chetan (M): conscious; animated; distinguished, elegant; sentient, mind; soul
Chetas (M): intelligence, consciousness; splendor; soul; heart; mind
Chetrama (M): pervading conciousness
Chidambaram (M): hall of consciousness, Śiva's shrine
Chinmaya (M): full of consciousness; the supreme spirit
Chitra (F): beautiful, wonderful; a picture; striking; excellent
Chitrajyoti (F): wonderfully glorious; shining brilliantly
Chitralata (F): wonderful vine
Chitralekha (F): beautiful outline; a picture
Chitrali (F): a wonderful lady
Chitramayi (F): full of wonders; like a beautiful picture
Chitrangada (F): with wonderful limbs; with bejewelled arms
Chitrangi (F): of charming body
Chitrapushpi (F): variegated blossom; Hibiscus
Chitrarati (F): grantor of excellent gifts
Chitrashri (F): with divine beauty
Chitrini (F): having marks of excellence; ornamented; talented
Chitta (F): thoughtful, intelligent; spiritual
Chudakarna (M): shaven head; mendicant
Chudala (F): having a lock of hair on the crown; a saintly queen
Chudamani, Chudika, Chudikadevi (F): most excellent, best; jewel
Chuhal (F): joyous
Chula (M): man; nucleus of a comet
Chulika (F): an introduction
Chulin (M): ṛishi; crowned; a crest
Chulitaka (F): a poet
Chuni (F): a small ruby; precious
Chuninda (M): chosen as the best
Chushini (F): female attendant of Dūrgā
Chutaka (F): a mango tree
Chutalatika (F): woman of the mango tree

D

Dadhichi (M): a sage
Dahanapriya (F): beloved of fire; wife of Agni
Daksha (M-F): the skillful one; Gaṇeśa
Dakshayani (F): gold, golden ornament; daughter of a perfect being; Dūrgā
Dakshen, Dakshesh (M): clever; Śiva
Daksheyu (F): striving for perfection; perfect
Dalaja (F): produced from petals; honey
Dalakosa (F): treasure of petals; jasmine flower
Dalapati (M): army commander
Damini (F): lightning; beauty
Danadada (F): giving generously; an *apsarā* or *gandharva*
Danda (M): staff
Dandapani (M): carrier of a staff; Lord Murugan
Danta (F): tamed, mild; an *apsarā*
Danti (F): patience, self-restraint
Danvir (M): generous
Darpan (M): a mirror
Darshan (M), Darshani (F): holy sight, blessing; Dūrgā
Darshatashri (F): of obvious beauty
Das, Dasa, Dasan (M): devotee, servant of God
Dasrasu (F): mother of the *aśvins*

Dattadevi (F): Goddess of gifts; mother of Chandragupta II
Dattatreya (M): Given by Atri; the three-headed Divinity of Brahmā-Vishṇu-Śiva
Daya (F): compassion, sympathy
Dayal (M): compassionate
Dayamay (M): compassionate God
Dayananda (M): joy of compassion
Dayandhi (M): very compassionate
Dayanvita (F): surrounded by mercy; merciful
Dayashankar (M): source of compassion, Śiva
Dayavati (F): full of mercy
Dayita (F): worthy of compassion; beloved, cherished
Dehini (F): of the body, corporeal; bearer of the body; the Earth
Desapali (F): protected by the country, belonging to the country, a native; a musical rāga
Desna (F): gift, offering
Deva (M): a divine being or light; angel
Devabrata (M): brother of Gods
Devadasa (M): devotee of God
Devadatta (F): given by the Gods; the mother of Gautama Buddha's cousin
Devadhani (F): Indra's divine city
Devadutta (M): God-given
Devagarbha (F): the womb of the Gods; a river of ancient India
Devagiri (F): divine knowledge; a *rāgiṇī*
Devago (F): divine protectress; Śakti
Devahuti (F): invocation of the Gods
Devajami (F): sister of the Gods
Devajaya (F): wife of the Gods
Devajyoti (M-F): God's light
Devak (M), Devaki (F): divine, glorious; pious
Devakanchana (F): divine gold
Devakanya (F): celestial maiden
Devakiri (F): tongue of the Gods
Devakri (F): myth; a rāga
Devakulya (F): divine pitcher; belonging to the Gods; the holy Gaṅgā
Devakusuma (F): divine flower; cloves
Devala (F): attached to the Gods; music personified
Devalata (F): divine vine; the double jasmine
Devalekha (F): a divine line; with a divine outline; a celestial beauty
Devam (M): God; Śiva
Devamala (F): divine garland
Devamani (F): jewel of the Gods
Devamata (F): mother of the Gods
Devamati (F): godly minded; virtuous; venerated
Devamatra (F): equivalent to a God; a mother in Skanda's retinue
Devamayi (F): divine illusion
Devamitra (F): friend of the Gods
Devamshu (M): part of God
Devanadi (F): river of the Gods
Devananda (M-F): God's joy
Devanangana (F): divine woman
Devanatha (M): king; lord of devas
Devanga (M): with God's limbs
Devansha (M): part of God
Devapratima (F): image of the Gods; an idol
Devapriya (M): loved by the Gods
Devaradhana (F): worship of the Gods
Devaraja (M): Indra, king of devas
Devaranjan (M): loved by the devas
Devarati (F): delight of the Gods
Devarupa (F): divine form
Devasena (F): with an army of

Gods, Murugan's consort
Devasenapati (M): commander of the devonic army; Murugan
Devasmita (F): with a divine smile
Devavanchana (F): with divine speech
Devavani (F): divine voice
Devavarnini (F): describer of the Gods
Devavati (F): owned by the Gods
Devaviti (F): enjoyment for the Gods
Devayani (F): chariot of the Gods; invested with divine power
Devayosa (F): the wife of a God
Devayu (M): with divine life
Devendra, Deven (M): chief of the Gods; Indra
Devesi (F): a chief of the Goddesses; Dūrgā
Devi (F): angel, a name of Pārvatī
Devika (F): minor Deity; God-like
Devikadevi (F): invested with divine qualities
Dharabhuja (M): earth enjoyer; a king
Dhama, Dhaman (M): ray; strength; splendour, majesty; house, place of pilgrimage; a rishi
Dhamadhipa (M): lord of Rays; Sūrya
Dhamakesin (M): ray-haired; Sūrya
Dhamanidhi (M): treasure of splendour; Sūrya
Dhamavat (M): owner of a house; powerful, strong
Dhanadhipa (M): lord of wealth; Kubera
Dhanajita (M): wealth; winning
Dhanaka (M): avarice; a farmer; coriander; a Yayati king and son of Durdhama
Dhanapala (M): guardian of wealth; a king
Dhanapati (M): lord of wealth; Kubera
Dhanaraja, Dhanraj (M): king of wealth
Dhanavanta, Dhanavat (M): containing wealth; the sea
Dhanavardhana (M): increasing wealth
Dhanayush (M): with a rich life; a son of Pururavas
Dhanesha, Dhanesh, Dhaneshvara (M): lord of wealth; Kubera
Dhanin (M): wealthy; a messenger of the *asuras*; Kubera
Dhansukha (M): wealthy
Dhanu (M): the bow; the zodiac sign of Sagittarius
Dhanuraja (M): king of archers; an ancestor of Sakyamuni
Dhanurdhara, Dhanurgraha (M): bearer of a bow; the zodiac sign of Sagittarius; Śiva
Dhanurvaktra (M): bow-mouthed; an attendant of Skanda
Dhanurvedin (M): knower of the bow; versed in archery; Śiva
Dhanusha (M): the bow; a ṛishi
Dhanushaksha (M): bow-eyed; a sage
Dhanva (M): with a bow; a king of Kāśī , father of Dhanvantari
Dhanvanta (M): wealthy
Dhanvantari (M): moving in a curve; the physician of the Gods; founder of āyurveda, a river
Dhanya (F): virtuous; good; bestowing wealth
Dharamvira (M): protector of religion
Dharana (M): bearing, holding, keeping; resembling; Śiva
Dharanija (M): born of the Earth
Dharen (M): one who supports

Dharendra (M): king of the Earth; the Himālayas
Dharma (M): path of life; virtue; religion; duty, observance; right
Dharmachandra (M): moon of dharma; religious; virtuous, venerated
Dharmachara, Dharmacharin (M): observing dharma; virtuous; upright; Śiva
Dharmada (M): bestower of dharma; a follower of Skanda
Dharmadasa (M): one who serves religion
Dharmadeva (M): lord of dharma
Dharmagopa (M): protector of dharma
Dharmagosha (M): voice of dharma
Dharmamitra (M): nectar of dharma; friend of dharma
Dharmanandana (M): son of dharma; King Yudhishṭhira
Dharmandhu (M): well of dharma; deeply religious; venerated
Dharmanitya (M): constant in dharma
Dharmapala (M): guardian of dharma
Dharmaprabhasa, Dharmaprakasha (M): light of dharma; virtuous; religious; venerated
Dharmaputra (M): son of dharma
Dharmaranya (M): grove of dharma; a Brahmin devotee of Sūrya
Dharmasakha (M): friend of dharma
Dharmasarathi (M): charioteer of dharma;
Dharmasavarni (M): resembling dharma
Dharmashoka (M): Aśoka the dutiful; Emperor Aśoka
Dharmasila (M): follower of dharma
Dharmasindhu (M): ocean of dharma
Dharmasingha (M): lion of dharma; one who guards, protects and practices dharma deeply
Dharmasthavira (M): stable in dharma
Dharmasuta (M): son of dharma
Dharmasyas (M): glory of dharma
Dharmavahana (M): vehicle of dharma; Śiva
Dharmavardhana (M): increasing dharma; Śiva
Dharmavarna (M): colored in dharma; virtuous
Dharmavira (M): champion of dharma; defender of religion
Dharmavivardhana (M): promoter of dharma; a son of Aśoka
Dharmayu (M): one who lives for dharma; a Puru king
Dharmayupa (M): a pillar of dharma
Dharmendra, Dharmesha, Dharmeshvara (M): lord of dharma
Dharmendu (M): light of dharma
Dharmishta (M): staying in dharma; virtuous, righteous
Dharmottara (M): entirely devoted to dharma
Dharsanatman (M): with a fierce nature; Śiva
Dharuna (M): bearing, supporting, holding; Brahmā
Dhata (M): establisher, creator, founder; supporter; one of the twelve *adityas*
Dhataki (M): resembling the creator; a son of Vitihotra
Dhatri (M): establisher, creator, founder; supporter

Dhatriputra (M): Dhatri's son; Sanatkumāra, son of Brahmā
Dhaumya (M): smokey, grey; name of a ṛishi
Dhavak (M): runner; quick, swift, flowing
Dhavala (M-F): dazzling white; pure; handsome; beautiful
Dhavalachandra (M-F): white moon
Dhavalapaksha (M): white winged; the light half of the mouth
Dhavita (M-F): whitish; washed, purified, clean
Dhavlesh (M): lord of white; Śiva
Dhira, Dheera (M-F), Dhiren (F): courageous; Gaṇeśa
Dhyana (M): meditation
Didda (F): eyeball; a celebrated princess of Kashmir
Didhiti (F): firm, stable; devotion; inspiration; religious reflection
Didivi (F): shining, bright; risen as a star; Bṛihaspati
Didyotisu (F): wishing to shine
Digambara, Digvasas, Digvastra (M): sky clad; Śiva and Skanda
Digangana (F): quarter of the sky identified as a young maiden
Digisha (M): lord of direction
Dikkanya (F): quarter of the sky, identified as a young maiden
Diksha (F): initiation; consecration, dedication
Dikshita, Dikshitar (M): initiated; consecrated
Dilipa (M): one who gives, accepts and protects; a righteous king
Dimbesvari (F): Goddess of creation; Dūrgā
Dinabandhu (M): friend of the poor; Supreme Spirit
Dinakara (M): that which causes the day; the sun; an *aditya*
Dinakaratmaja (F): daughter of Dinakara; the river Yamuna
Dinamani (M): day jewel; the sun
Dinapati (M): day lord; the sun
Dinaraja (M): day king; the sun
Dinaratna (M): day jewel; the sun
Dinesha, Dinesh (M): day lord; sun
Dipa, Deepa (F): illuminating; light; a lamp, lantern
Dipaka (M): illuminating; kindling; inflaming; lamp; saffron
Dipakalika (F): flame of a lamp
Dipakarni (M): with shining ears; attentive
Dipakshi (F): bright-eyed
Dipali (F): a row of lights
Dipana (F): illuminating; impassioning; that which kindles
Dipanjali (F): a lamp for praying; waved before the Deity during ritual worship
Dipavali (F): row of lights
Dipavati (F): containing lights; a mythical river
Dipen (M): lord of the lamp; light of the lamp
Dipika (F): a small lamp, light, moolight; fire plant
Dipin (M): illuminating; exciting
Dipita (M): inflamed; illuminated; manifested; excited
Dipra (F): radiant, flaming, shining
Dipsikha (F): the flame of a lamp
Dipta (M): illuminated; blazing; hot; brilliant
Dipti, Deepti (F): brightness; light; illuminating; enlightening
Dirgha (M): lofty; long; tall; deep; Śiva
Dirgharoman (M): long-haired; an attendant of Śiva
Disa (F): region; direction; the point of the compass

Dishta (M): settled; directed, appointed, assigned, fixed
Disti (F): direction; good fortune; happiness; auspicious juncture
Diti (F): glow, brightness, light; splendor, beauty; a daughter of Daksha
Ditikara (M): bringing glow; irradiating, illuminating
Ditimat (M): possessed with a glow, bright; splendid; brilliant
Divakara (M): day maker, the sun
Divali (F): row of lights
Divapati (M): day lord; the sun
Divija (M-F): born of the sky; heaven born; celestial
Divoja (M): descended from heaven
Divolka (F): fallen from the sky; a meteor
Divya (F): divine, celestial, heavenly; charming, beautiful; an *apsarā*
Divyadeha (M): with a divine body
Divyadevi (F): divine Goddess
Divyajyoti (F): divine light
Divyakrititi (F): of divine form; beautiful
Divyanari, Divyastri (F): celestial maiden; an *apsarā*
Divyayamuna (F): the divine Yamuna river
Dodahi (F): flute
Dodiya (F): royal family
Doma (F): a singer
Dora (F): string of an instrument
Duhsadhin (M): door keeper
Dulal (M): dear one
Duradhara (M): invincible; inaccessible
Durantadeva (M): the God who removes difficulties, Gaṇeśa
Durasan (M): one who opens or unlocks doors; giver, granter
Durgadas, Durgadasa (M): devotee of Dūrgā
Durgesha, Durgesh (M): lord of *dūrvā*, the sacred grass; Śiva
Durjaya (M): invincible
Durodhara (M): door opener
Durvadeva (M): lord of *dūrvā*, the sacred grass; Śiva
Durvara (M): irresistable
Durvasas (M): a sage
Dushyantan (M): destroyer of evil; a lunar dynasty emperor
Duskala (M): destroyer of time; Śiva
Dustara (M): invincible
Duvas (M): worship

E

Easan, Eashan, Eesan, Easvan, Eashvan (M): the Supreme Ruler
Edha (F): prosperity, happiness
Egattala (F): the Goddess of Chennai, India
Eka (F): singular; peerless, unique; Dūrgā
Ekabhakti (F): the worship of one Deity
Ekachandra (F): the only moon; the best one; a mother in the retinue of Skanda
Ekacharini (F): a woman devoted to a single man; obedient; a loyal, chaste woman
Ekadanta (M): having one tusk; Gaṇeśa
Ekadeva (M): the one great God
Ekaja (F): born alone; the only child
Ekajata (F): with a single twisted lock of hair; a tantric Goddess
Ekakini (F): lonely, alone
Ekala (M): solitary, solo singer
Ekamati (F): concentrated
Ekamukha (F): single-faced

(rudraksha bead); with one mouth; extremely auspicious
Ekananga (F): lover; the daughter of Yashoda and foster sister of Kṛishṇa
Ekanayana (M): the planet Venus
Ekangika (F): made of sandalwood; fair; frequent; auspicious; dear to the Gods
Ekanta (F): a lovely woman; devoted to one
Ekantika (F): devoted to one aim
Ekaparna (F): single-leafed; living on a single leaf; the daughter of Himavana and Mena, the sister of Dūrgā, Aparna and Ekapatala and the wife of sage Devala
Ekarishi (M): chief ṛishi
Ekastaka (F): a collection of eight; the time for consecration; the eighth day after the full moon in the month of Magha
Ekatala (M): harmony, unison
Ekavaktra (F): single-faced; a mother of Skanda
Ekavali (F): string of pearls
Ekavira (F): outstandingly brave; a daughter of Śiva
Ekikarana (M): singularizing
Ekisa (F): one Goddess; the primal Goddess
Ekiya (M): a part of one whole, a friend
Eksika (F): eye
Ela (F): born of Ila; the Earth; cardamom
Elana (M-F): orange
Elavali (M-F): small delicate plant
Elika (M-F): small cardamom seed
Eloksi (F): with hair as thick as the cardamom creeper
Enajina (M): deer skin (sacred to lord Śiva)
Enaksi (F): doe-eyed
Eni (F): a deer; spotted; a flowing stream
Enipada (F): with deer-like feet; fleet-footed
Esanika (F): fulfilling desire; a goldsmith's balance scale
Esha (F): wish, desire; aim
Eshana (M): wishing, seeking
Eta, Etaha (F): shining; flowing
Etaka (M): a kind antelope or deer
Etasa (M): many-hued; colorful
Ethari (M): now, this moment
Eti (F): arrival

G

Gagan (M): sky
Gajanan (M): Lord Gaṇeśa
Gajapati, Gajendra or Gajaraja (M): lord or king of elephants
Gaman (M): speed; voyage
Ganadhara (M): chief of a group
Gananatha, Ganapati (M): lord of celestial attendants; Śiva; Gaṇeśa
Gandhika (M): fragrant
Ganesh, Ganesha, Ganesa, Ganesan (M): lord of the *gaṇas* or categories, Gaṇeśa
Ganeshvara, Ganesvara, Ganesvaran (M): lord of categories; Gaṇeśa
Ganga (F): Goddess of River Gaṅgā
Gangala (M): precious stone
Gangesh (M): lord of the Gaṅgā, Śiva
Gangeya (M): Son of Mother Gaṅgā; Murugan
Gauri (F): fair, brilliant, beautiful; Parvatī
Gauriputra (M): the son of Gaurī; Gaṇeśa
Gayatri (F): phrased verse; a sacred

Vedic mantra; a hymn to the sun; Sarasvatī as consort of Brahmā and mother of the *Vedas*
Girapati (M): lord of speech; Brahmā
Giratha (M): learned; Bṛihaspati
Giri (M): mountain; honorific title given to ṛishis; number eight; cloud; ball
Giribandhava (M): friend of mountains; Śiva
Giridhanvana (M): the rainbow of mountains; Śiva
Giridhvaja (M): with the mountain as its banner; Indra's thunderbolt
Girijanatha, Girijapati, (M): lord of Pārvatī; Śiva
Girijavara (M): consort of Pārvatī; Śiva
Giriksita (M): mountain dweller; Śiva
Girilala, Girinandana (M): son of the mountain lord; Gaṇeśa; Kārttikeya
Girimana (M): mountain-like; a powerful elephant
Girinatha, Girindra, Giripati, Girish (M): lord of the mountains; Śiva
Giripriya (M-F): lover of mountains; Śiva
Giriraj (M): king of mountains; Himavana
Girisa (M): lord of speech; Bṛihaspati
Gita, Geeta (F): song
Gitapriya (M): lover of music; an attendant of Skanda; Śiva
Gitavidyadhara (M): scholar of music; a *gandharva* who was a great musician
Godavari (F): granting water; bestowing prosperity; a river
Godhika (F): Sita's lizard; emblem of Goddess Gauri
Gomati (F): a famous river
Gopana (M-F): protected, secured
Gopta (M): guardian
Gora (M-F): fair skinned, handsome
Gorakh, Gorakhdeva (M): self-disciplined
Goral (F): beautiful; fair skinned
Gori (F): beautiful, Pārvatī
Grahapati (M): lord of celestial bodies; Gaṇeśa
Gudapushpa (F): sweet flower
Gudiya (F): doll
Guha, Guhan (M): secret one; a cave; dweller in the heart's cave; Murugan
Guhanatha (M): lord of the spiritual heart, Murugan
Guhapriya (F): liking secret places; Indra's daughter
Gulab (M): rose
Gulabee (F): pink, rosy, pleasing
Gulal (F): auspicious, colorful powder used in the Holi festival
Gulika (F): ball; anything round; pearl
Gulmini (F): clustering; creeper
Gulshan (M): garden
Gunadhaya (M): rich in virtues
Gunaja (F): daughter of virtue; the Priyangu creeper
Gunakali (F): possessing virtues; a raga
Gunakara (M): endowed with all virtues
Gunal, Gunala (M-F): virtuous
Gunalakshmi (F): Lakshmī the virtuous
Gunamaya (F): endowed with virtues

Gunanidhi (M): a treasure house of virtues
Gunasundari (F): made beautiful with virtues
Gunatita (M): transcending all qualities; Gaṇeśa, Śiva
Gunavara (F): best in qualities; meritorious; virtuous;
Gunavati (F): virtuous; a river of ancient India
Gunavina (F): virtuous
Guncha (F): blossom; flower bud
Gunchaka (F): boquet of flowers
Guniyala (F): a virtuous woman
Gunja (F): a small red berry plant
Gunjana (F): buzzing of a bee
Gunratna (M): a jewel of virtue
Gunvan, Gunvanta (M): virtuous
Gurudasa (M): devotee, servant of the teacher
Guruparan (M): He who initiated His Father; Murugan
Gurupritа (M): love of the teacher

H

Haima (M): snow, frost; dew; golden; the Himālayas; Śiva
Hakesa (M): lord of sound
Hamsa, Hansa (M): swan; goose
Hamsika (F): beautiful swan
Hansaja (M): son of a swan; a warrior in Skanda's band
Hansanada (M): the cry of the swan
Hanugiri (M): the mountain of Hanuman
Hara, Harak, Haran (M): He who takes away; consumer; absorber; divisor; Śiva and Agni
Harachudamani (M): the crest gem of Śiva
Haradeva (M): lord of Śiva
Harahara (M): Śiva's necklace
Haramanas (M): the mind of Śiva; the soul of God
Haranetra (M): the eye of Śiva
Hararupa (M): with the form of Śiva
Harasekhara (M): the crest of Śiva
Harasiddha (M): eternal of Śiva
Harasunu (M): son of Śiva; Kārttikeya
Harasvarupa (M): in Śiva's image
Haratejas (M): Śiva's fiery energy
Harena (F): devotee of lord Śiva
Haresvara (M): Śiva and Vishṇu conjoined, Hari-Hara
Harinakshi (F): eyes as beautiful as a doe
Harita (F): green
Harnita (F): deer-like
Harsha (F): joy, delight
Harshika, Harshila, Harshina (F): joyful
Haryasva (M): with bay horses; Indra and Śiva
Hasanti (F): smiling
Hasini (F): laughter
Hastimukha (M): elephant-faced; Gaṇeśa
Hatakesha (M): lord of gold, Śiva
Havana (M): fire sacrifice, Agni
Havisha (M-F): worthy of oblation; Śiva
Hema (M-F): gold; a dark horse
Hemabala (M): power of gold; the pearl
Hemachandra (M): golden moon
Hemadri (M): golden mountain
Hemaguha (M): golden cave
Hemakanta (M): bright as gold
Hemakeli (M): golden sport; Agni
Hemakesha (M): with golden hair; Śiva
Hemakshi (F): with golden eyes
Hemal (M-F), Hemali (F): golden

Hemamalin (M): garlanded with gold; Sūrya
Heman (M): golden, yellow; the Jasmine blossom
Hemanatha (M): lord of gold, Śiva
Hemanga, Hemanya (M): golden-bodied, a brahmin; a lion
Hemapushpam (M): golden-flowered
Hemavati (F): golden, Pārvatī
Hemendra (M): lord of gold, Indra
Hemina (F): golden
Hemlata (M-F): golden creeper
Henal (F): made from the *henna* powder
Heramba (M): son of wealth; Gaṇeśa
Hetal (F): full of love
Himachala (M): abode of snow; the Himālaya mountain
Himadri (F): peak of snow; the Himālaya mountain; Pārvatī
Himajyoti (M-F): with snow-like light; Chandra
Himakara (M): snow-handed; causing cold; white; the moon
Himasaila (M): snow mountain; the Himālayas
Himatanaya (M-F): son of the moon
Himayati (M): one who favors; champion
Himmat (M): courage
Hinadosa (M): without fault
Hindi (F): wanderer; Dūrgā
Hindika (F): astrologer
Hindikanta, Hindipriya (M): beloved by Dūrgā; Śiva
Hinduka (M): wanderer; Śiva
Hingula, Hinguli (F): vermillion
Hinkara (M): chanting of hymns; the invocation of a Deity
Hinvati (F): to gladden; delight
Hira (F): diamond; Lakshmī
Hiradevi (F): queen
Hiranga (M): diamond-bodied; Indra's thunderbolt
Hiranya (M): gold; most precious
Hiranyavaha (M): bearing gold; Śiva; the river Sona
Hiresa (M): king of gems
Hiroka; Hiroki (F): poet
Hitasha (M): He who consumes oblations; Agni
Hitesin (M): benevolent
Hitesvara (M): God of welfare; caring for others
Homa (M): oblation
Honna (M): to possess
Hosang (M): to be one's own self
Hotravahana (M): with the chariot of invocation
Hullura, Hulluri (M-F): king of the Nāgas
Humbadevi (F): Goddess of jubilation
Hundana, Hundani (M-F): attendent of Śiva
Hundanesa (M): a ram; tiger; Śiva
Hushka (M): a king
Huta, Huti (M): one to whom an oblution into fire is offered; Śiva
Hutapriya (F): beloved of fire
Hutasa, Hutasi (M-F): subsisting by fire; fire consumer
Hutasana (F): a *yoginī*; having the nature of fire
Huvishka (M): a king

I

Iditri (F): one who praises
Ijana (M): one who has sacrificed
Ikshanika (M): a fortune teller
Ilina (M): from Ili, a weapon
Indivar (M-F): blue lotus
Indra (M): king of the devas

Irajan (M): born of the wind
Irilan (M): He who has no end
Isan, Isha, Ishan, Ishvan, Eesan, Eesha (M): Supreme ruler, Śiva
Ishva (M): a spiritual teacher
Isi, Isani, Eesi, Eesani (F): ruler; Parvatī
Isvaran, Eashvaran (M): lord of the Universe; a millionaire

J

Jagadagauri (F): fairest of the universe, Pārvatī
Jagadamba, Jaganmata (F): mother of the world, Dūrgā; Lakshmī
Jagadambika (F): little mother of the universe; Dūrgā
Jagadhatri (F): sustainer of the universe; Pārvatī
Jai, Jay, Jaya (M): victory
Jalabalika (F): maiden of water; daughter of the waters; lightning as the daughter of the clouds
Jalada (M): giving water; raincloud
Jaladhi (F): living in water; ocean; a crocodile
Jaladhipa (M): lord of the waters
Jalaj; Jalaja (F): born of water, the lotus; Lakshmī
Jalakanta (F): beloved of water; the ocean; wind
Jalakusuma (F): water flower; the lotus
Jalal (M): glory
Jalalata (F): creeper of water; a wave; a watervine
Jalapushpa (F): water lily
Jambalini (F): maiden of water, name of a river
Janabalika (F): daughter of the people; very bright; lightning
Janak, Janaka (M): progenitor; a father; name of a famous king
Janaki (F): daughter of Janaka
Janamitra (M): people's friend
Janava (M): protector of men
Janesha (M): king of people
Jantananda, Jnatanandana (M): bliss of knowing
Japa (M-F): repetition of mantras; chanting; incantation
Japendra, Japesa, Japesha (M): lord of chanting; Śiva
Jasarani (F): queen of fame
Jatarupa (F): beautiful, brilliant, golden
Jatin (M): pertaining to a mendicant
Jayapal (M): fruit of victory; a king
Jayendra, Jeyendra (M): lord of victory
Jayin (M): victorious
Jeman (M): possessing victory
Jenya (M): of noble origin; true
Jetasri (F): Goddess of gains; a rāga
Jetva (M): to be gained
Jhankar (F): a sweet sound
Jhanvi, Janvika (F): Gaṅgā, daughter of ṛishi Jahinu
Jharna (F): a small brook
Jiva, Jeeva (M-F): soul
Jivan, Jivana (M): source of life; the sun; Śiva
Jivanatha (M): lord of life
Jivantha, Jivatha (M): long-lived; virtuous; life, breath; peacock
Jivini (M): the sun; a brahmin; praise
Jnanada (M): giver of knowledge
Jnanadarpana (M): mirror of knowledge
Jnanadatta (M): given by knowledge
Jnanadeva (M): being of knowledge
Jnanadipa (M): lamp of knowledge
Jnanadirgha (M): far-knowing; farseeing
Jnanagarbha (M): source of knowl-

edge
Jnanakara (M): maker of knowledge
Jnanaketu (M): light of wisdom
Jnanakirti (M): having marks of intelligence
Jnanameru (M): mountain of knowledge
Jnanamurti (M): knowledge personified
Jnanapati (M): lord of knowledge
Jnanaprabha, Jnanaprakasha (M): brilliant with knowledge
Jnanaraja (M): king of knowledge
Jnanasiddhi (M): master of knowledge
Jnanavajra (M): knowledge-thunderbolt
Jnanavapi (M): pool of knowledge
Jnani (M): enlightened one
Jnata (F): intelligent
Jnatri (M): knower
Jogendra, Jogindra (F): lord of yoga; Śiva
Jogesha, Jogesh (F): king of yoga
Jogini (F): *yoginī*
Jogisha (F): lord of yoga
Josha (F): pleased; force, power
Josika (F): cluster of buds; maiden
Josita (F): pleased
Jovaki (F): firefly
Jugnu (M): firefly; ornament
Juhi (F): jasmine flower
Juhu (M): tongue; flame; Brahmā and Sūrya
Jurni (F): fire-brand
Jushka (M): lover; worshiper; meritorious
Jushta (M), Jushti (F): love; service
Jutika (F): a kind of camphor
Juvasdeva (M): divine quickness in thought, word and deed
Jyoti, Jyothi, Jothi (M-F): light

K

Kadhapriya (F): ever-loved; ever-friendly
Kailash, Kailas (M): Śiva's sacred mountain abode
Kaileshvari (F): Goddess of water; the family Goddess; Dūrgā
Kairavini (F): water-born; the white lotus plant
Kaivalya (M): established in liberation; Murugan
Kakalika (F): with a low and sweet voice
Kakubha (F): peak, summit; splendour, beauty; wreath of Champaka flowers
Kala (F): a small part of anything; a skill; ingenuity
Kaladhara, Kaladharan (M): wearer of the crescent; Śiva
Kalamali (F): dispelling darkness; splendid; sparkling
Kalandika (F): bestower of art and skills; wisdom, intelligence
Kalapini (F): as blue as the peacock's tail
Kalavati (F): moonlight; well versed in the arts, *kalās*
Kali (F): blackness, the Goddess
Kalikantha (F): with a pleasing voice; the dove
Kallolini (F): always happy; a surging stream or river
Kalyanavati (F): full of virtue; princess
Kalyani (F): beneficial, lucky; excellent; propitious; a sacred cow
Kamakanta (F): beloved of Kāma; jasmine
Kamakshi (F): lovely-eyed
Kamala (M-F), Kamal, Kamla (F): born of a lotus, spring; desirous,

beautiful, excellent; wealth; pale red; rose colored; Brahmā
Kamaladevi (F): lady of the lotus
Kamalini (F): lotus plant, collection of lotuses; beautiful; fragrant; auspicious; dear to the Gods
Kamini (F): embodiment of love; Gaṇeśa
Kamini, Kamra (F): desirable, beautiful; loving
Kanak, Kanchan (F): gold
Kanakambara (F): clad in gold, golden; a flower
Kanakasundari (F): as beautiful as gold
Kanda, Kandan, Kandiah (M): of integrated form; Murugan
Kandanatha (M): quick lord; Murugan
Kannaki (F): chaste and devoted wife, Sītā
Kanti (F): glory, beauty; wish; decoration
Kanya (F): maiden
Kapil (M), Kapila (F): reddish; a great ṛishi
Karishma (F): miracle
Karpani (F): gladness
Karttikeya (M): giver of courage; Murugan
Karttiki (F): full moon in the month of Kārttika; pious, holy
Karunya (F): merciful, compassionate; praiseworthy
Kashi, Kasi (M): shining, splendrous; Vārānasī, Śiva's holy city
Kashvi (F): shining; beautiful
Kathir, Katir (M): formless light, Murugan
Kathiresan (M): lord of light; Murugan
Kaumari (F): virginal
Kavita (F): poem; poet
Kavyamata (F): mother of poetry, mother of a brilliant one
Kedara, Kedaradeva (M): field, meadow; peak of Himālayan mountain; Śiva
Kedaranatha (M): lord of fields and meadows; Śiva as worshiped in Himālayas
Kedaresa (M): lord of fields and meadows; statue of Śiva in Kāśī
Kedarin (M): region of the Himālayas, Śiva
Kekavala (M): peacock
Kekaya (M): chief of a warrior tribe; full of water
Kelaka (M): dancer, tumbler
Kelasa (M): crystal
Kenati (F): wife of Kāma
Kenava (M): of a teacher
Kenipa (M): sage
Kerkhi (M): gold necklace
Kesara (M), Kesari (F): mane; saffron
Kesarin (M): having a mane; a lion; prince
Kesayanti (M): attendant of Skanda
Kesin (M): long-haired; lion, Rudra
Ketaka (M): banner, flag; gold ornament
Ketali (F): one with shelter
Ketana (M-F): house, shelter; flag, banner
Ketayan, Ketayitri (M): one who summons, counsels, advises
Ketu (M): a bright appearance; chief, leader, eminent person; the moon's south node
Ketubha (M): cloud
Ketubhuta (M): having a symbol
Ketumala (M): garland of light
Keturatna (M): a bright jewel
Ketusringa (M): with shining horns; a king of ancient Bhārat

Ketutara (M): a comet
Ketuvarman (M): flag shooter; one whose flag flies everywhere
Keva (F): lotus
Kevala (M): alone; absolute, exclusive, pure, whole, perfect
Kevalin (M): seeker of the Absolute
Keya (M-F): monsoon flower; speed
Keyura (M): armlet
Keyuraka (M): one who wears an armlet
Kimaya (F): divine
Kinjala (F): brook; lotus
Kinjalk (F): essence of a lotus
Kinnari (F): female singer; stringed musical instrument; a singer in Indra's court
Kiranamalin (M): garlanded with rays; Sūrya
Kiranamayi (F): full of rays
Kiranapani (M): ray-handed; Sūrya
Kiranapati (M): lord of rays; Sūrya
Kirata (M): Śiva in his form as a warrior of the Kirata tribe
Kirati (F): one who dwells in the mountains; Dūrgā and Gaṅgā
Kirin, Kirina (M-F): one who praises; poet, writer; speaker
Kirmi (F): an image of gold
Kirnali (F): beam of light
Kirtana (M): praise; repeating
Kirtenya (M): worthy of praise
Kirti (F): fame, glory; the Goddess of fame and reputation
Kirtida (F): giver of fame
Kirtideva (M): lord of light; lord of fame
Kirtidhara (M): bearer of fame
Kirtimalini (F): garlanded with fame; an attendant of Skanda
Kirtiman, Kirtimanta (M): famous
Kirtimukha (M): famous face; a *gaṇa* born from the hair of Śiva
Kirtisena (M): with a glorious army
Kishala (F): bud; blossom
Kishori (F): small girl
Kodandin (M): armed with a bow, Śiva
Komala (M-F): tender, soft, delicate, sweet; handsome, beautiful
Kotijit (M): conquering millions; Kālīdāsa
Kotikasya (M): abode of millions
Kotira (M): horned; Indra
Kotishvara (M): lord of millions
Kovida (M): knowledgeable, wise
Kripa (F): compassion; grace; blessing
Kripalavi (M-F): the compassionate one; Murugan
Kritini (F): the skillful one; Gaṇeśa
Kriya (M): action; temple worship
Kuhupala (M): lord of the moon; Śiva
Kuja (M): the *gaṇa* who wears the *rudrāksha mālā*
Kuladeva (M): Deity of the family
Kuladevi (F): family Goddess
Kuladipa (M): light of the family
Kulagan (M): beautiful one; Murugan
Kulamani (F): jewel of the family
Kulandai (M): beautiful one; Murugan
Kuleshvari (F): family Goddess
Kulishvara (M): family God; Śiva
Kumar, Kumara, Kumaran (M): youth; prince; Murugan
Kumaradevi (F): Goddess of children; a princess who was the wife of Chandragupta
Kumari (F): maiden; virgin girl
Kumudanatha (M): the moon
Kundalin (M): wearing large earings; Śiva
Kundan (M): glittering, sparkling;

gold; pure, refined
Kunjeshvara (M): lord of the forest
Kuntanatha (M): lord of vegetation
Kusavarta (M): of a passage of the Gaṅgā; of a *muni*; Śiva
Kusha (F): a kind of sacred grass
Kusumita (F): flower in full bloom
Kuvala (M): enricher of knowledge; water lily; pearl; water
Kuvalayesha (M): lord of the Earth; ruler of waters; lord of lilies
Kuvalya (M): the blue lotus

L

Lakshmi (F): wealth, prosperity; Goddess of wealth
Lambodara (M): of large belly; Gaṇeśa
Lekha (M): document; Deity, God
Lekhabhra (M): bright as light; shining
Lekharaja (M): lord of the Gods; the Supreme Being
Lelihana (M): darting out the tongue; serpent; Śiva
Lesha (M): small portion; a short song
Lila, Leela (F): the divine play
Linika (F): absorbed, dedicated
Lochan, Lochana (M): eyes
Lokesh (M): lord of regions
Lokpriya (M): popular among all
Lomesh (M): a sage
Lubdhaka (M): hunter; the star Sirius
Lunadosha (M): sinless; an attendant of Śiva
Lunakarna (M): with pierced ears
Lusha (M): saffron; name of a ṛishi

M

Madhu, Madhur, Madhuri (F): honey
Mahadev, Mahadeva, Mahadevan (M): Great God; Śiva
Mahadevi (F): great Goddess
Mahakala (M): great time; Śiva
Mahan (M): great one; Śiva
Mahati (M-F): the consummation of glory; Murugan
Mahendra (M): supreme ruler
Mahesh, Mahesa, Mahesan, Maheshvara (M): great lord; Śiva
Mahesvari, Maheshvari (F): great Goddess
Mala (F): rosary, prayer beads
Mallik (M): king; lord
Mallika (F): jasmine
Manasa (F): mental power; Pārvatī
Manesh (M): king of mind
Mangala (F): auspicious one
Mani (M-F): jewel
Manick, Manik, Manickan, Manickam (M): ruby-like
Manil (M): a beautiful bird
Manin (M): mind
Manish (M): intellect
Manjari (F): a bouquet
Manjeet (M): conqueror of mind
Manju (F): pollen grains; attractive
Manoj (M): born of the mind
Manu (M): intelligent; the first man
Mardav (M): softness; letting go of ego
Markendeya (M): winning over death; devotee of Śiva
Maruti (M): son of the wind; Hanuman
Matta (M-F): the embodiment of happiness; Murugan
Mayil (F): peacock
Mayilvaganam (M): peacock

mount; Murugan
Mayini (F): source of illusory power
Midhusha (M): bountiful; son of Indra
Midhushi (F): liberal; bountiful; Śakti
Midhushtama (M): most liberal; Sūrya
Mihika (F): mist, fog; snow
Mihikansu (M): mist-rayed; the moon
Mihira (M): causing heat, light and rain; sun, clouds, wind, air; a sage
Mihirakula (M): born in the solar dynasty; a king
Mihirana (M): born of the sun; Śiva
Milana, Milan (M): union; meeting; contract
Milap (M): embrace
Milita (F): partly opened, as in a flower blossom
Mina, Meena (F): fish; gem; goblet of wine
Minaketana (M): fish-bannered; Kāma
Minakshi, Meenakshi (F): fish-eyed; a species of Durva grass; Pārvatī
Minalaya (M): the ocean
Minanatha (M): master of fish
Minaraja (M): king of fish
Minesh, Mineshvara (M): lord of fish; Śiva
Mira (F): ocean;
Mirata (M): mirror
Misraka (M): mixed; manifold
Misri (M): mixed; sweet
Mita (F): measured, gauged; tried and tested; a friend; established
Mitadhvaja (M): with a strong flag
Mitali (F): friendship
Mithi (M): knowledged; truthful
Mithilesa (M): lord of Mithila
Mithuna (M): forming a pair; the zodiac sign of Gemini; honey and clarified butter
Miti (F): friend
Mitra (M): friend, companion
Mitrabahu (M): helped by friends
Mitradeva (M): lord of friends
Mitradharman (M): with faith in friends
Mitragupta (M): protected by friends
Mitrajit (M): winning friends
Mitrajna (M): knower of friends; knower of the sun
Mitrakrit (M): friend maker
Mitrasaha (M): indulgent towards friends
Mitrasena (M): with an army of friends
Mitravaha, Mitravan, Mitravinda (M): having friends
Mitravardhana (M): cherished by friends
Mitravarman (M): warrior among friends
Mitrayu (M): friendly; attractive; prudent
Mitrodaya (M): sunrise
Mitula (M): measured, limited, moderate
Mitushi (F): with limited desires
Mivara (M): leader of an army
Moda (M): pleasure, enjoyment, joy; fragrance
Modaka (M), Modaki (F): pleasing, delighting; a sweet goodie
Modakara (M): one who accomplishes joy; full of joy, delighted; a ṛishi
Mohana, Mohi, Mohin, Mohita (M), Mohini (F): infatuating; beautiful; bewildering; one of the five arrows of Kāma; Śiva or

Kṛishṇa
Mohantara (M): very infatuating
Mohona (F): endearing
Moksha (M): emancipation, liberation; Mount Meru
Mokshadvara (M): gate of liberation; Sūrya
Mokshin, Mokshita (M): free, liberated
Mora, Morara (M): peacock
Moti (M): pearl
Motia (M): jasmine
Muchira (M): generous, liberal; virtuous; the wind; the Deity
Mudabhaja (M): desirer of happiness
Mudanvita (M): pleased, delighted, filled with joy
Mudavarta (M): surrounded by happiness
Muddaya (M): to be happy; to delight
Mudgala (M): ever happy
Muhurta (M): moment, instant
Mukesh, Mukesa (M): lord of liberation; Śiva
Mukhachandra (M): moon face; with a face like the moon
Mukhaja (M): born of the mouth
Mukhakamala (M): with a face as lovely as a lotus
Mukhendu (M): with a face as lovely as the moon
Mukta (M): freed, emancipated, delivered; opened; a pearl
Muktaguna (M): qualities of a pearl
Muktananda (M): the joy of liberation
Muktapida (M): crowned with pearls
Muktapushpa (M): pearly flower
Muktaratna (M): pearl gem
Muktasena (M): with a free army
Muktesh, Muktesa (M): lord of emancipation
Mukunda (M): precious stone; one who liberates
Mukutesvara (M): lord of the crown
Mula (M): root or core
Mulaka (M): prince
Mulapurusha (M): male representative of a family
Mularaja (M): lord of creation; the original root
Mulashanti (M): a Vedic treatise
Mulika (M): principal, primary
Muni (M): silent one; sage; ascetic
Munichandra (M): moon among ascetics
Munikumara (M): young ascetic
Munindra (M): chief of munis; Śiva
Muniratna (M): jewel among sages
Munisa (M): chief of munis
Munistuta (M): praised by sages; Gaṇeśa
Murajaka (M): a drum; one of Śiva's attendants
Murdhan, Murdhanya (M): the top or summit, beginning or first
Murthi, Murthy, Murti (M): form; temple image
Muruga, Murugan (M): beautiful; tender youth; the God of spiritual striving, lord of ascetics; Kārttikeya
Murugesa (M): lord of the detached; Murugan
Mushika (M): Gaṇeśa's *vahana,* the mouse
Muthu (M): nice; gentle

N

Nabhan (M): heart center; Śiva residing in the lotus of the heart
Nabhanyu (M), Nabhanya (F):

springing forth from the heavens; ethereal, celestial, heavenly
Nabhasa (M), Nabhasi (F): misty; of the sky; celestial
Nabhashvati (F): born of the sky; lightning; thunder
Nabhasindhu (F): river of the sky; the Ākāshagaṅgā or celestial Gaṅgā, the Milky Way
Nachiketa, Nachiketan (M): not conscious; fire
Nada (M): sound
Nadabindu (M): seed sound; the primal sound, *Aum*
Nadinatha, Nadipati, Nadisha (M): lord of rivers; the ocean
Naga (M): mountain; serpent; elephant
Nagapati (M): overlord of the mountains; Himavan
Nagadhiraja (M): The paramount king of the mountains; Himavan
Nagamma (F): poetess
Naganandini (F): mountain-born; Pārvatī
Nagapushpika (F): flower of the mountains; yellow Jasmine
Nagaraja (M): king of serpents; Śiva who wears serpents as a mark of immortality and control of the instinctive mind
Nagarini (F): urban; sophisticated
Nagasri (F): princess
Nagendra (M): chief of serpents; Chief of mountains; Himavan
Nagesh, Nagesa, Nageshvar, Nageshvara (M): lord of serpents; lord of mountains; Himavan, Śiva; Mahārishi Patāñjali
Nageshvari (F): Goddess of serpents; Manasa
Nagija (F): blossom of the flower Mesua Roxburghii
Naka (M-F): vault of heaven; sky; Sūrya
Nakaloka (M): the heavenly worlds
Nakanadi (F): river of the sky; the Ākāshagaṅgā or celestial Gaṅgā, the Milky Way
Nakanari (F): heavenly woman
Nakanatha, Nakadhipa, Nakapati, Nakesa, Nakesh, Nakeshvara (M): lord of the sky; Indra
Nakanayaka (M): God of Jupiter
Nakapala (M): sky guardian
Nakavanita (F): dwelling in the sky
Nakin (M): having heaven; a God
Nakshatra (M-F): one of 27 principle asterisms (star clusters, also called Lunar Mansions) in the Hindu system of astrology, usually referring to one's birthstar
Nakula (M): mongoose; lord Śiva who, like the mongoose, is immune to the venom of serpents
Nala (F): made of reeds, a lotus flower
Nalada (F): nectar of a flower
Nalakini (F): multitude of flowers; lotus lake
Nalami (F): fragrant nectar; lute of Śiva
Nalika (F): spear, arrow; lotus flower
Nalini (F): lotus-like; lotus; beautiful; fragrant; gentle; sacred
Nalita (F): Arum Colocassia
Namasya (M-F): worshipful, worthy of salutation
Namdeesh (M): the ocean
Namita (F): one who worships, devotee
Namya (F): venerable
Nanda (F): delight; prosperity
Nandadevi (F): Goddess of happiness; lofty Himalayan peak

Nandana (M): rejoicing; gladdening
Nandi, Nandikesh (M): happy, joyful; Śiva's bull; Śiva expressing his blissful nature
Nandika, Nandini, Nandanti (F): gladdening, delightful, blissful; a daughter; Dūrgā and Gaṅgā
Nandirudra (M): joyful Rudra; Śiva
Nandishvara (M): lord of Nandi; Śiva
Nandita (F): one who pleases
Nanthakumar (M): eternal youth
Naradhara (M): supporter of mankind; Śiva
Narapriya (M): beloved of mankind; favorable to mankind
Naravira (M): heroic man
Narendra, Naresh, Naresa, Nareshvara (M): chief of mankind
Nari (F): feminine; wife, mother; daughter of Mount Meru
Narika (F): spiritual; watery
Narishta (M): dear to women; Arabian jasmine
Naritirtha (F): five sacred bathing places for women
Narmada (F): giver of pleasure; a holy river
Narmadeshvara (M): lord of the river Narmada; Śiva
Narmadyuti (F): bright with joy; happy, merry
Nartaki, Nataki, Natakiya (F): dancer
Narvakya (F): words of the wife
Narya (M): heroic; manly, human
Natana, Natya (M): dancing
Nataraj, Nataraja, Natarajan (M): king of dancers; Śiva
Natesa, Natesh, Nadesan, Nateshvar, Nadeshvar (M): lord of dancers; Śiva
Nateshvari (F): Goddess of dance; Pārvatī
Nath, Natha, Nathan (M): protector, master, lord, chief; blessing
Nathoka (M): a poet
Nati (F): bowing, humble
Natyapriya (M): fond of dance; Śiva
Nava (M): shout of joy
Navamallika (F): the new creeper; jasmine
Navangi (F): new, fresh body; lovely, beautiful
Navika (M): captain, sailor; chief of a vessel
Navina, Naviya, Navya (F): new, fresh, young
Nayaja (F): daughter of wisdom
Nayaka (M-F): chief, leader, guide
Nayanapriti, Nayanatara (F): star of one's eye; beloved; very dear
Nayavati (F): bearer of prudence
Nayika (F): noble lady
Nehal, Nehanshu (M-F): affectionate, loving
Neman (M): of excellent conduct
Neminathan (M): lord of the thunderbolt
Nesan (M): devotee, friend
Nesarajan (M): king of affection
Neta (M): lord, leader, ruler
Netanatha (M): lord of leaders
Netra (M): eye; leader, guide
Netrakosha (M): treasure of the eye; bud of a flower
Netramusha (M): capturing the eye; beautiful; unusual
Nichita (F): full; flowing down; Gaṅgā
Nidhra (M): moon; circumference of a wheel; the lunar mansion Revati
Niharika (F): Milky Way
Nika (M-F): tree; irrigation channel
Nikhil (M): the Sun God, Sūrya

Nila, Neela (M-F), Nilan (M), Nilani (F): dark blue; indigo; sapphire; Indian fig tree
Nilabha (F): of bluish hue; moon
Nilachandra (F): blue moon
Nilagala (F): blue-necked; Śiva
Nilagiri Ternatea: mountain; blue variety of flower Clitoria
Nilaja (F): blue steel
Nilakamala (F): blue lotus or water lily
Nilakantala (F): blue earings
Nilakantha, Nilakanta (M), Nilakanthi (F): blue-throated; Śiva
Nilalohita (M-F): red and blue; Śiva and Murugan
Nilama (M): dark blue; sapphire; indigo
Nilapadma (F): blue lotus
Nilapushpa (F): blue-flowered; a species of Eclipta
Nilasi (F): Vitex Negundo flower
Nilata (F): blueness
Nili (F): indigo; a Goddess
Nilima, Neelima (F): blueness
Nilini (F): the indigo plant
Nilmani, Neelmani (F): blue diamond, sapphire
Niloda (F): with blue water; a river
Nina (F): ornamented; slender
Nira (F), Neera: consisting of water
Niraj, Niraja (M-F): illuminating
Nirajakshi (F): lotus-eyed; beautiful
Nirajayati (F): shining upon, illuminating
Niranjana (M): without blemish; Gaṇeśa
Nirmala (M-F), Nirmalan (M): without impurity
Nirmalanatha (M): lord without bonds; Śiva
Nirupa (M-F): formless; air; ether; a God
Nirvikar (M): flawless
Nisha (F), Neesha: night; dream
Nishasari (F): night bird; owl
Nishtha (F): faith; conviction; fidelity
Nita (F), Neeta, Niti: guided, correct, modest
Nitha (M): leader; a king of the Vṛishṇi dynasty
Nitya (M-F): eternal, without end
Nivan (F): one of the ten horses of the moon

O

Odati (F): dawn; refreshing
Oghavati (F): a swift stream
Ojasvini (F): brave; bright
Omala (F): bestower of the root mantra, *Aum*
Omisa (F): Goddess of birth, life and death
Omkar, Omkara (M): the root mantra, *Aum*
Omvati (F): possessing the power of the root mantra, *Aum*

P

Pachata (M): cooked, boiled; Sūrya, Agni and Indra
Padma (F): lotus; lotus-hued one; Lakshmī
Padmabandhu (M): friend of the lotus; Sūrya.
Padmagarbha (M): born of a lotus; Brahmā, Vishṇu, Śiva and Sūrya
Padmaja (F): born of a lotus; Lakshmī
Padmakara (M): holding a lotus; Sūrya
Padmala (F): lotus-seated; Lakshmī
Padmalochana (F): lotus-eyed

Padmamalini (F): lotus-garlanded; Lakshmī
Padmanjali (F): offering of lotuses
Padmaraga (M): lotus-hued; ruby
Padmashri (F): divine lotus; as beautiful as a lotus
Padmin (M-F), Padmini (F): lotus-like; one who plucks the lotus; one who likes the lotus; elephant
Palaka (M): protector; prince, sovereign
Palaksha (M): white
Palani (M): renunciate; Murugan
Palin (M): protecting, guarding; keeping
Pallava (M), Pallavi (F): sprout, shoot; spray; bud, blossom
Panava (M): small drum; cymbal; prince
Panavin (M): possessing a small drum; Śiva
Panchaka (M): consisting of five elements; an attendant of Skanda
Panchaksha (M): five-eyed; an attendant of Śiva
Panchala (M): consisting of five; surrounded by five rivers; a rāga; a *nāga*; Śiva
Panchama (M): dextrous, clever; beautiful, brilliant
Panchamukha (M): five-faced, Śiva and Gaṇeśa
Panchasya (M): five-faced; lion; Śiva
Pandura (M): pale; yellow-white, an attendant of Skanda
Panika (M): hand; an attendant of Skanda
Panikarna (M): hands and ears conjoined; attentive, pro-active; Śiva
Panita (M): admired, praised
Pannagesha (M): lord of the creeping ones; lord of serpents; Śiva
Panshula (M): Śiva's staff; Śiva covered with sandalwood powder
Papuri (M): bountiful; liberal, abundant
Paraga (M): pollen of a flower; fragrant; fame, celebrity
Paraj (M): gold
Param (M): supreme; Śiva
Paramaka (M): highest, best
Paramakshara (M): the supreme syllable; *Aum*
Paramani (M): excellent jewel
Paramesha, Parameshvara (M): supreme lord; Śiva
Parameshvari (F): supreme Goddess
Paramika (F): highest, best, greatest; one who fulfills desires
Parimala (F): fragrance, perfume
Parinaha (M): circumference; width; Śiva
Parisatya (M): pure truth
Parishruta (M): famous, celebrated; an attendant of Skanda
Parshupani (M): axe holder; Gaṇeśa
Parvataja (M): born of mountains
Parvati (F): of all mountains; mountain stream
Pashunatha, Pashupati, Pasunatha, Pasupati (M): lord of cattle; lord of souls; Śiva
Patanjali (M): worshipful; name of a ṛishi
Paturupa (M): very clever
Pavana, Pavanta (M): pious; sacred; pure; fire; incense; protecting
Peruman (M): the great one; Śiva
Pesani, Peshani, Peshanidevi (F): well-formed; beautiful
Peshal, Peshala, Peshaladevi (F): delicate
Piki (F): Indian cuckoo
Pillaiyar (M): Gaṇeśa, the noble child
Pinaki (F): Śiva's box

Pinga, Pingala (F): of yellow hue, golden, fiery; turmeric, saffron; Lakshmī
Pingakshi (F): tawny-eyed, a Deity presiding over the family
Piroja (F): turquoise
Pitayuthi (F): an array of yellow; yellow jasmine
Pitika (F): saffron; yellow jasmine; honey
Pivanari (F): strong, robust, voluptuous
Piyushadyuti (F): nectar-rayed; the moon
Piyushakanika (F): nectar drop
Polami (F): consort of Indra
Pollavi (F): mango leaf
Ponnambalam (M): golden hall
Ponnamma (F): golden mother
Posha (M-F): thriving, prosperity, increasing
Poshaniya (F): to be protected
Poshayitri (F): one who nourishes, cherishes or rears
Poshita (F): cherished
Poshya (F): thriving; abundant, copious
Potriya (M-F), Potriyan (M): purifying
Poya (M-F): a kind of wind instrument
Prabha (F): lustre, radiance; Pārvatī
Prabhava (M-F), Prabhavan (M): lord Supreme; Murugan
Prabhavanatha (M): prominent, distinguished, powerful lord
Pradip, Pradeep (M): source of light
Prajapati (M): father of creation; Śiva and Murugan
Prakash, Prakasha (M): light
Prakriti (F): nature; cosmos
Prana (M-F): the life of life; energy; Murugan
Prasad, Prashad (M): blessed offerings
Prasannatma, Prasannatman (M): effulgent, kindly-souled; Gaṇeśa
Pratap (M): glory
Pravina, Praveena (F): sagacious; competent
Prem, Prema (M-F): love
Priya (F): darling, beloved
Puja (F): worship, honor, adoration,
Pundarika (F): lotus-like; white umbrella; a mark on the forehead; tiger
Pundarisraja (F): garland of lotuses
Punita (F): sacred; pious; holy
Punya (F): virtue, good work, merit; purity; holy basil
Punyavati (F): full of virtues, righteous; fortunate; happy; beautiful
Purani (F): fulfilling, completing, satisfying
Puranjani (F): understanding, intellegence
Purna, Poorna, Purnama, Purnima (F): full, complete; full moon
Purnamrita (F): full of nectar; a digit of the moon
Pushan (M): nourisher; protector; a Vedic God
Pushpa (F): flower; blossom
Pushpamanjari (F): flower boquet
Pushpendu (F): moon of flowers; white lotus
Pushpi (F): blossom; flower-like; tender, soft; beautiful; fragrant

R

Raga (F): act of coloring; feeling, passion; harmony, melody
Ragamaya, Ragavati (F): full of passion; full of love; beloved; dear full of color; red

Ragini (F): melody; attachment; love
Rahuratna (F): jewel of Rahu; the hyacinth flower
Raj, Raja, Rajan (M): king; Śiva
Rajadeva (M): kind of devas; Murugan
Rajadhidevi (F): Goddess of the kings; queen; a daughter of Sūrya
Rajakala (F): a royal piece; a digit of the moon
Rajakanya, Rajakumari (F): daughter of a king; princess
Rajakesari (F): shining gold; lion among kings
Rajal (F): queenly
Rajamani (F): crown jewel; royal gem
Rajamukhi (F): royal countenance
Rajani, Rajni (F): dark one; night; turmeric; queen; a holy river in ancient India
Rajanvati (F): abode of kings; Earth
Rajapushpa (F): royal flower
Rajasri, Rajasi (F): royalty; grandeur; a *gandharva*
Rajesh, Rajeshvara (M): lord of kings; Śiva
Rajeshvari (F): Goddess of a state; Pārvatī
Rajita (F): illuminated, resplendent, bright, brilliant
Rajivini (F): a collection of blue lotuses
Rajvi (F): ruling
Rajyadevi (F): Goddess of a state; royal woman; queen
Rajyalakshmi (F): wealth of a state; royal Lakshmī
Rakanisha (F): full-moon night
Rakesh (F): lord of the full moon
Rakhi (F): symbol of protection; full moon in Śravaṇa
Rakini (F): night, a tantric Goddess
Rakta (F): painted; red; beloved, dear; pleasant
Raktahansa (F): red swan; contented soul
Raktapadma (F): red lotus
Rakti (F): redness; pleasing, loveliness; affection, devotion
Rama (M): enchanting; a great king
Rambha (F): lovable, pleasing, agreeable; staff
Rameshvara (M): lord of Rāma; Śiva
Ramita (F): pleasing; omnipresent
Ramya (F): enchanting, pleasing, beautiful, enjoyable
Rangabhuti (F): born of love; full-moonnight in the month of Aśviṇi
Rangaja (F): vermilion; born of love
Rani (F): queen
Ranjana (F): pleasing, to worship
Ranjika (F): one who pleases; exciting love; charming, pleasing; red sandalwood
Ranna (M): delight; sound; joy; quill or bow of a lute
Rashmi (F): a ray of light
Rasi (F): wealth, quantity, number; a star constellation
Rasika (F): with discrimination; aesthetic; sentimental; passionate; tasteful, elegant
Ratna, Ratnam (F): wealth; jewel
Ratnamalavati (F): with a necklace of jewels
Ratnavara (F): best among precious things; gold
Ratridevi (F): Goddess of night
Ratu (F): truthful; true speech; the celestial Gaṅgā
Ravi (M): the Sun God
Ravichandrika (F): glory of the sun;

moonlight; a rāga
Ravichandra, Ravichandran (M): the sun and moon conjoined
Rebha (F): singer of praise
Reem (F): seed Goddess
Rejakshi (F): with eyes of fire
Rekha (F): line, streak
Renuka (F): born of dust
Resaman, Reshma (F): storm, whirlwind
Reva (F): agile, swift, quick
Revati (F): prosperity; wealth; 27th constellation
Ribhu, Ribuksha, Ribhwan (M): clever, skillful
Riddhi (F): wealth or good fortune personified; Pārvatī, Lakshmī
Riddhika (F): giver of wealth; Lakshmī
Ridhkaran (F): prosperity; Lakshmī
Rijhav (M): happy, pleased
Rijhayal (M-F): winsome; cultured
Rijhwar (M): lover, adorer
Riju (M): straight forward
Rijukratu, Rijumati (M): performing right sacrifices or works; sincere; Indra
Rijuta (F): honesty, sincerity
Riksh (M): fixed star, constellation
Rikshpati (M): lord of the stars; the moon
Rikshvan (M): forest of bears; a mountain in India
Rima (F): emancipated, released
Rishav (F): pertaining to a sage
Rishi (M): seer; sage
Rishit (M-F): happy, pleased, stout
Rishyamuk (M): beautiful mountain
Rit (F): season
Rita (F): flow; cosmic order; truth; righteous; correct; brave; honest
Ritangoli (F): a strengthening medicine
Ritaparna (M): truth-winged
Ritayin (M): truthful
Ritayu, Ritayus (M): follower of the sacred law
Riti (M-F): stream
Ritika (M-F): brass; bell metal
Ritunatha (M): lord of the seasons; spring personified
Rocha, Rochaka, Rochan, Rochana, Rochita, Rochisa, Rochmana (M), Roshini (F): shining, radiant; glorious; giving pleasure, agreeable, charming
Rochismat (M): possessing light
Rodas (M): heaven and earth
Rohaka, Rohana, Rohanta, Rohil, Rohin, Rohini (M): ascending, climbing; blossom; mountain; tree; a *nakshatra* or star
Rohinibhava (M): a son of Rohiṇī; planet Mercury
Rohinikanta, Rohiniramana (M): beloved of Rohiṇī; the moon
Rohinisa (M): lord of Rohiṇī; the moon
Rohit, Rohita, Rohitaka (M): red; ornament made of precious stones; rainbow; blood; saffron; Sūrya
Rohitaksha (M): red-eyed; Sūrya
Rohitasva (M): red horse; possessor of red horses; Agni
Rola (M): painting
Roladeva (M): lord of painting
Roma (M): hair
Romaharsha (M): goose bumps
Romaharshana, Romir (M): causing goose bumps; causing the hair to stand erect
Romali (F): line of hair
Romani (F): romantic
Romika (M): salt; magnet
Rosana, Roshan (M): passionate;

touchstone; quicksilver
Rosavaroha (M): diminisher of anger
Rudra (M): awesome; Śiva
Rupa, Rupali (F): beautiful

S

Sabanatha, Sabanathan, Sabapati (M): lord of dance; Śiva
Sabaratnam (M-F): jewel of dancers, Śiva
Sachi, Sachideva (M): a friend
Sadashiva, Sadasiva, Sadasivam (M): eternally auspicious; Śiva
Sagar (M): ocean; king of solar dynasty
Sahaja (M): natural
Sahil (M): guide
Sajan (M): beloved
Sakhi, Sakhila (F): sympathizer; friendly; companion
Sakti, Shakti (F): power, energy
Samapriya (M-F): lover of *Sāma Veda*; Śiva
Sambasiva; Sambasivam (M): Śiva the benevolent
Sambhava (M): born, manifested
Sambu, Shambu, Shambo (M): causing happiness; Śiva
Samudra (M): ocean; blue
Sanatan, Sanatana (M): eternal
Sangita, Sangeeta, Sangeet (F): music
Sanjay (M): completely victorious
Sanjiv, Sanjiva (M): possessed with life; vital
Sankara, Sankar, Shankara (M): causing prosperity; Śiva
Sanmitra (M): a close friend
Santosha, Santosh (M), Santoshi (F): contentment; peace
Sarada, Sharada, Sharda (F): vīṇā or lute bearer; Sarasvatī
Sarasvati (F): a region abounding in pools; full of essences; Goddess of learning
Saravan, Saravana, Saravanan, Saravanabhava (M): a reed-filled pond; quietude of mind; Murugan
Sarita (F): river, stream; Dūrgā
Saroj, Saroja (F): found in lakes; lotus flower
Sarvatanaya (M): son of Śiva
Sarvatmaka (M): the soul of all; Gaṇeśa
Satika (F): water
Satina (F): real, essential; peace; water; bamboo
Satvan, Satvi (F): strong, powerful, living
Satvika (M-F): perfect goodness; purity; Śiva
Satya (M-F): truth
Saumya (M-F): pleasant; Gaṇeśa
Savar (M): water; Śiva
Seduka (M): existent; a king of ancient India
Sekhara (M): crown of the head; crest, peak; best, chief
Selva, Selvan (M), Selvi (F): prosperous one
Selvamani (M): beautiful jewel
Selvaraj (M): handsome king
Sena (M): army; leader; body
Senabindu (M): pivot of the army
Senachitta (M): war-minded
Senahan (M): destroying armies
Senajit (M): vanquishing armies
Senaka (M): soldier
Senani (M): leader, general, chief; Murugan
Senapala (M): protector of the army
Senapati (M): commander of generals; leader of an army

Senaskandha (M): army of Skanda; a battalion
Sendan (M): red-hued; Murugan
Senika (M): soldier
Sentilnatha (M): red lord
Sephalendu (M): moon among the brave
Sephara (M): charming; delightful
Sevadhi (M): treasure receptacle; wealth; jewel
Seval (M): rooster; emblem of Lord Murugan
Sevara (M): treasury
Seya, Seyana (M): obtaining, achieving
Seyon, Ceyon (M): youthful; Murugan
Shabnam (F): dewdrop
Shaila (F): small mountain
Shaktidhara, Saktidhara (M-F), Saktidharan (M): wielder of power; Murugan
Shama (F): tranquility
Shambhava (M): the benevolent one; Śiva
Shanmukha; Shanmuga, Shanmugan, Samugam (M): the six-faced one; Murugan
Shanmukhanatha, Shanmuganatha (M): lord of six faces; Murugan
Shanta, Santa (F): peaceful
Shanti (F): peace
Sharva (M-F): the archer; Śiva
Shashishekhara, Shashishekharan (M): wearer of the moon in His hair; Śiva
Shashvata (M): eternal, unchanging; Śiva and Gaṇeśa
Shinjini (F): an anklet
Shirali (F): peacock's crown
Shirina (F): sweet
Shivapriya, Sivapriya (M-F): the gracious beloved; Śiva
Shrida, Shreeda (M-F): the bestower of wealth; Gaṇeśa
Shripati (M): lord of wealth; Gaṇeśa
Shubha (F): auspicious
Shubra, Subram (F): brilliance
Shuddha (M-F): the pure one; Gaṇeśa
Shulapani (M): holder of a spear; Śiva
Siddhama (F): blesssed mother; Dūrgā
Siddhan (M): perfected one; Murugan
Siddhartha (M): one who has accomplished his aim
Siddhasena (M): with a divine army; Kārttikeya
Siddhayogin (M): perfected or accomplished yogī; Śiva
Siddheshvara (M): lord of blessed or accomplished ones; Śiva
Siddheshvari (F): Goddess of the blessed
Siddhi (F): magical power; luck; accomplishment
Siddhida (F): conferring felicity or powers; Śiva
Siddhima (F): one of achievement
Sikha (F): peak, pinnacle, crest; plume, topknot
Sikhandi (F): crested; yellow jasmine
Sila (F): calm, tranquil; good-natured
Silamban (M): mountain king; Murugan
Silavati (F): virtuous, moral
Silpi, Shilpi (M), Silpika, Shilpika (F): craftsman; scultor
Silpita, Shilpita (F): sculptured; well crafted and proportioned
Sindura (F): a kind of tree
Sita, Seeta (F): white

Sitara (F): star
Siva, Sivan, Shiva (M-F): auspicious; with a long ā it becomes feminine, meaning the energy of Śiva
Sivaji, Shivaji (M): auspicious one; Śiva
Sivajnana (M), Sivajnanam: Śiva's wisdom
Sivakanta (F), Shivakanta: beloved of Śiva
Sivakumara, Sivakumaran, Shivakumara (M): son of Śiva
Sivalinga, Sivalingam (M): Śiva's holy mark
Sivananda, Shivananda (M): bliss of Śiva
Sivanatha, Sivanathan, Shivanatha (M): Śiva lord
Sivanesan (M): Śiva's friend
Sivani, Shivani (F): beloved of Śiva
Sivapadam (M): Śiva's sacred feet
Sivaprakasha, Shivaprakasha (M): light of Śiva; light of prosperity
Sivaprasada, Shivaprasada (M): given by Śiva
Sivaraja, Sivarajan, Shivaraja (M): Śiva the king
Sivarman, Shivarman (M): protected by Śiva
Sivasambu (M): Śiva the benevolent
Sivasankara, Shivashankara (M): Śiva the prosperous
Sivasri, Shivasri (M): glory of Śiva
Sivasundari, Shivasundari (F): Śiva's beauty, Pārvatī
Sivasvamin, Shivasvamin (M): Śiva as master, benign lord
Sivatmika, Shivatmika (F): soul of Śiva, consisting of the essence of Śiva
Sivavallabha, Shivavallabha (F): loved by Śiva; Indian white rose; Pārvatī
Skanda (M): hopper; king; clever; quicksilver; Kārttikeya; Śiva
Skandanatha (M): quick lord; Kārttikeya
Sobhaka, Shobhaka (M): brilliant; beautiful
Sobhana, Sobhan (M): handsome; excellent; Śiva
Sohan (M): good-looking; charming
Sohil (M): beautiful
Sokkan (M): beautiful one, Śiva
Soma (M-F), Soman: the moon
Somachandra (M), Somachandran: tranquil moon
Somadeva (M): God of the moon
Somadhara (M), Somadharan: moon-bearing; sky; heaven
Somaja (M): son of the moon, the planet Mercury
Somakanta (M): as lovely as the moon; beloved of the moon; moonstone
Somakhya (M): as virtuous as the moon, the red lotus
Somamshu (M): moonbeam
Somanandin (M): delighted by the moon; an attendant of Śiva
Somanatha (M): lord of the moon
Somashekhara, Somasegaram (M): moon-crested, Śiva
Somaskanda (M): warrior of the moon
Somasundara (M-F), Somasundaram (M): beautiful moon; Śiva
Somendra (M): moon
Somesa, Someshvara (M): lord of Soma; the moon
Sona, Sonala, Sonali (F): redness; fire; gold
Sonam (M): gold-like, beautiful; lucky
Sopan (M): way to moksha
Sovala (M): powerful

Soven (M): beautiful
Srikantha (M-F): beautiful-throated one; Śiva
Sthanavi (M-F): pillar of the universe; Śiva
Subala (M): good boy
Subali (F): very strong, powerful
Subandhava (F): good friend; Śiva
Subas (M): smile
Subbalakshmi (F): divine fortune
Subha (F): splendor, beauty; ornament, decoration; light, lustre; desire
Subhadra (F): glorious, splendid; auspicious; Dūrgā
Subhaga (F): good fortune; wild jasmine; sacred basil; honored mother; beloved by husband
Subharya (F): prosperous; graceful
Subhash, Subhasha, Subhashana (F): eloquent
Subodh, Subodha (F): knowledgeable; wise
Subrahmanya, Subramanian, Subramaniam (M): effulgent radiance; Murugan
Subuddhi (F): of good intellect; understanding, wise; clever
Suchara (F): very skillful; good performer; with a beautiful gait
Suchaya (F): casting a beautiful shadow; splendid
Sudama (F): bountiful
Sudaralakshmi (F): Goddess of beauty
Sudarsha, Sudarshan (M), Sudarshini (F): lovely in appearance; easily seen, conspicuous; beautiful
Sudhakara (M): receptacle of nectar; the moon
Sudhi (F): good sense, intelligence
Suditi (F): bright flame
Sugandha (M-F), Sugandhi (F): sweet smelling fragrance; sacred basil; lion; virtuous; pious; Supreme Being
Suguna (M): with good qualities
Suhasini (F): smiling beautifully
Sukaksha (M): abode of good; a ṛishi
Sukanta (M): very handsome
Sukantha (M), Sukanthi (F): sweet-voiced
Sukha (F): piety, virtue; ease, comfort; pleasure
Sukhajata (M): happy; Śiva
Sukratu (M): one who does virtuous deeds; benevolent; Śiva
Sukumara (M), Sukumari (F): very tender; very delicate; with soft, delicate skin
Sula, Sulan, Shula, Shulan (M): Śiva's trident
Suman (M-F): flower
Sumana (M): of good disposition; great-hearted; charming; handsome
Sumeru (M): vexalted, excellent; Śiva
Sunartaka (M): good dancer; Śiva.
Sundara, Sundaran, Sundaram (M), Sundari (F): beautiful, handsome, noble; a Śaivite saint
Sundareshvara (M): lord of beauty; Śiva
Sunita (F), Suniti: well conducted, well behaved, polite, civil; wise
Suprasada (M): best offerings; auspicious; gracious; Śiva
Surabhi (F): sweet-smelling; agreeable; shining; charming, pleasing; famous; good, beautiful; beloved; wise, virtuous; Champaka tree; nutmeg
Suragana (M): with servants of God;

Śiva
Surala (F): one who brings the Gods; Gaṅgā
Suramohini (F): attracting the Gods
Surananda (F): joy of the Gods; a river
Surapriya (F): dear to the Gods
Suravani (F): Earth as the mother of the Gods
Surendra (M): king of the Gods
Suresh, Suresha, Suresan, Sureshvara (M): king of the Gods; Brahmā, Śiva, Indra and Murugan
Suri, Surina (F): wise; learned one
Surupa (M): well formed; handsome; wise, learned; Śiva
Surya (M): the Sun God
Susaha (M): bearing well, Śiva
Sushubha (F): very beautiful; very auspicious
Susmita (M): with a pleasant smile
Suvarna (M), Svarna: of beautiful color; gold; famous; of noble birth; Śiva
Suvasa (M): well clad; Śiva
Svaha (F): Goddess of fire
Swaminathan (M): lord of renunciates, Murugan

T

Tanuja (F): daughter
Tanuka (F): slender
Tanvi (F): young woman
Tara (F): star; destiny
Taraka (M-F): the great protector; Śiva
Tarala (F): splendid; honeybee
Tarani (F): ray of light; boat
Tarika (F): belonging to the stars
Tarini (F): one who saves others, a raft; Goddess Tara
Taruna (M): young boy
Taruni (F): young girl; woman
Tejadeva (M): God of power; Agni
Tejapala (M): controller of power
Tejaschanda (M): very bright; sharp and powerful
Tejasinha (M): lion of power; a son of Ranadara
Tejasvat, Tejasvin (M): sharp edged; splendid; powerful; bright, beautiful; energetic, spirited; strong, heroic; dignified, famous
Tejeyu (M): possessed with splendor
Tejindra (M): glorious chief
Tejistha (M): very sharp; hot; bright
Tejita (M): sharpened; whetted
Tejomurti (M): consisting totally of light
Tejonidhi (M): abounding in glory
Tejorasi (M): array of splendor; Mount Meru
Tejorupa (M): consisting of splendor; Brahmā
Thakur (M): leader, God, lord
Thamby (M): little brother
Tilabhavani (F): beautiful dot; jasmine
Tilaka (M-F): mark on the forehead; ornament
Tirtha (F): passage; way; ford; place of pilgrimage; sacred object
Tirthadeva (M): lord of the pilgrimage; Śiva
Tirthaka (M): sanctified
Tiru, Thiru (M-F): holy; often used as a prefix meaning "Mister."
Todara (M): removing fear
Todika (F): splitting; breaking; a *rāgiṇī*
Tokavati (F): woman with children
Tokaya (F): to present a new-born child
Tokini (F): having offspring

Tokma (F): fresh; young shoot; green
Tola (M-F): being very poised; with a deer skin belt
Tolana (M-F): lifting up
Tomadhara (F): a water cloud
Tomara (M-F): lance; vel; javelin
Tomaradhara (M-F): javelin thrower; fire
Torana (M): arch; a triangle supporting a large balance; Śiva
Tosha (M-F), Toshan (M): satisfaction; contentment; pleasure; joy
Toshadeva (M): pleasant, contented God
Toshak (M): one who pleases
Toshashana (M-F): pleasing or gratifying others
Toshashaniya (F): pleasing
Toshin, Toshita (M): satisfied; pleased
Totala (F): repeating; Dūrgā and Gaurī
Toyadhi (M): containing water; water receptacle, the ocean
Toyalaya (F): a constellation
Toyanjali (F): cupped hands holding water
Toyaraj (M): king of waters, ocean
Toyesa, Toyesha (M): lord of water, Varuna
Toyika (F): a place that was made famous by a festival
Tudi (F): satisfying
Tuhara (M): remover of darkness, a soldier of Skanda
Tuhi (F): a cuckoo's cry
Tuja (F): thunderbolt
Tuka (M): young; boy; astronomer
Tula (M): balance; scale, the zodiac sign of Libra
Tuladhara (M): bearer of balance; poised; just
Tulakuchi (M): balanced; with a good heart
Tulasi (F): matchless; sacred basil
Tulini (F): cotton
Tumbavina (M): having the gourd for a lute; Śiva
Tungabala (M): very strong
Tungabhadra (F): very noble; sacred
Tungavena (F): loving heights
Tungeshvara (M): lord of mountains, a temple of Śiva
Tungishvara (M): lord of the night; Śiva
Turni (M): quick, clever; zealous; expeditious; the mind
Turvasha (M): overpowering; victorious, hero king extolled in the *Ṛig Veda*
Turya (F): the fourth state; superconscious; superior powers
Tushara (F): frost, snow; cold
Tusharakanti (M): beloved of the snow mountains; Śiva
Tushta, Tushya, Tusita (M): satisfied, pleased, contented
Tushti (F): satisfaction
Tuvijata (M): of powerful nature, Indra and Varuna
Tuvikshatra (F): ruling powerfully
Tuvikurmi (M): powerful in working; Indra
Tuvimanyu (M): zealous
Tyagaraj, Tyagaraja (M): king of renunciates; Śiva

U

Udara (M-F): generous
Udaya (M-F): to rise; prosperity; sunrise
Udayana (M-F): rising; king of Avanti
Udbhava (M-F): source, origin;

birth
Uddalaka (M): burnt open; a kind of honey
Uddara (M-F): liberation
Udita (F): grown; awakened; shining; risen
Udyana (F): garden, park
Ujala (F): bright
Ujasa (M): light
Uma (F): mother; Pārvatī
Umadevi (F): divine mother
Umapati (M): Śiva, lord of Umā
Umeda (F): hope, wish
Upala (F): a jewel
Upamanyu (M): a devoted pupil
Upasana (M): adoration, worship; religious meditation
Usha (F): dawn
Utpala (F): lotus, water lily
Utsava (M-F): festival
Uttama (F): good, superior, best
Uttara (F): highest; uppermost
Uttarkumar (M): excellent son

V

Vadanya (M): bountiful; liberal
Vadishvara (M): God of disputants; peace maker
Vagindra (M): lord of speech
Vagisha (M), Vagishvara: lord of speech; master of language; Brahmā, Gaṇeśa
Vaidyanatha (M): lord of knowledge; Murugan
Vajrendra (M): lord of the thunderbolt; Indra
Vakrabhuja (M): crooked-armed; Gaṇeśa
Vakrapada (M): crooked-legged; Gaṇeśa
Vakratunda (M): with a curved trunk; Gaṇeśa
Vallabhananda (M): rejoicing in being loved
Vallabhendra (M): Indra among the beloved; best beloved
Vallabheshvara (M): most beloved; God among the beloved
Valli (M): creeper, vine; lightening; Earth
Valmiki (M): name of a ṛishi
Vamadeva (M): noble lord; lovely lord; Śiva
Vanadeva (M): forest God
Vananatha (M): controller of the forest; lion
Vandan (M): salutation
Vani (F): speech; praise; music; Sarasvatī
Vanija (M): merchant, trader; the zodiac sign of Libra; Śiva
Vaniprada (M): grantor of the power of speech; Gaṇeśa
Varada, Varadan (M): benevolent; bestower of boons; Gaṇeśa and Murugan
Varanatha, Vararaja (M): lord of the waters; Varuna
Varathanatha (M): most excellent lord
Varavriddha (M): eldest among the best; Śiva
Varen (M): best
Varendra (M): lord of the nobles; chief, sovereign
Varesh, Vareshvara (M): best God; God of boons; Śiva
Varin, Variyas (M): water; river; Śiva
Varuna (M): lord of the sea; enveloping sky; guarding of the West; a Vedic God
Varuni (F): lord Varuṇa's consort
Vasant (M): spring; cupid
Vasanta (F): bestower of desires; companion of Kāma

Vasanti (F): of the spring season; vernal
Vasishta (M): most excellent; a ṛishi
Vasu (M): dwelling in all beings; divine; precious; God; gem, gold; water; wealthy; ray of light; excellent, good, beneficient
Vasuki (F): one who resides under earth; wife of Tiruvalluvar
Vasunanda (M): delighting the Gods
Vasurupa (M): of divine form; Śiva
Vasvananta (M): infinite wealth
Vayu (M): air; God of wind
Vedadarshin (M): perceiver of knowledge; a seer
Vedagarbha (M): the quintessence of the *Vedas*; Murugan
Vedagatha (M): singer of the texts; ṛishi
Vedagupta (M): one who preserved the *Vedas*
Vedesa (M): lord of *Vedas*
Vedisa (M): lord of the wise
Vegin (M): hawk; falcon
Vel (M): lance
Velan, Veylan (M): lance-bearer, Murugan
Velmurugan (M): Murugan with lance
Venidasa (M): of a man; braid of hair
Venika (M): of a people; braid of hair
Vetaka (M): of a man
Vetrin (M): staff-bearer, Murugan
Vettri (M): one who knows the nature of soul and God; sage
Vibudheshvara, Vibudheshvaran (M): lord of the wise; Gaṇeśa
Vidya (F): knowledge
Vighnaraja, Vighnarajan (M): the ruler of obstacles; Gaṇeśa
Vijaya; Vijay (M-F): victorious, triumphant
Vimala, Vimali (F): stainless, pure; Sarasvatī
Vina (F): an indian lute; lyre
Vinadevi (F): Goddess of the vīṇā, Sarasvatī
Vinadhara (M): carrier of the vīṇā; Śiva
Vinapani (F): vīṇa bearer, Sarasvatī
Vinay, Vinaya (F): guiding; modesty, control; taking away
Vinayaka, Vinayaga (M): remover [of obstacles]; Gaṇeśa
Vinita (F): trained; modest
Vira (M-F): hero; brave, powerful
Virabhadra (M): foremost of heroes; Śiva
Virupaksha (M-F): the all-seeing one; Śiva
Visakan, Vishakan (M); Vishakha (M-F): branched, divided; a constellation; Murugan;
Vishva, Vishvan (M): pervasive; world, universe
Vishveshvara (M): all-pervading ruler of the cosmos; Śiva
Vodhavya (F): to be led home or married
Vodhri (M-F): one who bears or carries; guide; charioteer
Vola (M-F): myrrh
Vollaha (M): chestnut-colored horse
Vopula (M): a man
Voraka, Volaka (M): writer
Vorata (M-F): jasmine
Vovam (F): white lotus
Vovi (F): deer
Vrishanka (M): whose emblem is a bull; Śiva
Vyaghrapada (M): tiger-foot

Y

Yaganiya (M): to be worshiped
Yaja (F): worshiper, sacrificer; brahmin
Yajaka (M): worshiping; liberal
Yajamana (M): sacrificing; worshiping; patron of priests
Yajata (M-F): holy, divine; dignified; worthy of worship; adorable; the moon; officiating priest of a sacrifice; Śiva
Yajisnu (M): worshiping the Gods
Yajna, Yajnya, Yagna, Yagnya (F): sacred fire ritual
Yajnavaha (M): conducting the sacrifice to the gods; an attendant of Skanda
Yajnavahana (M): having sacrifice or worship as a vehicle; Śiva and Vishṇu
Yajnikadeva (M): lord of sacrifices
Yajnodaya (M): risen from the sacred fire
Yamajit (M): conqueror of Yama; Śiva
Yamal (F): brace; pair, twin
Yamantaka (M): destroyer of Yama; Śiva
Yami, Yamin (F): night; one who has curbed his passions
Yamika (F): moonlit night
Yamininatha (M): lord of the night; the moon
Yamuna (F): a sacred river in India
Yamunajanaka (M): father of Yamuna; the sun
Yasachandra (M): as famous as the moon
Yash, Yashil (F): glory, fame
Yashila (F): successful
Yashna (F): prayer
Yashomati (F): having fame
Yasksini (F): a celestial being
Yasodeva (M): lord of fame and beauty; a son of Rāmachandra
Yati (F), Yatin, Yatish (M): restraint; control; guidance; ascetic; Śiva
Yatinatha, Yatishvara (M-F): lord of ascetics; Śiva as a forest sage
Yatu (M): going; traveller; wind; time
Yogadanda (M): staff of yogic striving
Yoganatha, Yoganathan (M): Śiva, lord of union, yoga
Yogendra (M): Śiva, lord of yoga
Yogesh, Yogeshvara (M), Yogeshvari (F): master of yoga; Śiva, Dūrgā
Yogin (M): ascetic; Śiva
Yugandhara (F): the earth
Yuthika (F): white jasmine
Yuti (F): one who units
Yuvati (F): young girl

Hindudharma
Saṁskārāḥ Svīkaraṇam
हिन्दुधर्म संस्काराः स्वीकरणम्

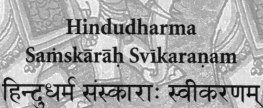

Embracing Hindu Culture

Embracing Hindu Culture

Cues and Clues

THOSE SEEKING TO ADOPT THE HINDU culture fully who have been raised in non-Hindu environments will face many changes. The refinements of Hindu culture must be carefully studied and practiced. Western culture gives freedom to the individual, irrespective of the hurts he may cause to elders, spouse and children. Eastern culture gives freedom within the bounds of duty to elders, spouse and children. The sense of duty is the foundation of Hindu culture, and in performing duty one finds freedom within oneself through the higher accomplishments of yoga. Arriving at this state of unity requires study, worship, *sādhana* and effort to mold oneself into the beliefs and culture of the religion one seeks to adopt. The gentle Hindu culture is the embodiment of the profound philosophy. Therefore, to become fully Hindu means fully adopting the attitudes, customs and protocols of Hinduism. Of course, the best way to absorb the subtle nuances is to associate with and live among high-minded Hindus and learn from their example.

The Meaning of Culture

Each of the religions of the world has its own culture, with many beautiful, refined qualities. Each religious culture naturally embodies the beliefs and worship of that religion, as followers live out their convictions and goals at all levels of life. The same is true of philosophies that are nonreligious, such as existentialism, humanism, materialism and communism. Each of these, too, has a culture. Each country has its combined culture as well. Today in the West and in Asia as well there exist many sub-cultures, some of which are made up of anti-establishment, anti-religious people who consciously defy others by being uncultured by the standards of the mainstream society. That is actually part of their culture.

A Few Cultural Cues and Clues

To be cultured, in the highest sense, means to be in control of oneself and exemplify the highest qualities of one's society, religion or philosophy. For Hindus and those of other Eastern faiths this means to consistently conduct oneself in accordance with the higher nature. The Hindu culture is a culture of love, respect, honoring others and humbling one's own ego so that the inner nature, which is naturally pure and modest, will shine forth. There are countless ways the Hindu attitudes of compassion, respect and self-effacement are expressed. Below we briefly describe some of the most important for new converts and adoptives to incorporate into their lifestyle.

RESPECT AND REVERENCE

1. **RESPECT FOR ELDERS:** Respect for elders is a keystone of Hindu culture. This genuine acknowledgment of seniority is demonstrated through endearing customs, such as sitting to the left of elders, bringing gifts on special occasions, not sitting while they are standing, not speaking excessively, not yawning or stretching, not putting one's opinions forward strongly, not contradicting or arguing, seeking their advice and blessings, giving them first choice in all matters, even serving their food first.
2. **NAME PROTOCOL:** Youngers never use the proper name of their elders. In the Tamil tradition, a younger brother, for example, refers to his brother as *annan,* or *periannan* (older brother), not by name. The elder, however, may use the name of the younger. Children are trained to refer to all adults as auntie or uncle. Adults, too, refer to each other as elder or younger brother or simply as

brother (likewise for women). Only men the same age will occasionally address each other by first name. A Hindu wife never speaks the name of her husband. When referring to him she uses terms such as "my husband," "him" or, for example, "Jothi's father." When addressing yogīs, swāmīs or *sādhakas*, one uses the title, not personal pronouns, such as *you* or *your* (nor by the name alone). For example, one would never ask, "What do you want?" Instead, one would inquire, "What does Swāmī want?"

3. **TOUCHING FEET IN RESPECT:** One touches the feet of holy men and women in recognition of their great humility and inner attainment. A dancer or a musician touches the feet of his or her teacher before and after each lesson. Children prostrate and touch the feet of their mother and father at special times, such as New Year's day, birthdays and before departing on a journey.
4. **BEHOLDING THE DIVINE:** Newcomers to Hinduism will quickly become familiar with the concept of *darśana,* meaning, "seeing," and referring to beholding with inner or outer vision, a temple image, Deity, holy person or place, with the desire to inwardly contact and receive the grace and blessings of the venerated being or beings. This is the spirit of Hindu worship. Even beholding a photograph in the proper spirit is a form of *darśana.* Not only does the devotee seek to see the Divine, but to be seen as well, to stand humbly in the awakened gaze of the holy one, even if for an instant, such as in a crowded temple when thousands of worshipers file quickly past the enshrined Lord. Gods and gurus are thus said to "give" darśana, and devotees "take" *darśana,* with the eyes being the mystic locus through which energy is exchanged. It is a direct and personal two-sided apprehension—highly sought-after experience of Hindu faith.
5. **DAKSHIṆĀ:** It is tradition to provide *dakshiṇā,* a monetary fee or gift to a priest given at the completion of any rite.

Dakshiṇā is also given to gurus as a token of appreciation for their spiritual blessings.

Purity

Purity and its opposite, pollution, are vitally important in Hindu culture. While they imply a strong sense of physical cleanliness, their significance extends to social, ceremonial, mental, emotional, psychic and spiritual contamination. Freedom from all forms of contamination is a key to Hindu spirituality, and is one of the *yamas.* Physical purity requires a clean and well-ordered environment, yogic purging of the internal organs and frequent cleansing with water. Mental purity derives from meditation, right living and right thinking. Emotional purity depends on control of the mind, clearing the subconscious and keeping good company. Spiritual purity is maintained through following the *yamas* and *niyamas,* study of the *Vedas* and other scriptures, pilgrimage, meditation, japa, *tapas* and ahiṁsā. Ritual purity requires the observance of certain *prāyaśchittas,* or penances, for defilement derived from foreign travel, contact with base people or places, conversion to other faiths, contact with bodily wastes, attending a funeral, etc.

Purity is of three forms—purity in mind, speech and body, or thought, word and deed. Purity is the pristine and natural state of the soul. Impurity, or pollution, is the obscuring of this state by adulterating experience and beclouding conceptions. In daily life, the Hindu strives to protect this innate purity by wise living, following the codes of dharma. This includes harnessing the sexual energies, associating with other virtuous Hindu devotees, never using harsh, angered or indecent language, and keeping a clean and healthy physical body.

Clearly, Eastern culture regards purity as more than just physical. Something may be perfectly clean yet be impure or polluted by thoughts of another or by undesirable vibrations. Customs of purity are often based on hygiene and health. Here are several ways purity is preserved in Hindu culture.

1. **PURITY AND FOOD:** Purity is central to food and nutrition, as the nature of one's nourishment deeply affects the entire physical, mental and emotional nature. In a marketplace, one does not touch food one doesn't intend to buy. One cooking food for others would never taste of the dish from a spoon and then put the spoon back in the pot. If food is to be tasted while cooking, a small portion is placed in the right hand. Similarly, one would not touch the lips to a water vessel that is also used by others. Nor would one offer something to another from which one has taken a bite or a sip.
2. **SANCTIFIED FOOD OFFERINGS:** However, the opposite of this is true in the case of the *satguru's* food leavings. Food that he has tasted of is revered as sacred *prasāda* or *ucçhishṭa.* This and the water from the washing of his feet are sought after and imbibed by devotees for the great spiritual blessings that they contain toward *moksha.*
3. **FLOWER OFFERINGS:** One does not sniff flowers picked for offering to the Deities; even the smell is for the Gods, not for us. Flowers that fall to the ground should not be offered.
4. **OFFERINGS:** Offerings, such as an *archana* basket, flowers or garlands, are carried with both hands on the right side of the body, so as to not be breathed on. All items are washed in preparation and, if carried more than a short distance, wrapped or covered.
5. **THE LEFT HAND:** In Asian culture the left hand is considered impure because it is used (with water) in the place of toilet paper for personal hygiene after answering the call of nature. Handing another person anything with the left hand may be considered a subtle insult.
6. **SHOES:** Shoes are considered impure. The cultured Hindu

never wears shoes or sandals inside a temple or shrine, nor in his home or the homes of other Hindus. Carrying shoes in the hands from one part of the premises to another is also avoided. An ultimate insult is to be struck with a shoe.

7. **CAUTION WITH FOOTWEAR:** It is very important to apologize immediately if one touches someone with their shoe or sandal. This is done by touching the right hand to where the foot touched the other person and then touching one's right hand lightly to his own left eye and then the right. This same remedy applies to inadvertently hitting someone with the hand or foot or bumping into them.

EXCHANGE OF PRĀṆA

1. **GIVING AND RECEIVING WITH BOTH HANDS:** Giving and accepting things from one to another, presenting offerings to the Deity, etc., is most properly done with both hands. The reason for this is that with the gift, *prāṇa* is also given through both hands, thus endowing more energy to the object. The recipient of the gift receives it with both hands along with the *prāṇa* from the gracious giver. It is known that this exchange of energies is vital for friendship, harmony and the total release of the gift to the recipient.
2. **NOT POINTING THE FINGER:** Pointing with the forefinger of the right hand or shaking the forefinger in emphasis while talking is never done. This is because the right hand possesses a powerful, aggressive *prāṇic* force, an energy that moves the forces of the world. Pointing the index finger channels that force into a single stream. The harshness of this energy would be severely felt in the nerve system of the recipient. More properly, rather than pointing or shaking the index finger to give direction or emphasize a verbal statement, the entire hand is used as a pointer, with the palm up and the thumb held along-

side the forefinger.

3. **SHAKING HANDS:** The traditional way that Hindu men greet one another is with the *añjali mudrā,* then, with palms still held together, extending their hands to one another, in a two-handed handshake, in a deliberate transfer of *prāṇa.* The hands of one man, usually the less senior, are gently clasped between the other's. Each looks smilingly into the other's face while bowing slightly in humility. This handshake is not firm, but relaxed and gentle.
4. **GREETING WOMEN:** However, Hindu men never shake hands with women in the above manner or in any other way. Women are greeted by placing hands in *añjali mudrā,* the prayerful gesture.
5. **NOT THROWING THINGS:** Throwing any object to another person is considered extremely improper, even if the persons know each other very well. Cultured Hindus consider this crude and even mildly violent, even if done in efficiency or jest.
6. **CARE IN SITTING:** It is improper to sit with one's legs outstretched toward a temple, shrine or altar, or even toward another person. This is a grave insult. Crossing one leg over the knee when sitting in a chair should be avoided, though crossing at the ankles is permitted. One must always try to follow the example of traditional elders. Worshiping, meditating or sitting in the kneeling pose is not acceptable among Hindus.
7. **DOORWAYS:** Conversations are not held inside or through doorways. This is considered inauspicious. Similarly, to exchange or give or lend an object, one steps inside the room first, or the recipient steps out of the room so that both parties are in the same room.

MODESTY

1. **MODESTY:** Interaction in public between men and women is much more restrained in Asian culture than in Western culture. In Asian culture, for the most part, men socialize with men, and women with women. Men never touch women in public, such as helping a woman out of a car, unless the lady is very elderly or infirm.
2. **DISPLAYING AFFECTION:** Married couples in Asia do not hug, hold hands or kiss in public. Even embracing at airports and train stations is considered out of the question. Men, however, frequently walk hand in hand.

THE ROLE OF WOMEN

In traditional Hindu culture, women are held in the highest regard—far more respected, in truth, than in the West. But this does not imply the kind of equality or participation in public interactions that are common in the West. The qualities traditionally most admired in an Asian woman are modesty of manner, shyness and self-effacement. Self-assertive or bold tendencies are regarded with circumspection. Feminine refinements are expressed and protected in many customs, including the following:

1. **WOMANLY RESERVE:** In mixed company, a Hindu woman will keep modestly in the background and not participate freely in conversation. This, of course, does not apply to situations among family and close friends. When male guests are in the home, women of the household will appear when it is proper for them to do so. Visitors do not expect or ask to meet them. Women are not expected to speak out or make themselves a part of the conversation.
2. **WALKING BEHIND ONE'S HUSBAND:** The wife walks a step or two behind her husband, or if walking by his side, a step or two back, always giving him the lead. In the West, the reverse of this is often true.

3. **SERVING AT MEALS:** At meals women follow the custom of serving the men first before enjoying their own meal.
4. **CHAPERONING:** It is customary for a woman to always be accompanied when she leaves the home. Living alone, too, is unusual.
5. **WOMEN IN PUBLIC:** Generally it is improper for women to speak with strangers on the street and especially to strike up a casual conversation. Similarly, drinking alcohol or smoking in public, no matter how innocent, are interpreted as a sign of moral laxity and are not acceptable.

GUESTS IN THE HOME

1. **HOME VISITS:** Close friends can visit one another anytime without being announced or making arrangements first. When they drop in, at least a refreshing drink is always served.
2. **HOSTING GUESTS:** Children generally leave the room, with a smile, when guests enter. The mother remains close by to serve as needs arise. The father, if present, will speak with the guest. If he is not present, the mother and a mature son will fulfill this role; and if no son is present, the mother may act as hostess, but only with the accompaniment of someone close to the family.
3. **WIFE HOME ALONE:** If the lady of the house is home alone and a male visitor comes to see her husband, it is not proper for her to invite him in, nor for him to expect to enter. Rather, he will leave a message and depart.
4. **GIVING GIFTS:** Gifts are always given when one visits a home or stays overnight as a guest. The value of the gift varies greatly, depending upon circumstances. It is proper to give a separate gift for the wife and the husband. The wife is given the nicest item.

BODY LANGUAGE

All Hindus know that "Life is meant to be lived joyously!" All is God, and God is everywhere and in all things. This understanding and appreciation is exemplified in every aspect of Hindu deportment.

1. **KINDLY WORDS AND COUNTENANCE:** Hindus strive to keep a pleasant expression on their face, a gentle smile and a kind word for everyone they meet through the day. They know in their heart of hearts that God is everywhere and that all in the universe is perfect at every point in time. This knowledge gives them strength and courage to face their daily karmas positively and graciously.
2. **REFINED GESTURES:** Hindus know that every movement of the body, the face, hands, eyes, mouth, head, etc., has a meaning. Youth are taught to be sensitive to the thoughts and feelings of others in their body language. It is wise for new adoptives and converts to realize that they are communicating even when they are not speaking. For example, standing with arms folded across one's chest. This can convey in body language a sense of aloofness and non-participation.
3. **EYES:** Eyes are also a primary means of communicating, and the meanings are fairly straightforward. They usually indicate degrees of interest in what the speaker is saying. Smiling with your eyes as well as your mouth conveys sincerity. There are three levels of smiling (and infinite shades and degrees in between). Having the eyes open only slightly indicates mild interest. Eyes more open and a bigger smile indicates more interest and enthusiasm. Having the eyes open wide with a big smile or nod, possibly accompanied by some verbal expression, indicates greater interest or great happiness.

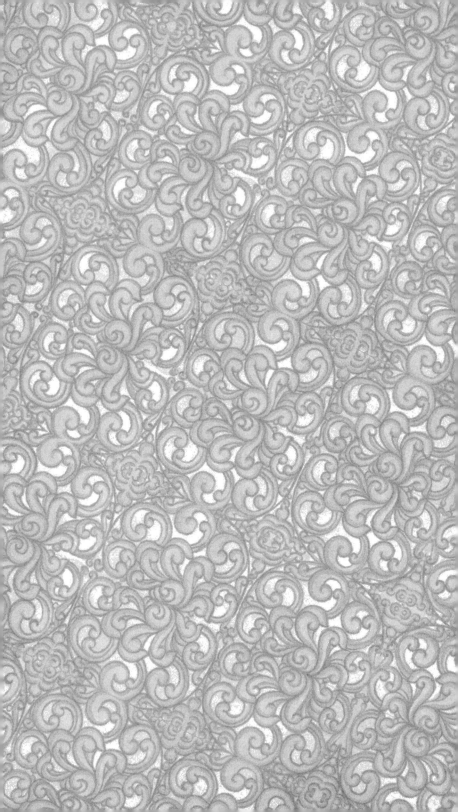

Hindudharmavishayaka
Nava Praśnāḥ

हिन्दुधर्मविषयक नव प्रश्नाः

Nine Questions About Hinduism

Nine Questions About Hinduism

IN THE SPRING OF 1990, A GROUP OF teenagers from the Hindu Temple of Greater Chicago, Lemont, sent a formal request to me for "official answers" to nine questions they had been commonly asked about their religious heritage by their American peers. These same questions had perplexed the Hindu youth themselves, and their parents, they confided, had no convincing answers. We took up the challenge and provided the following answers to the nine questions. We begin with advice on the attitudes to hold when responding.

First, ask yourself, "Who is asking the question?" Millions of Americans are sincerely interested in Hinduism and the many Asian religions. Therefore, when asked questions about Hinduism, do not take a defensive position, even if the questioner seems confrontational. Instead assume that the person really wants to learn. With this in mind, it is still important never to answer a question about religion too boldly or too immediately. This might lead to confrontation. Offer a prologue first and then come to the question, guiding the inquirer toward understanding. Your poise and deliberateness give the assurance that you know what you are talking about. It also gives you a moment to think and draw upon your intuitive knowing. Before going deeply into an answer, always ask the questioner what his religion is. Knowing who is asking, you can address his particular frame of mind and make your answer most relevant. Another important key: have confidence in yourself and your ability to give a meaningful and polite response. Even to say, "I am sorry.

I still have much to learn about my religion and I don't yet know the answer to that," is a meaningful answer. Honesty is always appreciated. Never be afraid to admit what you don't know, for this lends credibility to what you do know.

Here are four prologues that can be used, according to the situation, before you begin to actually answer a question. 1) "I am really pleased that you are interested in my religion. You may not know that one out of every six people in the world is a Hindu." 2) "Many people have asked me about my spiritual tradition. I don't know everything, but I will try to answer your question." 3) "First, you should know that in Hinduism it is not only belief and intellectual understanding that is important. Hindus place the greatest value on experiencing each of these truths personally." 4) The fourth type of prologue is to repeat the question to see if the person has actually stated what he wants to know. So, repeat the question in your own words and ask if you have understand his query correctly. If it's a complicated question, you might begin by saying, "Philosophers have spent lifetimes discussing and pondering questions such as this, but I will do my best to explain in a simple way."

Have courage. Speak from your inner mind. Sanātana Dharma is an experiential path, not a dogma, so your experience in answering questions will help your own spiritual unfoldment. You will learn from your answers if you listen to your inner mind speak. This can be a lot of fun. The attentive teacher always learns more than the student.

After the prologue, address the question without hesitation. If the person is sincere, you can say, "Do you have any other questions?" If he wants to know more, then elaborate as best you can. Use easy, everyday examples. Share what enlightened souls and scriptures of Hinduism have said on the subject. Remember, we must not assume that everyone who asks about Hinduism is insincere or is challenging our faith. Many are just being friendly or making conversation to get to know you. So don't be on the defensive or take it all too seriously. Smile when you give your response. Be open. If the second or third question is on something you know nothing about, you can say, "I don't know. But if you are really interested, I will find out or mail you some literature or lend you one of my books." Smile and have confidence as you give these answers. Don't be shy. There is no question that can be put to you in your birth karmas that you cannot rise up to with a fine answer to fully satisfy the seeker. You may make lifelong friends in this way.

The nine answers below are organized with a one-line response, followed by a longer answer, then a more detailed explanation. You may be surprised to find how many people are content with the most simple and short answer, so start with that first. You may use the explanation as background information for yourself, or as a contingency response in case you end up in a deeper philosophical discussion. Memorize the answers and use them as needed. So now we begin with the questions your classmates and friends may have been asking you all the time.

Question One: Why does Hinduism have so many Gods?
A: While acknowledging many Gods, all Hindus believe in a one Supreme God who creates and sustains the universe.

Longer answer: Hindus believe in one God, one humanity and one world. We believe that there is one Supreme God who created the universe and who is worshiped as Light, Love and Consciousness. People with different languages and cultures have understood the one God in their own distinct way. This is why we are very tolerant of all religions, as each has its own pathway to the one God. One of the unique understandings in Hinduism is that God is not far away, living in a remote heaven, but is inside each and every soul, in the heart and consciousness, waiting to be discovered. This knowing that God is always with us gives us hope and courage. Knowing the One Great God in this intimate and experiential way is the goal of Hindu spirituality.

Explanation: Hinduism is both monotheistic and henotheistic. Hindus were never polytheistic, in the sense that there are many equal Gods. Henotheism better defines the Hindu view of a single Supreme God with many other divinities. We Hindus believe there is one all-pervasive God who energizes the entire universe. We can see Him in the life shining out of the eyes of humans and all creatures. This view of God as existing in and giving life to all things is called "panentheism." It is different from pantheism, which is the belief that God is the natural universe and nothing more. It is also different from strict theism which says God is only above the world, apart and transcendent. Panentheism is a beautiful concept. It says that God is both in the world and beyond it, both immanent and transcendent. That is the Hindu view. Hindus also believe in many devas or Gods who perform various functions, like executives in a large corporation. These should not be confused with God. There is one Supreme God only. What is sometimes confusing to non-Hindus is that Hindus of various sects may call the one God by many different names, according to their regional tradition. Truth for the Hindu has many names, but that does not make for many truths. Hinduism gives us the freedom to approach God in our own way, without demanding conformity to any dogma.

Advice: There is much confusion about this subject, not only among Hindus but among those on the outside looking in. Learn the right terms and the subtle differences in them, and you can explain the profound ways that Hindus look at Divinity. Others will be delighted with the richness of the ancient Indian concepts of God. You may wish to tell inquiring minds that some Hindus believe only in the formless Absolute Reality as God; others believe in God as personal Lord and Creator. This freedom makes the concept of

God in Hinduism, the oldest living religion, the richest in all of Earth's existing faiths.

Question Two: Why do Hindus believe in reincarnation?
A: We Hindus believe the soul is immortal and reenters a fleshy body time and time again in order to resolve experiences and learn all the lessons that life in the material world has to offer.

Longer Answer: *Carnate* means "of flesh." And *reincarnate* means to "reenter the flesh." Yes, Hindus believe in reincarnation. To us, it explains the natural way the soul evolves from immaturity to spiritual illumination. I myself have had many lives before this one and expect to have more. Finally, when I have it all worked out and all the lessons have been learned, I will attain enlightenment and *moksha*, liberation. This means I will still exist, but will no longer be pulled back to be born in a physical body. Even science is discovering reincarnation. There have been many cases of individuals remembering their past lives. These have been researched by scientists, psychiatrists and parapsychologists during the past decades and documented in very good books and videos.

Explanation: At death the soul leaves the physical body. But the soul does not die. It lives on in a subtle body called the astral body. The astral body exists in the nonphysical dimension called the astral plane. Here we continue to have experiences until we are reborn again in another physical body as a baby. Each reincarnating soul chooses a home and a family which can best fulfill its next step of maturation. After enlightenment we do not have to reexperience the baseness of Earthly existence, but continue to evolve in our inner bodies. Similarly, after we graduate from school we never have to go back to the fifth grade. We have gone beyond that level in understanding. Young children speak of vivid past-life memories, which fade as they grow older, as the veils of individuality shroud the soul's intuitive understanding. Great mystics speak of their past lives as well. Reincarnation is believed in by the Jains and the Sikhs, by the Indians of the Americas, and by the Buddhists, certain Jewish sects, the Pagans and the many indigenous faiths. Even Christianity originally taught reincarnation, but formally renounced it in the twelfth century. It is, in fact, one of the widest held articles of faith on planet Earth.

Question Three: What is karma?

A: Karma is the universal principle of cause and effect, action and reaction which governs all life.

Longer Answer: Karma is one of the natural laws of the mind, just as gravity is a law of matter. It simply means "cause and effect." What happens to us that is apparently unfortunate or unjust is not God punishing us. It is the result of our own past actions. The *Vedas*, Hinduism's revealed scripture, tell us if we sow goodness, we will reap goodness; if we sow evil, we will reap evil. The divine law is: whatever karma we are experiencing in our life is just what we need at the moment, and nothing can happen but that we have the strength to meet it. Even harsh karma, when faced in wisdom, can be the greatest catalyst for spiritual unfoldment.

Explanation: We cannot give anything away but that it comes back to us. A few years ago in Chennai an American devotee said to me, "Shall I give money to the beggar?" I said, "Give him ten rupees. You may need the fifty rupees when karma pays you back, just as he needs the ten rupees now." The karmic law pays higher interest than any bank when you give freely with no strings attached. Karma is basically energy. I throw energy out through thoughts, words and deeds, and it comes back to me, in time, through other people. We Hindus look at time as a circle, as things cycle around again. Professor Einstein came to the same conclusion. He saw time as a curved thing and space as well. This would eventually make a circle. Karma is a very just law. Karma, like gravity, treats everyone the same. Because we Hindus understand karma, we do not hate or resent people who do us harm. We understand they are giving back the effects of the causes we set in motion at an earlier time. At least we try not to hate them or hold hard feelings. The Hindu law of karma puts man at the center of responsibility for everything he does and everything that is done to him.

Karma is a word we hear quite often on television. "This is my karma," or "It must have been something I did in a past life to bring such good karma to me." In some schools of Hinduism karma is looked upon as something bad. A Hindu guest from Guyana, South America, visited us in Hawaii and mentioned that karma means "sin," and that this is what the Christians in his country are preaching that it means. Some non-Hindus also preach that karma means "fate," which we know is untrue. The idea of inexorable fate, or a preordained destiny over which one has no control, has nothing to do with Sanātana Dharma. Karma actually means "cause and effect."

The process of action and reaction on all levels—physical, mental and spiritual—is karma. Here is an example: I have a glass of water in front of me on a table. Because the table is not moving, the water is calm. Shake the table; the water ripples. This is action and reaction, the basic law of nature. Another example: I say kind words to you; you feel peaceful and happy. I say harsh words to you, and you become ruffled and upset. The kindness and the harshness will return to me, through others, at a later time. This is karma. It names the basic law of the motion of energy. An architect thinks creative, productive thoughts while drawing plans for a new building. But were he to think destructive, unproductive thoughts, he would soon not be able to accomplish any kind of positive task even if he desired to do so. This is karma, a natural law of the mind. We must also be very careful about our thoughts, because thought creates, and thoughts make karmas—good, bad and mixed.

Question Four: Why do Hindus regard the cow as sacred?
A: The cow represents the giving nature of life to every Hindu. Honoring this gentle animal, who gives more than she takes, we honor all creatures.

Longer Answer: Hindus regard all living creatures as sacred—mammals, fishes, birds and more. To the Hindu, the cow symbolizes all other creatures. The cow represents life and the sustenance of life. It also represents our soul, our obstinate intellect and unruly emotions. But the cow supersedes us because it is so giving, taking nothing but grass and grain. It gives and gives and gives, as does the liberated soul give and give and give. The cow is so vital to life, the virtual sustainer of life for humans. If you lived in a village and had only cows and no other domestic animals or agricultural pursuits, you and your family could survive with the butter, the cream, yogurt, ghee and milk. The cow is a complete ecology, a gentle creature and a symbol of abundance.

Explanation: Who is the greatest giver on planet Earth today? Who do we see on every table in every country of the world—breakfast, lunch and dinner? It is the cow. The golden arches and their rivals have made fortunes on the humble cow. When we were in Moscow in March, 1990, we learned that McDonald's had opened eleven of its cow-vending outlets there. The generous cow gives milk and cream, yogurt and cheese, butter and ice cream, ghee and buttermilk. It gives entirely of itself through sirloin, ribs, rump, porterhouse and beef stew. Its bones are the base for soup broths. It gives the world leather belts, leather seats, leather coats and shoes, beef jerky, cowboy hats—you name it. The cow is the most prominent giving animal in the world today. The only cow-question for Hindus is, "Why don't more people respect and protect this remarkable creature?"

Question Five: Are Hindus idol worshipers?

A: No, Hindus are not idle worshipers. They worship with great vigor and devotion!

Longer Answer: Seriously, Hindus are not idol worshipers in the sense implied. We Hindus invoke the presence of God, or the Gods, from the higher, unseen worlds, into stone images so that we can experience His divine presence, commune with Him and receive His blessings. But the stone or metal Deity images are not mere symbols of the Gods. They are the form through which their love, power and blessings flood forth into this world. We may liken this mystery to our ability to communicate with others through the telephone. We do not talk to the telephone; rather we use it as a means of communication with another person. Without the telephone, we could not converse across long distances; and without the sanctified icon in the temple we cannot easily commune with the Deity. Divinity can also be invoked and felt in a sacred fire, or in a tree, or in the enlightened person of a *satguru*. In our temples, God is invoked in the sanctum by highly trained priests. Through the practice of yoga, or meditation, we invoke God inside ourself. Yoga means to yoke oneself to God within. The image or icon of worship is a focus for our prayers and devotions. Another way to explain icon worship is to acknowledge that Hindus believe God is everywhere, in all things, whether stone, wood, creatures or people. So, it is not surprising that they feel comfortable worshiping the divine in His material manifestation. The Hindu can see God in stone and water, air and ether, and inside his own soul.

Explanation: Humorously speaking, Hindus are not idle worshipers. I have never seen a Hindu worship in a lazy or idle way. They worship with great vigor and devotion, with unstinting regularity and constancy. There's nothing idle about our ways of worship! (A little humor never hurts.) But, of course, the question is about "graven images." All religions have their symbols of holiness through which the sacred flows into the mundane. To name a few: the Christian cross, or statues of Mother Mary and Saint Theresa, the holy Kaaba in Mecca, the Sikh *Ādi Granth* enshrined in the Golden Temple in Amritsar, the Arc and *Torah* of the Jews, the image of a meditating Buddha, the totems of indigenous and Pagan faiths, and the artifacts of the many holy men and women of all religions. Such icons, or graven images, are held in awe by the followers of the respective faiths. The tooth of the Buddha in Sri Lanka's town of Kandy is another loved and respected image. The question is, does this make all such religionists idol-worshipers? The answer is, yes and no. From our perspective, idol worship is an intelligent, mystical practice shared by all of the world's great faiths.

The human mind releases itself from suffering through the use of forms and symbols that awaken reverence, evoke sanctity and spiritual wisdom. Even a fundamentalist Christian who rejects all forms of idol worship, including those of the Catholic and Episcopal churches, would resent someone who showed disrespect for his *Bible*. This is because he considers it sacred. In Hinduism one of the ultimate attainments is when the seeker transcends the need of all form and symbol. This is the yogī's goal. In this way Hinduism is the least idol-oriented of all the religions of the world. There is no religion that is more aware of the transcendent, timeless, formless, causeless Truth. Nor is there any religion which uses more symbols to represent Truth in preparation for that realization.

Question Six: Are Hindus forbidden to eat meat?

A: Hindus teach vegetarianism as a way to live with minimum of hurt to other beings. But in today's world not all Hindus are vegetarian.

Longer Answer: Vegetarians are more numerous in the South of India than in the North. This is because of the

North's cooler climactic conditions and past Islamic influence. Our religion does not lay down rigid "do's and don'ts." There are no commandments. Hinduism gives us the wisdom to make up our own mind on what we put in our body, for it is the only one we have—in this life, at least. Priests and religious leaders are definitely vegetarian, so as to maintain a high level of purity and spiritual consciousness to fulfill their responsibilities, and to awaken the more refined areas of their nature. Soldiers and law-enforcement officers are generally not vegetarians, because they have to keep alive their aggressive forces in order to perform their work. To practice yoga and be successful in meditation, it is mandatory to be vegetarian. It is a matter of wisdom—the application of knowledge at any given moment. Today, about twenty or thirty percent of all Hindus are vegetarians.

Explanation: This can be a very touchy subject. When you are asked this question, there are several ways that you can go, depending on who is asking and the background in which they were raised. But there is an overlying principle which gives the Hindu answer to this query. It is called ahiṁsā, refraining from injuring, physically, mentally or emotionally, anyone or any living creature. The Hindu who wishes to strictly follow the path of noninjury to all creatures naturally adopts a vegetarian diet. It's really a matter of conscience more than anything else.

When we eat meat, fish, fowl and eggs, we absorb the vibration of the instinctive creatures into our nerve system. This chemically alters our consciousness and amplifies our lower nature, which is prone to fear, anger, jealousy, confusion, resentment and the like. Many Hindu swāmīs advise followers to be well-established vegetarians prior to initiation into mantra, and then to remain vegetarian thereafter. But most do not insist upon vegetarianism for those not seeking initiation. Swāmīs have learned that families who are vegetarian have fewer problems than those who are not.

There are many scriptural citations that counsel not eating meat, such as in the *Vedas, Tirukural* and *Manu Dharma Śāstras.* For guidance in this and all matters, Hindus also rely on their own guru, community elders, their own conscience and their knowledge of the benefits of abstaining from meat and enjoying a wholesome vegetarian diet. Of course, there are good Hindus who eat meat, and there are not-so-good Hindus who are vegetarians.

Today in America and Europe there are millions of people who are vegetarians simply because they want to live a long time and be healthy. Many feel a moral obligation to shun the mentality of violence to which meat-eating gives rise. There are some good books on vegetarianism, such as *Diet for a New America* by John Robbins. There is also a fine magazine dedicated to the subject, called *Vegetarian Times.*

Question Seven: Do Hindus have a Bible?
A: Our "Bible" is called the *Veda.* The *Veda* is comprised of four ancient and holy scriptures which all Hindus revere.

Longer Answer: Like the Taoist *Tao te Ching,* the Buddhist *Dhammapada,* the Sikh *Ādi Granth,* the Jewish *Torah,* the Christian *Bible* and the Muslim *Koran*—the *Veda* is the Hindu holy book. The *Veda* is the ultimate scriptural authority for Hindus. Its words and wisdom permeate Hindu thought, ritual and meditation. They open a rare window into ancient Indian society, proclaiming life's sacredness and the way to oneness with God.

Explanation: For untold centuries unto today, the *Veda* has remained the sustaining force and authoritative doctrine, guiding followers in ways of worship, duty and enlightenment. The *Veda* is the meditative and philosophical focus for millions of monks and a billion seekers. Its stanzas are chanted from memory by priests and laymen daily as liturgy in temple worship and domestic ritual. All Hindus wholeheartedly accept the *Veda,* yet each draws selectively, interprets freely and amplifies abundantly. Over time, this tolerant allegiance has woven the varied tapestry of Indian Hindu Dharma. Today, the *Veda* is published in Sanskrit, English, French, German and other languages. But it is the metaphysical and popular *Upanishads*, the fourth section of the *Veda*, which have been most amply and ably translated.

Question Eight: Why do many Hindus wear a dot near the middle of their forehead?

A: The dot worn on the forehead is a religious symbol. It is also a beauty mark.

Longer Answer: The dot worn on the forehead is a sign that one is a Hindu. It is called the *bindi* in the Hindi language, *bindu* in Sanskrit and *pottu* in Tamil. In olden days, all Hindu men and women wore these marks, and they both also wore earrings. Today it is the women who are most faithful in wearing the *bindi*. The dot has a mystical meaning. It represents the third eye of spiritual sight, which sees things the physical eyes cannot see. Hindus seek to awaken their inner sight through yoga. The forehead dot is a reminder to use and this spiritual vision to perceive and better understand life's inner workings, to see things not just physically, but with the "mind's eye" as well. There are many types of forehead marks, or *tilaka*, in addition to the simple dot. Each mark represents a particular sect or denomination of our vast religion. We have four major sects: Śaivism, Vaishṇavism, Śāktism and Smārtism. Vaishṇava Hindus, for example, wear a v-shaped *tilaka* made of clay. Elaborate *tilakas* are worn by Hindus mainly at religious events, though many wear the simple *bindi*, indicating they are Hindu, even in the general public. By these marks we know what a person believes, and therefore know how to begin conversations.

For Hindu women, the forehead dot is also a beauty mark, not unlike the black mark European and American women once wore on the cheek. The red *bindi* is generally a sign of marriage. A black *bindi* is often worn before marriage to ward off the evil eye. As an exotic fashion statement, the dot's color complements the color of a lady's sari. Ornate bindis are worn by actresses in popular American TV shows.

Explanation: Men and women of a particular faith wishing to identify themselves to one another often do so by wearing distinctive religious symbols. Often these are blessed in their temples, churches or synagogues. In some countries Muslim girls cover their face with a veil. Christians wear a cross on a necklace. Jewish boys wear small leather cases that hold scriptural passages, and the round cap called *yalmuka.*

Do not be ashamed to wear the *bindi* on your forehead in the United States, Canada, Europe or any country of the world. It will distinguish you from all other people as a very special person, a Hindu, a knower of eternal truths. You will never be mistaken as belonging to another nationality or religion. For both boys and girls, men and women, the dot can be small or large depending on the circumstance, but should always be there in appropriate circumstances. Naturally, we don't want to flaunt our religion in the face of others. We observe that Christian boys and girls take off or conceal their crosses in the corporate business world. Recently a Canadian TV documentary distinguished the *bindi* by calling it a "Cool Dot." Times are changing, and to proudly wear the symbols that distinguish and define us is totally cool.

Question Nine: Are the Gods of Hinduism really married?
A: To the more uneducated people who are not able to understand high philosophy, Hinduism is taught in story form. Those of the higher philosophy know that each God is complete within Himself, neither male nor female.

Longer Answer: Hinduism is taught on many different levels to many different people, and to the more uneducated people who are not able to understand the high philosophy, Hinduism is taught in story form. These stories, called *Pur-*

āṇas, are the basis of dance, plays, storytelling around the fire in the homes to children as they are growing up to amplify how they should live. Because the temple is the center of every Hindu community, and everyone is focused on the temple and the Gods within the temple, the Gods are the major players in these stories. Hindus who understand the higher philosophy seek to find God on the inside while also worshiping God in the temples. Simple folk strive to be like a God, or like a Goddess. The stories illustrate how a family should live, how they should raise their children, and much, much more.

Explanation: Those who are privileged to the higher philosophies know that Gods are neither male nor female, which is the yoga of *iḍā* and *piṅgalā* blending into *sushumṇā* within each individual. They know that Gods do not marry, that they are complete within themselves. This unity is depicted by Ardhanārīśvara, Śiva as half man and half woman and in the teaching that Śiva and Śakti are one, that Śakti is Śiva's energy. Hindus are very peaceful people, they believe in ahiṁsā, not hurting physically, mentally or emotionally, but in times of war, the stories become violent, stimulating young men to get out and fight, showing how the Gods killed the demons, and how battles were won. Before the printing press, there were few books and these were owned only by a few families. Hinduism was conveyed through stories and parables. Therefore, Hindus are a visual community, holding pictures in their mind on how they should behave in peacetime, how they should behave in wartime. Some modern swāmīs now urge devotees not to pay any attention to the Purāṇic stories, saying that they have no relationship with the world today—that they are misleading and confusing. Instead, they encourage followers to deepen themselves with the higher philosophies of the Vedic *Upanishads* and the realizations of Hindu seers.

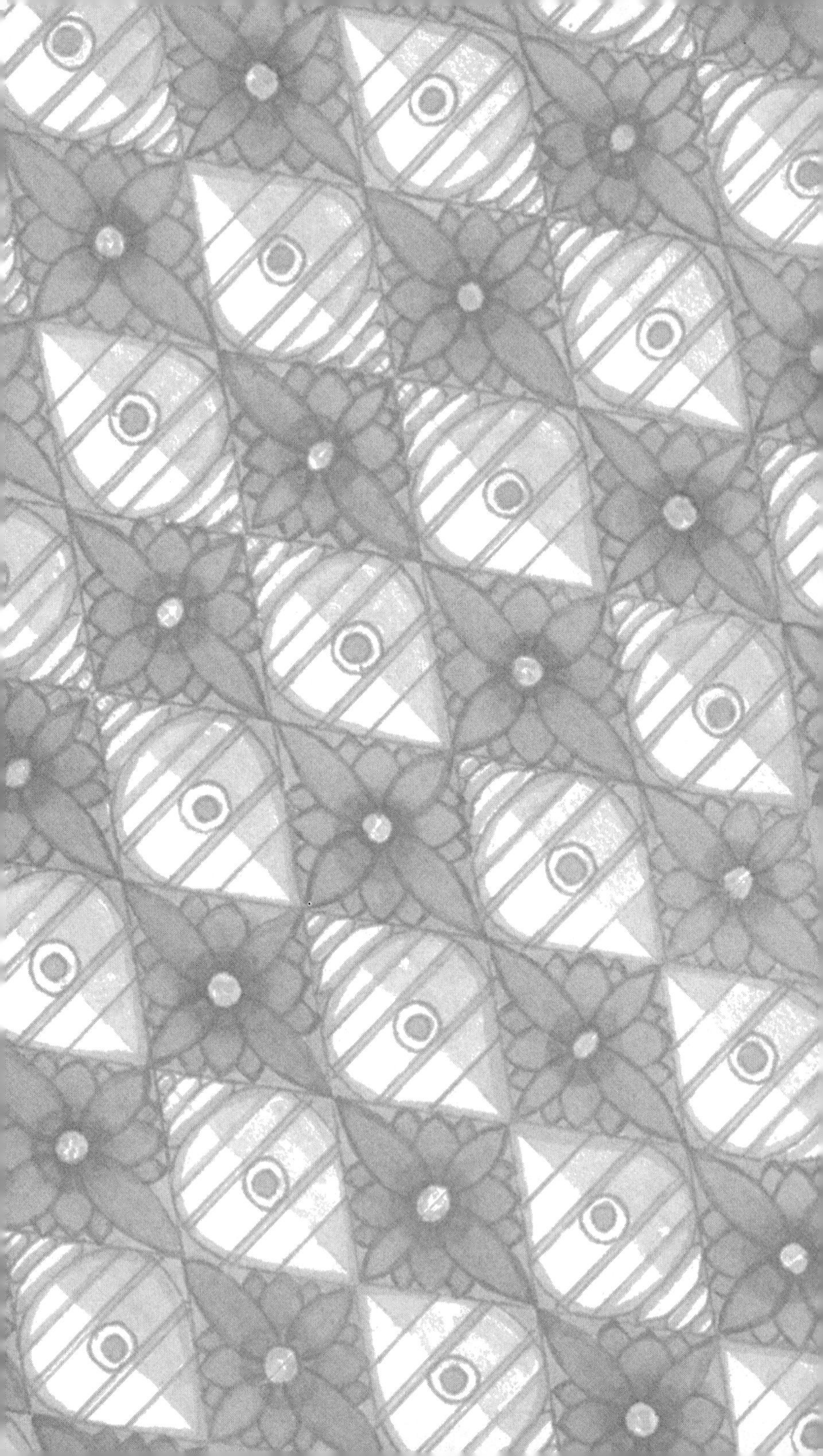

Conclusion

Nirvahaṇam

निर्वहणम्

IN CONCLUSION, WE CAN SPEAK FRANKLY ABOUT THE SUBJECT OF CONVERSION, ADOPTION AND BEING BORN INTO A RELIGION. DURING THE TIME of the intense conversions of my followers—who then joined Śaiva Siddhānta Church and are to this day loyal, mature members, having raised their children, and now their children are raising their children, a third generation is emerging—what impressed me was the attitude of ownership that each priest, minister and rabbi had when approached by a former parishioner. This attitude does not exist in Sanātana Dharma. It never has and never will.

During this time, and much less in conversions that followed in the late 80's and 90's, the clergy of the various religions read and reread their own Jewish laws, Catholic canon, Protestant books of discipline and Mormon doctrines in regard to apostasy. In short, these texts all state in one way or another that any follower is automatically excommunicated who, through study or personal inner experience, has accepted the beliefs and follows the ways of another religion. It is as simple as that. We could have at that point said to would-be converts that it is really not necessary to go back to your archbishop, priest, minister or elder, since you are already an apostate.

The only problem was that was on the human level it was simply not polite, good manners, to drift way, never facing up to the serious matter of severance and beginning a new life in a new religion. And it was simply not ethical. There was and still is another factor, that of strengthening the would-be convert in his new-found religion and its beliefs, culture and new-found friends. This was done by sending him back to his former pastor, congregation, relatives, friends and their surrounding community, to take part in their ceremonies and give them a fair chance to bring him back into the fold by talking him out of his apostate views. This was then, and still is, an ethical procedure.

Yes, that is all true, you may think but inwardly ask, "Has anyone who underwent this return ever turned around and decided to stay in their born religion?" The answer is frankly, yes. We have experienced this a few times and were glad for it. This proved to us the ethicality of our approach to conversion from one religion or ism to another.

Adoptives and born Hindus with little prior religious commitments have it easier, but they are generally subconsciously programmed with various ism's, such as communism, existentialism, atheism, materialism, scientism and secular humanism. To effect the same level of reconciliation, we required them to approach college and university professors as well as other mentors to hear their views and argue out the turn of events in their lives giving them a chance to turn the prospective Hindu back to their teachings.

We have in our midst the New Age movement. It has made a difference in the Western world, but the unfortunate truth is that it offers little or nothing for the children. New Age parents have no heritage to pass on to the next generation. To New Age groups visiting our ashram on this Garden Island in the mid-Pacific I give a simple analogy. I explain that there are many paths to the top of the mountain, some lead to the top and others half way up. But the New Age approach is to take none of these, but instead to go around and around the base of the mountain, sampling the most basic out-front teaching and disciplines each faith puts forward. This, I point out, is a nonproductive procedure.

My postulation generally has had little impact on New

Age seekers who were and still are totally committed to being noncommitted in any way. No matter. It has become an open secret that the movement called the New Age is, in fact, nothing more and nothing less than a modern discovery of the venerable, age-old Sanātana Dharma, which in today's world is imbedded in many languages, as Hinduism in English, Indu Samayam in Tamil, Hindutva in Sanskrit, Hindouisme in French, Hinduismo in Spanish, Religione Hindú in Italian, Hinduismus in German and more.

Why do we call it do-it-yourself conversion? Because if you really want to accelerate the natural spiritual, evolutionary laws of the soul, which slowly bring the realizations of the essence of the Sanātana Dharma, the eternal truths inherent in every soul, you have to do it yourself.

There are millions of Hindus out there, born to a Hindu mother and father, who due to modern and powerful influences have diverted to other ways. One of our goals in this book is to welcome them back to the religion of their birth. One of our broader goals is to teach them about their grandfather's path in words that make sense to them, with a style that is comfortable to them. For this, we at Himālayan Academy have developed many tools, including children's books for their kids and grand-kids. Many don't take religion seriously until they see the result of their attitudes of indifference and worldliness in their own offspring.

Then there is our international magazine, HINDUISM TODAY, which speaks of their religion's place in this contemporary world; as well as our books on meditation and personal spiritual experience; books on philosophy and theology and the *Vedas;* books on culture and lifestyle; and books on Lord Gaṇeśa and vegetarianism. And now the book you hold in your hands: a book on how anyone, born-Hindu or born-Nothing, can join the the eternal path, which has no equal, the ancient path which has none older than it, the innermost path which is the straightest way to God.

Sanskrit Pronunciation

Ucchāraṇa Vyākhyā

उच्चारण व्याख्या

VOWELS

Vowels marked like ā are sounded twice as long as the short vowels. The four dipthongs, e, ai, o, au, are always sounded long, but never marked as such.

अ a as in about
आ ा ā ...tar, father
इ ि i ...fill, lily
ई ी ī ...machine
उ ु u ...full, bush
ऊ ू ū ...allude
ऋ ृ ṛi ...merrily
ॠ ॄ ṛī ...marine
ऌ lṛi ...revelry
ए े e ...prey
ऐ ै ai ...aisle
ओ ो o ...go, stone
औ ौ au ...*Haus*

GUTTURAL CONSONANTS

Sounded in the throat.

क् k ...kite, seek
ख् kh ...inkhorn
ग् g ...gamble
घ् gh ...loghouse
ङ् ṅ ...sing

PALATAL CONSONANTS

Sounded at the roof of the mouth.

च् ch ...church
छ् çh ...chain
ज् j ...jump
झ् jh ...he*dg*ehog
ञ् ñ ...hinge

CEREBRAL CONSONANTS

Pronounced with the tongue turned up and back against the roof of the mouth. These are also known as retroflex.

ट् ṭ ...true
ठ् ṭh ...nuthook
ड् ḍ ...drum
ढ् ḍh ...redhaired
ण् ṇ ...none

DENTAL CONSONANTS

Sounded with the tip of the tongue at the back of the upper front teeth.

त् t ...tub
थ् th ...anthill
द् d ...dot
ध् dh ...adhere
न् n ...not

LABIAL CONSONANTS

Sounded at the lips.

प् p ...pot
फ् ph ...path
ब् b ...bear
भ् bh ...abhor
म् m ...map

SEMIVOWELS

य् y ...yet (palatal)
र् r ...road (cereb.)
ल् l ...lull (dental)
व् v ...voice (labial),

but more like *w* when following a consonant, as in the word *sw̲āmī.*

ह् h ...hear (guttural)

SIBILANTS

श् ś ...sure (palatal)
ष् sh ...shut (cerebral)
स् s ...saint (dental)

ANUSVĀRA ं (ṁ)

Represents the nasal of the type of letter it precedes; e.g.: अंग = *aṅga.* Transliterated as ṁ, or the actual nasal, e.g., ñ. At the end of words it is often म् *(m).*

AYOGAVAHA ᳵ ᳶ

An accentuated Vedic form of *anusvāra* preceding र ष श स ह. The ᳵ is used following short vowels, and ᳶ follows long vowels.

VISĀRGA (ः) ḥ

Pronounced like *huh* (with a short, stopping sound), or *hih,* after i, ī and e.

AVAGRAHA ऽ

Marks the deletion of initial a after e or o (because of *sandi).* Thus: तेऽब्रुवन्

DAṆḌA

। marks end of sentence.
॥ marks end of stanza.

SPECIAL CHARACTERS

ज्ञ् jñ ...a nasalized sound, like *gya* or *jya.*
क्ष् = क्+ ष् ksh

CONVENTIONS

1. चछ is transliterated as cçh, and चच as cch.
2. Geographical names, e.g., *Himalaya,* generally are given without diacriticals.

Glossary

Śabdāvalī

शब्दावली

aadheenakarthar: The *aadheenam* head, or pontiff, also called the *Guru Mahāsannidhānam.* See: *aadheenam.*

aadheenam: ஆதீனம் Endowment, foundation, institution, establishment, estate, property. A Śaivite Hindu monastery and temple complex in the South Indian Śaiva Siddhānta tradition. Also known as *maṭha* or *pīṭha,* as in Kailāsa Pīṭha. The *aadheenam* head, or pontiff, is called the *Guru Mahāsannidhānam* or *Aadheenakarthar.*

actinic: Spiritual, creating light. Adjective derived from the Greek *aktis,* "ray." Of or pertaining to consciousness in its pure, unadulterated state.

advaita: अद्वैत "Non-dual; not two-fold." Nonduality or monism. The philosophical doctrine that Ultimate Reality consists of a one principal substance, or God. Opposite of *dvaita,* dualism. Advaita is the primary philosophical stance of the Vedic *Upanishads* and of Hinduism, interpreted differently by the many ṛishis, gurus, pandits and philosophers. See: *dvaita-advaita.*

Advaita Siddhānta: अद्वैत सिद्धान्त "Nondual ultimate conclusions." Śaivite philosophy codified in the *Āgamas* which has at its core the nondual (*advaitic*) identity of God, soul and world. This monistic-theistic philosophy, unlike the Śaṅkara, or Smārta view, holds that *māyā* (the principle of manifestation) is not an obstacle to God Realization, but God's own power and presence guiding the soul's evolution to perfection. See: *Śaiva Siddhānta.*

advaitin: अद्वैतिन् An adherent to the philosophy of *advaita.*

Āgama: आगम The tradition that has "come down." An enormous collection of Sanskrit scriptures which, along with the *Vedas,* are revered as *śruti* (revealed scripture). The *Āgamas* are the primary source and authority for ritual, yoga and temple construction. Each of the major denominations—Śaivism, Vaishṇavism and Śāktism—has its unique *Āgama* texts.

Agastya: अगस्त्य One of 18 celebrated Śaiva *siddhas* (adepts), and accepted as the first grammarian of Tamil language. He is said to have migrated from North India to the South. His name appears in the *Mahābhārata, Rāmāyaṇa* and the *Purāṇas* and was known to ancient Indonesians.

ahiṁsā: अहिंसा "Noninjury," nonviolence or nonhurtfulness. Refraining from causing harm to others, physically, mentally or emotionally. Ahiṁsā is the first and most important of the *yamas* (restraints). It is the cardinal virtue upon which all others depend.

Amarnāth: अमर्नाथ् "Immortal Lord." A sacred cave in Kashmir in which a *svayambhū* Śivaliṅgam is formed naturally of an ice stalagmite, which waxes and wanes with the moon.

amma: அம்மா "Mother." An endearing term in the Tamil language.

Amman: அம்மன் "Mother." Usually refers to Mariyamman, the "smallpox Goddess," protectress from plagues, a popular *grāmadevatā* ("village Deity" or tutelary Deity of a locale). See: *Śakti, Śāktism.*

amṛita: अमृत "Immortality." Literally, "without death *(mṛita)*." The nectar of divine bliss which flows down from the *sahasrāra* chakra when one enters very deep states of meditation.

ānanda: आनन्द "Bliss." The pure joy, ecstasy or enstasy, of God-consciousness or spiritual experience. In its highest sense, ānanda is expressed in the famous Vedic description of God: *Sat-chit-ānanda,* "existence-consciousness-bliss"—the divine or superconscious mind of all souls.

añjali mudrā: अञ्जलिमुद्रा "Reverence gesture." Also called *praṇāmāñjali.* A gesture of respect and greeting, in which the two palms are held gently together and slightly cupped. Often accompanied by the verbal salutation *namaskāra,* meaning "reverent salutation." See: *mudrā, namaskāra.*

annan: அண்ணன் "Brother."

Antarloka: अन्तर्लोक "Inner plane," or "in-between world." The astral plane. See: *loka.*

appa: அப்பா "Father." An endearing term in the Tamil language.

archana: अर्चन A special, personal, abbreviated pūjā done by temple priests in which the name, birthstar and family lineage of a devotee are recited to invoke individual guidance and blessings. *Archana* also refers to chanting the names of the Deity, which is a central part of every pūjā. See: *pūjā.*

archana basket: A basket brought to the temple containing special items to offer before the Deity. Archana baskets ready prepared are often available for purchase outside larger temples in India. Standard items include incense, fruits, a husked coconut, rock sugar, loose flowers and a flower garland. See: *archana, pūjā.*

***ardha*-Hindu:** अर्धहिन्दु "Half-Hindu." A devotee who has adopted Hindu belief and culture to a great extent but has not formally entered the religion through ceremony and taking a Hindu first and last name. Also refers to Easterners born into the faith who adopt non-Hindu names.

Ardhanārīśvara: अर्धनारीश्वर "Half-female Lord." Lord Śiva in androgynous form, male on the right side and female on the left, indicating that: 1) Śiva (like all Mahādevas) is genderless; 2) Śiva is All, inseparable from His energy, Śakti; 3) in Śiva the *iḍā* (feminine) and the *piṅgalā* (masculine) *nāḍīs* (psychic nerve currents) are balanced so that *sushumṇā* is ever active. See: *kuṇḍalinī, nāḍī, Śakti, Śiva.*

Ārya: आर्य "Honorable, noble" or "respectable one; a master, lord."

Ārya Samāj: "Noble conclave." A renaissance movement founded in Mumbai during the pre-independence era of India in 1875 by Swāmī Dayānand Sarasvatī (1824-1883) with the ideal of moving Hindu Dharma away from fictitious beliefs and returning to the pure teachings of the *Vedas.*

āsana: आसन "Seat; posture." In *haṭha* yoga any of numerous poses prescribed to balance and tune up the subtle energies of mind and body for meditation and to promote health and longevity. See: *haṭha yoga, rāja yoga, yoga.*

ashram *(āśrama):* आश्रम "Place of striving." From *śram,* "to exert energy." Hermitage; order of life. Holy sanctuary; the residence and teaching center of a sādhu, saint, swāmī, ascetic or guru; often includes lodging for students. Also names life's four stages.

aśoka tree: अशोक "Not causing sorrow." The tree Jonesia Aśoka, moderate in size, belonging to the leguminous class with magnificent red flowers.

āśrama dharma: आश्रमधर्म "Laws of life's orders," or "duties of life's stages." Human or developmental dharma. The natural process of maturing from childhood to old age through fulfillment of the duties of each of the four stages of life—*brahmachārī* (student), *gṛihastha* (householder), *vānaprastha* (elder advisor) and *sannyāsa* (religious solitaire).

asura: असुर "Evil spirit; demon." (Opposite of *sura,* meaning "deva; God.") A being of the lower astral plane, Naraka. *Asuras* can and do interact with the physical plane, causing major and minor problems in people's lives. *Asuras* do evolve and do not remain permanently in this state.

atavistism (atavistic): The return of a trait or recurrence of previous behavior after a period of absence.

ātman: आत्मन् "The soul; the breath; the principle of life and sensation." The soul in its entirety—as the soul body *(ānandamaya kośa)* and its essence (Parāśakti and Paraśiva). One of Hinduism's most fundamental tenets is that we are the ātman, not the physical body, emotions, external mind or personality. See: *Paramātman.*

Aum: ॐ or ओम् Often spelled *Om.* The mystic syllable of Hinduism, placed at the beginning of most sacred writings. A symbol of loving Gaṇeśa. As a mantra, it is pronounced *aw* (as in *law*), *oo* (as in *zoo*), *mm.* The dot above, called *anusvāra,* represents the Soundless Sound, Paranāda. In common usage in several Indian languages, *aum* means "yes, verily" or "hail." See also: *nāda.*

avatāra: अवतार "Descent." A God born in a human (or animal) body. A central concept of Śāktism, Smārtism and Vaishṇavism. See: *Ishṭa Devatā, Vaishṇavism.*

avidyā: अविद्या Spiritual "ignorance." Wrongful understanding of the nature of reality. Mistaking the impermanent for the everlasting.

Baptist: A member of an evangelical Protestant church of congregational polity, following the reformed tradition in worship, and believing in individual freedom, in the separation of church and state, and in baptism of voluntary, conscious believers.

bhajana: भजन Spiritual song. Individual or group singing of devotional songs, hymns and chants. See also: *kīrtana.*

bhakta: भक्त "Devotee." A worshiper. One who is surrendered to the Divine.

bhakti: भक्ति "Devotion." Surrender to God, Gods or guru. Bhakti extends from the simplest expression of devotion to the ego-decimating principle of *prapatti,* which is total surrender. Bhakti is the foundation of all denominations of Hinduism, as well as yoga schools throughout the world. See: *bhakti yoga, darśana, prapatti, prasāda.*

bhakti yoga: भक्तियोग "Union through devotion." Bhakti yoga is the practice of devotional disciplines, worship, prayer, chanting and singing with the aim of awakening love in the heart and opening oneself to God's grace. Bhakti may be directed toward God, Gods or one's spiritual preceptor. See: *prapatti.*

Bhārata: भारत The ancient and original name of Indian lands and the constitutional name of independent India (Bhārat in Hindi). Also, Bhāratavarsha "land of Bhārata," a legendary monarch and sage.

Bhārata Nātyam: भारतनात्यम् பரதநாட்டியம் One of the ancient dance forms of India dating back to the second century BCE. This dance type originated in the Hindu temples of Southern India and is one of the most graceful and sophisticated dance styles.

Bhāratkhand: भारत्खन्ड् "Land of Bhārat," India.

bhāshya: भाष्य "Speech, discussion." Commentary on a text. Hindu philosophies are largely founded upon the interpretations, or *bhāshyas,* of primary scripture.

bindu: बिन्दु "A drop, small particle, dot." 1) The seed or source of creation. 2) Small dot worn on the forehead between the eyebrows or in the middle of the forehead, made of red powder *(kuṅkuma)*, sandalpaste, clay, cosmetics or other substance. It is a sign that one is a Hindu. Mystically, it represents the "third eye," or the "mind's eye," which sees things that the physical eyes cannot see. See also: *tilaka.*

brahmacharya: ब्रह्मचर्य "Path to God," or "moving in God." Sexual purity—restraint of lust and the instinctive nature. See: *yama-niyama.*

brahmacharya vrata: ब्रह्मचर्य व्रत Vow of celibacy, often taken by Hindu youth at age 12 upon entering the *brahmacharya āśrama.* The *vrata* may also be taken by Hindu men and women later in life, such as upon entrance into the *sannyāsa āśrama* or after the death of a spouse. See: *āśrama dharma, brahmacharya.*

Brahman: ब्रह्मन् "Supreme Being; expansive spirit." From the root *bṛih,* "to grow, increase, expand." Name of God or Supreme Deity in the *Vedas,* where He is described as 1) the Transcendent Absolute, 2) the all-pervading energy and 3) the Supreme Lord or Primal Soul. These three correspond to Śiva in His three perfections. Thus, Śaivites know Brahman and Śiva to be one and the same God. ***—Nirguṇa Brahman:*** God "without qualities *(guṇa),*" i.e., formless, Absolute Reality, Parabrahman, or Paraśiva—totally transcending *guṇa* (quality), manifest existence and even Parāśakti, all of which exhibit perceivable qualities. ***—Saguṇa Brahman:*** God "with qualities;" Śiva in His perfections of Parāśakti and Parameśvara—God as superconscious, omnipresent, all-knowing, all-loving and all-powerful. See: *Parameśvara, Parāśakti, Paraśiva.*

brahmin (brāhmaṇa): ब्राह्मण "Mature or evolved soul." The class of pious souls of exceptional learning. From *Brāhman,* "growth, expansion, evolution, development, swelling of the spirit or soul." The mature soul is the exemplar of wisdom, tolerance, forbearance and humility.

Buddha: बुद्ध "The Enlightened." Usually the title of Siddhārtha Gautama (ca 624–544 BCE), a prince born of the Śākya clan—a Śaivite Hindu tribe in eastern India on the Nepalese border. He renounced the world and became a monk. After his enlightenment he preached the doctrines upon which his followers later founded Buddhism. See also: *Buddhism.*

Buddhism: The religion based on the teachings of Siddhārtha Gautama, known as the Buddha (ca 624–544 BCE). He refuted the idea of man's having an immortal soul and did not preach of any Supreme Deity. Instead he taught that man should seek to overcome greed, hatred and delusion and attain enlightenment through realizing the Four Noble Truths and following the Eightfold Path. See also: *Buddha.*

Carnatic (vocal) music: Also spelled *karnatic.* One of the world's oldest and richest musical traditions dating back to *Sāma Veda,* carnatic music is denotes the classical style of South India which evolved from ancient Hindu traditions and was relatively unaffected by the Muslim influences that, since the late twelfth and early thirteenth centuries, characterized the Hindustani music of northern India.

caste: A hierarchical system, called *varṇa dharma* (or *jāti dharma),* established in India in ancient times, which determined the privileges, status, rights and duties of the many occupational groups, wherein status is determined by heredity. There are four main classes *(varṇas)*—brāhmin, kshatriya, vaiśya and śūdra—and innumerable castes, called *jāti.* See: *varṇa dharma.*

chakra: चक्र "Wheel." A) In iconography, a disk-shaped weapon among the insignia of loving Gaṇeśa (and of Lord Vishṇu as well). It is a symbol of the sun and of the mind. Wielded as a weapon, it is the intellect divinely empowered. B) Metaphysically, any of the nerve plexuses or centers of force and consciousness located within the *inner bodies* of man. In the physical body there are corresponding nerve plexuses, ganglia and glands. The seven principal chakras can be seen psychically as colorful, multi-petaled wheels or lotuses. They are situated along the spinal cord from the base to the cranial chamber. Additionally, seven chakras, barely visible, exist below the spine. They are seats of instinctive consciousness, the origin of jealousy, hatred, envy, guilt, sorrow, etc. They constitute the lower or hellish world, called Naraka or *pātāla.*

charyā mārga: चर्यामार्ग See: *charyā pāda.*

charyā pāda: चर्यापाद "Conduct stage." Stage of service and character building. See: *pāda, Śaiva Siddhānta, Śaivism.*

Chettiar: செட்டியார் An ethnic group of South India and Sri Lanka of the vaiśya caste.

creed: *Śraddhādhāraṇā.* An authoritative formulation of the beliefs of a religion. Historically, creeds have arisen to protect doctrinal purity when religions are transplanted into foreign cultures.

dakshiṇā: दक्षिणा A fee or honorarium given to a priest at the completion of any rite; also a gift given to gurus as a token of appreciation for their infinite spiritual blessings.

damaru: डमरु The thin-waisted rattle drum of Śiva. It is the symbol of Divine Creation, which begins with the soundless sound, *paranāda,* whence arises the mantra *Aum.* See: *Naṭarāja, Śiva, Aum.*

darshan *(darśana):* दर्शन "Vision, sight." Seeing the Divine. Beholding, with inner or outer vision, a temple image, Deity, holy person or place, with the desire to inwardly contact and receive the grace and blessings of the venerated being or beings. Also: "point of view," doctrine or philosophy.

deva: देव "Shining one." A being inhabiting the higher astral plane, in a subtle, nonphysical body. Deva is also used in scripture to mean "God or Deity." See: *Mahādeva.*

Devī: देवी "Goddess." A name of Śakti, used especially in Śāktism. See: *Śakti, Śāktism.*

dharma: धर्म "Righteousness." From *dhṛi,* "to sustain; carry, hold." Hence dharma is "that which contains or upholds the cosmos." Dharma, religion, is a complex and comprehensive term with many meanings, including divine law, law of being, way of righteousness, ethics, duty, responsibility, virtue, justice, goodness and truth. Essentially, dharma is the orderly fulfillment of an inherent nature or destiny. Relating to the soul, it is the mode of conduct most conducive to spiritual advancement, the right and righteous path.

dhyāna: ध्यान "Meditation." See: *meditation, rāja yoga.*

dīkshā: दीक्षा "Initiation." Solemn induction by which one is entered into a new realm of awareness and practice by a teacher or preceptor through the bestowing of blessings and the transmission of *prāṇas.* Denotes initial or deepened connection with the teacher and his lineage and is usually accompanied by ceremony.

dīkshitar: दीक्षितर् Hereditary Śivāchārya temple priests of Chidambaram Temple in Tamil Nadu.

Durgā: दुर्गा "She who is incomprehensible or difficult to reach." A form of Śakti worshiped in Her gracious as well as terrifying aspect. See: *Śakti, Śāktism.*

dūrvā: दूर्वा A type of grass, also called *aruhu* and *harali,* sacred to Gaṇeśa, traditionally offered to Him in *pūjā. Cynodon dactylon.*

dvaita-advaita: द्वैत अद्वैत "Dual-nondual; twoness-not twoness." Among the most important terms in the classification of Hindu philosophies. *Dvaita* and *advaita* define two ends of a vast spectrum. —***dvaita:*** The doctrine of dualism, according to which reality is ultimately composed of two irreducible principles, entities, truths, etc. God and soul, for example, are seen as eternally separate. —**dualistic:** Of or relating to dualism, concepts, writings, theories which treat dualities (good-and-evil, high-and-low, them-and-us) as fixed, rather than transcendable. —**pluralism:** A form of nonmonism which emphasizes three or more eternally separate realities, e.g., God, soul and world. —***advaita:*** The doctrine of nondualism or monism, that reality is ultimately composed of one whole principle, substance or God, with no independent parts. In essence, all is God. —**monistic theism:** A dipolar view which encompasses both monism and dualism. See: *monistic theism.*

enstasy: A term coined in 1969 by Mircea Eliade to contrast the Eastern view of bliss as "standing inside oneself" (enstasy) with the Western view as ecstasy, "standing outside oneself." A word chosen as the English equivalent of *samādhi.* See: *rāja yoga, samādhi.*

existentialism: A philosophy that emphasizes the uniqueness and isolation of the individual experience in a hostile or indifferent universe, regards human existence as unexplainable, and stresses freedom of choice and responsibility for the consequences of one's acts.

existentialist: Pertaining to, or believing in existentialism.

festival: A time of religious celebration and special observances. Festivals generally recur yearly, their dates varying slightly according to astrological calculations. They are characterized by acts of piety (elaborate pūjās, penance, fasting, pilgrimage) and rejoicing (songs, dance, music, parades, storytelling and scriptural reading).

fundamentalist: Any religious or philosophical group or individual marked by extreme dogmatism and intolerance. Fundamentalists believe in a literal interpretation of their scripture as the exclusive truth, the one and only way which all souls must follow to attain salvation, and in allegiance to their Messiah or Prophet as the one true representative of God. A religious fanatic.

gaṇa(s): **गण** "Number," hence "throng," "troop," "retinue;" a body of followers or attendants." A troop of demigods—God Śiva's attendants, devonic helpers under the supervision of Lord Gaṇeśa. See: *Gaṇeśa.*

Gaṇeśa: **गणेश** "Lord of Categories." (From *gaṇ,* "to count or reckon," and *Īśa,* "lord.") Or: "Lord of attendants *(gaṇa),*" synonymous with *Gaṇapati.* Gaṇeśa is a Mahādeva, the beloved elephant-faced Deity honored by Hindus of every sect. He is the Lord of Obstacles (Vighneśvara), revered for His great wisdom and invoked first before any undertaking, for He knows all intricacies of each soul's karma and the perfect path of dharma that makes action successful. He sits on the *mūlādhāra* chakra and is easy of access.

Gaṅgā Sādhana: **गंगासाधन** A practice for unburdening the mind, performed by releasing the energy of unwanted thoughts. An internal cleansing *sādhana* of sitting quietly by a river or stream and listening to the *Aum* sound as the water flows over the rocks. When a thought arises, it is mentally placed into a leaf held in the right hand, then gently tossed into the water. Then a flower is offered to thank the water for carrying away the thought. This is a subconscious cleansing process of letting go of hurts, anger, problems or whatever it is that rises in the mind to disturb the meditation.

Gautama: **गौतम** The name of the founder of the Nyāya school of Śaivism, author of the *Nyāya Sūtras.* Also, the Buddha (Siddhārtha Gautama). See: *Buddha, Buddhism.*

ghee: **घी** Hindi for clarified butter; *ghṛita* in Sanskrit. Butter that has been boiled and strained. An important sacred substance used in temple lamps and offered in fire ceremony, *yajña.* It is also used as a food with many āyurvedic virtues.

Goddess: Female representation or manifestation of Divinity; Śakti or Devī. *Goddess* can refer to a female perception or depiction of a causal-plane being (Mahādeva) in its natural state, which is genderless, or it can refer to an astral-plane being residing in a female astral body. To show the Divine's transcendence of sexuality, sometimes God is shown as having qualities of both sexes, e.g., Ardhanārīśvara, "Half-woman God;" or Lord Naṭarāja, who wears a feminine earring in one ear and a masculine one in the other.

Gods: Mahādevas, "great beings of light." In *Loving Gaṇeśa,* the plural form of *God* refers to extremely advanced beings existing in their self-effulgent soul bodies in the causal plane. The meaning of *Gods* is best seen in the phrase, "God and the Gods," referring to the Supreme God—Śiva—and the

Mahādevas who are His creation. See: *Mahādeva.*

gotra: गोत्र "Cowshed." Family lineage or subcaste stemming from a *ṛishi* or *satguru* and bearing his name. Originally described as several joint families sharing a common cowshed. See: *caste, varṇa dharma.*

grace: "Benevolence, love, giving," from the Latin *gratia,* "favor, goodwill." God's power of revealment, *anugraha* śakti ("kindness, showing favor"), by which souls are awakened to their true, Divine nature. Grace in the unripe stages of the spiritual journey is experienced by the devotee as receiving gifts or boons, often unbidden, from God. The mature soul finds himself surrounded by grace. He sees all of God's actions as grace, whether they be seemingly pleasant and helpful or not. See: *prapatti.*

guru bhakti: गुरुभक्ति Devotion to the teacher. The attitude of humility, love and ideation held by a student in any field of study. In the spiritual realm, the devotee strives to see the guru as his higher Self. By attuning himself to the *satguru's* inner nature and wisdom, the disciple slowly transforms his own nature to ultimately attain the same peace and enlightenment his guru has achieved. Guru bhakti is expressed through serving the guru, meditating on his form, working closely with his mind and obeying his instructions. See: *guru, satguru, guru-śishya system.*

Gurudeva: गुरुदेव "Divine" or "radiant preceptor." An affectionate, respectful title for the guru. See: *guru.*

guru-disciple: See: *guru-śishya system.*

Guru Mahāsannidhānam: गुरु महासन्निधानम् Spiritual head of a traditional *aadheenam.* See: *aadheenakartar.*

guru paramparā: गुरुपरंपरा "Preceptorial succession" (literally, "from one teacher to another"). A line of spiritual gurus in authentic succession of initiation; the chain of mystical power and authorized continuity, passed from guru to guru. See: *sampradāya.*

Guru Pūrṇimā: गुरु पूर्णिमा Occurring on the full moon of July, Guru Pūrṇimā is for devotees a day of rededication to all that the guru represents. It is occasioned by *pādapūjā*—ritual worship of the guru's sandals, which represent his holy feet. See: *guru-śishya system.*

***guru-śishya* system:** गुरुशिष्य "Master-disciple" system. An important educational system of Hinduism whereby the teacher conveys his knowledge and tradition to a student. Such knowledge, whether it be Vedic-Āgamic art, architecture or spirituality, is imparted through the developing relationship between guru and disciple. See: *guru, guru bhakti, satguru.*

harijan: हरिजन् "Child of God." See: *varṇa dharma.*

haṭha yoga: हठयोग "Forceful yoga." Haṭha yoga is a system of physical and mental exercise developed in ancient times as a means of preparing the body and mind for meditation. See: *kuṇḍalinī, nāḍī, yoga.*

Himālayan Academy: The educational institution of Śaiva Siddhānta Church, founded by Satguru Sivaya Subramuniyaswami in 1957.

Hindu: हिन्दु A follower of, or relating to, Hinduism. Generally, one is understood to be a Hindu by being born into a Hindu family and practicing the faith, or by professing oneself a Hindu. Acceptance into the fold is recognized through the name-giving sacrament, a temple ceremony called *nāmakaraṇa saṁskāra,* given to born Hindus shortly after birth, and to Hindus by choice who have proven their sincerity and been accepted by a Hindu community. See: *Hinduism.*

Hindu astrology: See: *jyotisha.*

Hinduism (Hindu Dharma): हिन्दुधर्म India's indigenous religious and cultural system, followed today by nearly one billion adherents, mostly in India, but with large diaspora in many other countries. Also called Sanātana Dharma (Eternal religion) and Vaidika Dharma (Religion of the *Vedas.*) Hinduism is the world's most ancient religion and encompasses a broad spectrum of philosophies ranging from pluralistic theism to absolute monism. It is a family of myriad faiths with four primary denominations: Śaivism, Vaishṇavism, Śāktism and Smārtism. These four hold such divergent beliefs that each is a complete and independent religion. Yet, they share a vast heritage of culture and belief—karma, dharma, reincarnation, all-pervasive Divinity, temple worship, sacraments, manifold Deities, the guru-*śishya* tradition and a reliance on the *Vedas* as scriptural authority.

Hinduism Today: The Hindu family magazine founded by Satguru Sivaya Subramuniyaswami in 1979, issued bimonthly by Himālayan Academy to affirm Sanātana Dharma and record the modern history of a billion-strong global religion in renaissance, reaching 150,000 readers in over 100 countries. See: *Himālayan Academy.*

Hindu solidarity: Hindu unity in diversity. A major contemporary theme according to which Hindu denominations are mutually supportive and work together in harmony, while taking care not to obscure or lessen their distinctions or unique virtues. The underlying belief is that Hinduism will be strong if each of its sects and lineages is vibrant. See: *Hinduism.*

homa: होम "Fire-offering." A sacred ceremony in which the Gods are offered oblations through the medium of fire in a sanctified fire pit, *homakuṇḍa,* usually made of earthen bricks. *Homa* rites are enjoined in the *Vedas, Āgamas* and *Dharma* and *Gṛihya Śāstras.* See: *yajña.*

icçhā śakti: इच्छाशक्ति "Desire; will." See: *Śakti.*

iḍā nāḍī: इडानाडी "Soothing channel." The feminine psychic current flowing along the spine. See: *kuṇḍalinī, nāḍī, piṅgalā.*

initiation (to initiate): *Dīkshā.* Entering into; admission as a member. In Hinduism, initiation from a qualified preceptor is considered invaluable for spiritual progress. See: *dīkshā, śaktipāta.*

Ishṭa Devatā: इष्टदेवता "Cherished or chosen Deity." The Deity that is the object of one's special pious attention.

Īśvara: ईश्वर "Highest Lord." Supreme or Personal God. See: *Parameśvara.*

Itihāsa: इतिहास "So it was." Epic history, particularly the *Rāmāyaṇa* and *Mahābhārata* (of which the famed *Bhagavad Gītā* is a part). This term sometimes refers to the *Purāṇas,* especially the *Skānda Purāṇa* and the *Bhāgavata Purāṇa* (or *Śrīmad Bhāgavatam*). See: *smṛiti.*

Iyengar: A South Indian Vaishṇavite brahmin caste.

Iyer: ஐயர் A common name for brahmin priests, often a Smārta brāhmin.

Jainism *(Jaina):* जैन An ancient non-Vedic religion of India made prominent by the teachings of Mahāvīra ("Great Hero"), ca 500 BCE. The Jain *Āgamas* teach reverence for all life, vegetarianism and strict renunciation for ascetics. Jains focus great emphasis on the fact that all souls may attain liberation, each by his own effort. Their great historic saints, called Tīrthaṅkaras ("Ford-Crossers"), are objects of worship, of whom Mahāvīra was the 24th and last. Jains number about six million today, living mostly in India.

japa: जप "Recitation." Practice of concentrated repetition of a mantra, often while counting the repetitions on a *mālā* or strand of beads. It is recommended as a cure for pride and arrogance, anger and jealousy, fear and confusion. It fills the mind with divine syllables, awakening the divine essence of spiritual energies.

jina: जिन "Conqueror." The root of the word *Jain,* implying conquest over the bondage imposed by the phenomenal world. See: *Jain.*

jīva: जीव "Living, existing." From *jīv,* "to live." The individual soul, ātman, bound by the three *malas (āṇava,* karma and *māyā).* The individuated self *(jīva-ātman)* as opposed to the transcendental Self *(parama ātman).* See: *ātman, jīvanmukta, soul.*

jīvanmukta: जीवन्मुक्त "Liberated soul." One who has attained *nirvikalpa samādhi*—the realization of the Self, Paraśiva—and is liberated from rebirth while living in a human body. (Contrasted with *videhamukta,* one liberated at the point of death.) This attainment is the culmination of lifetimes of intense striving, *sādhana* and *tapas,* requiring total renunciation, *sannyāsa* (death to the external world, denoted in the conducting of one's own funeral rites), in the current incarnation. While completing life in the physical body, the *jīvanmukta* enjoys the ability to re-enter *nirvikalpa samādhi* again and again. See: *jīvanmukti, jñāna, moksha, Self Realization, videhamukti.*

jīvanmukti: जीवन्मुक्ति "Liberation while living." The state of the *jīvanmukta.* Contrasted with *videhamukti,* liberation at the point of death. See: *jīvanmukta, moksha, reincarnation, videhamukti.*

jñāna: ज्ञान "Knowledge; wisdom." (Tamil: *jñānam*) The matured state of the soul. It is the wisdom that comes as an aftermath of the kuṇḍalinī breaking through the door of Brahman into the realization of Paraśiva, Absolute Reality. Jñāna is sometimes misunderstood as book knowledge, as a maturity or awakening that comes from simply understanding a complex philosophical system or systems. See: *God Realization, Self Realization, samādhi.*

jñāna mārga: ज्ञानमार्ग See: *jñāna pāda.*

jñāna pāda: ज्ञानपाद् "Stage of wisdom." According to the Śaiva Siddhānta ṛishis, jñāna is the last of the four successive *pādas* (stages) of spiritual unfoldment. It is the culmination of the third stage, the *yoga pāda.* Also names the knowledge section of each *Āgama.* See: *jñāna, pāda.*

Judaic-Christian: Concerned with two of the three religions descended from Abraham, Judaism and Christianty, especially in the sense of their shared beliefs.

Judaism: The religion of over 12 million adherents worldwide (over half in the United States), first of the Abrahamic faiths, founded about 3,700 years ago in Canaan (now Israel) by Abraham, who started the lineage, and in Egypt by Moses, who emancipated the enslaved Jewish tribes. Its major scripture is the *Torah.*

jyotisha: ज्योतिष From *jyoti,* "light." "The science of the lights (or stars)." Hindu astrology, the knowledge and practice of analyzing events and circumstances, delineating character and determining auspicious moments, according to the positions and movements of heavenly bodies. In calculating horoscopes, *jyotisha* uses the sidereal (fixed-star) system, whereas Western astrology uses the tropical (fixed-date) method.

jyotisha śāstrī: ज्योतिषशास्त्री One who is versed in the *jyotisha śāstras* and qualified to cast and analyze horoscopes and give counsel and advice on karmic events and timing of innovations in people's lives. See: *jyotisha.*

jyotishī: ज्योतिषी *See: jyotisha śāstrī.*

K

Kabir: कबिर्दस् Saint Kabirdas (1440-1518), an Indian mystic and world-renowned poet who attempted to bridge Hindu and Muslim thought and preached the essential equality of all men. He was a forerunner of Sikhism, the faith established by his disciple Nānak. The Sikh holy scripture *Ādi Granth* contains over 500 verses by Kabir.

Kailāsa: कैलास "Crystalline" or "Abode of bliss." The four-faced Himalayan peak in Western Tibet; the earthly abode of Lord Śiva. Associated with Mount Meru, the legendary center of the universe, it is an important pilgrimage destination for all Hindus, as well as for Tibetan Buddhists.

Kailāsa Paramparā: कैलासपरंपरा "Crystaline lineage." A spiritual lineage of *siddhas*, a major stream of the Nandinātha Sampradāya, proponents of the ancient philosophy of monistic Śaiva Siddhānta, of whom Sivaya Subramuniyaswami is the current representative. See also: *Yogaswāmī.*

Kālī: काली "Black" Goddess. A form of Śakti in Her fierce aspect worshiped by various sects within Śāktism. She is dark, nude, primordial and fiercely powerful, as of a naked energy untamed. But from the perspective of devotees, She is the incomparable protectress, champion of *sādhana* and mother of liberation. The Goddess Durgā, seated on a tiger, has similar characteristics and is often identified with Kālī. See: *Śakti, Śāktism.*

karma: कर्म "Action, deed." One of the most important principles in Hindu thought, karma refers to 1) any act or deed; 2) the principle of cause and effect; 3) a consequence or "fruit of action" *(karmaphala)* or "after effect" *(uttaraphala)*, which sooner or later returns upon the doer. What we sow, we shall reap in this or future lives. Selfish, hateful acts *(pāpakarma* or *kukarma)* will bring suffering. Benevolent actions *(puṇyakarma* or *sukarma)* will bring loving reactions. Karma is a neutral, self-perpetuating law of the inner cosmos, much as gravity is an impersonal law of the outer cosmos. See: *moksha, soul.*

karma yoga: कर्मयोग "Union through action." Selfless service. See: *yoga.*

karmic: Relating to or caused by karma.

Kārttikeya: कार्त्तिकेय Child of the Pleiades, from *Kṛittikā*, "Pleiades." Second son of Śiva, the brother of Gaṇeśa. A great Mahādeva worshiped in all parts of India and the world. Also known as Murugan, Kumāra, Skanda, Shaṇmukhanātha, Subrahmaṇya and more, He is the God who guides that part of evolution which is religion, the transformation of the instinctive into a divine wisdom through yoga. He holds the holy *vel* of jñāna śakti, His Power to vanquish ignorance.

Kāśī: काशी See: *Vārāṇasī.*

kathā: कथा "Story; discussion." Also, the literary form involving the telling of stories. *Kathakas* are bards, storytellers.

kīrtana: कीर्तन "Praising." Devotional singing and dancing in celebration of God, Gods or guru. An important form of congregational worship in many

Hindu denominations. See: *bhajana.*

kośa: कोश "Sheath; vessel, container; layer." Philosophically, five sheaths through which the soul functions simultaneously in the various planes or levels of existence.

Kṛishṇa: कृष्ण "Black." Also related to *kṛishṭiḥ,* meaning "drawing, attracting." One of the most popular Gods of the Hindu pantheon. He is worshiped by Vaishṇavas as the eighth avatāra, incarnation, of Vishṇu. He is best known as the Supreme Personage depicted in the *Mahābhārata,* and specifically in the *Bhagavad Gītā.* In Gauḍīya Vaishṇavism, Kṛishṇa is the Godhead.

Kṛittikā Dīpa: कृत्तिकादीप A joyous one-day festival on the Kṛittikā *nakshatra* (Pleiades constellation), in November-December, when God Śiva is worshiped as an infinite pillar of light. Great bonfires are lit at night on hills and in villages in India and elsewhere to represent the divine, all-permeating light of Parāśakti. See: *festival.*

kriyā: क्रिया "Action." In a general sense, kriyā can refer to doing of any kind. Specifically, it names religious action, especially rites or ceremonies. See: *pāda.*

kriyā pāda: क्रियापाद "Stage of religious action; worship." The stage of worship and devotion, second of four progressive stages of maturation on the Śaiva Siddhānta path of attainment. See: *pāda.*

kshatriya: क्षत्रिय "Governing; sovereign." The social class of lawmakers, law-enforcers and the military. See: *varṇa dharma.*

kulapati: कुलपति A married man who is the head of his joint family and its extended family. His wife is a *kulamātā.* A husband and wife who are part of a *kulapati's* extended family are known as *mukhya* and *grihiṇī* respectively.

Kumāra: कुमार "Virgin youth; ever-youthful." A name of Lord Kārttikeya as an eternal bachelor.

kumbhābhisheka: कुम्भाभिषेक "Water-pot ablution." The formal consecration of a new temple and its periodic reconsecration, usually at twelve-year intervals, following renovation, extensive cleaning and renewal. The rites culminate with the priests' pouring sanctified water over the temple spires, which resemble an inverted pot, or *kumbha.*

kuṇḍalinī: कुण्डलिनी "She who is coiled; serpent power." The primordial cosmic energy in every individual which, at first, lies coiled like a serpent at the base of the spine and eventually, through the practice of yoga, rises up the *sushumṇā nāḍī.* As it rises, the kuṇḍalinī awakens each successive chakra. *Nirvikalpa samādhi,* enlightenment, comes as it pierces through the door of Brahman at the core of the *sahasrāra* and enters! See: *chakra, samādhi, nāḍī.*

Lakshmī: लक्ष्मी "Mark or sign," often of success or prosperity. Śakti, the Universal Mother, as Goddess of wealth. The mythological consort of Vishṇu. Usually depicted on a lotus flower. Prayers are offered to Lakshmī for wealth, beauty and peace. See: *Goddess, Śakti.*

liberal Hinduism: A synonym for Smārtism and the closely related neo-Indian religion. The latter form carries forward basic Hindu cultural values—such as dress, diet and the arts—while allowing religious values to subside. Neo-Indian religion encourages Hindus to follow any combination of theological, scriptural, *sādhana* and worship patterns, regardless of sectarian or religious origin. See: Smārtism.

liberation: *Moksha,* release from the bonds of *pāśa,* after which the soul is liberated from saṁsāra (the round of births and deaths). In Śaiva Siddhānta, *pāśa* is the three-fold bondage of *āṇava,* karma and māyā, which limit and confine the soul to the reincarnational cycle so that it may evolve. *Moksha* is freedom from the fettering power of these bonds, which do not cease to exist, but no longer have the power to fetter or bind the soul. See: *mala, moksha, reincarnation, Self Realization.*

liṅga: लिङ्ग "Mark." See: *Śivaliṅga.*

Madurai Aadheenam: மதுரை ஆதீனம் The oldest (1,400 years) of the major aadheenams of South India, founded by Śaivite Saint Tirujñāna Sambandar, located two blocks from the huge Madurai Meenakshi-Sundareśvara temple, one of the most famous Śiva-Śakti shrines in the world. Madurai Aadheenam is currently an active center of Śaiva Siddhānta philosophy under the direction of Śrila-Śrī Arunagirinātha Śrī Gñānasambanda Deśika Paramāchāriya, 292nd abbot of the monastery.

Mahādeva: महादेव "Great shining one; God." Referring either to God Śiva or any of the highly evolved beings who live in the Śivaloka in their natural, effulgent soul bodies. See: *Gods, Parameśvara, Śiva.*

Mahāśivarātri: महाशिवरात्रि "Śiva's great night." Śaivism's foremost festival, celebrated on the night before the new moon in February-March. Fasting and an all-night vigil are observed as well as other disciplines: chanting, praying, meditating and worshiping Śiva as the Source and Self of all that exists. See: *festival.*

mala: मल "Impurity." An important term in Śaivism referring to three bonds, called *pāśa—āṇava,* karma, and māyā—which limit the soul, preventing it from knowing its true, divine nature. See: *liberation, pāśa.*

manana: मनन "Thinking; deep reflection."

mandira: मन्दिर "Abode." A temple or shrine; sanctuary. See: *temple.*

mantra: मन्त्र "Mystic formula." A sound, syllable, word or phrase endowed with special power, usually drawn from scripture. Mantras are chanted loudly during pūjā to invoke the Gods and establish a force field. To be truly effective, such mantras must be given by the preceptor through initiation.

mantra dīkshā: मन्त्रदीक्षा Initiation which gives blessings to chant a sacred mantra given by a *satguru* or priest at an auspicious time after serious preparations and *sādhana* well performed by the devotee. Also called *samaya dīkshā.* See: *dīkshā, mantra.*

Manu Dharma Śāstra: मनुधर्मशास्त्र "Sage Manu's law book." An encyclopedic treatise of 2,685 verses on Hindu law assembled as early as 600 BCE. These "Laws of Manu" are the oldest and considered the most authoritative of the greater body of *Dharma Śāstras.* See: *caste, dharma, Dharma Śāstras.*

mārga: मार्ग "Path; way." From *mārg,* "to seek." See: *pāda.*

māyā: माया From the verb root *mā,* "to measure," "to limit," "give form." The principle of appearance or manifestation of God's power or "mirific energy," "that which measures." The substance emanated from Śiva through which the world of form is manifested. Hence all creation is also termed *māyā.* It is the cosmic creative force, the principle of manifestation, ever in the process of creation, preservation and dissolution. See: *loka.*

meditation: *Dhyāna.* Sustained concentration. Meditation describes a quiet, alert, powerfully concentrated state wherein new knowledge and insights are awakened from within as awareness focuses one-pointedly on an object or specific line of thought. See: *rāja yoga, yoga.*

Meru: मेरु See: *Kailāsa.*

mlecçha: म्लेच्छ "One who speaks indistinctly (like a foreigner)." A foreigner or barbarian, one who does not conform to Hindu culture; a non-Hindu.

moksha: मोक्ष "Liberation." Release from transmigration, *saṁsāra,* the round of births and deaths, which occurs after karma has been resolved and *nirvikalpa samādhi*—realization of the Self, Paraśiva—has been attained. Same as *mukti.* See: *kuṇḍalinī, liberation.*

monism: "Doctrine of oneness." 1) The philosophical view that there is only one ultimate substance or principle. 2) The view that reality is a unified whole without independent parts. See: *advaita.*

monistic: Expressive of the belief that reality is of one kind or substance.

monistic theism: Advaita Īśvaravāda. Monism is the doctrine that reality is a one whole or existence without independent parts. Theism is the belief that God exists as a real, conscious, personal Supreme Being. Monistic theism is the dipolar doctrine, also called panentheism, that embraces both monism and theism, two perspectives ordinarily considered contradictory or mutually exclusive, since theism implies dualism. Monistic theism simultaneously accepts that 1) God has a personal form, 2) that He creates, pervades and *is* all that exists, and 3) that He ultimately transcends all existence and that the soul is, in essence, one with God. See: *advaita, theism.*

moringa: A medicinal tree, *Moringa longituba,* which produces a red flower.

mudrā: मुद्रा "Seal." Esoteric hand gestures which express specific energies or powers. Usually accompanied by precise visualizations, mudrās are a vital element of ritual worship (pūjā), dance and yoga. See: *añjali mudrā, haṭha yoga, namaskāra.*

mukti: मुक्ति "Release." A synonym for *moksha.* See: *moksha.*

***mūlādhāra* chakra:** मूलाधारचक्र "Root support center," from *mūla,* "root," and *ādhāra,* "supporting." The psychic center located at the base of the spine and governing memory, time and space. The first of seven nerve plexuses or centers of force and consciousness in the psychic nerve system of man, located along the spinal column from its base to the cranial chamber.

muni: मुनि "Sage." A sage or *sādhu,* especially one vowed to complete silence or who speaks but rarely and who seeks stillness of mind. A hermit. The term is related to *mauna,* "silence."

mūrti: मूर्ति "Form; manifestation, embodiment, personification." An image or icon of God or one of the many Gods used during worship.

Murugan: முருகன் "Beautiful one," a favorite name of Kārttikeya among the Tamils of South India, Sri Lanka and elsewhere. See: *Kārttikeya.*

nāda: नाद "Sound; tone, vibration." Metaphysically, the mystic sounds of the Eternal, of which the highest is the transcendent or Soundless Sound, Paranāda, the first vibration from which creation emanates. From Paranāda comes Praṇava, Aum, and further evolutes of *nāda.* These are experienced by the meditator as the *nādanāḍī* śakti, "the energy current of sound," heard pulsing through the nerve system as a constant high-pitched *hum,* much like a *tambūra,* an electrical transformer, a swarm of bees or a *śruti* box. Most commonly, *nāda* refers to ordinary sound. See: *Aum.*

nāḍī: नाडी "Conduit." A nerve fiber or energy channel of the subtle (inner) bodies of man. It is said there are 72,000. These interconnect the chakras. See: *chakra, kuṇḍalinī, rāja yoga.*

nāga: नाग "Serpent," often the cobra; symbol of the kuṇḍalinī coiled on the four petals of the *mūlādhāra* chakra. See: *kuṇḍalinī, mūlādhāra chakra.*

nakshatra: नक्षत्र "Star cluster." Central to astrological determinations, the *nakshatras* are 27 star-clusters, constellations, which lie along the ecliptic, or path of the sun. An individual's *nakshatra,* or birth star, is the constellation the moon was aligned with at the time of his birth. See: *jyotisha.*

nāmakaraṇa: नामकरण "Name-giving." See: *saṁskāra.*

namaskāra: नमस्कार "Reverent salutations." Traditional Hindu verbal greeting and mudrā where the palms are joined together and held before the heart or raised to the level of the forehead. The mudrā is also called *añjali.*

Nandī: नन्दी "The joyful." A white bull with a black tail, the *vāhana,* or mount, of Lord Śiva, symbol of the powerful instinctive force tamed by Him. See: *vāhana.*

Naṭarāja: नटराज "King of Dance," or "King of Dancers." God as the Cosmic Dancer. Perhaps Hinduism's richest and most eloquent symbol, Naṭarāja represents Śiva, the Primal Soul, Parameśvara, as the power, energy and life of all that exists. This is Śiva's intricate state of Being in Manifestation. See: *nāda, Parameśvara, Parāśakti, Paraśiva.*

Nātha: नाथ "Master, lord; adept." Names an ancient Himalayan tradition of Śaiva-yoga mysticism, whose first historically known exponent was Nandikeśvara (ca 250 BCE). *Nātha*—Self-Realized adept—designates the extraordinary ascetic masters (or devotees) of this school. The *Nāthas* are considered the source of *haṭha* as well as *rāja yoga.*

Nātha Sampradāya: नाथसंप्रदाय "Transmitted doctrine (or theology) of the masters." *Sampradāya* means a living stream of tradition or theology. Nātha Sampradāya is a philosophical and yogic tradition of Śaivism whose origins are unknown. This oldest of Śaivite *sampradāyas* existing today consists of two major streams: the Nandinātha and the Ādinātha. See: *Kailāsa Paramparā, Nātha, Śaivism, sampradāya.*

Nehru, Pandit Motilal: मोतिलल् नेहृ (1861-1931) Indian nationalist politician who was an associate of Mahatma Gandhi and an influential leader in the years leading to India's independence. His son Jawaharlal Nehru (1889-1964), also greatly involved in the movement for self-governance, was the political heir to Gandhi and the first Prime Minister of independent India (1947-1964).

Neo-Vaishṇavas: A term used by the International Society for Kṛishṇa Consciousness (ISKCON) referring to non-Indian devotees of Śrī Kṛishṇa.

New Year: The majority of Hindus in India celebrate the New Year according to traditional, pre-colonial calendars, several of which are still in use. There are, therefore, various New Year's days in different states of India, the two major ones being Dīpāvalī in October-November, observed in North India, and the day when the sun enters Mesha (Aries) in April, celebrated in Tamil Nadu, Bengal and Nepal.

Nirguṇa Brahman: निर्गुणब्रह्मन् "God without qualities." See: *Brahman.*

nirvāṇa: निर्वाण "Extinction." In Buddhism it is the indescribable ultimate attainment or disinterested wisdom and compassion. In Hinduism it is the emancipation from ignorance and the end of all attachment. Also an ideal condition of rest, harmony, stability, or joy.

nirvikalpa samādhi: निर्विकल्पसमाधि "Undifferentiated trance, enstasy *(samādhi)* without form or seed." The realization of the Self, Paraśiva, a state of oneness beyond all change or diversity; beyond time, form and space. See: *enstasy, rāja yoga, samādhi, Self Realization.*

niyama: नियम "Restraint." See: *yama-niyama.*

offering basket: See: *archana basket.*
orthodox: "Of right (correct) opinion." Conforming to established doctrines or beliefs. Opposite of *heterodox,* "different opinion."

pāda: पाद "The foot (of men and animals); quarter-part, section; stage; path." Names the four major sections of the Āgamic texts and the corresponding stages of practice and unfoldment on the path to *moksha.* **—*charyā pāda*** ("Good conduct stage"): Stage one, learning to live righteously and serve selflessly, performing karma yoga. Traditional acts of *charyā* include cleaning the temple, lighting lamps and collecting flowers for worship. Worship at this stage is mostly external. **—kriyā *pāda*** ("Religious action; worship stage"): Stage of bhakti yoga, of cultivating devotion through performing pūjā and regular daily *sādhana.* A central practice of the kriyā *pāda* is performing daily pūjā. **—yoga *pāda:*** ("Stage of uniting"): Having matured in the *charyā* and kriyā *pādas,* the soul now turns to internalized worship and rāja yoga under the guidance of a *satguru.* It is a time of *sādhana* and serious striving when realization of the Self is the goal. **—jñāna *pāda*** ("Stage of wisdom"): Once the soul has attained Realization, it is henceforth a wise one, who lives out the life of the body, shedding blessings on mankind. This stage is also called the San Mārga, "true path." See: *jñāna, yoga.*
pāda pūjā: पादपूजा "Foot worship." Ceremonial worship of the guru's sandals or holy feet, often through ablution with precious substances and offering of fruit and flowers. After the ceremony, the water of the bath, the fruit and other precious substances are partaken of as *prasāda* by the devotees. See: *guru, guru bhakti, prasāda, ucçhishṭa.*
pañcha mahāyajñas: पञ्चमहायज्ञ The householder's five daily sacrifices*:* to Gods, ancestors, ṛishis, creatures and men.
pañcha nitya karma(s): पञ्चनित्यकर्म "Five constant duties." A traditional regimen of religious practice for Hindus: 1) *dharma* (virtuous living), 2) *upāsanā* (worship), 3) *utsava* (holy days), 4) *tīrthayātrā* (pilgrimage) and 5) *saṁskāras* (sacraments.) See: *dharma, festival, saṁskāra, tīrthayātrā.*
Pañcha Silanyāsa: पञ्चसिलन्यास The five-stone placement ceremony in consecration of a temple's grounds prior to erecting the temple edifice.
pandit *(paṇḍita):* पण्डित "Learned one." Hindu religious scholar or theologian, well versed in philosophy, liturgy, religious law and sacred science.
panentheism: "All-in-God doctrine." The view that the universe is part of the

being of God, as distinguished from *pantheism* ("all-is-God doctrine"), which identifies God with the total reality. In contrast, panentheism holds that God pervades the world, but is also beyond it. He is immanent and transcendent, relative and Absolute. This embracing of opposites is called dipolar. For the panentheist, God is in all, and all is in God. Panentheism is the technical term for monistic theism. See: *dvaita-advaita, monistic theism.*

Paramātman: परमात्मन् "Supreme Self," or "transcendent soul." Paraśiva, Absolute Reality, the one transcendent Self of every soul. Contrasted with *ātman,* which includes all three aspects of the soul: *Paraśiva, Parāśakti* and *ānandamaya kośa.* See: *ātman, kośa, soul.*

Parameśvara: परमेश्वर "Supreme Lord or Ruler." God Śiva in the third perfection as Supreme Mahādeva, Śiva-Śakti, mother of the universe. In this perfection as Personal, father-mother God, Śiva is a person—who has a body, with head, arms and legs, etc.—who acts, wills, blesses, gives *darśana,* guides, creates, preserves, reabsorbs, obscures and enlightens. In Truth, it is Śiva-Śakti who does all. The term *Primal Soul,* Paramapurusha, designates Parameśvara as the original, uncreated soul, the creator of all other souls. Parameśvara has many other names and epithets, including those denoting the five divine actions—Sadāśiva, the revealer; Maheśvara, the obscurer; Brahmā, the creator; Vishṇu the preserver; and Rudra the destroyer. See: *Naṭarāja.*

Parāśakti: पराशक्ति "Supreme power; primal energy." God Śiva's second perfection, which is impersonal, immanent, and with form—the all-pervasive, Pure Consciousness and Primal Substance of all that exists. There are many other descriptive names for Parāśakti—Satchidānanda ("existence-consciousness-bliss"), light, silence, divine mind, superconsciousness and more. The attainment of Parāśakti is called *savikalpa samādhi.* See: *Śiva.*

Paraśiva: परशिव "Transcendent Śiva." The Self God, Śiva in His first perfection, Absolute Reality. God Śiva as *That* which is beyond the grasp of consciousness, transcends time, form and space and defies description. Attainment of this is called Self Realization or *nirvikalpa samādhi.* See: *samādhi, Śiva.*

Pārvatī: पार्वती "Mountain's daughter." One of many names for the Universal Mother. Prayers are offered to Her for strength, health and eradication of impurities. Mythologically, Pārvatī is wedded to Śiva. See: *Goddess, Śakti.*

pāśa: पाश "Tether; noose." The whole of existence, manifest and unmanifest. That which binds or limits the soul and keeps it (for a time) from manifesting its full potential. *Pāśa* refers to the soul's three-fold bondage of *āṇava,* karma and māyā. See: *liberation, mala, Pati-paśu-pāśa.*

patha: पथ "Path."

Pati-paśu-pāśa: पति पशु पाश Literally: "master, cow and tether." These are the three primary elements *(padārtha,* or *tattvatrayī)* of Śaiva Siddhānta philosophy: God, soul and world—Divinity, man and cosmos—seen as a mystically and intricately interrelated unity. Pati is God, envisioned as a cowherd.

Paśu is the soul, envisioned as a cow. *Pāśa* is the all-important force or fetter by which God brings souls along the path to Truth. See: *pāśa, Śaiva Siddhānta, soul.*

penance: *Prāyaśchitta.* Atonement, expiation. An act of devotion (bhakti), austerity *(tapas)* or discipline *(sukṛitya)* undertaken to soften or nullify the anticipated reaction to a past action. Penance is uncomfortable karma inflicted upon oneself to mitigate one's *karmic* burden caused by wrongful actions *(kukarma).* It includes such acts as prostrating 108 times, fasting, self-denial, or carrying *kavadi (public penance),* as well as more extreme austerities, or *tapas.* Penance is often suggested by spiritual leaders and elders. See: *prāyaśchitta, tapas.*

periannan பெரியண்ணன் "Big brother" or "elder brother."

piṅgalā: पिंगला "Tawny channel." The masculine psychic current flowing along the spine. See: *kuṇḍalinī, nāḍī, rāja yoga.*

pitṛi-tarpaṇa: पितृ तर्पण Ceremonial offerings to departed ancestors, constituting one of the *pañcha mahāyajñas.* See: *pañcha mahāyajñas.*

plague: To distress, afflict, trouble or torment.

pottu: பொட்டு See: *bindu, tilaka.*

prakṛiti: प्रकृति "Primary matter; nature." See: *purusha, tattva.*

prāṇa: प्राण Vital energy or life principle. Literally, "vital air," from the root *praṇ,* "to breathe." Usually *prāṇa* refers to the life principle; but sometimes it denotes energy, power or the animating force of the cosmos. See: *kośa, tattva.*

praṇāma: प्रणाम "Obeisance; bowing down." Reverent salutation in which the head or body is bowed. ***—ashṭāṅga praṇāma*** ("Eight-limbed obeisance"): the full prostration for men, in which the hands, chest, forehead, knees and feet touch the ground. (Same as *śashṭāṇga praṇāma.*) ***—pañchāṅga praṇāma*** ("Five-limbed obeisance"): the woman's form of prostration, in which the hands, head and legs touch the ground (with the ankles crossed, right over the left). A more exacting term for prostration is *praṇipāta,* "falling down in obeisance." See: *bhakti, namaskāra, prapatti.*

prāṇāyāma: प्राणायाम "Breath control." See: *rāja yoga.*

prāṇic: Relating to *prāṇa.* See: *prāṇa.*

prapatti: प्रपत्ति "Throwing oneself down." Bhakti—total, unconditional submission to God, often coupled with the attitude of personal helplessness, self-effacement and resignation. See: *bhakti, grace, pāda, surrender.*

prasāda: प्रसाद "Clarity, brightness; grace." 1) The virtue of serenity and graciousness. 2) Food offered to the Deity or the guru, or the blessed remnants of such food. 3) Any propitiatory offering. See: *sacrament.*

prāyaśchitta: प्रायश्चित्त "Predominant thought or aim." Penance. Acts of atonement. See: *penance.*

preceptor: Highly respected teacher and head of a spiritual order and clan; the equivalent of the word *satguru.*

priya: प्रिय "Beloved, dear to."

proselytize: To induce someone to convert to another religious faith.

pūjā: पूजा "Worship, adoration." An Āgamic rite of worship performed in the home, temple or shrine, to the *mūrti* (Deity image), *śrī pādukā* (holy sandals), or other consecrated object, or to a person, such as the *satguru.* Its inner purpose is to purify the atmosphere around the object worshiped, establish a connection with the inner worlds and invoke the presence of God, Gods or one's guru. During pūjā, the officiant *(pujārī)* recites various chants praising the Divine and beseeching divine blessings, while making offerings in accordance with established traditions. Pūjā, the worship of a *mūrti* through water, lights and flowers in temples and shrines, is the Āgamic counterpart of the Vedic *yajña* rite, in which offerings are conveyed through the sacred *homa* fire. These are the two great streams of adoration and communion in Hinduism.

punarjanma: पुनर्जन्म "Reincarnation." From *punaḥ,* "again and again," and *janma,* "taking birth." See: *reincarnation.*

Purāṇa: पुराण "Ancient (lore)." Hindu folk narratives containing ethical and cosmological teachings relative to Gods, man and the world. They revolve around five subjects: primary creation, secondary creation, genealogy, cycles of time and history.

Radhākṛishṇan, Dr. S.: राधाकृष्णन् (1888-1975) A President of India (1962-1967), an outstanding scholar, philosopher, prolific writer, compelling speaker and effective spokesman of Hinduism. Along with Vivekānanda, Tagore, Aurobindo and others, he helped bring about the current Hindu revival, making Hinduism better known and appreciated at home and abroad, especially in the intellectual world. He was a proponent of panentheism. See also: *Vedānta.*

Rādhā Rāṇi: राधाराणि "Queen of prosperity." Mythologically, Rādhā Rāṇi is a consort of Lord Kṛishṇa. In Hindu mythology, Rādhā is the creative, life-sustaining, auspicious, benevolent, loving and redemptive Goddess, chief among the Gopis. In the bhakti tradition of Kṛishṇa she symbolizes the soul's yearning for salvation and union with God.

rāga: राग "That which enraptures." In the structure of melody in Indian music, a specific collection of sounds or notes. *Rāga* is similar to "scale" in Western notation, but *rāga* includes the unique emotional or mystical mood created when the melody is heard.

Rājarājeśvarī: राजराजेश्वरी "Royal lady." The Goddess of world-sustaining transcendental knowledge. She whose glances delight the universe. A form of Pārvatī.

rājaṛishi: राजऋषि "Kingly seer."

rāja yoga: राजयोग "King of yogas." Also known as *ashṭāṅga* yoga, "eight-limbed yoga." The classical yoga system of eight progressive stages to Illumination as described in various yoga *Upanishads*, the *Tirumantiram* and, most notably, the *Yoga Sūtras* of Patañjali. The eight stages are: *yama* (restraints), *niyama* (observances), āsana (posture), *prāṇāyāma* (breath control), *pratyāhara* (withdrawal), *dhāraṇa* (concentration), *dhyāna* (meditation) and *samādhi* (enstasy, mystic oneness). See: *enstasy, samādhi, yoga.*

Rāmakṛishṇa: रामकृष्ण (1836–1886) One of the great saints and mystics of modern Hinduism, and an exemplar of monistic theism—fervent devotee of Mother Kālī and staunch monist who taught oneness and the pursuit of *nirvikalpa samādhi*, realization of the Absolute. He was *guru* to the great Swāmī Vivekānanda (1863–1902), who internationalized Hindu thought and philosophy.

reincarnate: To take birth in another body, having lived and died before.

reincarnation: "Re-entering the flesh." *Punarjanma;* metempsychosis. The process wherein souls take on a physical body through the birth process. The cycle of reincarnation ends when karma has been resolved and the Self God (Paraśiva) has been realized. This condition of release is called *moksha.* Then the soul continues to evolve and mature, but without the need to return to physical existence. See: *karma, moksha, saṁsāra, soul.*

religion: From Latin *religare*, "to bind back." Any system of belief in and worship of suprahuman beings or powers and/or a Supreme Being or Power. Religion is a structured vehicle for soul advancement which often includes theology, scripture, spiritual and moral practices, priesthood and liturgy. See: *Hinduism.*

Ṛig Veda: ऋग्वेद "*Veda* of verse *(ṛik).*" The first and oldest of the four *Veda* compendia of revealed scriptures *(śruti)*, including a hymn collection *(Saṁhitā)*, priestly explanatory manuals *(Brāhmaṇas)*, forest treatises *(Āraṇyakas)* elaborating on the Vedic rites, and philosophical dialogs *(Upanishads).* The oldest and core portion is the *Saṁhitā*, believed to date back, in its oral form, as far as 8,000 years. It embodies prayerful hymns of praise and invocation to the Divinities of nature and to the One Divine. See: *śruti, Veda.*

ṛishi: ऋषि "Seer." A term for an enlightened being, emphasizing psychic perception and visionary wisdom. In the Vedic age, ṛishis lived in forest or mountain retreats, either alone or with disciples. These ṛishis were great souls who were the inspired conveyers of the *Vedas.*

S

Sabbath: The last day of the week designated by the fourth Commandment as a day of worship and rest, observed by Jews and Christians.

sacrament: 1) Holy rite, especially one solemnized in a formal, consecrated manner which is a bonding between the recipient and God, Gods or guru. This includes rites of passage *(saṁskāra)*, ceremonies sanctifying crucial events or stages of life. 2) *Prasāda.* Sacred substances, grace-filled gifts, blessed in sacred ceremony or by a holy person. See: *prasāda, saṁskāra.*

sādhaka: साधक From *sadh*, "going straight to the goal." A spiritual aspirant; a devotee who performs *sādhana.* A serious seeker who has undertaken spiritual disciplines, is usually celibate and under the guidance of a guru. He wears white and may be under simple vows, but is not a yogī or *sannyāsin.* See: *sādhana.*

sādhana: साधन "Effective means of attainment." Self-effort, spiritual discipline; the way. Religious or spiritual disciplines, such as pūjā, yoga, meditation, japa, fasting and austerity. The effect of *sādhana* is the building of willpower, faith and confidence in oneself and in God, Gods and guru. See: *pāda, rāja yoga, spiritual unfoldment.*

sādhana mārga: साधनमार्ग "The way of *sādhana.*" A phrase used by Sage Yogaswāmī to name his prescription for seekers of Truth—a path of intense effort, spiritual discipline and consistent inner transformation, as opposed to theoretical and intellectual learning. See: *pāda, sādhana, spiritual unfoldment.*

Saguṇa Brahman: सगुणब्रह्मन् Brahman "with qualities." Describes Śiva's perfections of Satchidānanda and Maheśvara, the Primal Soul and His Divine Mind—that part of God which is divine, all-knowing, all-loving, all-powerful and omnipotent. See: *Brahman.*

Śaiva: शैव "Auspicious." Of or relating to Śaivism or its adherents, of whom there are about 400 million in the world today. Same as *Śaivite.* See: *Śaivism.*

Śaiva Siddhānta: शैवसिद्धान्त "Final conclusions of Śaivism." The most widespread and influential Śaivite school today, predominant especially among the Tamil people in Sri Lanka and South India. It is the formalized theology of the divine revelations contained in the twenty-eight *Śaiva Āgamas.* For Śaiva Siddhāntins, Śiva is the totality of all, understood in three perfections: Parameśvara (the Personal Creator Lord), Parāśakti (the substratum of form) and Paraśiva (Absolute Reality which transcends all). Souls and world are identical in essence with Śiva, yet also differ in that they are evolving. A pluralistic stream arose in the middle ages from the teachings of Aghoraśiva and Meykandar, which denies that souls ever attain perfect sameness or unity with Śiva. See: *Śaivism.*

Śaiva Siddhānta Church *(Śaiva Siddhānta Dharmasabhā):* शैव सिद्धान्त धर्मसभा "Church of God Siva's Revealed Truth," founded in 1949 by Satguru Sivaya Subramuniyaswami.

Śaivism (Śaiva): शैव The religion followed by those who worship Śiva as supreme God. Oldest of the four denominations of Hinduism. The earliest historical evidence of Śaivism is from the Indus Valley civilization (purported to be 6,000 to 8,000 years old) in the form of the renowned seal of Śiva as Lord Paśupati, seated in a yogic pose. In the *Rāmāyaṇa*, Lord Rāma worshiped Śiva, as did his rival Rāvaṇa. In 624 BCE Buddha was born a Śaivite Hindu prince in a royal family, and records of his time speak of the Śaiva ascetics who wandered the hills looking much as they do today.

Śaivite (Śaiva): शैव Of or relating to Śaivism or its adherents, of whom there are about 400 million in the world today. See: *Śaivism.*

Śākta: शाक्त "Powerful," Of or relating to *Śāktism.* A follower of the Śākta Hindu religion. See: *Śāktism.*

Śakti: शक्ति "Power, energy" (from the root *śak,* "to be able"). The active power or manifest energy of Śiva that pervades all of existence. Śakti is most easily experienced by devotees as the sublime, bliss-inducing energy that emanates from a holy person or sanctified Hindu temple. See: *kuṇḍalinī, Śāktism.*

śaktipāta: शक्तिपात "Descent of grace." Guru *dīkshā,* initiation from the preceptor; particularly the first initiation, which awakens the *kuṇḍalinī* and launches the process of spiritual unfoldment. See: *dīkshā, grace, kuṇḍalinī.*

Śāktism *(Śākta):* शाक्त "Doctrine of power." The religion followed by those who worship the Supreme as the Divine Mother—Śakti or Devī—in Her many forms, both gentle and fierce. Śāktism is one of the four primary denominations of Hinduism. See: *Śakti, tantrism.*

samādhi: समाधि "Enstasy," which means "standing within one's Self." "Sameness; contemplation; union, wholeness; completion, accomplishment." *Samādhi* is the state of true yoga, in which the meditator and the object of meditation are one. *Samādhi* is of two levels. The first is *savikalpa samādhi* ("enstasy with form or seed"), identification or oneness with the essence of an object. Its highest form is the realization of the primal substratum or pure consciousness, Satchidānanda. The second is *nirvikalpa samādhi* ("enstasy without form or seed"), identification with the Self, in which all modes of consciousness are transcended and Absolute Reality, Paraśiva, beyond time, form and space, is experienced. This brings in its aftermath a complete transformation of consciousness. See: *kuṇḍalinī, Paraśiva, rāja yoga, Self Realization.*

samāpatti: समापत्ति The second in the stages of the Path of Attainment in Buddhism, a continuation of *dhyāna* (meditation), the first stage, leading through a progressive nullification of psychic, mental and emotional activity to a state which is perfect solitude, neither perception nor nonperception.

Sāma Veda: सामवेद "Song of wisdom." Third of the four *Vedas.* Ninety percent of its 1,875 stanzas are derived from the *Ṛig Veda.* It is a collection of hymns specially arranged and notated for chanting with a distinctive melody and cadence by the Udgātā priests during *yajña,* fire ceremony, together with stanzas from the *Yajur Veda.* This *Veda* forms the oldest known form of Indian music. See: *śruti, Vedas.*

sampradāya: संप्रदाय "Tradition," "transmission;" a philosophical or religious doctrine or lineage. A living stream of tradition or theology within Hinduism, passed on by oral training and initiation. The term derives from the verb *sampradā,* meaning "gift, grant, bestowing or conferring; handing down by tradition; bequeathing." See: *guru paramparā.*

saṁsāra: संसार "Flow." The phenomenal world. Transmigratory existence, fraught with impermanence and change. The cycle of birth, death and rebirth; the total pattern of successive earthly lives experienced by a soul.

saṁskāra: संस्कार "Impression, activator; sanctification, preparation." 1) The imprints left on the subconscious mind by experience (from this or previous lives), which then color all of life, one's nature, responses, states of mind, etc. 2) A sacrament or rite done to mark a significant transition of life. These make deep and positive impressions on the mind of the recipient, inform the family and community of changes in the lives of its members and secure inner-world blessings. See: *sacrament.*

Sanātana Dharma: सनातनधर्म "Eternal religion" or "everlasting path." It is the original designation for the Hindu religion. See: *Hinduism.*

Sanātani: सनातनि "Of the eternal." A Hindu, a follower of the eternal path.

saṅgama: सङ्गम "Association; fellowship." Also *saṅga.* Coming together in a group, especially for religious purposes. See: *satsaṅga.*

saṅkalpa: संकल्प "Will; purpose; determination." A solemn vow or declaration of purpose to perform any ritual observance. Most commonly, *saṅkalpa* names the mental and verbal preparation made by a temple priest as he begins rites of worship. See: *pūjā.*

Śaṅkara: शङ्कर One of Hinduism's most extraordinary monks (788–820) and preeminent guru of the Smārta Sampradāya. He is noted for his monistic philosophy of Advaita Vedānta, his many scriptural commentaries, and formalizing ten orders of sannyāsins with pontifical headquarters at strategic points across India. He only lived 32 years, but traveled throughout India and transformed the Hindu world in that time. See: *Smārtism, Vedānta.*

Śaṅkarāchārya pīṭha: शङ्कराचार्यपीठ Advaita monasteries established by Śaṅkara (ca 788–820) as centers of Smārta authority in India, each with a distinct guru *paramparā* and a reigning pontiff entitled Śaṅkarāchārya, and one of the four Upanishadic *mahāvākyas* as a mantra. East coast: Govardhana Maṭha, in Puri (center of the Āraṇya and Vāna orders). Himalayas: Jyotiḥ Maṭha, near Badrināṭh (Giri, Pārvata and Sāgara orders). West coast: Śārada Maṭha, in Dvāraka (Tīrtha and Āśrama orders). South: Śṛingeri Maṭha (Bhārati, Pūrī and Sarasvatī orders). A fifth prominent *pīṭha,* associated with Sṛingeri Maṭha, is in Kanchipuram, also in the South. See: *Smārtism, Śaṅkara.*

Sāṅkhya: सांख्य "Enumeration, reckoning." See: *tattva.*

San Mārga: सन्मार्ग "True path." The straight spiritual path leading to the ultimate goal, Self Realization, without detouring into unnecessary psychic exploration or pointless development of siddhis. A *San Mārgī* is a person "on the path," as opposed to a *saṁsārī,* one engrossed in worldliness. *San Mārga* also names the *jñāna pāda.* See: *pāda, sādhana mārga.*

San Mārga Sanctuary: A meditation *tīrtha* at the foot of the extinct volcano, Mount Waialeale, on Hawaii's Garden Island, Kauai. Here pilgrims follow the ½-mile path, San Mārga, to a natural Śivaliṅga, walk the path of the Tamil Nayanars around picturesque lotus lakes and ponds and visit the six shrines of the Kailāsa Paramparā on the banks of Śaravaṇabhāva Lake in Ṛishi Valley. Paths lead visitors to the sacred Wailua River, then up stone stairs to the Chola-style white-granite Iraivan Temple, hand-carved in Bangalore, India. In the sanctum sanctorum, the Supreme God, Śiva (Parameśvara-Parāśakti-Paraśiva), will be enshrined as a massive 700-pound, single-pointed earthkeeper quartz crystal. San Mārga Sanctuary, founded in 1970, is among many public services of Śaiva Siddhānta Church, one of America's senior Hindu religious institutions. See: *Subramuniyaswami, tīrtha.*

sannidhāna: **सन्निधान** "Nearness; proximity; taking charge of." A title of heads of monasteries: Guru Mahāsannidhāna. See: *sānnidhya.*

sānnidhya: **सान्निध्य** "(Divine) presence; nearness, proximity." The radiance and blessed presence of *śakti* within and around a temple or a holy person.

Sanskrit *(Saṁskṛita):* **संस्कृत** "Well-made;" "refined," "perfected." The classical sacerdotal language of ancient India, considered a pure vehicle for communication with the celestial worlds. It is the primary language in which Hindu scriptures are written, including the *Vedas* and *Āgamas.* Employed today as a liturgical, literary and scholarly language, but no longer used as a spoken vernacular.

Sarasvatī: **सरस्वती** "The flowing one." Śakti, the Universal Mother; Goddess of the arts and learning, mythological consort of the God Brahmā. Sarasvatī, the river Goddess, is usually depicted wearing a white sārī and holding a *vīna,* sitting upon a swan or lotus flower. Prayers are offered to her for refinements of art, culture and learning. *Sarasvatī* also names one of seven sacred rivers (Sapta Sindhu) mentioned in the *Ṛig Veda.* See: *Goddess, Śakti.*

sārī: (Hindi, **साड़ी**) The traditional outer garment of a Hindu woman, consisting of a long, unstitched piece of cloth, usually colorful cotton or silk, wrapped around the body, forming an ankle-length skirt, and around the bosom and over the shoulder.

śāstra: **शास्त्र** "Sacred text; teaching." 1) Any religious or philosophical treatise, or body of writings. 2) A department of knowledge, a science; e.g., the *Dharma Śāstras* on religious law, *Artha Śāstras* on politics.

Satan: The devil; evil personified. A being who in Christian and other Semitic religions opposes God's will and tempts souls into wickedness. In Hinduism, all is seen as the manifestation of God, and there is no Satan.

Satchidānanda (Sachchidānanda): **सच्चिदानन्द** "Existence-consciousness-bliss." A synonym for *Parāśakti.* Lord Śiva's Divine Mind and simultaneously the pure superconscious mind of each individual soul. Perfect love and omniscient, omnipotent consciousness, the fountainhead of all existence, yet containing and permeating all existence. Also called pure consciousness, pure form, substratum of existence, and more. One of the goals of the meditator or *yogī* is to experience the natural state of the mind, Satchidānanda, subduing the *vṛittis* through *yogic* practices. See: *tattva.*

satguru (sadguru): **सद्गुरु** "True weighty one." A spiritual preceptor of the highest attainment—one who has realized the ultimate Truth, Paraśiva, through *nirvikalpa samādhi*—a *jīvanmukta* able to lead others securely along the spiritual path. He is always a *sannyāsin*, an unmarried renunciate. All Hindu denominations teach that the grace and guidance of a living *satguru* is a necessity for Self Realization. He is recognized and revered as the embodiment of God, Sadāśiva, the source of grace and of liberation. See: *guru, guru bhakti, guru-śishya system.*

Satguru Pūrṇimā: **सत्गुरु पूर्णिमा** See: *Guru Pūrṇimā.*

satsaṅga: **सत्संग** "Holy gathering." Association of devotees for temple or home worship, celebration, selfless service and religious studies.

satya: **सत्य** "Truthfulness." See: *yama-niyama.*

savikalpa samādhi: **सविकल्पसमाधि** "Enstasy with form" or "seed." See: *rāja yoga, samādhi.*

Self (Self God): God Śiva's perfection of Absolute Reality, Paraśiva—That which abides at the core of every soul. See: *Paramātman, Paraśiva.*

Self Realization: Direct knowing of the Self God, Paraśiva. Self Realization is known in Sanskrit as *nirvikalpa samādhi;* "enstasy without form or seed;" the ultimate spiritual attainment (also called *asamprajñata samādhi).* Esoterically, this state is attained when the mystic kuṇḍalinī force pierces through the *sahasrāra* chakra at the crown of the head. See: *liberation, kuṇḍalinī, Paraśiva, rāja yoga, samādhi.*

Semitic: Of or relating to the Semites or their languages (Arabic, Hebrew, Amharic, and Aramaic) or their cultures.

severance: A breaking off or separation.

Shaṇmukha: **षण्मुख** "Six-faced." A name for Lord Murugan or Kārttikeya, denoting the multiplicity of His divine functions. See: *Kārttikeya.*

Sharma: **शर्म** A North Indian Brahmin caste.

Shum: A Nātha mystical language of meditation revealed in Switzerland in 1968 by Sivaya Subramuniyaswami. Its primary alphabet looks like this:

Sikhism: "Discipleship." Religion of nine million members founded in India about 500 years ago by the saint Guru Nānak. A reformist faith which rejects idolatry and the caste system, its holy book is the *Ādi Granth,* and its main holy center is the Golden Temple of Amritsar.

śishya: **शिष्य** "A pupil or disciple," especially one who has proven himself and has formally been accepted by a guru.

Śiva: शिव "The auspicious, gracious or kindly one." Supreme Being of the Śaivite religion. God Śiva is All and in all, simultaneously the creator and the creation, both immanent and transcendent. As personal Deity, He is creator, preserver and destroyer. See: *Naṭarāja, Parameśvara, Paraśiva, Śaivism.*

Śivaliṅga: शिवलिङ्ग "Mark (or sign) of Śiva." The most prevalent icon of Śiva, found in virtually all Śiva temples. A rounded, elliptical, aniconic image, usually set on a circular base, or *pīṭha.* The Śivaliṅga is the simplest and most ancient symbol of Śiva, especially of Paraśiva, God beyond all forms and qualities. The *pīṭha* represents Parāśakti, the manifesting power of God. See: *mūrti, Śaivism.*

Sivam: சிவம் Same as Śiva.

Sivathondar: சிவதொண்டர் One who performs Sivathondu, selfless service to God Śiva.

Sivathondu: சிவதொண்டு "Service to Śiva." Akin to the concept of *karma yoga.* See: *karma yoga.*

Smārta: स्मार्त "Of or related to *smṛiti,*" the secondary Hindu scriptures. Of or related to Smārtism; a follower of Smārtism. See: *Smārtism.*

Smārtism: स्मार्त Sect based on the secondary scriptures *(smṛiti).* The most liberal of the four major denominations of Hinduism, an ancient Vedic *brāhminical* tradition (ca 700 BCE) which from the 9th century onward was guided and deeply influenced by the Advaita Vedānta teachings of the reformist Ādi Śaṅkara. Its adherents rely mainly on the classical *smṛiti* literature, especially the *Itihāsas (Rāmāyaṇa* and *Mahābhārata,* the latter of which includes the *Bhagavad Gītā), Purāṇas* and *Dharma Śāstras.* These are regarded as complementary to and a means to understanding the *Vedas.* See: *Śaṅkara.*

smṛiti: स्मृति That which is "remembered;" the tradition. Hinduism's nonrevealed, secondary but deeply revered scriptures, derived from man's insight and experience. *Smṛiti* speaks of secular matters—science, law, history, agriculture, etc.—as well as spiritual lore, ranging from day-to-day rules and regulations to superconscious outpourings. 1) The term *smṛiti* refers to a specific collection of ancient Sanskritic texts. 2) In a general sense, *smṛiti* may refer to any text other than *śruti* (revealed scripture) that is revered as scripture within a particular sect.

snāna: स्नान "Bathing." Ceremonial ablution, especially in sacred waters, traditionally prescribed as an obligatory Hindu duty.

soul: The real being of man, as distinguished from body, mind and emotions. The soul (known as ātman or *purusha*) is the sum of its two aspects: 1) the form or body of the soul and 2) the essence of the soul—Pure Consciousness *(Parāśakti* or *Satchidānanda)* and Absolute Reality *(Paraśiva).* See: *ātman, Paramātman, spiritual unfoldment.*

spiritual unfoldment: The unfoldment of the spirit, the inherent, divine soul of man. The gradual expansion of consciousness as kuṇḍalinī śakti slowly rises through the *sushumṇā*. The term *spiritual unfoldment* indicates this slow, imperceptible process, likened to a lotus flower's emerging from bud to effulgent beauty. See: *kuṇḍalinī, liberation, pāda, sādhana.*

śraddhā: श्रद्धा "Faith; belief."

śraddhā śuddhi: श्राद्धाशुद्धि See: *śuddhi.*

śruti: श्रुति "That which is heard." Aurally, or clairaudiently, received scripture. Hinduism's revealed scriptures, of supreme theological authority and spiritual value. They are timeless teachings transmitted to ṛishis, or seers directly by God Śiva and the Gods thousands of years ago. *Śruti* is thus said to be *apaurusheya,* "impersonal," or rather "suprahuman." *Śruti* essentially consists of the *Vedas* and the *Āgamas,* preserved initially through oral tradition and eventually written down in Sanskrit. Most mantras are drawn from *śruti,* used for rites of worship, both public and domestic, as well as for personal prayer and japa. See: *Āgama, smṛiti, Veda.*

Subramuniyaswami: சுப்பிரமுனியசுவாமி Current and 162nd *satguru* (1927–) of the Nandinātha Sampradāya's Kailāsa Paramparā. He was ordained Sivaya Subramuniyaswami by Sage Yogaswāmī on the full-moon day of May 12, 1949, in Jaffna, Sri Lanka, at 6:21 PM. This was just days after he had attained *nirvikalpa samādhi* in the caves of Jalani. The name *Subramuniya* is a Tamil spelling of the Sanskrit *Śubhramunya* (not to be confused with *Subramaṇya).* It is formed from *śubhra* meaning "light; intuition," and *muni,* "silent sage." *Ya* means "restraint; religious meditation." Thus, *Subramuniya* means a self-restrained soul who remains silent or, when he speaks, speaks out from intuition.

śuddhi: शुद्धि "Purification." Also, *śraddhā śuddhi,* "purification of faith." The rite of accepting back into the Hindu fold individuals who have been converted to other faiths or otherwise require purification to rejoin the Hindu congregation. An alternate term to *vrātyastoma,* "oath affirmation."

śūdra: शूद्र "Worker, servant." The social class of skilled artisans, workers and laborers. See: *varṇa dharma.*

śūnya: शून्य "The void, the distinctionless absolute."

Sūrya: सूर्य "Sun." One of the principal Divinities of the *Vedas,* also prominent in the epics and *Purāṇas.* Śaivites revere Sūrya, the Sun God each morning as Śiva Sūrya. Smārtas and Vaishṇavas revere the golden orb as Sūrya Nārāyaṇa.

sushumṇā nāḍī: सुषुम्णानाडी "Most gracious channel." Central psychic nerve current within the spinal column. See: *kuṇḍalinī, nāḍī, samādhi.*

sūtra: सूत्र "Thread." An aphoristic verse; the literary style consisting of such maxims. From 500 BCE, this style was widely adopted by Indian philosophical systems and eventually employed in works on law, grammar, medicine, poetry, crafts, etc.

svayambhū mūrti: स्वयम्भूमूर्ति "Self-existent image." A Deity image discovered in nature, and not carved or crafted by human hands. See: *mūrti.*

swāmī: स्वामी "Lord; owner." He who knows or is master of himself. A respectful title for a Hindu monk, usually a *sannyāsin*. The term swāmī is sometimes applied more broadly to include nonmonastics dedicated to spiritual work. See: *sannyāsin*.

Tagore, Rabīndranāth: रबीन्द्रनाथ् तगोरे One of India's most highly acclaimed modern-day writers and poets (1861–1941), son of Devendranāth Tagore. He wrote in Bengali and in English. His most famous poetic religious work is *Gītāñjali*, which centers around dialogs between the soul and God Vishṇu. He received the Nobel Prize for literature in 1913.

tāṇḍava: ताण्डव "Violent dance." Any vigorous dance sequence performed by a male dancer. There are many forms of *tāṇḍava*. Its prototype is Śiva's dance of bliss, *ānanda tāṇḍava*. The more sublime, female dance is called *lāsya*, from *lasa*, "lively." Dance in general is *nartana*. See: *Naṭarāja*.

tantra: तन्त्र "Loom, methodology." 1) Most generally, a synonym for *śāstra*, "scripture." 2) A synonym for the Āgamic texts, especially those of the Śākta faith, a class of Hindu scripture providing detailed instruction on all aspects of religion, mystic knowledge and science. The tantras are also associated with the Śaiva tradition. 3) A specific method, technique or spiritual practice within the Śaiva and Śākta traditions. See: *tantrism*.

tantric *(tāntrika):* तान्त्रिक Adjectival form for practices prescribed in the tantra traditions. The name of a follower of any of the tantric traditions. See: *tantra*.

tantrism: The enlightenment path outlined in the Tantra scriptures. 1) Tantrism is sometimes considered a parallel stream of history and tradition in Hinduism, running alongside and gradually interweaving with the Vedic *brāhminical* tradition. 2) Tantrism refers to traditions, mainly within Śaivism and Śāktism, that focus on the arousal of the kuṇḍalinī force and which view the human body as a vehicle of the Divine and an instrument for liberation. Tantrism's ultimate aim is a channeling of the kuṇḍalinī life force through the *sushumṇā*, the gracious channel, upwards into the *sahasrāra* chakra and beyond, through the door of Brahman *(brahmarandhra)* into Paraśiva, either before or at the time of death. The stress is on the transformation of all spheres of consciousness, spiritual, psychic, emotional and material. It is a path of *sādhana*. 3) ***—Śākta Tantrism:*** Brings a strong emphasis on the worship of the feminine force. Depending on the school, this may be symbolic or literal in rites involving sexual intercourse, etc. Śākta Tantrism's main principle is the use of the material to gain the spiritual. In certain schools, historically, this implies embracing that which is normally forbidden and manipulating the forces to attain transcendent consciousness rather than lower consciousness. See: *kuṇḍalinī*, *rāja yoga*,

Śāktism, tantra.

tapas: तपस् "Warmth, heat," hence psychic energy, spiritual fervor or ardor. Austerity, asceticism, penance. State of accelerated unfoldment and working with the forces through spiritual practices. A state of humble submission to the divine forces and surrender to the processes of inner purification which occurs almost automatically at certain stages. Denotes religious austerity, intense meditation, penance, bodily mortification; connotes spiritual purification and transformation as a "fiery process" that "burns up" impurities, ego, *vāsanas* and past karmas that obstruct God Realization. See: *kuṇḍalinī, penance, sādhana.*

Tatha astu: तथास्तु A pronouncement meaning, "Be it so."

tattva: तत्त्व "That-ness" or "essential nature." *Tattvas* are the primary principles, elements, states or categories of existence, the building blocks of the universe. Ṛishis describe this emanational process as the unfoldment of thirty-six *tattvas,* stages or evolutes of manifestation, descending from subtle to gross. At *mahāpralaya,* cosmic dissolution, they enfold into their respective sources, with only the first two *tattvas* surviving the great dissolution.

tejas: तेजस् "Brilliance, fire, splendor." Heat or fire, one of the five elements—earth, water, fire, air, ether. *Tejas* also names the glow of *tapas* in the shining expression of the *tapasvin. Tejas* is increased through *brahmacharya,* control of the sexual energies by lifting the heat into the higher chakras. See: *brahmacharya, tapas.*

temple: *Mandira.* An edifice in a consecrated place dedicated to the worship of God or the Gods. From the Latin *templum,* "temple, sanctuary; marked space." Hindu temples, over one million worldwide, are revered as sacred, magical places in which the three worlds most consciously commune—structures especially built and consecrated to channel the subtle spiritual energies of inner-world beings. The temple's psychic atmosphere is maintained through regular worship ceremonies (pūjā) invoking the Deity, who from the Third World uses His installed image *(mūrti)* as a temporary body through which bless those living on the earth plane, the First World. See: *darshan, tīrthayātrā.*

theism: Belief that God exists as a real, conscious, personal Supreme Being, creator and ruler of the universe. May also include belief in the Gods.

theistic dualism: Any dualistic philosophy that is also theistic. Theism is the belief that God exists as a real, conscious, personal Supreme Being. Dualism describes a philosophy which view reality as ultimately composed of two irreducible principles, entities or truths, such as God and soul, which are seen as eternally separate.

tilaka: तिलक "Sesamum-like mark," from *tila,* "sesame seed." Distinctive marks made on the forehead or the brow with clay, ashes or sandalwood paste as an indication of sectarian affiliation. Vaishṇavas wear a vertical v-shaped *tilaka* made of clay. The Śaivite *tilaka,* called *tripuṇḍra,* consists of three horizontal lines of white holy ash with a dot, usually red, below the middle of the forehead. See: *bindu, Hinduism.*

tīrtha: तीर्थ "Passageway; ford." A bathing *ghat* or place of pilgrimage, especially on the banks of sacred waters. Also refers to water offered in pūjā.

tīrthayātrā: तीर्थयात्रा "Journeying to a holy place." Pilgrimage. One of the five sacred duties *(pañcha nitya karmas)* of the Hindu is to journey periodically to one of the innumerable holy spots in India or other countries. Preceded by fasting and continence, it is a time of austerity and purification, when all worldly concerns are set aside and God becomes one's singular focus. See: *pañcha nitya karmas*

Tirukural: திருக்குறள் "Holy couplets." A treasury of Hindu ethical insight and a literary masterpiece of the Tamil language, written by Śaiva Saint Tiruvalluvar (ca 200 BCE) near present-day Madras. See: *Tiruvalluvar.*

Tiruvalluvar: திருவள்ளுவர் "Holy weaver." Tamil weaver and householder saint (ca 200 BCE) who wrote the classic Śaivite ethical scripture Tirukural. See: *Tirukural.*

tithing: *Daśamāṁśa.* "One-tenth sharing." Religion's dues. The spiritual discipline, often a *vrata,* of paying one-tenth of one's gainful and gifted income to a religious organization of one's choice, thus sustaining spiritual education and upliftment on Earth. The Sanskrit *daśamāṁśa* is called *makimai* in the Tamil tradition. See: *tithing vow.*

tithing vow: *Daśama bhāga vrata.* "One-tenth-part vow." A promise tithers make before God, Gods and their family or peers to tithe regularly each month—for a specified time, or for life.

tripuṇḍra: त्रिपुण्ड्र "Three marks." The Śaivite sectarian mark, consisting of three horizontal lines of *vibhūti* (holy ash) on the brow, often with a dot *(bindu)* at the third eye. The three lines represent the soul's three bonds: *āṇava,* karma and māyā. Holy ash, made of burnt cow dung, is a reminder of the temporary nature of the physical body and the urgency to strive for spiritual attainment and closeness to God. See: *bindu, tilaka.*

triśūla: त्रिशूल "Trident." A three-pronged spear or trident wielded by Lord Śiva and certain Śaivite ascetics. Also held by loving Gaṇeśa, it symbolizes God's three fundamental śaktis or powers—*icçhā* (desire, will, love), kriyā (action) and jñāna (wisdom).

ucçhishṭa: उच्छिष्ट "Leavings; remainder." Religiously, the precious leavings from the guru's food plate or the waters from the bathing of his feet or sandals (or of a Deity) which are ingested by devotees as *prasāda.* See: *prasāda, satguru.*

upadeśa: उपदेश "Advice; religious instruction." Often given in question-and-answer form, the *satguru's* spiritual discourses.

Upanishad: उपनिषद् "Sitting near devotedly." The fourth and final portion of the *Vedas*, expounding the secret, philosophical meaning of the Vedic hymns. The *Upanishads* are a collection of profound texts which are the source of Vedānta and have dominated Indian thought for thousands of years. They are philosophical chronicles of ṛishis expounding the nature of God, soul and cosmos, exquisite renderings of the deepest Hindu thought. See: *śruti, Veda, Vedānta.*

upāsanā: उपासना "Sitting near." Worship or contemplation of God. One of the *pañcha nitya karmas.* "five constant duties."

utsava: उत्सव "Festival." Religious celebrations or holy days and their observance in the home and temple. *Utsava* is one of the five constant duties, *pañcha nitya karmas.* See: *festival, pañcha nitya karmas.*

vahana: वहन "Vessel, conveyance." The mount, or vehicle, of a Deity, often an expression of an aspect of the Deity.

Vaidika Dharma: वैदिकधर्म "The way of the *Vedas.*" An alternate term for Hinduism. See: *Hinduism.*

Vaikuṇṭha: वैकुण्ठ "Vishṇu's heaven." See: *Vaishṇavism.*

Vaishṇava: वैष्णव "Way of Vishṇu." Of or relating to Vishṇu. A follower of Lord Vishṇu or His incarnations, such as Kṛishṇa or Rāma. See: *Vaishṇavism.*

Vaishṇavism *(Vaishṇava):* वैष्णव One of the four major religions or denominations of Hinduism, representing roughly half of the world's one billion Hindus. It gravitates around the worship of Lord Vishṇu as Personal God, His incarnations and their consorts. Vaishṇavism stresses the personal aspect of God over the impersonal, and *bhakti* (devotion) as the true path to salvation. Foremost among Vaishṇava scriptures are the *Vaishṇava Āgamas.*

Vaishṇavite: A follower of Vishṇu or His incarnations. See: *Vaishṇavism.*

vaiśya: वैश्य "Landowner; merchant." The social class of bankers, businessmen, industrialists; employers. Merchant class, originally those whose business was trade as well as agriculture. See: *varṇa dharma.*

vāma: वाम 1) "Pleasant; beautiful; benignant; striving after"—as in Vāmadeva, a name of Śiva. 2) "Left; crooked; acting in the opposite way"—as in *vāma mārga,* the left-handed *tantric* path." See: *left-handed, tantrism.*

vānaprastha āśrama: वानप्रस्थ आश्रम "Forest-dweller stage." See: *āśrama dharma.*

Vārāṇasī: वाराणसी Also known as Kāśī or Banāras. (Derived from the name of two rivers, the Varaṇā, "warding off," and Asī, "sword.") One of the most holy of Śaivite cities, and among the oldest cities in the world. Located in North India on the Ganges River. Hindus consider it highly sanctifying to die in Kāśī, revering it as a gateway to *moksha.*

varṇa: वर्ण "External appearance, covering; type, species, kind, color; caste. See: *varṇa dharma.*

varṇa dharma: वर्णधर्म "The way of one's kind." The hereditary social class system, generally referred to as *caste,* established in India in ancient times. Within *varṇa dharma* are the many religious and moral codes which define human virtue. *Varṇa dharma* is social duty, in keeping with the principles of good conduct, according to one's community, which is generally based on the craft or occupation of the family. Strictly speaking it encompasses two interrelated social hierarchies: 1) *varṇa,* which refers to the four classes: brāhmin, kshatriya, vaiśya and śūdra; and 2) *jāti,* the myriad occupational subgroups, or guilds, which in India number over 3,000. Hence this dharma is sometimes called *jāti* dharma. The class-caste system is still very much a part of Indian life today. Many modern Hindus propose that social status is now (and was originally) more properly determined by a person's skills and accomplishments than by birth. Mobility between *jātis,* or castes, within Hindu communities worldwide is limited but not impossible, and is accomplished through marrying into a new *jāti,* or changing professions through persistence, skill and education. *Śāstrīs* say that once a person breaks out of his *varṇa* or *jāti* of birth and changes "caste," it takes three generations for his family to become fully established in that new strata of society, provided the continuity is unbroken.

—***varṇa:*** The four *varṇas* are as follows. —***brāhmin (brāhmaṇa):*** "Mature, evolved soul." Scholarly, pious souls of exceptional learning. Hindu scriptures traditionally invest the *brāhmin* class with the responsibility of religious leadership, including teaching and priestly duties. —***kshatriya***: "Governing; endowed with sovereignty." Lawmakers and law enforcers and military, also known as *rājanya.* —***vaiśya***: "Landowner, merchant." Businessmen, financiers, industrialists; employers. Those engaged in business, commerce and agriculture. —***śūdra***: "Worker, servant." Skilled artisans and laborers. It is in keeping with *varṇa dharma* that sons are expected to follow the occupation of their father, as that is the occupation that was chosen prior to birth.

—***jāti:*** "Birth; position assigned by birth; rank, caste, family, race, lineage." *Jāti,* more than *varṇa,* is the specific determinant of one's social community. Traditionally, because of rules of purity each *jāti* is excluded from social interaction with the others, especially from interdining and intermarriage. In modern times there is also a large group (one-seventh of India's population in 1981) outside the four *varṇas.* These are called scheduled classes, untouchables, *jātihīta* ("outcaste"), *chandālas* (specifically those who handle corpses) and *harijan,* a name given by Mahātma Gāndhi, meaning "children of God." "Untouchable" *jātis* included the *nishāda* (hunter), *kaivarta* (fisherman) and *kārāvara* (leather worker).

The *varṇa dharma* system—despite its widespread discrimination against *harijans,* and the abuse of social status by higher castes—ensures a high standard of craftsmanship, a sense of community belonging, family integrity and religio-cultural continuity. Caste is not unique to Hinduism and India. By other names it is found in every society. The four *varṇas,* or classes, and myriad *jātis,* occupational castes, or guilds, form the basic elements of human interaction. See: *dharma, jāti.*

varṇāśrama dharma: **वर्णाश्रमधर्म** "The way of one's caste and stage of life." Names the social structure of four classes *(varṇa),* hundreds of castes *(jāti)* and four stages of life *(āśramas).* It is the combined principles of *varṇa dharma* and *āśrama dharma.* See: *āśrama dharma, dharma, varṇa dharma.*

Veda: **वेद** "Wisdom." Sagely revelations which comprise Hinduism's most authoritative scripture. They, along with the *Āgamas,* are *śruti,* "that which is heard." The *Vedas* are a body of dozens of holy texts known collectively as the *Veda,* or as the four *Vedas: Ṛig, Yajur, Sāma* and *Atharva.* In all they include over 100,000 verses as well as additional prose. Each *Veda* has four sections: *Saṁhitās* (hymn collections), *Brāhmaṇas* (priestly manuals), *Āraṇyakas* (forest treatises) and *Upanishads* (enlightened discourses). See: *śruti, Upanishad.*

Vedānta: **वेदान्त** "Ultimate wisdom" or "final conclusions of the *Vedas.*" Vedānta is the system of thought embodied in the *Upanishads* (ca 1500-600 BCE), which give forth the ultimate conclusions of the *Vedas.* Through history there developed numerous Vedānta schools, ranging from pure dualism to absolute monism. See: *monistic theism, panentheism.*

Vedāntin: **वेदान्तिन्** An adherent of Vedānta.

Vedic astrology: See: *jyotisha.*

veshti: **வேஷ்டி** A long, unstitched cloth like a sarong, wound about the waist and reaching below the ankles. Traditional Hindu apparel for men. It can be wrapped in many different styles. A Tamil word derived from the Sanskrit *veshṭana,* "encircling." Also called *vetti* (Tamil) or *dhoti* (Hindi).

videhamukti: **विदेहमुक्ति** "Disembodied liberation." Release from reincarnation through *nirvikalpa samādhi*—the realization of the Self, Paraśiva—at the point of death. See: *jīvanmukti, moksha, Paraśiva, Self Realization.*

vīṇā: **वीणा** Large South Indian popular musical instrument usually having seven strings and two calabash gourd resonance boxes.

Vīra Śaivism (Śaiva): **वीरशैव** "Heroic Śaivism." Made prominent by Basavaṇṇa in the 12th century. Also called Liṅgāyat Śaivism. Followers, called Liṅgāyats, Liṅgavantas or Śivaśaraṇās, always wear a Śivaliṅga on their person. Vīra Śaivites are proudly egalitarian and emphasize the personal relationship with Śiva, rather than temple worship. Today Vīra Śaivism is a vibrant faith, particularly strong in its religious homeland of Karnataka, South Central India. By rejecting the *Vedas,* they continue to stand outside mainstream Hinduism, but in their profound love of Śiva and acceptance of certain *Śaiva Āgamas,* as well as the main truths of the Vedic wisdom, they have identified themselves as a unique Śaiva sect. Though they have established their faith as a distinct and independent religion in Indian courts of law, they are still widely embraced as devout brothers and sisters of the Hindu dharma. See: *Śaivism.*

visarjana: विसर्जन "Departure."

Vishṇu: विष्णु "The All-Pervasive." Supreme Deity of the Vaishṇavite religion. God as personal Lord and Creator, the All-Loving Divine Personality, who periodically incarnates and lives a fully human life to reestablish dharma whenever necessary. In Śaivism, Vishṇu is Śiva's aspect as Preserver. See: *Vaishṇavism.*

Viśvaguru: विश्वगुरु "World as teacher." The playful personification of the world as the guru of those with no guru, headmaster of the school of hard knocks, where students are left to their own devices and learn by their own mistakes rather than by following a traditional teacher.

viśvagrāsa: विश्वग्रास "Total absorption." The final merger, or absorption, of the soul in Śiva, by His grace, at the fulfillment of its evolution. It is the ultimate union of the individual soul body with the body of Śiva—Parameśvara—within the Śivaloka, from whence the soul first emanated. *Jīva* has totally become Śiva—not a new and independent Śiva, as might be construed, for there is and can only be one Supreme God Śiva. See: *ātman, samādhi, soul.*

Vivekānanda, Swāmī: विवेकानन्द "Of blissful discrimination." blissful disciple of Śrī Rāmakṛishṇa who was overtaken by an ardent love of Hinduism and a missionary zeal that drove him onward. He attained *mahāsamādhi* at age 39 (1863–1902). Most notable among his achievements was a trip around the world on which he gave brilliant lectures, especially in Europe and America, that created much respect for Hinduism. In India he founded the Rāmakṛishṇa Mission which thrives today internationally with over 100 centers and nearly 1,000 *sannyāsins.* He is credited, along with Tagore, Aurobindo, Rādhākṛishṇan and others, with sparking the modern Hindu revival.

vow: See: *vrata.*

vrata: व्रत "Vow, religious oath." Often a vow to perform certain disciplines over a period of time, such as penance, fasting, specific mantra repetitions, worship or meditation. *Vratas* extend from the simplest personal promise to irrevocable vows made before God, Gods, guru and community.

vrātyastoma: व्रात्यस्तोम "Vow pronouncement." The purification rite, outlined in the *Taṇḍya Brāhmaṇa,* to welcome back into a Hindu community those who have become impure. It is performed for Hindus returning to India from abroad and for those who have embraced other faiths.

yama-niyama: यम नियम "Restraints-observances." The first two of the eight limbs of rāja yoga, constituting Hinduism's fundamental ethical codes, the ten *yamas* and ten *niyamas* are the essential foundation for all spiritual progress. The *yamas* are the ethical restraints; the *niyamas* are the religious practices. Here are the ten traditional *yamas* and ten *niyamas.* —***yamas:*** 1) **ahiṁsā:** "Noninjury." 2) ***satya:*** "Truthfulness." 3) ***asteya:*** "Nonstealing." 4) ***brahmacharya:*** "Sexual purity." 5) ***kshamā:*** "Patience." 6) ***dhṛiti:*** "Steadfastness." 7) ***dayā:*** "Compassion." 8) ***ārjava:*** "Honesty, straightforwardness." 9) ***mitāhāra:*** "Moderate appetite." 10) ***śaucha:*** "Purity." —***niyamas:*** 1) ***hrī:*** "Remorse." 2) ***santosha:*** "Contentment." 3) ***dāna:*** "Giving." 4) ***āstikya:*** "Faith." 5) **Īśvarapūjana:** "Worship of the Lord." 6) ***siddhānta śravaṇa:*** "Scriptural listening." 7) ***mati:*** "Cognition." 8) ***vrata:*** "Sacred vows." 9) **japa:** "Recitation." 10) ***tapas:*** "Austerity." See: *rāja yoga.*

yantra: यन्त्र "Restrainer," "limiter," a mystic diagram composed of geometric and alphabetic figures—usually etched on small plates of gold, silver or copper. Sometimes rendered in three dimensions in stone or metal. The purpose of a *yantra* is to focus spiritual and mental energies according to computer-like *yantric* pattern, be it for health, wealth, childbearing or the invoking of one God or another. It is usually installed near or under the temple Deity.

yātrā: यात्रा See: *tīrthayātrā.*

yoga: योग "Union." From *yuj,* "to yoke, harness, unite." The philosophy, process, disciplines and practices whose purpose is the yoking of individual consciousness with transcendent or divine consciousness. One of the six *darśanas,* or systems of orthodox Hindu philosophy. Yoga was codified by Patañjali in his *Yoga Sūtras* (ca 200 BCE) as the eight limbs *(ashṭāṅga)* of rāja yoga. It is essentially a one system, but historically, parts of rāja yoga have been developed and emphasized as yogas in themselves. Prominent among the many forms of yoga are haṭha yoga (emphasizing bodily perfection in preparation for meditation), kriyā yoga (emphasizing breath control), as well as karma yoga (selfless service) and bhakti yoga (devotional practices) which could be regarded as an expression of rāja yoga's first two limbs *(yama* and *niyama).* See: *bhakti yoga, haṭha yoga, rāja yoga.*

Yogaswāmī: யோகசுவாமி "Master of yoga." Sri Lanka's renowned spiritual master (1872–1964); a *siddhar* of the Nandinātha Sampradāya's Kailasa Paramparā who initiated Satguru Sivaya Subramuniyaswami in 1949. See: *Kailāsa Paramparā.*

yogī: योगी One who practices yoga, especially kuṇḍalinī yoga or rāja yoga. (More properly *yogin.* Feminine, *yoginī.*)

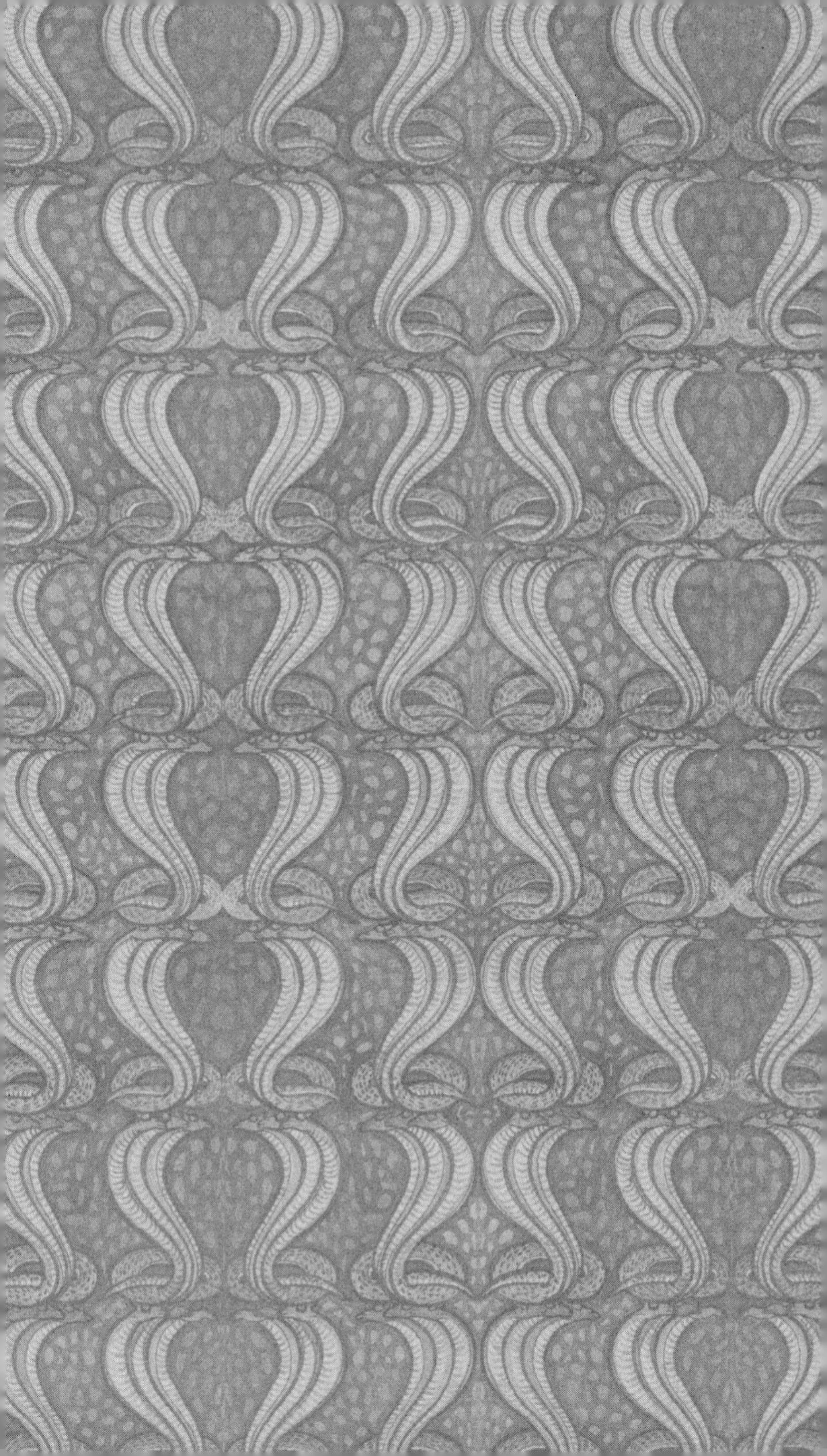

Index

Anukramaṇikā

अनुक्रमणिका

A

Abrahamic religions: derivation of term, 240; no Satchidānanda, 140; similarities among, 246; undeclared apostates in, 141; Vedānta and, 139
Absolute: in Taoism, 196
Abundance: cow as symbol, 360
Abysses, mental: religion and, 172
Action: reaction and, 359
Address: forms of (in Hindu culture), 341
Adoptive Hindus: body language and, 348; case histories, 22, 25, 62–63
Adoptives (religious): converts vs., xvi; subconscious beliefs of, 370
Advaita Śaiva Siddhānta: Śaiva Siddhānta Church and, xix
Affection: displaying, 346
Africa: Hinduism in, ix
Afterlife: in Christianity, 216; none in materialism, 232; none in secular humanism, 238
Aggression: fundamentalism and, 229; meat-eating and, 363
Agnosticism: entering Hinduism from, xviii
Agricultural era: belief and, 144
Ahiṁsā: Hindu ideal, 180, 251; Jain ideal, 186–188; personal experiences, 88; practice of, 153, 157; purity and, 342; vegetarianism and, 363; vs. Christian beliefs, 250
Alahan: Asha, personal history, 35; Isani, personal history, 27; Valli, personal history, 15; Vel, personal history, 11
Alcohol: addiction to, 4; Hindu attitudes, 347
Alexander the Great: Hinduism and, 158
Amṛitānandamāyī, Māta: at Parliament of World Religions, xxv
America: Hinduism in, ix; name changes in, 284–285
Analogies: enlightenment and graduation, 357; karma and gravity, 358; stone image and telephone, 361; unfoldment and mountain, 370
Angels: Catholic, 45, 60–61; Christian, 46; Eastern Orthodox Christian, 18, 21; Jewish, 17
Anger: meat-eating and, 363
Animals: Christian Bible and, 82
Apostasy: and conversion, 139; automatic excommunication, 369; defined, 120; in Islam, 119; in Judaism, 119; letter of, 51; severance and, 261
Appar, Saint: protecting Sanātana Dharma, ix
Ardha-Hindus: need for leadership, 140; problems of, xx; two types, 110
Ardhanārīśvara: symbology of, 367
Arms: body language of, 348
Arunachaleśvara Temple: Rāmana and, 100

Arya Samaj: teachings of, 71
Asceticism: Buddhist attitude, 184; Eastern vs. Western views, 244; in Hinduism, 253; Jain ideal, 186–188; Sikh attitude, 192; Zoroastrian attitude, 206
Asia: culture of (discussion), 339
Associates: conversion and, 110
Astrology: good timing and, 13; names and, 22, 288, 291–292; Vedic, 98
Atheism: entering Hinduism from, xviii; return to Hinduism from, xxii
Atheistic philosophies: discussion, 232
Attainment: commitment and, 254
Attitudes: beliefs and, xxiii, 106, 173, 254
Aurobindo, Sri: and the *Vedas,* 85, 97; concept of man, 76; *The Life Divine,* 75
Austerity: in Hinduism, 176; in Jainism, 188
Āgamas: Hindu scripture, 156

B

Baha'i: beliefs of, 223
Bali: Hinduism in, ix
Baptism: inner significance of, 18
Baptist Church: fear of God in, 4; severance from (case history), 3
Behavior: beliefs, attitudes and, 254
Beings, unseen: devotee and, 106; Hindu belief, 180; New Age belief, 226; Taoist belief, 196; vs. Christian beliefs, 249
Beliefs: attitudes and, xxiii, 106, 173, 254; behavior, attitudes and, 254; evaluating, 173; examination of, 259
Beliefs, Hindu: religions opposed, xxiv; widespread in West, 154; severance and, 127
Belief systems (non-religious): severance from, 128
Bible, Christian: animals and, 82; names from, xxi
Bible, Hindu: question and answers, 364
Bindi (forehead dot): question and answers, 365; wearing in West, 366
Birth (country of): Hinduism and, 162–164
Birthstar: Hindu names and, 291
Blessings: Hindu names and, 288
Body: physical, soul and, 357; language, in Hindu culture, 348
Books: of Hindu names, 295
British (in India): creation of strife, 134
Buddha: intellectualization and, 87
Buddhism: differences from Hinduism, xxiv–xxv; early history, ix; entering Hinduism from, xviii; Hinduism and, 133, 151; in Italy, 164; rejection of (case history), 92; Self and, 96; severance from (case histories), 41; Subramuniyaswami and, xv; summarized, 182–184; use of images in, 362
Business world: religious symbols and, 366

C

Cambodia: Hinduism in, ix
Caste: Hindu names and, 288; newcomers and, 159
Catholicism: and conversion, 142; apostasy and, 261; conversion tactics, 81; entering Hinduism from, 261; equals excommunication, 369; Hindus educated in, xxii; mysticism and, 93; proselytization, 81;

questioning, 93; rejection of (case histories), 70, 92; severance from (case histories), 27, 35, 39, 41, 47, 60; Vedānta and, 139, 105; vegetarianism and, 82; yoga and, xv
Certificate: *nāmakaraṇa saṁskāra,* xvii, 263-264
Charyā: foundation for unfoldment, xii
Charyā mārga: dharma and, xiv
Chettiar, Kandiah: Subramuniyaswami and, xiii
Children: New Age movement and, 370; parents' worldliness and, 371; raising in Hinduism, xvi–xvii, xx, 27, 30–31, 34–35, 39, 369
Chinmāyānanda, Swāmī: meeting, 65
Christian rule: effect on Hinduism, 152
Christianity: and conversion, 142; apostasy equals excommunication, 369; compared with Hinduism, 248–250; compared with Judaism and Islam, 246–247; conversion tactics, 83; cost per convert, 165; cross on necklace identifying, 366; differences from Hinduism, xxiv–xxv; early history, ix, xi; entering Hinduism from, xviii; ethical conversion and, xx; names from, xxi; Paganism and, ix; practice vs. conversion, 82; return to Hinduism from, 285; summarized, 214–216; Today (magazine), 87, 160, 163, 248; universalism in, 222; use of images in, 362; yoga and, xiv, 137
Cleanliness: purity and, 342
Commandments: none in Hinduism, 363
Commitment: attainment and, 254; avoiding (New Age ideal), 227; conversion and, xvi; drifting vs., 127; importance of, xxiii; loyalty and, 105–110; name change and, 289
Communication: non-verbal, 348
Communism: Ram Swarup and, 75, 78–79; rejection of (case history), 70; return to Hinduism from, xxii; summarized, 233–235
Communist Manifesto: Marx, 75
Community, Hindu: acceptance by, 5, 13, 17, 21, 50, 116; conversion and, 107; merging with, xxvi, 260, 284, 289; Subramuniyaswami's acceptance into, xiii
Company, religious: conversion and, 107
Compassion: Buddhist ideal, 184; Christian ideal, 214; God as (Hinduism), 252; Jain ideal, 186; New Age ideal, 226
Confirmation: severance required, 259
Conflict, religious: confusion and, 105; resolving, xviii
Confrontation: avoiding, 353
Confucianism: summarized, 198–200
Confusion: meat-eating and, 363
Consciousness, group: separatism vs., 108
Contemplation: religion and, 172
Conversion: announcement of, 266; follow-up, 167; forced or deceitful, 141–142, 144–146; guidelines, website, 262; laws and, 146; Mahābhārata and, 160; name change and, 285, 290; predatory, 143
Conversion, ethical: history of, xv; six steps, 259–266; vs. predatory, xx
Conversion tactics: Catholic, 80–81; Christian, 83; unscrupulous, 144
Converts: adoptives vs., xv; body language and, 348
Covenant with God: in Abrahamic religions, 246; Jewish belief, 211–212

Cow, sacredness of: question and answers, 360
Creation: Eastern and Western views, 241; Hindu vs. Christian beliefs, 249; oneness of (Taoist belief), 196
Creator: God as (Eastern and Western views), 241; sacredness, 211
Creatures: sacredness of all, 360
Cremation: burial vs., 154
Culture: beliefs and, 124, 254
Culture, Hindu: embracing, 339–340; living, 260; Subramuniyaswami's upbringing in, xi; resource books, 371
Cycles of universe: Eastern religions, 241; Hindu, 249, 251

D

Dakshiṇā: Hindu tradition of, 342; *nāmakaraṇa saṁskāra* and, 263
Dalai Lama: on 'personal God' concept, xxiv
Dandapani, Shyamadeva and Peshanidevi: personal histories, 47
Darśana: explanation, 341
Death, physical: soul and, 357
Deeds, consequence of: Hindu vs. Christian beliefs, 249
Defensiveness: avoiding, 353, 355
Deities: in each religion, 174; in Eastern religions, 245; in Shintoism, 204; spiritual practice and, 99
Deity: invoking, 361
Destiny: karma vs., 359
Devas: angels and, 174, 245; guardian, 107; Hindu, 11, 21, 30, 46; in Hinduism, 180, 249, 251
Devil: in Christianity, 215
Devotee: role in conversion, 124
Devotion: Hinduism, 176, 178–180, 249, 252–253; Islam, 190; Judaism, 212; Saiism, 223; Shintoism, 202; Sikhism, 192
Dharma: family vs. monastic, 34; in Buddhism , 184; in Eastern religions, 242; in Hinduism, 176, 251; karma and, 152, 157; progressive stages of, xiv; purity and, 342
Dialogue (religious): Catholic evangelization and, 143
Diaspora, Hindu: reincarnation and, 117
Discipline: in Hinduism, 178, 180, 250; in Jainism, 188; in Taoism, 195; in Zoroastrianism, 208
Disciplines: commitment and, xxiii; mix-and-match (New Age belief), 226
Divine: beholding, 341, 378
Dīkshā, Subramuniyaswami's, xiv
Documents: importance of, 266; name change on, xxvi, 259
Doorways: inauspiciousness of, 345
Dot (forehead): question and answers, 365; wearing in West, 366
Double standard: avoiding, 265, 289; problems created, 283
Doubts: of a Catholic, 93; religious, 72, 75
Drifting, religious: commitment vs., 127
Drug culture: involvement with, 43; summarized, 224–225
Drugs: addiction to, 4
Duty: Hindu culture and, 339

E

Eastern views: compared with Western, 240–245
Ecology movement: summarized, 227, 229
Ecumenism: single path vs., 133

Education, religious: importance, 122
Einstein: theories of, 358
Elders: respect for, 340
Emir, Rudite J.: personal history, 65
Emotions (lower): meat-eating and, 363; religion and, 174
Energies: exchange of, 344
Energy: karma as, 358–359
Enlightenment: Eastern and Western views, 241, 244-245; existentialist attitude, 236; Hindu goal, 179; means to (drug culture belief), 224; soul's evolution and, 357; Zoroastrian attitude, 207
Eswaran, Sivaram: history, 22
Eternal: Taoist belief, 196
Ethics: conversion and, 123–124, 133, 146–147
Europe: Hinduism in, ix
Evangelization: Catholic, 142; Christian priority, 214
Evil: Eastern and Western views, 243; good vs. (Zoroastrianism), 206–208; in Abrahamic religions, 246; in Christianity, 216, 249; in existentialism, 236; in fundamentalist sects, 230; in Islam, 220; in Judaism, 211–212; nonexistence of (Shintoism), 204; not intrinsic (Hinduism), 251; personification of (Zoroastrianism), 206–207; unnaturalness of (Confucianism), 200
Evolution: of the soul, 32, 155, 178, 180, 186, 245, 249, 357
Evolutionism: H.G. Wells and, 74
Excommunication: apostasy and, 369; defined, 120; heresy, apostasy and, 121
Existentialism: beliefs of, 145; entering Hinduism from, xviii; rejection of (case histories), 70, 92; summarized, 235–236
Eye, third: forehead dot and, 365
Eyes: communicating with, 348

F

Fabian (Indian Ambassador to Italy): on conversion, 164
Faiths, miscellaneous: summarized, 222–224
Families: vegetarianism and, 363
Family: *nāmakaraṇa saṁskāra* for, 264; reactions of, 4, 6–8, 10, 21–22, 25, 29–30, 34, 36, 39, 45, 50, 56, 59; and friends, role in conversion, 126; life, monastic path vs., 34
Fate: karma vs., 359
Fear: meat-eating and, 363
Feet: apology for contact, 344; *satguru's*, water from washing, 343; touching in respect, 341
Finger: refraining from pointing, 344
Fire: invoking Divinity in, 361; use in worship (Zoroastrian belief), 208
Flowers: offerings of, 343
Food: purity and, 343
Footwear: apology for contact, 344
Forehead: dot, question and answers, 365; marks on, 154
Frawley, David: personal history, 92
Free will: in Confucianism, 200; in existentialism, 236; in materialism, 233; in Zoroastrianism, 208
Freedom, cultural: Hindu vs. Western, 339
Freemasonry: severance from (case history), 47
Fundamentalism: summarized, 229–230

G

Gaṇeśa: personal experiences, 7, 19, 58, 66–67
Gandhi, Maneka: *The Penguin Book of Hindu Names*, 295
Gender: Gods and, 366
Gestures: of giving and receiving, 344; refining body language, 348
Gifts: giving and receiving, 344; host and hostess, 347
Gitānanda Ashram: Italy, 162
Giving: gestures of, 344; karmic benefits, 358
Goals: Eastern vs. Western, 240
God: and Deva, Eastern and Western views, 245; and Gods, invoking, 361; body language and, 348; Buddhist views, xxiv, 240 ; Eastern and Western views, 240–243, 245; existence of, 153–154; Gods and (Hinduism), 356; Hindu and Christian beliefs, 248; immanence of, 361; immanent, religions opposed, xxiv; in Abrahamic religions, 246–247; in Buddhism, 183; in Christianity, 216, 250; in Communism, 234; in Confucianism, 199–200; in fundamentalist sects, 229; in Hinduism, 176–178, 180, 251–253; in Islam, 220; in Jainism, 187–188; in Judaism, 210, 212; in Rajneeshism, 223; in Saiism, 223; in Sikhism, 191–192; in Taoism, 195; in Zoroastrianism, 207–208; means to Realization (Hinduism), 180; nature of, 156; one, 232; one Supreme (Hinduism), 355; personal, religions opposed, xxiv; realization of (Hinduism), 178; realization, *sushumṇā* and, 140; religions and, 157; unproven or unknowable (secular humanism), 237
Godbole, Shreeram Tyambak: on assimilation into Hinduism, 160
Goddess: in Hinduism, 179, 251–252; in Shintoism, 203–204; worship of, 68, 72
Gods: and Goddesses, personal experiences of, 69, 88, 98–99; gender and, 366; in Buddhism, 184; in Hinduism, 180, 249, 251; in Jainism, 187; in Shintoism, 202–204; in Taoism, 196; many, question and answers, 355
Goel, Sita Ram: at Kauai Aadheenam, 90; personal history, 70; return to Hinduism, xxii
Good conduct: Christian ideal, 214; Confucian ideal, 198; Eastern and Western views, 243, 245; Hindu ideal, 176, 180, 250; Islamic ideal, 218; Jain ideal, 188
Good works (Christian): conversion and, 143–144
Gopalakṛishṇan, Dr. R: on conversion, 164
Grace: drug culture attitude, 225; Eastern and Western views, 241; in Abrahamic religions, 246; in Christianity, 215, 220, 249; in Eastern religions, 245; in Hinduism, 178–179, 253; in Sikhism, 191; in Vaishṇavism, 177
Great Britain: name changes in, 285
Greek Orthodoxy: severance from (case history), 18
Greeks: entering Hinduism, 158, 160
Guests: Hindu customs, 347
Guru: drugs as (drug culture belief), 224; Eastern and Western views, 241; in Buddhism, 183; in Hinduism, 176, 179; in Sikhism, 190–192; necessity of, 153; New Age attitudes, 227; release required from, xix; Subramuniyaswami's

search for, xiii
Gurudeva: meetings with, 26, 34, 36, 43, 49, 59, 64

H

Half-Hindus: problems of, xx
Hand(s): left, impurity of, 343; refined gestures of, 344; right, aggressive energy in, 344; shaking: Hindu customs, 345
Haran, Kriya: personal history, 39
Harmony: Confucian ideal, 198
Health: *prāṇāyāma* and, 96; vegetarianism and, 364
Heaven: Eastern and Western views, 243; in Abrahamic religions, 246; in Buddhism, 183; in Christianity, 214–216; in Confucianism, 198–200; in Hinduism, 177; in Islam, 219–220; in Jainism, 187; in Judaism, 212; in Taoism, 195–196; in Zoroastrianism, 207–208
Hell: Eastern and Western views, 242–243; for the unbaptized, 83; in Abrahamic religions, 246; in Christianity, 214–216; in Hinduism, 176; in Islam, 219–220, 247; in Jainism, 187; in Judaism, 212; in Western religions, 241; in Zoroastrianism, 207–208
Henotheism: in Hinduism, 356
Heresy: defined, 120; excommunication and, 120
Himālayan Academy: outreach; programs, 371; services, xvii
Hindu: recognizing oneself as, xxiv
Hindu culture: adoption of (discussion), 339; connecting with dharma, 101; distinguishing features, 340; living, 260; VHP's definition of Hinduism, 154
Hinduism: acceptance into, 158–160, 167; beliefs of, 153; central concepts, x; changing sects within, 120; compared with Christianity, 248–250; comparison of sects, 251–254; embracing, 123; entering, good and poor reasons, xxiii; entering, traditional requirements, xx; levels of teaching, 366; modernization and, 70; naming customs, 288; nine beliefs, 156; no severance from, 118–119; power of tradition, xviii; questions and answers, 353; reconversion to, 285; sects of, shared beliefs, 151; sects of, conversion into, x; Subramuniyaswami's upbringing in, xi; summarized, 176–180; universalism in, 222; Western perceptions, 92
HINDUISM TODAY (magazine): contemporary Hinduism, 371; Ram Swarup and, 91
Hindus: born, subconscious beliefs of, 370; by belief, 154; Catholic schools and, xxii; defined, xix, 154; five obligations of, 157; forehead dot identifying, 365; proselytization by, 141; welcoming back, 371
Holiness: symbols of, 362
Holy days: Hindu observance of, 157
Homa: nāmakaraṇa saṁskāra, 262
Humanitarianism: beliefs of, 223
Humility: in Hindu culture, 340
Husband: wife walking behind, 346
Huyler, Stephen P.: story, 68

I

Idealogies: culture and, 339; nonreligious, severing from, 262
Idol worship: questions and answers, 361

Idols: Protestantism and, 65
Illumination (spiritual): soul's evolution into, 357
Images: graven, question and answer, 361; stone, telephone analogy, 361
Immanence: of God, 251
Immaturity: soul's evolving from, 357
Immortality: Eastern and Western views, 245; in Christianity, 216; in Jainism, 187; in Zoroastrianism, 208; none (existentialist belief), 236; soul's (Shintoism), 203
Impurity: avoidance of, 342; of footwear, 344; of left hand, 343
Incarnation: of God (Vaishṇava belief), 178–179; Hindu sects, 252
India: Sanātana Dharma and, 86
Indian Supreme Court: defining Hindu beliefs, 155
Inheritance: religions and, x
Initiation: Hindu names and, 288; requirements for, xix; severance required, 259; vegetarianism and, 363
Instinctive mind: control of, 138
Intellectual mind: control of, 138
Intellectualization: Buddha and, 87
Interest: nonverbal indicators, 348
Ishṭa Devatā: choice of, 135; tradition and, 136
ISKCON: declaration of non-Hinduism, 290
Islam: apostasy in, 119–120; compared with Judaism and Christianity, 246–247; conversions into, 142; differences from Hinduism, xxiv–xxv; early history, ix, xi; entering Hinduism from, xviii; return to Hinduism from, 285; summarized, 218–220; universalism in, 222; use of images in, 362; woman's veil identifying, 366; yoga and, xv
Islamic rule of India: effect on Hinduism, 152
Italy: Buddhism in, 164; Hinduism in, 162–163

J

Jainism: differences from Hinduism, xxiv; early history, ix; Hinduism and, 151; summarized, 186–188; universalism in, 222
Japa: purity and, 342
Jealousy: meat-eating and, 363
Jesus: Christian beliefs, 214–216; other sages and, 94
Jñāna *mārga:* dharma and, xiv
Judaism: apostasy in, 119, 261, 369; boys' yalmuka identifying, 366; compared with Christianity and Islam, 246–247; differences from Hinduism, xxiv–xxv; entering Hinduism from, xviii; (Hasidic), reincarnation in, xxv; idol worship and, 106; severance from (case histories), 11, 15; summarized, 210–212; use of images in, 362
Judgment (of souls by God): Abrahamic religions, 246; Christianity, 214, 216; Eastern and Western views, 242; Hindu vs. Christian views, 249; Islam, 219–220; Judaism, 212; Western religions, 242; Zoroastrianism, 206–207

K

Kami: Shinto belief, 202–203
Kandar, Diksha: personal history, 18
Karma: belief in, apostasy and, 123; examples of, 359; facing positively, 348; in Buddhism, 184; in Eastern religions, 240, 242, 249; in Hinduism, 176, 178–180, 251; in Jain-

ism, 187–188; in Scientology, 223; law of, 153–154, 156; non-Hindu religions and, xv; question and answers, 358; religions opposed to, xxv
Karmic attachments: conversion and, 107
Katir, Easan: personal history, 25
Kindliness: Hindu attitude, 348
Kriyā *mārga: charyā* and, xii; dharma and, xiv
Kundrakuddi Aadheenam: reconversions, 165

L

Laws: conversion and, 146
Leaders: Hindu, call to welcome aspirants, xxvii; Hindu, vegetarianism of, 363; prior, severing from, 259, xvi
Liberation: Eastern and Western views, 244; human goal, 153, 156; in Buddhism, 184; in Eastern religions, 240, 242–243; in Hinduism, 177, 179–180, 249, 251; in Jainism, 186–187; soul's evolution to, 357
Life: cow as symbol, 360; eternal, Hindu vs. Christian beliefs, 249; long, vegetarianism and, 364; meaning of (drug culture belief), 225; meaninglessness of (existentialist belief), 235; prosaic, 79; purpose of (materialist belief), 233; reverence for, Hindu vs. Christian beliefs, 250; reverence for, in Jainism, 186, 188; sacredness of (Hindu belief), 180
Life (single): Christian belief, 216; Communist belief, 234; in Abrahamic religions, 246; secular humanist belief, 238; Western belief, 240
Lifestyle: conversion and, 109–110; resource books, 371
Limbo state: full conversion and, 128
Living with Śiva: Nandinātha Sūtras of, 260
Lord Gaṇeśa: resource books, 371. *See* Gaṇeśa
Love: Buddhist ideal, 184; Christian ideal, 216, 250; Confucian ideal, 198–199; God as (Eastern and Western views), 241-242; Hindu ideal, 176, 180, 252; Jain ideal, 186; New Age ideal, 226; Sikh ideal, 192
Loyalty (religious): declaration of, 263; identifying, xvii; importance of, 115

M

Madurai Aadheenam: reconversions, 165, 285
Mahābhārata: acceptance into Hinduism, 160
Malaysia: changing one's name in, 24
Man: Divine within (Rajneeshism belief), 223; finitude of (Taoist belief), 196; identity with God (Hinduism), 176, 178; intrinsic Divinity of (Confucianism), 202; intrinsic goodness of (Eastern and Western views), 243; meaninglessness of (existentialist belief), 235; nature of (Buddhist belief), 184; perfection of (Jain belief), 186; plight of, Eastern and Western views, 242; relationship with Spirit and earth (indigenous tribalism), 224; sinful nature of (Christian belief), 216
Mankind: intrinsic goodness of (Christian belief), 216
Mantra: vegetarianism and, 363

Manu Dharma Śāstras: vegetarianism in, 364
Mārgas: progressive nature of, xii, xiv, 138
Marriage: arranged, 27; forehead dot and, 366; religions and, x
Marx, Karl: *Communist Manifesto,* 75
Master Course: study programs for non-Hindus, xvii
Masurāśrama: reconversions to Hinduism, 165
Materialism: entering Hinduism from, xviii; rejection of (case history), 70; summarized, 232–233
Matter: principle of, 153; the only reality (materialism), 232
Māyā: Hindu belief, 251; overcoming, 179; principle of, 153
Meals: serving men first, 347
Meat-eating: effects on consciousness, 363; question and answers, 362
Meditation: commitment and, xxiii; in Buddhism, 182–184; in Hinduism, 176, 179–180, 250; in Taoism, 195; invoking Divinity through, 361; New Age beliefs, 226; non-Hindu religions and, xv; obstacles to, 138; personal experiences, 88, 95; purity and, 342; religion and, 172; resource books, 371; vegetarianism and, 363
Mentors; severance from, 260; attitude of ownership, 369
Messiah: in Christianity, 214; in fundamentalist sects, 229; in Judaism, 211–212; in Western religions, 245; in Zoroastrianism, 206
Metaphysics, Western: practicality vs., 79
Milan: 1997 conference on conversion, 162
Mind, group: levels of, 107
Missionary spirit: Hinduism and, 160
Modernization: Hinduism and, 70
Modesty, public: Asian culture, 346
Moksha: in Eastern religions, 242; in Hinduism, 177–178, 180, 251; in Jainism, 187–188; in Sikhism, 191; soul's evolution to, 357
Monastic life: Catholic, 81; Hindu, 18, 21–22, 26
Monasticism: family path vs., 34; in Buddhism, 183; in Jainism, 186–187
Monotheism: in Abrahamic religions, 246; in Hinduism, 356
Moon: Hindu names and, 291–292
Morality: drug culture attitudes, 225; Eastern and Western views, 245; in Buddhism, 183; in fundamentalist sects, 230; in Hinduism, 178; in Jainism, 188; in Judaism, 210–211; in secular humanism, 237; in Shintoism, 204; in Sikhism, 192; in the ecology movement, 228; materialist attitudes, 233; vegetarianism and, 364
Mormonism: apostasy equals excommunication, 369; severance from (case history), 41
Mystical experiences: drugs and, 224
Mysticism: beliefs, 223; Catholicism and, 93; Communist attitudes, 234

N

Nakshatra: Hindu names and, 288, 291; *nāmakaraṇa saṁskāra* and, 263; sounds of each, 291-294
Name change: initial concern, xxi; legal, xiv, 10, 262; legal process, 10; legalities of (Malaysia), 24; letter announcing, 55; obstacles to, 283; sample documents, 275–277, 279;

Subramuniyaswami's, xiv
Name-giving: announcing, 266; personal experiences, 34
Names: astrology and, 22, 288, 291–292; Christian, 285; customs worldwide, 284–287; double standard in, 289; family and given, 286; Hindu listing 297-335; importance of, 22, 24, 117, 174; protocol of use, 340; resources, 295; sources of, 288; Westernization and, 290
Nandinātha Sūtras: upholding, 260
Nature: sacredness of (Shinto belief), 204; ecology movement belief, 227
Navaratnam, K.: Hindu beliefs, 153
Nāmakaraṇa saṁskāra: announcement of, 266; arranging for, xxvi; certificate of, xxvi; details, 262–264; examples, 265, 278; for family, 264; letter of release and, 261; personal experiences, 10, 13, 17, 21, 25, 30, 38, 46, 53, 64; Subramuniyaswami's, xiii; website, xxvi
Nārāyaṇa Guru: reconversions to Hinduism, 165
New Age: Hinduism and, 161; discussion, 370; seekers, entering Hinduism, xviii; severance from (case history), 41; summarized, 225–227
Newcomers: Hindu acceptance of, xvi, 151
Non-Hindus: study programs for, xvii
Noninjury: vegetarianism and, 363
Nonsectarianism: and dilution, 135; futility of, 134–135
Nonviolence: ecology movement ideal, 228; Hindu ideal, 176; Jain ideal, 186

O

Objectivity: worship vs., 69
Obligations (prior religious): commitment and, xvi
Occultism: beliefs, 224
Offering(s): basket, 263; handling of, 343
Oneness: in Eastern religions, 242; in Hinduism, 176–178; in Taoism, 196; New Age belief, 226

P

Paganism: use of images in, 362
Pandya and Pandya-Bhanot: *Pick a Pretty Indian Name for Your Baby,* 295
Panentheism: in Hinduism, 356
Pantheism: panentheism vs., 356
Parliament of the World's Religions: 1993 centennial, xxiv
Parsi religion: yoga and, xv
Passport: name change on, xxvi, 259, 264
Path, spiritual: monastics vs. householders, 34
Pāda: Hindu names and, 291
Pādapūjā: personal experience of, 62
Personal Lord: God as (Hinduism), 179
Philosophy: commitment and, xxii; practicality vs., 79; resource books, 371; stories vs., 366
Pilgrimage: Hindu observance, 157; purity and, 342; yearly performance, 260
Plane, astral: reincarnation and, 357; sleep and, 106
Point-counterpoint: for educated choice, 260; Hindusim and Christianity, 248; severance and, xviii, 13

Pointing: refraining from, 344
Polytheism: henotheism vs., 356
Pope: New Age and Hinduism, 161; John Paul II, converting Asia, 142
Pottu (forehead dot): question and answers, 365
Practices: essential, 157
Prasāda: of *satguru*, 343
Prayers: written, 8, 19, 30, 43, 59
Prāṇāyāma: practicing, 95
Prāṇa: exchange of, 344
Preceptor, spiritual: Eastern vs. Western views, 245; Hindu vs. Christian beliefs, 250; importance of, 254; Jainism, 187
Preparation: successful severance and, 12
Priests, Hindu: vegetarianism of, 363
Promiscuity, sexual: overcoming, 4
Pronunciation, Sanskrit: guide, 372
Property: religions and, x
Prophet(s): in Abrahamic religions, 246; in Christianity, 250; in Islam, 218–220; in Judaism, 210, 212; in Western religions, 241, 243, 245; in Zoroastrianism, 207–208; Ram Swarup on, 89
Proselytization: among strayed Hindus, 141; Catholic, 81; destructive effects of, xi; ethics of, 121; Hinduism and, 119, 129; Islamic priority, 219
Protestantism: apostasy equals excommunication, 369; idols and, 65; symbology, 66; Vedānta and, 139
Protocol: conversion and, 147
Purāṇas: discussion of, 367
Purity: and Hindu culture, 342; necessity of, 153; three forms of (discussion), 342; vegetarianism and, 363
Pūjā: daily performance, 260
Questions: answers to, 353

R

Rajneeshism: beliefs, 223
Rāmakṛishṇa, Śrī: personal impressions of, 86
Rāmana: Arunachaleśvara temple and, 100; Lord Skanda and, 98
Rāmanāshram: visit to, 98
Rādhākṛishṇan, Dr. S: missionary spirit of Hinduism, 160
Rāmakṛishṇa: Mission, reconversions to Hinduism, 165; Śrī, and ecumenism, 133
Reality: nature of, Eastern and Western views, 245; Ultimate, New Age belief, 226
Realization: temple worship and, 136; urgency vs., 137
Receiving: gestures of, 344
Reconversion: follow-up, 167; to Hinduism, efforts, 165
Reincarnation: belief in, apostasy and, 123; cycle of, 153–156, 177; Eskimo belief, 287; Hindu vs. Christian beliefs, 249; Buddhism, 182–184; in Eastern religions, 240; in Hinduism, 176, 178, 180, 251; in Jainism, 186–187; in many religions, 358; non-Hindu religions and, xv; none in materialism, 232; none in secular humanism, 238; process of, 357; question and answers, 357; religions opposed to, xxv; Western Hindus and, 117
Relationships, human: five kinds (Confucianism), 199–200; free sex (drug culture ideal), 225; no hope of harmony (existentialism), 236
Release: letter of, 261
Religion: freedom of, 125; importance of commitment, xxiii; name changes and, 285; rediscovering former, xviii, xxii, 370; responding

to questions, 353–354; returning to former, 6, 18, 36, 45, 51, 60; severing from, xvi. *See* Severance; two ways to enter, 115; yoga, *sādhana* and, 136
Religions: Abrahamic conversion practices, xx; Abrahamic, similarities of, 240; beliefs and, xxiii; culture and, 339; Eastern and Western compared, 240–241; ecology movement beliefs, 228; essential distinction among, xxv; Hindu tolerance of, 355; legal rights and, x; materialist attitudes, 232; myth of sameness, 171; unique names in, 284; use of images in, 362
Religious leaders, former: reactions of, 7–8, 11–12, 17, 19, 29, 32, 34, 38, 41, 45, 53, 61, 125
Religious practices: graded forms of, 153
Resentment: meat-eating and, 363
Resources: Hindu names, 295; religious and cultural, 371; vegetarianism, 364
Respect: in Hindu culture, 340; successful severance and, 12
Responsibility: karma and, 359
Resurrection: Christian belief, 216; of physical body, in Abrahamic religions, 246
Reverence: in Hindu culture, 340; symbols awakening, 362
Rights: human, secular humanist ideals, 237; legal, religions and, x
Ritual, domestic: *Veda* in, 364
Robbins, John: *Diet for a New America*, 364
Robertson, Pat: New Age and Hinduism, 161
Roles: in ethical conversion, 123–124
Rumi, Jalal al-Din: quote, 172

S

Saṁsāra: in Buddhism, 182; in Hinduism, 157, 178–179; in Jainism, 188
Sabanathan, Chamundi: personal history, 62
Saiism: beliefs, 223
Sainthood: Eastern and Western views, 244
Śaiva Siddhānta: *mārgas* in, xiv
Śaiva Siddhānta Church: name changes and, 289; Hindus entering, xix
Śaivism: beliefs, 251; conversion to, x
Śakti: in Hinduism, 252; Śiva and, 177, 367
Śāktism: beliefs, 251; conversion into, x; Śaiva Siddhānta Church and, xix
Salvation: Eastern and Western views, 243–245; Hindu vs. Christian beliefs, 250; in Abrahamic religions, 247; in Buddhism, 183; in Christianity, 214–216; in Confucianism, 199; in fundamentalist sects, 229; in Hinduism, 180; in Islam, 219–220; in Jainism, 186, 188; in Shintoism, 203; in Sikhism, 190, 192; in Zoroastrianism, 207; many ways to, 155, 157
Samādhi: levels of, 177
Sampradāyas, Hindu: conversion among, 120
Sanātana Dharma: India and, 86; names of, 371; soul and, 89
Śaṅkara, Ādi: protecting Sanātana Dharma, ix
Sannyāsin: Subramuniyaswami's *dīkshā* as, xiv
Sanskrit: guide to pronunciation, 372; Vedic study and, 97
Sarasvatī: Śrī Śrī Śrī Jayendra, features of Hinduism, 153; Swāmī

Chidānanda, at Parliament of World Religions, xxv
Saravan, Hitesvara: story, 3
Sartre, Jean-Paul: existentialism and, 145
Satan: in Abrahamic religions, 246; in Judaism, 211; in Western religions, 243
Satchidānanda: Self-Realization and, 177; unknown in Abrahamic religions, 140
Satguru: Hinduism, 178, 180, 250–251; Sikhism, 191; invoking Divinity in, 361; necessity of, 156; *prasāda* of, 343
Satsaṅga: attending, 4, 28, 30; regular worship, 260
Sādhakas: addressing, 341
Sādhana: commitment and, xxii; daily performance, 260; Eastern vs. Western views, 244; Gaṅgā, 7; in Hinduism, 178–179, 223, 252–253; religion and, 136
Schooling: at home, 31, 35, 39
Schools, Catholic: evangelization and, 143; Hindus in, xxii
Scientology: beliefs, 223
Scriptural study: purity and, 342
Scriptures: Abrahamic, 246; attitude of fundamentalist sects, 229; Buddhismt, 182, 184; Christian, 216; Christianity, 214, 216, 248, 250; Confucianism, 198, 200; Eastern and Western views, 241; Hindu, 151, 156176, 179–180, 248, 251, 253; Hindu, vegetarianism in, 364; Islam, 218–220; Jainism, 186, 188; Judaism, 210–212; Shintoism, 202, 204; Sikhism, 190–192; Taoism, 194, 196; Western religions, 244; Zoroastrianism, 206, 208
Sect (Hindu): selection of, xxvi; names and, 288
Sectarianism: importance of, 122; religion and, 134; wisdom of, 137
Sects: Buddhist, 182; Christian, 214; Hindu, conversion among, xix, xxi, 120, 259, 251; forehead marks and, 365; Islamic, 218; Jain, 186; Judaic, 210; not in Confucianism, 198; Shinto, 202; Sikh, 190; Taoist, 194; Zoroastrian, 206
Secular humanism: involvement with, 43; summarized, 236–238
Seekers: Swāmī Tilak on, 167
Self Realization: Buddhism and, 96; Hinduism and, 251; non-Hindu religions and, xv; Satchidānanda and, 177; Subramuniyaswami's search for, xv
Self-declaration: as a Hindu, xix
Self-pity: immersion in, 73
Sendan, Aran: personal history, 60
Separatism: tragedy of, 108; transcending, 109
Severance: announcing, 266; conversion and, xvi; experience of, xxiii; from former mentors, 260; from Islam, 119–120; from Judaism, 119; individual's responsibility, xviii; letters of (examples), 267–274; necessity for, 369; not from Hinduism, 118–119; refusal to grant, 261; required for conversion, 259; roles in, 121; true, requirements, 126
Severance case histories: Baptist Church, 3; Catholicism (Roman), 39, 47, 60; emotional difficulties, 125; Freemasonry, 47; Greek Orthodoxy, 18; Judaism, 11, 15; many prior religions, 41; Taoism, 57
Sexual energies: purity and, 342
Seyon, Amala: personal history, 31
Shamanism: summarized, 222
Shanmugan, Damara: personal history, 41

Shastri, Vamadeva: story, 92
Shintoism: summarized, 202–204
Shoes: impurity of, 344
Sight, spiritual: forehead dot, 365
Sikhism: Hinduism and, 151; summarized, 190–192; use of images in, 362
Sin: Eastern and Western views, 243; in Abrahamic religions, 246–247; in Christianity, 214–216, 249; in fundamentalism, 230; in Islam, 219–220; in Jainism, 187; in Judaism, 212; in Western religions, 242; in Zoroastrianism, 207; materialist attitudes, 233; original, in Abrahamic religions, 246
Sincerity: nonverbal indicators, 348
Sitting: dos and don'ts, 345
Śiva: Śakti and, 177; oneness with Śakti, 367; personal experiences, 28, 53; Naṭarāja, Subramuniyaswami's introduction to, xii
Sivanathan, Indivar: story, 57
Skanda: nature of, 99; personal experiences of, 98, 100
Smārtism: beliefs, 251–253; conversion into, x; Ishṭa Devatā and, 135; Śaiva Siddhānta Church and, xix; summarized, 178–179
Smoking: Hindu attitudes, 347; quitting, 30
Snake farm: conversion ploy, 144
Society: Communist ideals, 234
Song of the Sannyāsin: effect on Subramuniyaswami, xii
Soul: Eastern and Western views, 240–243, 245, 249; evolution of (Hindu belief), 180; existence of, 153; Hindu, distinguishing characteristics, 116, 118; Hindu in a non-Hindu birth, 117; in Christianity, 215–216; in existentialism, 236; in Hinduism, 251, 253; in Islam, 219–220; in Jainism, 186–187; in Judaism, 211–212; innate purity of, 342; nature and destiny of (Zoroastrian belief), 208; none (materialist belief), 232; Sanātana Dharma and, 89; seeing God in, 361
Soul-searching: true conversion and, 128
Spirit Worlds: Hindu vs. Christian beliefs, 249
Spiritual: experience, personal, resource books, 371; progress, means to (Eastern vs. Western views), 250; New Age belief, 226
Spiritualism: summarized, 222
Spirituality: vegetarianism and, 363
Sri Lanka: Buddhism in, xv
Strife: British and, 134
Subconscious mind: purity and, 342
Subramuniya Gotra: formation of, xvii
Subramuniyaswami, Satguru Sivaya: acceptance of *śishyas*, xvii; at Parliament of World Religions, xxv; childhood years, xi; Yogaswāmī and, 289
Success: religion and, 174
Suffering: Eastern and Western views, 242; in Buddhism, 182–184; in Christianity, 215–216; in existentialism, 236; in Western religions, 241, 245
Sundarar, Saint: protecting Sanātana Dharma, ix
Supreme: in Buddhism, 184; in Shintoism, 204; in Taoism, 196
Sushumṇā: and God Realization, 140
Sustenance: cow as symbol, 360
Swāmīs: addressing, 341; role in conversion, 123–124
Swarup, Ram: and HINDUISM TODAY, 91; Communism and, 75, 78–79; dharma and, 85; Hindu scripture

and, 84; meeting with, 91; on newcomers to Hinduism, 161
Symbology: Protestantism and, 65–66
Symbols: not in Sikhism, 191; religion and, 116; religious, wearing, 366; use in all religions, 362
Śaivism: beliefs, 252–253; summarized, 177–178
Śāktism: beliefs, 252–253; summarized, 177–178
Śishyas: acceptance by Subramuniyaswami, xvii
Śuddhi: purification ceremony, 101

T

Taoism: entering Hinduism from, xviii; severance from (case history), 57; similarities with Hinduism, 59; summarized, 194–196
Tapas: purity and, 342
Technological age: nonbelief and, 145
Temple(s): admission to, xvii, 264, 266, 289; Hindu, visiting, 26, 48–49, 63, 100; payment for facilities, 263; regular worship at, 260; religions opposed to, xxv; Subramuniyaswami's introduction to, xiii; worship, realizations and, 136
The Life Divine: Sri Aurobindo, 76
Theism: panentheism vs., 356
Theology: resource books, 371
Theosophy: summarized, 222
Thombare, Dr. Atulchandra S.: on conversion, 164
Thoughts: creative power of, 360
Throwing: refraining from, 345
Tilak, Swāmī: on truth-seekers, 167
Tilaka (forehead marks): discussion, 365
Tirukural: vegetarianism in, 364
Tolerance: Eastern vs. Western attitudes, 244
Tolerance, Hindu: of other views, 155, 157; attitude, 355, 359; ideal, 180; vs. Christian beliefs, 250
Touching: inadvertent, apology for, 344; public, Asian culture, 346
Tradition(s): importance of, 172; power of, xviii
Transcendence: of God, 220, 356
Tree: invoking Divinity in, 361
Tribalism: indigenous, beliefs, 224; religion and, 108–109
Trinidad: Hinduism in, x
Truth: seekers of, 167

U

Unfoldment: religion and, 172; spiritual, karma as catalyst, 358
Unione Induista Italiana: Swāmī Yogānandagiri and, 163
United States: name changes in, 285
Universalism: beliefs of, 223; Hinduism and, 68; separatism and, 108; summarized, 222
Universe: creation of, 355; cycles of, 155–156; divinity of (Shinto belief), 204; Eastern and Western views, 241; Hindu vs. Christian beliefs, 249; in Christianity, 216; in Hinduism, 180, 251; in Judaism, 212; in materialism, 232; in Shintoism, 202, 204; in Taoism, 196
Upadeśa: ethical conversion, 133
Upanishads: translation of, 365
Urgency: vs. realization, 137

V

Vaishṇava; Hindus, forehead mark of, 365; beliefs, 251–253; Śaiva Siddhānta Church and, xix; summarized, 177, 179
Vatican: expansionist agenda of, 143
Vedas: Hindu Bible, 364; Hindu scripture, 151, 155–156; karma in, 358; resource books, 371; Sri Aurobindo and, 97; study of, 97; vegetarianism in, 364
Vedānta: Abrahamic religions and, 139; Christianity and, 137; philosophy, non-Hindu religions and, 105
Vegetarian: becoming, 4, 28, 30, 49, 58, 64; *Times* (magazine), vegetarian resource, 364
Vegetarianism: Catholicism and, 82; health and moral reasons, 364; in Jainism, 186; question and answers, 362; resource books, 371
Vinayaga, Shama: story, 63
Violence: in Communism, 235; in fundamentalist sects, 229–230; in *Purāṇas,* 367; meat-eating and, 364
Virtue: Eastern and Western views, 243
Vishva Hindu Parishad: definition of a Hindu, xix, 154; reconversions to Hinduism, 165
Visitors: Hindu customs, 347
Vivekānanda, Swāmī: acceptance into Hinduism, 158–159; bringing Hinduism West, ix; effect on Subramuniyaswami, xii; on conversion to Hinduism, v
Vīra Śaivism: Hinduism and, 151
Vrātyastoma: reacceptance into Hinduism, 165

W

War: conversion and, 147; Sri Lankan, xiv
Website(s): conversion guidelines, 262; Gurudeva's, 3–5; Hindu name lists, 431
West: Hinduism in, ix
Western views: compared with Eastern, 240–245
Westernization: Hindu names and, 290
Wife: home alone, Hindu customs, 347; walking behind husband, 346
Witness: role in severance, 260–261; severance and, 11–12
Women: forehead dot and, 365; greeting, Hindu customs, 345; traditional role, 346–347
World: consciousness of (New Age belief), 226; secular humanist attitudes, 238; Wide Web, Hinduism and, 152
Worlds (three): severance and, 261; in Hinduism, 251; religion and, 174
Worship: Eastern and Western views, 242, 244; image, Western attitudes, 69; importance of, 153–157; in Confucianism, 198; in Hinduism, 176–178, 180, 249, 251–253; in Islam, 220; in Jainism, 188; in Judaism, 211–212; in Shintoism, 202, 204; in Sikhism, 190–191; in Taoism, 195; in Zoroastrianism, 206, 208; objectivity vs., 68–69; regular, 260; various faiths' attitudes, 223; *Vedas* and, 364
www.himalayanacademy.com/basics/conversion/: conversion information, xxvi

Y

Yamas and niyamas: purity and, 342
Yoga: *charyā* and, xii; Christianity and, 137; drug culture attitude, 225; Eastern vs. Western views, 244; experimentation with, 95; in Buddhism, 183; in Eastern religions, 244; in Hinduism, 176, 178–179, 253; in Jainism, 187; inner sight and, 365; meaning, 361; non-Hindu religions and, xv; practice of, non-Hindu religions and, 105; religion and, 136, 172; vegetarianism and, 363; *mārga,* dharma and, xiv
Yogaswāmī, Śiva: and ecumenism, 133; sectarianism, 134; Subramuniyaswami and, v, xiii, 289; Vivekānanda and, xii
Yogānandagiri, Swāmī: Hinduism in Italy, 162–164
Yogīs: addressing, 341
Zoroastrianism: differences from Hinduism, xxv; summarized, 206–208

Supplementary Studies

Granthavidyā

ग्रन्थविद्या

Books are available directly from the publishers or from distributors such as: 1) South Asia Books, P.O. Box 502, Columbia, MO 65205 (phone 314-474-0166); 2) Nataraj Books, P.O. Box 5076, Springfield, VA 22150 (phone 703-455-4996); 3) Treasures of the Heart, 1834 Ocean Street, Santa Cruz, CA 95060 (phone: 408-458-9654, e-mail: ramama@cruzio.com); 4) Hindu Heritage Books, 1085 Bathurst Street, Toronto M5R 3G8, Canada (phone: 416-532-2560). Titles especially recommended are marked with an asterisk. Those quoted from in *How to Become a Hindu* are marked with two asterisks.

SACRED LITERATURE

*Hume, Robert Ernest, *The Thirteen Principal Upanishads.* Oxford: O. Univ. Press, 1958.

*Mascaró, Juan, *The Upanishads* (selections). Narmondsworth: Penguin Books, 1965.

*Natarajan, B. (tr.), *Tirumantiram, A Tamil Scriptural Classic by Tirumular.* Madras: Sri Ramakrishna Math, 1991.

*Panikkar, Raimon, *The Vedic Experience.* Delhi: Motilal Banarsidass, 1989.

*Subramuniyaswami, Sivaya, *Weaver's Wisdom* (English trans. of *Tirukural).* Himalayan Academy, 1999.

SOURCEBOOKS ON HINDUISM

Arunachalam, M., *Peeps into the Cultural Heritage of Hinduism.* Tirupanandal: Kasi Mutt, 1987.

*Dye, Joseph M., *Ways To Shiva—Life and Ritual in Hindu India.* Philadelphia: Philadelphia Museum of Art, 1980.

*Klostermaier, Klaus K., *A Survey of Hinduism.* Albany: State Univ. of N.Y., 1998.

*Navaratnam, K., *Studies in Hinduism.* Jaffna: Maheswary Navaratnam, 1963.

*Radhakrishnan, S., *The Hindu View of Life.* New York: Macmillan, 1975.

Singh, Dr. Karan, *Essays on Hinduism.* Delhi: Ratna Sagar, 1990.

Sivananda, Swami, *All About Hinduism.* Shivanandanagar: The Divine Life Society, 1988.

*Subramuniyaswami, Sivaya, *Dancing with Śiva.* Kapaa, HI: Himalayan Academy, 1997.

*Subramuniyaswami, Sivaya, *Loving Gaṇeśa.* Kapaa, HI: Himalayan Academy, 2000.

CULTURE AND WORSHIP

Barth, Auguste, *The Religion of India.* London: Kegan Paul, 1921.

**Huyler, Stephen P., *Meeting God.* New Haven: Yale University Press, 1999.

Pandey, Raj Bali, *Hindu Samskaras.* Delhi: Motilal Banarsidass, 1969.

*Subramuniyaswami, Sivaya, *Living with Śiva.* Kapaa, HI: Himalayan Academy, 1991.

PERIODICALS, ETC.

*Chari, Seshadri, (ed.), *Organiser* (weekly journal), New Delhi: Hemandas Motwani for Bharat Prakashan.

*Ramachandran, T.R., *Tattvaloka,* Bangalore: Sri Abhinava Vidyateertha Mahaswamigal Education Trust, bimonthly.

**Subramuniyaswami, Sivaya, *Hinduism Today* (bimonthly magazine), Kapaa, HI: Himalayan Academy.

CONVERSION

**Frawley, David (Vamadeva Shastri), *How I Became a Hindu.* New Delhi: Voice of India, 2000.

**Goel, Sita Ram, *How I Became a Hindu.* New Delhi: Voice of India, 1982.

HINDU NAMES

**Gandhi, Maneka, *The Penguin Book of Hindu Names.* New Delhi: Penguin Books India, 1989.

*Pandya, Meenal A. and Pandya-Bhanot, Rashmee, *Pick a Pretty Indian Name for Your Baby.* Wellesley: Meera Publications, 1991.

INTERNET RESOURCES

http://www.kabalarians.com/gkh/yourbaby.htm Kabalarian Philosophy website on the importance of the name, including a list of over 400,000 Hindu baby names.

http://www.hindunet.org/baby_names/ Hindu Students' Council website including lists of Hindu baby names.

http://www.rajiv.org/iu/hindunam.txt Website with a list of Hindu names.

http://www.indiaexpress.com/specials/babynames/ India Express Network website with lists of Indian names of the Hindu, Sikh, Buddhist and Jain traditions.

http://members.tripod.com/~VishnuMavuram/names.html Vishnu Mavuram's website with an interactive Hindu names list.

http://www.himalayanacademy.com/basics/conversion/ *How to Become a Hindu* online.

http://www.himalayanacademy.com/books/ Himalayan Academy Publications, modern Hindu texts by Satguru Sivaya Subramuniyaswami and other authors, as well as many other resources.

http://www.himalayanacademy.com/academy/ Himalayan Academy's home page, including information about studying with Satguru Sivaya Subramuniyaswami.

http://www.gurudeva.org/ A Daily Chronicle of Kauai's Hindu Monastery, Satguru Sivaya Subramuniyaswami's daily inspirational spoken message from the Garden Island of Kauai.

http://www.hindu.org/ Hindu Resources Online, a vast collection of Hindu and Hindu-related websites and other Hindu religious/cultural resources available on the Internet.

http://www.flash.net/~dshanmug/ SHIVA, Saivite Hindu Information for the Visually Assisted, Hindu mystical books, magazines and lessons transcribed into English Braille and large print.

http://www.hindu.org/hhe/ Hindu Heritage Endowment, a multi-million dollar endowment for the promotion and preservation of charitable Hindu institutions worldwide.

Colophon

Antyavachanam

अन्त्यवचनम्

HOW TO BECOME A HINDU, A GUIDE FOR SEEKERS AND BORN HINDUS WAS DESIGNED AND ILLUSTRATED BY THE SWĀMĪS OF THE ŚAIVA Siddhānta Yoga Order at Kauai's Hindu Monastery on the Garden Island in Hawaii. This first edition was edited and produced using QuarkXPress on a Fast Ethernet network of Apple Power Macintosh G4 computers. The book was built on the foundation of *Śaivite Names,* published by the author in 1989 to serve the needs of his congregation and those interested in adopting the Hindu faith in a formal way. At the turn of the millennium, the author did his editing and additions on a wireless Ethernet-based series of Apple iBooks using Farallon's Timbuktu at an oceanside field office. The text is set in Adobe's Minion family of fonts: 11.5-point medium with 13.5-point linespacing for the body of the book and 9 on 11 for the glossary and index. For Devanāgarī and Tamil, we used fonts created by Ecological Linguistics in Washington, D.C., and by Śrīkṛishṇa Patel of Cupertino, California. Pages were output to film and printed by offset press on 60# Finch Opaque paper by Sheridan Books in Fredericksburg, Virginia.

The cover art is a watercolor by Tiru S. Rajam, 81, of Chennai, India, commissioned for this book in 2000. The painting on the title page is by the same artist, a venerable national treasure of South India, musical composer and traditional Tamil Śaivite artist whose work is permanently exhibited in the British Museum in London. The vivid oil portrait of Gurudeva on the back cover was a gift by India's renowned artist and national treasure, Sri Indra Sharma, 73, during his sojourn on Kauai in late 1997. He was also commissioned to execute the portrait of Jñānaguru Yogaswāmī on page iv, a painting described to be "just like he looked," said Śrīla Śrī Śivaratnapuri Tiruchiswāmīgal of Bangalore, who knew him well. Illustrations and patterns are by Tiru A. Manivelu and his son, M. Arumugam, of Chennai, India, commissioned in 2000.

The cover design and Himālayan Academy logo were created by San Francisco artist John Kuzich. Multi-level indexing and comprehensive proofreading were accomplished by Tirumati Chamundi Sabanathan of Santa Rosa, California, Selvan Erasenthiran Poonjolai of Kuala Lumpur, Malaysia and the monks at Kauai's Hindu Monastery. Sanskrit translations of the chapter titles and other expertise was provided by Mrs. Sudha P. Kulkarni of Mumbai.

Dozens of devotees and authors came forward to share intimate stories of their conversion to Hinduism. Their testimonies lend credence to the worldwide relevance of Hinduism and importance of ethical religious conversion in this modern age. Indeed, their own recognition of their Hinduness brought them ever closer to their soul and their spiritual destiny, a true unfoldment on the path that all souls eventually attain.

For all these noble, talented and selfless contributions, we offer our heartfelt appreciation. May many blessings come to each one who contributed to this great documentary. We conclude *How to Become a Hindu* with abundant praise to all the author's devotees who stayed the course through the years, slowly and gently adopting Hindu culture, setting the example for hundreds more souls who will find their roots in Hinduism for generations to come.

About the Author

Once in a while on this Earth there arises a soul who, by living his tradition rightly and wholly, perfects his path and becomes a light to the world. Satguru Sivaya Subramuniyaswami is such a being, a living example of awakening and wisdom, a leader recognized worldwide as one of Hinduism's foremost ministers. In 1947, as a young man of 20, he journeyed to India and Sri Lanka and was two years later initiated into *sannyāsa* by the renowned *siddha* yogī and worshiper of Śiva, Jñānaguru Yogaswāmī of Sri Lanka, regarded as one of the 20th century's most remarkable mystics. For over four decades Subramuniyaswami, affectionately known as Gurudeva, has taught Hinduism to Hindus and seekers from all faiths. He is the 162nd successor of the Nandinātha Kailāsa lineage and *satguru* of Kauai Aadheenam, a 51-acre temple-monastery complex on Hawaii's Garden Island of Kauai. From this verdant Polynesian *āśramā* on a river bank near the foot of an extinct volcano, he and his monastics live their cherished vision, following a contemplative and joyous existence, building a jewel-like white granite Śiva temple, meditating together in the hours before dawn, then working, when rainbows fill the sky, to promote the dharma together through Śaiva Siddhānta Church, Himālayan Academy and Hindu Heritage Endowment. Gurudeva is known as one of the strictest gurus in the world. His Church nurtures its membership and local missions on five continents and serves, personally and through books and courses, the community of Hindus of all sects. Its mission is to protect, preserve and promote the Śaivite Hindu religion as expressed through three pillars: temples, *satgurus* and scripture. Its congregation is a disciplined, global fellowship of family initiates, monastics and students who are taught to follow the *sādhana mārga*, the path of inner effort, yogic striving and personal transformation. Gurudeva is the recognized hereditary guru of 2.5 million Sri Lankan Hindus. His is a Jaffna-Tamil-based organization which has branched out from the Śrī Subramuniya Ashram in Alaveddy to meet the needs of the growing Hindu diaspora of this century. He has established a branch monastery on the island of Mauritius and gently oversees more than 40 temples worldwide. Missionaries and teachers within the family membership provide counseling and classes in Śaivism for children, youth and adults. HINDUISM TODAY is the influential, award-winning, international monthly magazine founded by Gurudeva in 1979. It is a public service of his monastic order, created to strengthen all Hindu traditions by uplifting and informing followers of dharma everywhere. Gurudeva is author of more than 30 books unfolding unique and practical insights on Hindu metaphysics, mysticism and yoga. His *Master Course* lessons on Śaivism, taught in many schools, are preserving the teachings among thousands of youths. Hindu Heritage Endowment is the public service trust founded by Gurudeva in 1995. It seeks to establish and maintain permanent sources of income for Hindu institutions worldwide. In 1986, New Delhi's World Religious Parliament named Gurudeva one of five modern-day Jagadāchāryas, world teachers, for his international efforts in promoting a Hindu renaissance. Then in 1995 it bestowed on him the title of Dharmachakra for his remarkable publications. The Global Forum of Spiritual and Parliamentary Leaders for Human Survival chose Subramuniyaswami as a Hindu representative at its unique conferences. Thus, at Oxford in 1988, Moscow in 1990 and Rio de Janeiro in 1992, he joined religious, political and scientific leaders from all countries to discuss privately, for the first time, the future of human life on this planet. At Chicago's historic centenary Parliament of the World's Religions in September, 1993, Subramuniyaswami was elected one of three presidents to represent Hinduism at the prestigious Presidents' Assembly, a core group of 25 men and women voicing the needs of world faiths. In 1996 Gurudeva upgraded the newspaper HINDUISM TODAY to a magazine, a quantum leap that placed it on newsstands everywhere. In 1997 he responded to President Clinton's call for religious opinions on the ethics of cloning and spearheaded the 125th anniversary of Satguru Yogaswāmī and his golden icon's diaspora pilgrimage to Sri Lanka. Recently Gurudeva has been a key member of Vision Kauai, a small group of inspirers (including the Mayor and former Mayor, business and education leaders and local Hawaiians) that meets to fashion the island's future based on spiritual values. If you ask people who know Gurudeva what is so special about him, they may point to his incredible power to inspire others toward God, to change their lives in ways that are otherwise impossible, to be a light on their path toward God, a father and mother to all who draw near.

You can visit Gurudeva's home page on the Web: www.gurudeva.org

There are a few unusual men who have had enough of the world and choose to dance, live and merge with Śiva as Hindu monks.

These rare souls follow the path of the traditional Hindu monastic, vowed to poverty, humility, obedience, purity and confidence. They pursue the disciplines of *charyā*, kriyā, yoga and jñāna that lead to Self Realization. Knowing God is their only goal in life. They live with others like themselves in monasteries apart from the world to worship, meditate, serve and realize the truth of the *Vedas* and *Āgamas.*

Guided by Satguru Sivaya Subramuniyaswami and headquartered at Kauai Aadheenam in Hawaii, USA, the Śaiva Siddhānta Yoga Order is among the world's foremost traditional Hindu monastic orders, accepting candidates from every nation on Earth. Young men considering life's renunciate path who strongly believe they have found their spiritual master in Gurudeva are encouraged to write to him, sharing their personal history, spiritual aspirations, thoughts and experiences. Holy orders of *sannyāsa* may be conferred in Gurudeva's order after ten to twelve years of training.

Satguru Sivaya Subramuniyaswami
Guru Mahāsannidhānam, Kauai Aadheenam
107 Kaholalele Road, Kapaa, Hawaii 96746-9304 USA

Hail, O sannyāsin, love's embodiment! Does any power exist apart from love? Diffuse thyself throughout the happy world. Let painful māyā cease and never return. Day and night give praise unto the Lord. Pour forth a stream of songs to melt the very stones. Attain the sight where night is not, nor day. See Śiva everywhere and rest in bliss. Live without interest in worldly gain. Here, as thou hast ever been, remain.

YOGASWĀMĪ'S NATCHINTANAI 228

The Hindu Heritage Endowment

Hindu thought and culture thread through almost every civilization on the planet, weaving a subtle tapestry of lofty philosophy and earthy pragmatic wisdom. Whose life has not been touched? Some have been raised in India and enjoy memories of warm extended families and cool temples resounding with ancient mantras. Others find peace of mind in Hindu yoga practices. Many find solace in the concepts of karma, dharma and reincarnation, which express their own inner findings and beliefs. If you are one who has been touched by Hindu thought and culture, you may wish to further enrich your life by giving back to India and helping to preserve her rich heritage for future generations. Hindu Heritage Endowment (HHE) provides such an opportunity. A public charitable trust founded by Sivaya Subramuniyaswami and recognized by the United States government, HHE was created to maintain permanent endowments for Hindu projects and institutions worldwide. Its endowments benefit orphanages, children's schools, *āśramas* and temples. They support priests and publish books, and they are designed to continue giving that financial support year after year, decade after decade, century after century. Whether you are inspired to give a few dollars to support orphanages, or bequest millions in your will, the staff at HHE is one-pointed in their dedication to seeing that qualified donations will be used effectively for the purposes intended. Write, give us a call, or look us up on the Internet. Find out how to enrich your life by helping to preserve the treasures of a profound heritage for generations as yet unborn.

Hindu Heritage Endowment, Kauai's Hindu Monastery, 107 Kaholalele Road, Kapaa, Hawaii, 96746-9304, USA. Phone: (800) 890–1008; outside of the US: (808) 822–3152; fax: (808) 822-3152; World Wide Web: http://www.himalayanacademy.com/endowment/

The Mini-Mela Giftshop

For all our books, visit store.himalayanacademy.com

Loving Gaṇeśa

Hinduism's Endearing Elephant-Faced God
By Satguru Sivaya Subramuniyaswami

NEW, SECOND EDITION. No book about this beloved elephant-faced God is more soul-touching. The Lord of Dharma will come to life for you in this inspired masterpiece. It makes approaching this benevolent Lord easy and inspiring. Learn about Gaṇeśa's powers, pastimes, mantras, nature, science, forms, sacred symbols, milk-drinking miracle and more. "A copy of *Loving Gaṇeśa* should be placed in every library and Hindu home"(Sri Om Prakash Sharma). Second Edition, 576 pages, paper, 5½" x 8½", (ISBN 0-945497-77-6), US$29.85.

Merging with Śiva

Hinduism's Contemporary Metaphysics
By Satguru Sivaya Subramuniyaswami

Here is the ultimate text for the really serious seeker. It may well go down in history as the richest and most inspired statement of meditation and God Realization ever, in any language. Yet, it's user-friendly, easy to follow, sensible and nonacademic! *Merging with Śiva* is 365 daily lessons, one for each day of the year, about the core of your own being. It's about God, about the mystical realm of the fourteen chakras, the human aura, karma, force fields, thought and the states of mind, the two paths, *samādhi* and so much more. Illustrated with fifty original South Indian paintings. First edition, 1999, 8.5" x 5.5," 1,408 pages, softcover (ISBN 0-945497-74-1), $39.75.

Dancing with Śiva

Hinduism's Contemporary Catechism
By Satguru Sivaya Subramuniyaswami

This remarkable 1,008-page sourcebook covers every subject, answers every question and quenches the thirst of the soul for knowledge of God and the Self. Clearly written and lavishly illustrated, expertly woven with 600 verses from the *Vedas, Āgamas* and other holy texts, 165 South Indian paintings, 40 original graphics, a 40-page timeline of India's history and a 190-page lexicon of English, Sanskṛit and Tamil. A spiritual gem and great value at twice the price. "The most comprehensive and sensitive introduction to the living spiritual tradition of Hinduism ...a feast for the heart and the mind (Georg Feuerstein)." Fifth edition, 1997, 8½" x 5½", softcover (ISBN 0-945497-97-0), $29.85.

Living with Śiva

Hinduism's Contemporary Culture
By Satguru Sivaya Subramuniyaswami

Hindu culture is nowhere illumined better than in this priceless collection of Gurudeva's honest, unflinching thoughts on every aspect of human life. At its core are 365 spiritual rules for the lion-hearted, verses on how Hindus approach God, family life, sex, relationships, money, food, health, social protocol, worship and more. This book proclaims and clearly explains the ancient wisdom by which followers of Sanātana Dharma lived and interrelated with one another in the days when love and peace, respect and wisdom prevailed, and it shows how that spiritual life can and should be lived today. Second edition, 2001, 8½" x 5½", 1008 pages, beautifully illustrated with original South Indian paintings, softcover (ISBN 0-945497-99-7), $39.75. **Available Spring 2001.**

The Master Course

Level One,
Śaivite Hindu Religion

What every Hindu parent needs: intelligent, nonviolent, traditional texts for their kids—an authentic, illustrated, seven-book series called *The Master Course*, teaching philosophy, culture and family life. Based on the holy *Vedas*, the world's oldest scripture, this course is the loving work of Sivaya Subramuniyaswami. An excellent resource for educators and parents, it explains the "why" of each belief and practice in simple terms in three languages. Prominent leaders of all sects have given enthusiastic endorsements. "A commendable, systematically conceived course useful to one and all with special significance to fortunate children who shall be led on the right path (Sri Sri Sri Tiruchi Mahaswamigal, Bangalore, India)." Book One (5- to 7-year-old level) is available in a Hindi-Tamil-English edition. Softcover, 8½" x 5½", 170 pages, $12.95. Book Two (6- to 8-year-old level), English-Tamil-Malay, 196 pages, $12.95.

The Vedic Experience

Back when we were gathering Vedic verses for *Dancing with Śiva,* we could hardly believe our eyes when we came upon this brilliant anthology from the Vedic *Saṁhitās, Brāhmaṇas, Āraṇyakas* and *Upanishads* and other scriptures. This Vedic epiphany tells the story of the universal rhythms of nature, history and humanity. The translation and abundant commentary are the work of renaissance thinker Raimon Panikkar—the fruit of twelve years of daily *sādhana* in Varanasi between 1964 and 1976 while he lived above a Śiva temple on the Holy Gaṅga. He considers it perhaps his most significant literary contribution. This classic makes the *Vedas* available to all. Motilal Banarsidass, Delhi, 1977, smythe-sewn and case bound, cloth cover, 8½" x 5½", 1,000 pages, $41.95.

Hinduism Today

The International Bi-monthly Magazine

Enjoy a bimonthly spiritual experience with the foremost international journal on Sanatana Dharma, published by Gurudeva and his swamis. Breaking news, ancient wisdom, modern trends, world-class photos, family resources, humor—you'll treasure every issue! "HINDUISM TODAY is a beautiful example of the positive possibility of the media being fulfilled, a bright ray of light in a darkened world" (Anne Shannon, Portland). Introductory offer (US only): one-year subscription, 6 stunning issues, for $35! And yes, the author of this book is founder and publisher of this global magazine. • ISSN 0896-0801; UPC: 0-74470-12134-3. Visit www.hinduismtoday.com.

Lemurian Scrolls

Angelic Prophecies Revealing Human Origins
By Satguru Sivaya Subramuniyaswami

Enliven your spiritual quest with this clairvoyant revelation of mankind's journey to Earth millions of years ago from the Pleiades and other planets to further the soul's unfoldment. Learn about the ensuing challenges and experiences faced in evolving from spiritual bodies of light into human form and the profound practices followed and awakenings achieved in ancient Lemuria. These angelic prophecies, read by Sivaya Subramuniyaswami from *ākāśic* records written two million years ago, will overwhelm you with a sense of your divine origin, purpose and destiny and motivate a profound rededication to your spiritual quest. An extraordinary metaphysical book which answers the great questions: Who am I? Where did I come from? Where am I going? First Edition, 1998, 7" x 10", 400 pages, beautifully illustrated with original drawings, smythe-sewn and case bound with printed color cover (ISBN 0-945497-70-9), $29.85.

Order Form

☐ Please send me free literature.

☐ I consider myself a devotee of Satguru Sivaya Subramuniyaswami. I kindly request to receive my first 52 *sādhanas* (spiritual discipline).

☐ I wish to subscribe to HINDUISM TODAY.
USA rates: ☐ 1 year, $35 ☐ 2 years, $65 ☐ 3 years, $95 ☐ Lifetime, $1001
(For international rates send e-mail to: subscribe@hindu.org)

I would like to order:

☐ *Merging with Śiva*, $39.75 ☐ *Loving Gaṇeśa*, $29.85 ☐ *Dancing with Śiva*, $29.85
☐ *Living with Śiva*, $39.75 ☐ *Vedic Experience*, $41.95 ☐ *Lemurian Scrolls*, $29.85
☐ *Śaivite Hindu Religion:* Book 1 (ages 5-7), $12.95; ☐ Book 2 (ages 6-8), $12.95

Prices are in U.S. currency. Add 20% for postage and handling in USA and foreign, $1.50 minimum. Foreign orders are shipped sea mail unless otherwise specified and postage is paid. For foreign airmail, add 50% of the merchandise total for postage.

☐ My payment is enclosed. Charge to: ☐ MasterCard ☐ Visa ☐ Amex

Card number: ____________________

Expiration, month: ________ year: ________ Total of purchase: ____________

Name on card: [PLEASE PRINT] ____________________

Signature: ____________________

Address: [PLEASE PRINT] ____________________

____

____

Phone: ____________ Fax: ____________

E-mail: ____________________

Mail, phone, fax or E-mail orders to:

Himalayan Academy Publications, Kauai's Hindu Monastery, 107 Kaholalele Road, Kapaa, Hawaii 96746-9304 USA. Phone (US only): 1-800-890-1008; outside US: 1-808-822-7032 ext. 238; Fax: 1-808-822-3152; E-mail: books@hindu.org; World Wide Web: store.himalayanacademy.com

Also available through the following (write or call for prices):

Sanāthana Dharma Publications, Bukit Panjang Post Office, P. O. Box 246, Singapore 916809. Phone: 65-362-0010; Fax: 65-442-3452; E-mail: sanatana@mbox4singnet.com.sg

Śaiva Siddhānta Church of Mauritius, La Pointe, Rivière du Rempart, Mauritius, Indian Ocean. Phone: 230-412-7682; Fax: 230-412-7177.

Iraivan Temple Carving Site, P.O. Box No. 4083, Vijayanagar Main, Bangalore, 560 040. Phone: 91-80-839-7118; Fax: 91-80-839-7119; E-mail: jiva@vsnl.com

Om Vishwa Guru Deep Hindu Mandir, Europe: Phone/Fax: 361-3143504; E-mail: ervin@mail.matav.hu

Mere words are insufficient to express the gratitude of the Hindu world for this educational masterpiece which gives further support to the principles of Sanatana Dharma. Ironically, many Hindus who are not from an orthodox Hindu background are today rediscovering how to become a Hindu, and this publication will no doubt steer them on the right pathway. ¶I find most interesting the testimonies of the converted in the chapter "Personal Encounters with Hinduism." I am certain this will have an effect on those Hindus who have deserted their dharma (especially to the corrupt influences of the Western world) and will ensure them a safe return into the loving embrace of Hinduism. ¶Secondly, the chapter "Does Hinduism Accept Newcomers" is a subject which I have to address quite frequently when non-Hindus and non-Indians come to discover the miracle of our Sunday morning worship at the Edinburgh Hindu Temple. Gurudeva has provided me with *diksha* to fortify my effort in handling this delicate matter. In the case of a Hindu marrying a non-Hindu, I use counseling and the medium of initiation (guru-*diksha)* to the non-Hindu, to add to my flock rather than lose both "to the competition." Sadly, in Trinidad, this is still a problem for some of the orthodox pandits. Hopefully, this publication will provide a clear approach to this subject. ¶Gurudeva's exploratory ventures into subject matter which has not been covered in print before show his continuing desire for unification of the beliefs of all God's children. Sanatana Dharma ki jai!

Pundit Ramesh Tiwari, President General, Edinburgh Dharmic Sabha, Chaguanas, Trinidad & Tobago

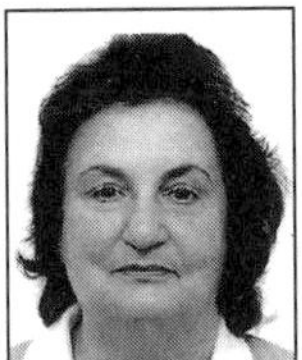

Those of us who enter Hinduism from another religion, and I include myself amongst this group, find themselves dedicating themselves fully to this glorious path of the soul. We commit solidly by changing our name, often legally, because we feel as if we are born again in this life. Within Satguru Sivaya Subramuniyaswami's book, *How to Become a Hindu,* there are numerous stories of ethical conversion to Hinduism, not only from devotees who have converted from other religions, but from those born within a Hindu family who have rediscovered Hinduism. I have found all these "encounters" of deep spiritual interest. Not only do they portray the movement of the soul as it climbs the ladder of self-awareness, they also show the evolution of the soul ripening to development and entering the true path of Self Realization. Indeed, the Divine leads us forward into unknown realms where we can even encounter the Gods themselves. Further, Gurudeva's book directs the aspirant through a system of enquiry to some extremely important factors of how to become a Hindu, as well as answering many important ethical questions. This gives the aspirant the opportunity to think clearly about this wonderful quest. ¶Most of us in this world of form require a guru as our soul searches for spiritual answers. As we move up the "rungs of the ladder" and even begin to think about converting from one religion to another, it can be "gut wrenching," as one of the stories in the book so aptly describes. This is why I believe

How to Become a Hindu fills an important vacuum. It is a practical guide for those among us who are seeking sound advice and true answers to soul-searching questions. It is a guidebook, a gift from a master, offering an excellent opportunity to learn. And further, it offers the soul the opportunity to plunge into a beautiful, exhilarating experience where it can eventually glow in the truth of wonderful transformation. ¶There are those of us who need a formal process, a period of discipline and development, where there is the opportunity also to join with others of like mind. This is an essential period, a time for learning and self-discovery, a perfect time to quietly listen to the guru (teacher) and learn to understand the glory of Hinduism before making the final commitment. ¶When we eventually reach the stage when we know deep within the soul and can also outwardly admit that we are Hindu, we can make massive strides forward on the glorious spiritual path. Gurudeva has explained all of this vividly in his book. The Divine is always here ready to help us with this commitment. ¶Even though I entered Hinduism from another religion, I cannot recall a period of my life when my soul did not feel Hindu. Hinduism is very special. It is the bedrock of my soul. It is my religion. It is my culture. It is my way of life. It covers and it shields this earthly form so that within that Divine light of understanding everything is known as Divinity. Hinduism has shown me that here, in this world of form, my soul has the outstanding opportunity to humbly place everything at the lotus feet of Lord Siva and His Shakti.

Mrs. Iswari Kamalabaskran, Lecturer in World Religions and Founder-Member and former Trustee and Secretary to the Board of Trustees of the London Highgate Murugan Temple and the Sri Rajarajeswary Amman Temple, Stoneleigh, Surrey, U.K.; Author of *The Light of Arunachaleswarar Siva* and *Arunagiri Valam–The Supreme Path of Grace.*

May through this guidebook mankind find peace, harmony and God Realization by understanding the sense and significance of religion. I believe that this recent publication of Sri Subramuniyaswamiji is conveying a true vision with tolerance and open-mindedness. It enlightens mankind about the Sanatana Dharma and the noble ideals of ahimsa, love and service to all living beings and God Realization. I wish that this book may inspire hundreds of thousands of sincere seekers and provide them with the right perspective for their spiritual path.

Paramhans Swami Maheshwarananda, named Saravbhom Sanatan Jagadguru by the World Religious Parliament; Spiritual Head, International Sri Deep Madhavananda Ashram Fellowship; Vienna, Austria

For decades, Western Orientalists, Christian missionaries and Marxist intellectuals have been trying to persuade us that Hinduism isn't a religion and that even if it were we couldn't convert to it. Now we know better, and Satguru Sivaya Subramuniyaswami in his book *How to Become a Hindu* has taken the bull by the horns in encouraging non-Indian Hindus of conviction to make a public commitment and say with pride that they are Hindus. He is to be commended for his courageous and creative religious leadership. His book is intelligent and very timely and must be read by all persons seriously interested in Indian philosophy and yoga—for there is no true philosophy or yoga without the worship of Ishwara.

Ishwar Sharan, author of *The Myth of Saint Thomas and the Mylapore Shiva Temple,* Tiruvannamalai, Tamil Nadu, India.

Satguru Sivaya Subramuniyaswami sets at rest the doubt that Hinduism is not a religion, saying it is a distinct world religion encompassing four major denominations: Vaishnavism, Saivism, Saktism and Smartism, all in one known as Sanatana Dharma. He rightly asserts that Hindu philosophy is free from missionary compulsions. With his own personal life experience, Swamiji has laid down six conditions for conversion to Hinduism, the first being a letter from the priest of the religion which one wants to give up, giving the consent for conversion. The implication of this condition is that he should convince the priest or guru about his new beliefs and convictions. The book is a manual for those who want to become Hindu. I am sure it will go a long way in achieving Gurudeva's life mission of spreading Hinduism, to bring the entire world within its fold with convictions and not compulsions.

Jagadguru Dharamraj His Holiness Swami Pragyanand Ji Maharaj, Pragya Peethadhiswar, Founder/Patron Pragya Mission International, New Delhi, India

How to Become a Hindu is a remarkable book with the objective of providing important tools and guidance to those who feel the need and have the desire to embrace this ancient religion. The book is an outcome of the author's own experience as an aspirant and a guru. ¶Can a person become a Hindu? This is a question that is often asked. Many years ago I and a few friends went into a restaurant after a conference. The young Indian waiter asked me whether I was a Hindu. When I confirmed what he said, he felt very happy. One of the friends told him that she also was a Hindu. The boy was astonished. He gazed at her and said, "You are not an Indian; how can you be a Hindu?" It is generally believed that one has to be born a Hindu. ¶The term "ethical self-conversion" is used by the author in the sense that embracing Hinduism should not be a matter of convenience. There must be a genuine feeling about the great values of Hinduism. This is very important because the emphasis in Hinduism is not just belief or even practicing but experiencing inner peace, joy and freedom. ¶The book has compared and contrasted Hindu beliefs and practices with other religions, including Judaism, Christianity and Islam, in a fair manner. There are personal testimonies and encounters with Hinduism which will prove valuable to those who still need proof about the motive of Christian missionaries, the sly methods they use and the advantage they take over people's circumstances. ¶The chapter "Beliefs of All the World's Religions" gives a bird's eye view of some basic beliefs that are held by their followers. This will be an eye-opener to those Hindus who hold the view that all religions are the same. This publication is indispensable for Hindu priests, parents, libraries, organizations and educational institutions.

Swami Nirliptananda is a sannyasin of the Bharat Sevashram Sangha, Calcutta, India. He hails from Guyana and is in charge of the branch of the Sangha in London, England.

Many of us went to India seeking personal enlightenment in the late '60s and early '70s. Now, a generation later, the West is dotted with ashrams, and Western teachers are carrying the Eastern lineages back home. Gurudeva Sivaya Subramuniyaswami's important book *How to Become a Hindu* asks many pertinent questions about the next phase of our development. It is also a monumental analysis of the differing ideas of all the major religions. ¶I have noticed that Western Buddhists easily call themselves Buddhist, while followers of Hindu gurus have enormous trouble with the "H" word. Gurudeva takes a refreshingly hard line, insisting that yogis come out of the closet and admit they are Hindus. Not everyone will agree with this approach, but the book is fascinating reading, and the questions become urgent when we think of the many children of devotees who grow up in an ashram environment. Shouldn't they have spiritual training, and shouldn't they know that they fit into the religious universe by way of the Hindu tradition? ¶Gurudeva's provocative ideas have sparked a healthy debate within our community here in Australia, and I'm grateful to him for cogently calling attention to an important area of self-definition and concern for the next generation. Every Western yogi could profitably read this book.

Sri Sri Swami Shankarananda, 55, heads the Shiva Ashram near Melbourne, Australia. He leads retreats and offers a course introducing the "Shiva Process," a contemplative tool for living in the world.

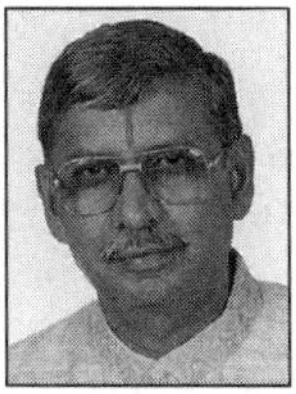

Whenever there arises a need to reeducate the masses, a great soul descends on this Earth and paves a path of divine inclination. Thousands of years ago such decension happened in the form of Maha Rishi Veda Vyasaji, who rewrote the knowledge of the *Vedas* as *Bhagavat Maha Purana* and paved a path to God Realization for all. About four hundred years ago, Tulasidas arrived on Earth to teach the path of Ramji *(Ram-Ayan)* to the bhaktas who had strayed from the true *marga* (path) of Sanatana Dharma. In the 20th century Gurudeva has graced this Earth to guide all divine souls to the Eternal Sanatana Dharma. ¶This great work by Gurudeva is a much needed book at the present time for the salvation of all those who have strayed from the true *marga*. I will call this book a true path of return for those who have adopted other religions by birth, or for those who are only half-Hindus, i.e., born in Hindu families but do not have firm beliefs in Hindu scripture. ¶Through case histories of renowned people and devotees, Gurudeva has placed signboards for weak devotees so that they may arrive safely at their true destination on this Earth. He has placed speed bumps for non-Hindus desirous to convert to Hindu Dharma, in the form of severance of all ties to their current religious practices. ¶This divine work should not only be in all the libraries on this Earth, but in all households—for Hindus to strengthen their beliefs and for non-Hindus to gain the true path of God Realization.

Pandit Rajendra Sharma, Priest of the Hindu Worship Society, Houston, Texas, is a third generation Fijian-born Hindu, trained by Sri Jagdish Shukla of Bharatiya Vidya Bhavan, Mumbai, India.

In 1990 I had a unique opportunity to be a witness to the signing of certificates for the conversion of new followers of our Hindu faith at the Concord Palani Andavar Temple. Gurudeva converts his followers in the most correct manner, morally, spiritually and legally. ¶As a young boy growing up in Jaffna, I received my primary school education in a Christian school. The teacher impressed upon me in religious classes that the Hindu Gods were all evil devils. We were told when passing the Hindu temples to spit and swear at these evil images. Many times I followed my teacher's instructions and indeed did these inappropriate deeds—until one day I spat at an image of Lord Ganesh and immediately fell to the ground and suffered a serious head wound. My cousin was studying in a Catholic convent with many other students who were born as Hindus. Every morning they were taken to the church for prayers. On the way the students passed a Hindu temple where they were told to spit and swear in the direction of the temple. This was a cruel and dishonest attempt at conversion to a different faith. Gurudeva only accepts converts if they are satisfied and accept his teachings. This indeed is the only ethical way to convert anybody to any faith.

Pundit K.N. Navaratnam, M.A.F.A., F.A.A.; Jyotisha Shastri, Jyotisha Marthand and National Astrologer of Australia; close devotee of Satguru Siva Yogaswami; Director of the Sivathondan Center, Hallam, Australia

I find that this is a book for the adoptive Hindu and the born Hindu. "How to remain a Hindu" may be added as a subtitle for this timely book. The rising tide of interest and enthusiasm for Indian thought, religions and philosophies was first confirmed to scholars who made the sudden discovery that Sanskrit was related to the Indo-European family of languages. With the advent of the modern printing press, Edwin Arnold's, the *Song Celestial* and *The Light of Asia* hastened the interest of men and women in the West. ¶As stated by Gurudeva in his introduction, the arrival of Swami Vivekananda at Chicago for the first Parliament of World Religions, and his extended tour of the States, as well as the arrival of swamis of the Ramakrishna Mission who followed him, helped to create a new awareness in Vedantic thought and exercised the minds of American poets and philosophers, like Emerson and others. In recent decades, the arrival of Swami Bhaktivedanta captured the minds of American youth, who turned "Boston Brahmin." This gave birth to the Hare Krishna movement, which began to spread all over the world, giving new impetus to Vedantic views and spreading the teachings of the *Gita.* As a result Sanatana Dharma established a foothold on the American continent. Emigrant Hindus from India and Sri Lanka have increased the number of Hindu temples in the West. ¶This new trend—the movement from East to West—reverses the movement which brought Christian missionaries Eastward eager to save "pagans and infidels." Rudyard Kipling's view that "East is east, West is west; never the twain will meet" has been proven wrong. New scientific discoveries have brought the world closer and affirmed Tirumular's concept, expressed two thousand years ago, that "Mankind is one family." The 21st century has witnessed the meeting of minds from East and West, North and South. Even the atomic scientist Oppenheimer was prompted to quote the words of the *Gita,* "I become as Death, the destroyer of worlds," when he realized the terrible power he had placed in the hands of politicians, a power that could annihilate the world! ¶*How to Become a Hindu* gives a clear picture of the process necessary for becoming a Hindu for those wishing to adopt Sanatana Dharma as their self-chosen way of life to attain moksha. ¶Every born Hindu should read Sita Ram Goel's account of his personal life and return to Sanatana Dharma in the chapter on personal encounters. I can tell you that there is many "a rootless intellectual" in Malaysia, as elsewhere, cut off from the language of their origin, alienated by a Western education, or converted to an alien religion at the point of the sword or for a "mess of pottagie," or by their biological urges, to abandon their ancestral religion. The axe handles of Indian society, the ex-Hindus who come to convert Hindus, are to be feared among this group of Indians. ¶There is another group of rootless intellectuals who attribute to Hinduism the statement that all religions are alike, and therefore it does not matter what religion one chooses. This is a fallacy, but it persists. Nowhere does Hinduism state that all religions are the same. It merely states, "All paths lead to the same goal," but each religion is distinct, with its own beliefs and basic characteristics. The late Saiva-periyar of Malaysia, K. Ramanathan Chettiar, who introduced me to Saiva Siddhanta, refuted this fallacy by saying, "Those who saw all religions as the same have no religion to speak of." He illustrated this further by stating, "All women are women, but only your wedded wife is your own." Let Hindus learn to respect their own religion, without despising it or abandoning it for another. ¶Gurudeva has, therefore, given a summary account of all existing religions, both theistic and atheistic, that have moved the minds of men and women. This section on comparative religion gives the reader an opportunity to exercise his/her judgment and decide for himself what he/she chooses to be or become. The nine questions asked of every Hindu by a non-Hindu, and the answers given, need to be taken note of in order to be able to answer these nine questions. Those Hindus who need to renew their faith, as well as ex-Hindus who wish to retrace their steps and return to the Hindu fold, will find this section invaluable. ¶This new publication is therefore a book on how to become a Hindu for non-Hindus, as well as a book on how to remain a Hindu for Hindus who lack faith in themselves, a faith which is undermined by their ignorance and indifference. There is no better book to convince aspirants who wish to become Hindus, and to explain how to go about it. There is no better book available in English for the untutored Hindu wanting to remain a Hindu and for the ex-Hindu wishing to return to Sanatana Dharma. We have a duty to extend to them our hand of welcome. ¶As Hindu culture and civilization is inextricably linked with Hindu religion—language, music, dance, customs and practices—the concluding chapter, "Embracing Hindu Culture," helps to depict the cultural traits and traditions expected of a Hindu, and practices which distinguish one as being a Hindu. We are all fortunate indeed that such a book has been conceived by Gurudeva to meet the needs of men and women of the new millennium.

Dr. S.M. Ponniah, Professor, INTI College; Member of the National Commission on Moral Education; Advisor to the Malaysian Hindu Sangam; Kuala Lumpur, Malaysia

Gurudeva Sivaya Subramuniyaswami is doing a yeoman's service to Hindus as a whole by reminding them of their ancient tradition through his books and lectures about the significance of the Hindu way of living. *How to Become a Hindu* is especially important for those who are living outside of India, immersed in various other traditions of the world, yet who want to understand and follow the Hindu lifestyle. This publication provides instruction on the basic values of Hindu society and will benefit both Hindus and those interested in adopting Hindu Dharma.

Chakrapani Ullal is a renowned Jyotisha Shastri, named by the Indian Council of Astrological Sciences as Jyotisha Kovid and Jyotisha Vachaspati; Los Angeles, California.

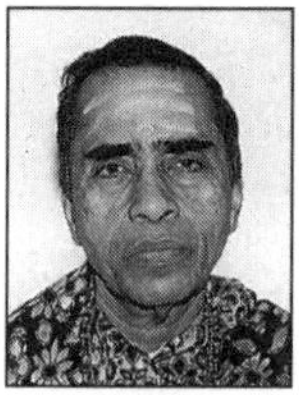

Hinduism does not believe in aggressive proselytizing, cultural invasion or spiritual colonialism. An inner, ethical conversion and a sincere and lasting commitment to the Hindu beliefs are the passports to embrace Hinduism. The inspiring real-life stories of nineteen ardent spiritual seekers belonging to different faiths and religious denominations, including Hinduism, illustrate in captivating detail the various steps of ethical conversion. The author then, with impressive thoroughness, takes the reader step by step to show how entrance into Hinduism means becoming a part of all its basic beliefs, traditions, culture, group-consciousness and spiritual unfoldment. The author then proceeds to discuss vital and burning questions like "Does Hinduism accept newcomers? What is that makes a person a Hindu? What are the beliefs of all the world's religions?" with deep-seeing ethical judgment. ¶"The Six Steps of Conversion" gives the reader a fairly comprehensive picture of what adoptives and converts to Hinduism should fulfill to enter Hinduism, whose eternal truths are the heritage of humanity. The formal ceremonies, *samskaras* and traditional rituals required to be fulfilled to embrace Hinduism are exhaustively dealt with in this section. A study of this work will be a rewarding experience to all seekers of self-knowledge and spiritual enlightenment.

Sri S. Harihara Sharma, Chief Priest, Sri Murugan Temple, Vancouver, Canada; Former Religious Program Producer, Sri Lanka Broadcasting Corporation

This is a book simple to the point of being straightforward yet significant to the point of being sensational, for it gives voice to a silent shift within modern Hinduism hitherto mentioned only *sotto voce.* "New occasions teach new duties. Time makes ancient good uncouth." In this respect this book is the ultimate "how to" book in relation to Hinduism. It tells us how to convert to it and retrospectively negates Albiruni's description of Hindus as a people who do not "receive anybody who does not belong to them, even if he wished to or was inclined to their religion." I do not consider it a mere coincidence that a book such as this should appear as we enter the new millennium, for it removes the dark shadow of hesitancy in respect to conversion to Hinduism lurking over the threshold as we cross it.

Arvind Sharma, Ph.D., Department of Religion, McGill University, Montreal, Canada

For many years Subramuniyaswami has taught Hinduism to Hindus and to seekers from all faiths. I was pleased and admiring at the recent contribution to the Hindu world by his esteemed illustration of *How to Become a Hindu.* The synopsis of different faiths brought out in this book and the letters of those who converted to Hinduism from other faiths carries a long way in his attempt. May the almighty Lord Siva give him all courage and long, healthy life to continue his worthy contribution.

Brahma Sri Samy Visvanatha Kurukkal, Prathisda Sironmani, Kriya Kirama Jothy, Swanupoothy, Sivachariya Thurantharar, Colombo, Sri Lanka

The world is heading towards doom under the guise of religion. It is very sad to note that some are instrumental in downgrading and also criticizing our respected Hindu philosophy, known as Sanatana Dharma, and are indulging in conversion to other religions, which they consider as their religious beliefs. We have fallen upon an age in which corruption is fairly universal. Hinduism is not a fanatic faith. It has a charity that is comprehensive. ¶This book will be a guide to all those who look at the Hindu religion with sarcasm. This Book cannot be described by mouth or by words. It can only be known by experiencing. The more you get sunk into the spiritual ocean created by this book, the more you get the priceless gems. All human beings should read this book and follow its teachings and experience its grace. The book inspires confidence and helps one to rise higher and higher in the spiritual ladder in the attempt to reach God. Learned scholar Satguru Sivaya Subramuniyaswami was born on Earth to protect the Hindu religion and also to spread the Hindu philosophy to all and sundry.

His Holiness Dr. Swami R.K. Murugesu, Founder-President, Sri Lankatheshwarar Deyana Mander, Nuwara Eliya, Sri Lanka

This book is not only an interesting literary novelty that clearly deals with the problem of conversion, providing interesting answers on this subject which definitely must be evaluated carefully for the future of Hinduism. We should all follow with great zeal the example of Satguru and be grateful to him for the superb work he is doing in defending that precious patrimony of humanity represented by Hindu religion. ¶It's true that Hinduism does not proselytize. However, nothing keeps it from defending itself from the obsessing and devouring invasion of those religions that live under the flag of proselytism. A line of defense can be the correct popularization, as in this book, of how you can become a Hindu and profess your religious beliefs appropriately. Hinduism would certainly be more solid and of greater utility for humanity if every Hindu professed his own religious beliefs with pride, asserting his spiritual principles, cultivating them in his own family and becoming an example for society. Or still, if every organization or group of Hindu devotees in the world collaborated with one another, without egoism and exaggerated pride, to carry out a common task of spreading Hinduism, its spiritual traditions and culture, without superficiality. ¶The problem of spreading Hinduism is not only related to the aggressiveness of other religions, but that unfortunately in Hinduism itself there are weaknesses and superficialities on the part of religious leaders who defend their own powers, their own individualism, etc., at times becoming superficial divulgers of Indian culture. This attitude is widespread in Europe, where swamis or religious leaders belonging to important organizations come exclusively to spread yoga, presenting it as a discipline that aims essentially to psychophysical benefits colored by a vague spirituality, however far from a religious and ascetic practice. This is to betray the Hindu spirit and the spirit of yoga. In truth, yoga is a spiritual practice, the scope of which is the realization of the Self, and is deep rooted in Hinduism. It is part of Hinduism. It is the experimental aspect which can be found in every *sampradaya*. We must admit that it has immense psychophysical benefits, but we should remember that they are only "positive incidents" which can happen along the spiritual path. Yoga, like the Hindu medical, scientific and artistic arts, cannot be eradicated from its Hindu roots. To cut yoga from its spiritual roots out of fear of having fewer followers if it is presented in its wholeness—a discipline with a philosophy and theology deeply rooted in Hinduism—would be to make this discipline dry, like branches with no lymph. Maybe the swamis who do so want to seem liberal, to show that they welcome anyone. But is this not a subtle and servile form of proselytism which yields only personal advantages? ¶What we call conversion is also the freedom to choose one's own spiritual language. Therefore, the Hindu has the duty of affirming his religious belief. He doesn't have to convince anyone, but he must favor whoever sincerely and of his own free choice wishes to enter into the great family of Sanatana Dharma. This courage is always present in Sri Satguru Sivaya Subramuniyaswami. ¶The book also deals with the assertion that "you cannot become a Hindu," which prevents sincere but unaware devotees from assuming Hinduism as their religion. Satguru deals very clearly and gives precise answers on this subject. ¶I truly recommend this text, which can be a stimulating experience not only for Hindus but also for those who wish to go deeper into Hinduism. We thank Satguru Sivaya Subramuniyaswami for his work and for the love he shows in upholding the cause of Hinduism.

Sri Svami Yogananda Giri, Founder and Spiritual Head of Unione Induista Italiana, Sanatana Dharma Samgha, Gitananda Ashram, Carcare, Italy

How to Become a Hindu is a simple and easy to understand manual to help guide those seeking to ratify their declared commitment to Hinduism in all its dimensions: spiritual, social, cultural, economic and educational. Satguru Sivaya Subramuniyaswami is a divine being in the human form who inspires everyone through this book. Regardless of whether you are a Christian, Muslim, Hindu, Jew or any other, you can understand the clear concepts expressed in this guide. Gurudeva is an ocean of mercy, compassion and divine knowledge. I highly recommend this book to each and every person to understand the clear concept of Hinduism.

Swami Brahmavidyananda, a disciple of Paramahansa Satyananda, has taught Hinduism in India, the US, South and Central America. He directs Satyananda Ashram and Institute of Holistic Yoga in Miami, Florida.

"Conversion" has engaged the attention of scholars and laity alike in recent decades.There are books devoted to the topic and there are conferences where it is debated by scholars. Religious heads are willing to discuss the topic, and magazines and newspapers are willing to engage in the issue. Thus a general awareness of conversion as an area of conflict has engaged the consciousness of people globally in recent decades. ¶The title can be misleading, for this book is not so much about the conversion into Hinduism (though it is used as the context for the discussion), but about helping those who feel uncomfortable in the religion they find themselves in and have no empathy for, while strongly attracted to the ways, lifestyle and philosophy of another religion. Though the author has himself adopted the Saiva Sampradaya of Hinduism, nowhere does the book advocate conversion to Saivism/Hinduism as one of the aims for which the book is written. The book has emerged out of a desire to help those who enter a new religion due to their liking for its way of practicing religion but who also seem to live in a limbo as far as religious identity is concerned. ¶Let us take for instance those Western swamis who don the sannyasin's robe, follow the rules prescribed for a sannyasin and yet find themselves identified as belonging to their earlier religion and not to Hinduism as such. We are all aware of the number of intellectually converted Westerners that started with Swami Vivekananda's historic 1893 speech at the Parliament of World Religions in Chicago and gathered momentum in the 1920s and 1930s and is still going on in one form or the other. Neither Swami Vivekananda nor the swamis coming after him have tried to integrate these "new entrants" completely into the Hindu fold. "Many hundreds of devotees are betwixt and between" (p. 124). As Gurudeva says, "My own personal observation is that without a complete and final severance from one's former religion or philosophy it is not possible to practice Hinduism fully and receive full spiritual benefit, because of subconscious psychological confrontations that inevitably occur when the former belief and commitment make battle with the newly found ones" (p.105). And in line with the many innovations set in motion by Gurudeva (the magazine HINDUISM TODAY being one important one) he has come up with the unique tool of Ethical Conversion to serve devotees who are "betwixt and between." ¶While some religions, like Islam and Christianity, do have a formalized code of conversion for new entrants into their religion, other religions like Hinduism have not paid much attention to this aspect. Thus a dichotomy of what one has truly become and what one cannot discard (due to lack of a structure by which to do it) has characterized a number of persons, particularly Western converts to Hinduism. If then one has truly chosen to convert to another religion, how should one complete the process begun and gain total identity as a person belonging to the chosen religion? This is the topic dealt with in different ways in the ten chapters of this book and which is termed "Ethical Self-Conversion." ¶Of human interest is chapter one, where those who have followed this process of "ethical conversion" narrate their stories in the first person. Personally I found this chapter fascinating. Chapter 6 presents briefly the main tenets of the world religions and is highly informative. Chapter 10 is of particular significance in the Western context as it can benefit both Hindus who will know how to answer some basic questions put to them regarding Hinduism and also the Westerner who can come to an understanding of Hinduism in his own idiom and language. It is good to remember that not all Hindus are familiar with their own religion, though born into it. This chapter is thus useful for the Diaspora Hindus as well, who are scattered like seeds all over the globe and are the ones who are asked these questions. Unless they know what they are talking about how can they convey the sense to others? ¶This is a book written in a fascinating style, using a mixture of history and personal narrative. It grips you from the start and leaves you with the feeling that, "Here at last is a book which is taking care of some of the practical problems of those who sincerely want to change from one religion into another." This is a book that tackles an issue of great interest and that can be read by anyone even remotely interested in the dynamics of inter-religious discourse.

Dr. T.S. Rukmani, distinguished academician, appointed the first Hindu Chair in the world, University of Durban, South Africa; second person to be appointed the first Chair of Hindu Studies in N. America at Concordia University, Montreal.

All these years during my travel around the world to spread the message of Lord Siva's words in many places, I was worried to notice the practices that are followed which are against the *Vedas* and *Agamas*. But Sri Gurudeva has clearly mentioned in this book that to be a complete Hindu (not an *ardha*-Hindu) one has to believe in the *Vedas* and *Agamas*. This is very important because without the basement how can a building be constructed? The *Vedas* and *Agamas* are the base of this great Sanatana Dharma. ¶In his introduction Swamiji has clearly explained his own evolution as a complete Hindu with his guru's blessings which many people around the world were eager to know. ¶The chapter which talks about encounters with Hinduism is a clear answer for the people who question whether Hinduism converts people. We do not believe in conversion through money or power, as do certain other religions, but we are obliged to accept the souls who would like to adopt our religion for the liberation of their souls. ¶Gurudeva has excellently explained the necessary steps that have to be followed to become a complete Hindu. This is useful not only for people from other religions, but it is also a very useful guide for the Hindus who are Hindus by just namesake (whom Gurudeva correctly defines as *ardha*-Hindu). ¶In the world, everything has to be fulfilled; nothing can be incomplete. Something incomplete cannot yield the full fruits of that faith. Can a person say that he is safe by crossing half the wall? How can an *ardha*-Hindu say that he belongs to the Sanatana Dharma? Just by displaying religious faith's pictures and symbols, a person cannot be secular in feeling. He would be a phony. He should be ready in his heart and mind. This Gurudeva has clearly explained: how the vibrations differ by keeping a picture of Jesus with that of our Lords. I always stress this point around the world: I accept Jesus as a messenger of the Lord, but how can he be kept together with the Mahadevas? Is the protocol right? This has to be understood clearly. ¶This book of Sri Gurudeva's is a must in all Hindu families and for the souls who are interested in following the Sanatana Dharma. This work is not a partial one in praise of the Hindu religion. The world will now know of Sri Gurudeva's experience for the last fifty years as an *acharya* and his extensive study not only of Hindu Dharma but also his detailed knowledge about other religions and beliefs. His explaining about the steps for conversion is not a day's work, but a life's experience. Even the subtle things, such as taking the religious certificate to India during pilgrimage, are handled carefully. ¶I am very happy to say that Gurudeva is the spokesperson for our Sanatana Dharma at the international level because of his dedication, devotion, the *satsang* that he has been blessed with, and, above all, the guidance of Lord Nataraja. He is rightly called the Jagadacharya. All the great *acharyas, aadheenams* and our Sivachariars of our holy India and around the world are with him to spread this message of Sanatana Dharma for the peace and happiness of the world.

Sivashri Dr. T.S. Sambamurthy Sivachariar, Head of the South India Archaka Sangam; Head Priest, Shree Kalikambal Kovil; Chennai, Tamil Nadu, South India